Growing up
in the new South Africa

WITHDRAWN

Growing up
in the new South Africa

CHILDHOOD AND ADOLESCENCE IN POST-APARTHEID CAPE TOWN

Rachel Bray • Imke Gooskens • Lauren Kahn • Sue Moses • Jeremy Seekings

HSRC
PRESS

Published by HSRC Press
Private Bag X9182, Cape Town, 8000, South Africa
www.hsrcpress.ac.za

First published 2010

ISBN (soft cover) 978-0-7969-2313-4
ISBN (pdf) 978-0-7969-2314-1
ISBN (e-pub) 978-0-7969-2315-8

Copyedited by Mark Ronan
Typeset by Baseline Publishing Services
Cover design by Michelle Staples
Printed by Paarlmedia
Jan van Riebeeck Drive, Paarl, South Africa

Distributed in Africa by Blue Weaver
Tel: +27 (0) 21 701 4477; Fax: +27 (0) 21 701 7302
www.oneworldbooks.com

Distributed in Europe and the United Kingdom by Eurospan Distribution Services (EDS)
Tel: +44 (0) 20 7240 0856; Fax: +44 (0) 20 7379 0609
www.eurospanbookstore.com

Distributed in North America by Independent Publishers Group (IPG)
Call toll-free: (800) 888 4741; Fax: +1 (312) 337 5985
www.ipgbook.com

Contents

Tables and figures

Preface

This book is the product of a collaborative effort by researchers in the Centre for Social Science Research (CSSR) at the University of Cape Town. It presents primarily qualitative research, and has its origins in a perceived need to go beyond quantitative research. The CSSR was established in 2001 with the goal of strengthening capacity in quantitative social science. One of the CSSR's major projects was the Cape Area Panel Study (CAPS), for which a 'panel' of almost 5 000 adolescents across Cape Town were interviewed repeatedly over several years as they grew into adulthood. CAPS was a joint project of the CSSR and scholars at the University of Michigan, and was co-directed by Jeremy Seekings (from the CSSR) and David Lam (from the University of Michigan). The first wave of interviews was conducted in 2002, and subsequent waves in 2003/04, 2005 and 2006. It soon became clear that progress in understanding transitions into adulthood would require a combination of qualitative and quantitative research, and so an ethnographic research project was initiated within the CSSR in 2004 by Rachel Bray and Jeremy Seekings. Rachel Bray led the ethnographic study and, with Imke Gooskens and Susan Moses, conducted 15 months of fieldwork in the Cape Town neighbourhoods of Masiphumelele, Fish Hoek and Ocean View respectively. This qualitative research proceeded in parallel to the successive waves of CAPS.

Analysis of the qualitative data from each neighbourhood was conducted both individually and collaboratively by Imke, Rachel and Sue. Jeremy analysed the quantitative data and participated in discussions about the qualitative research. Rachel and Jeremy took responsibility for integrating material into composite chapters, with Rachel taking primary responsibility for about two-thirds of the chapters and Jeremy for one-third. Just about every chapter, however, includes substantial contributions from Rachel, Sue, Imke and Jeremy. The one exception is Chapter 7, for which Lauren Kahn was primarily responsible. Lauren had conducted fieldwork among adolescent girls in the same neighbourhoods in Cape Town, focusing specifically on their friendships and sexual relationships. She incorporated findings from her own research and from the research by Rachel, Imke and Sue into a composite chapter. Every chapter was discussed repeatedly in collective workshops, and read and reread by each member of the team. Both Rachel and Jeremy restructured and rewrote almost every chapter.

Some sections of the book have appeared in other forms. Sue, Imke and Lauren drew on their analyses for their master's dissertations (Gooskens 2006; Kahn 2008; Moses 2005). Jeremy, Sue, Imke and Lauren contributed articles to a special issue of *Social Dynamics* (32[1] 2006). Rachel and Imke co-wrote an article on the ethics of conducting research with children in *Anthropology Southern Africa* (Bray & Gooskens 2006). Rachel drew on this and further ethnographic work with mothers and young children to co-write work on childcare, poverty and HIV/AIDS with Rene Brandt in, among others, the *Journal of Children and Poverty* (Bray & Brandt 2007). Most of these papers – and others – were published as working papers in the CSSR Working Paper Series.

Ariane de Lannoy, a PhD student in the CSSR, who is researching educational decision-making among young people in Cape Town, provided particular input to Chapter 6. Katherine Ensler, a visiting student from Princeton, assisted with observational research in high schools in Fish Hoek and Masiphumelele.

This research was only possible because of the enthusiasm shown by many children and adolescents in Fish Hoek, Ocean View and Masiphumelele, and by many of their family members and neighbours. We are especially grateful to the six teenage residents of the Valley who volunteered to join the team as young researchers: Riccardo Herdien, Thandolwethu Mbi, Karen Painter, Samantha Peacocke, Zahir Slarmie and Siyabulela White. All names used in the text are pseudonyms.

We were able to conduct research inside schools through the generous assistance of the principals and teachers at Fish Hoek Primary, Middle and Senior High; Marine Primary; Ocean View Secondary; Ukhanyo Primary; and Masiphumelele High. We are also grateful to the Western Cape Education Department for their permission – and especially to Dr Ronald Cornelissen. Staff and volunteers working in state services, NGOs and churches welcomed us into their work environments or gave their time for interviews or informal discussions. Nomatamsanqa Fani and Lindiwe Mthembu-Salter provided invaluable research assistance and translation services.

The research presented in this book was funded largely by the CSSR. The funders included the Andrew W Mellon Foundation, as part of its grant to establish the CSSR, and the Ford Foundation, through a grant to the AIDS and Society Research Unit (which is part of the CSSR) to support research that generates new forms of knowledge. Sue Moses received a generous scholarship from the Potter Charitable Trust, which also funded a workshop in early 2005. The major funder of CAPS was the US National Institute of Child Health and Human Development, through grants R01-HD39788 (research on 'Families, Communities and Youth Outcomes in South Africa') and R01-HD045581 (research on 'Family Support and Rapid Social Change in South Africa').

A number of academics provided important advice along the way, especially Andy Dawes, Pamela Reynolds, Fiona Ross and Susan Levine, and our colleagues in the CSSR who gave feedback on presentations in the CSSR seminar series.

This publication was supported with generous assistance from the University of Cape Town and the South African Netherlands Research Programme on Alternatives in Development (SANPAD).

The Fish Hoek valley

The research for this book was conducted in the Fish Hoek valley, with the participants in the study drawn from three of its major communities: Fish Hoek, Ocean View and Masiphumelele. This section provides a visual introduction to the area, as seen through the eyes of the young participants themselves. They took all the photographs presented here, and drew all of the maps with the exception of Map 1 and Map 7.

Situated in the southern part of the Cape Peninsula, the Fish Hoek valley (referred to as 'the Valley' throughout this book) originally consisted of a middle-class coastal village, and farmlands. Under apartheid it was almost entirely a 'white group area' which meant that 'non-white' people were permitted to live in the area only if they were employed as domestic workers or farm labourers.

In the 1960s Ocean View, a small working-class housing estate, was built in an isolated area in the Valley to accommodate 'coloured' people who were forcibly resettled there from other areas in the southern peninsula. The 1980s and 1990s saw significant growth throughout the Valley. The existing villages of Fish Hoek, Noordhoek and Kommetjie expanded, and new suburbs, such as Capri and San Michel, were developed. By the early 1990s, approximately half the population, occupying most of the Valley, was 'white' and just under half, confined to Ocean View, was 'coloured'. Masiphumelele was established in 1991 as a semi-formal settlement for the small number of African people already living in the Valley, either legally or illegally. By 2001, however, Masiphumelele, too, had grown to the point where it accommodated almost 25 per cent of the population in the Valley.

Today, the Valley has become a suburban expansion of Cape Town, and the population has doubled. There are many signs of post-apartheid change – almost everyone throughout the Valley has access to electricity, basic sanitation, schools and healthcare facilities. However, the spatial impress of apartheid remains: the majority of the coloured and African residents live within the narrow confines of Ocean View and Masiphumelele, whilst the richer, white residents live in the lush suburbs and smallholdings that have developed across the area, from one coast to the other.

Locating the Valley

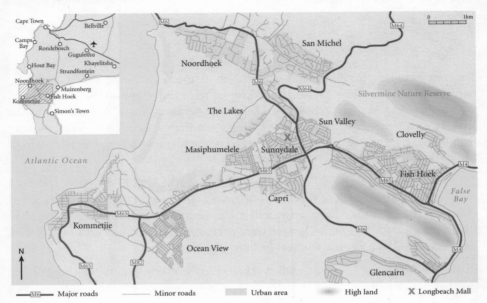

Map 1 *The Fish Hoek Valley*

This map shows the three neighbourhoods researched (reading from left to right): Ocean View, Masiphumelele and Fish Hoek, with the main arterial routes linking them to Greater Cape Town in the north. The insert shows the position of the Valley relative to Cape Town.

Local neighbourhoods

Photo 1 *Ocean View central*

Ocean View has a handful of formal shops, including a small supermarket, butchery and video-hire store, as well as informal shops operating out of people's homes. The only sports facilities are bare soccer fields. The young person who took Photo 2 makes quite clear the reason for the name of her neighbourhood.

Photo 2 *Ocean View residential*

Photo 3 *Masiphumelele central*

Masiphumelele has only informal spaza shops run from shacks, roadside sellers and shebeens (bars). Its soccer field is a patch of ground filled with rubble, which until recently was covered with temporary classrooms for the high school. Although there are some three-room brick homes recently built by the government, most people live in small, informally built shacks like the one shown in Photo 4.

Photo 4 *Masiphumelele residential*

Photo 5 *Fish Hoek central*

Fish Hoek has a wide range of supermarkets and shops; restaurants; an 80-year-old department store; a well-stocked library; tennis courts and lush sports fields with clubhouses. Quiet, tree-lined streets and solidly constructed homes characterise the residential area.

Photo 6 *Fish Hoek residential*

Mapping our neighbourhoods

Map 2 *Ocean View: Dangerous places*

A group of grade-9 boys from Ocean View mapped the areas in their neighbourhood that they consider to be dangerous.

In the top left corner they drew an area of informal housing named Mountain View where they say a lot of gangsters live, and you are likely to be robbed or stabbed if you go there. To the right is Soetwater, an area slightly outside of Ocean View, where people go drag racing. It is an unsafe place because cars crash and spectators get hurt.

On the right, behind a row of houses, is an open space near the rubbish dump, often used for illicit activities. Because it is unlit it is particularly dangerous after dark, when you risk being attacked if you stumble across someone lurking there.

In the centre of the map are the 'flats' (blocks of one- and two-roomed apartments), where many of the children live. These are dangerous because people drink and take drugs, resulting in fights and stabbings. The children who live there stay in after dark because 'gangsters come and sit on the stoep (veranda) and smoke dagga and make a noise. They often don't want to leave. Sometimes adults help to chase them away, but if there are no adults home then we shoot stones and marbles with a catapult at them or throw hot water over them and then they go away.'

'Nella's Pap', in the bottom left-hand corner of the map is one of the many shebeens in Ocean View. The boys say they are dangerous mainly after dark, when people get drunk and become violent.

Map 3 *Masiphumelele: Our yard*

Praise, a girl aged 12, drew this map of her immediate surrounds in Masiphumelele.

She describes her map:

> I live in this shack [bottom left quadrant]. We've got a stove and a fridge in our kitchen, and my parents have a bed with a beautiful cover. We share our yard with other families [points to other shacks in her drawing]. Our houses are built close together and they are all different sizes – some of them are big [points to the house in the top right quadrant] and some are very small [indicates the house in the centre].

> I like staying here because all my friends are here and they can come to my house and I can go to their houses. Sometimes my friends' places can also feel like my own home, so I have drawn the furniture in their houses too.

> We all use the toilet and the shower and tap here [points to bottom right quadrant]. And after we've washed our clothes we hang them up between our houses [indicates the line of washing in her drawing]. My friends and I always help each other and the other aunties to hang up the washing and take it down again.

Map 4 *Fish Hoek: My community*

Drawn by 13-year-old Helen, this map depicts her immediate 'world' in Fish Hoek and its surrounds. Her map includes several friends' houses, none of which are within walking distance: they are spread across an area which ranges from a five-minute to a 20-minute drive from her home.

Below her house in the centre-left of the map, Helen includes in her world the beach and the railway station, roughly a five-minute drive away. In the centre she has drawn a nearby shop she sometimes walks to with her mother. To the right is Fish Hoek itself, where she has shown the school she attends, her church and two of her friends' houses. For Helen, getting to any of these places entails a ten- to fifteen-minute drive with one of her parents.

In the top right corner of her map, Helen's world expands beyond the Fish Hoek Valley to include the place where her father works in Constantia, a wealthy suburb 20 minutes' drive away from her home. On the other side of the mountain, in Noordhoek, she has shown another friend's house and the Longbeach Mall, where she goes shopping with her parents on weekends (a ten-minute drive).

How we spend our time

Photo 7 *Ocean View: The Fiesta Girls*

Mina and her friends have given themselves a group or gang name 'because we do everything together'. Here they are outside the flats where they live in Ocean View.

Below, the Fiesta Girls and other friends play karrom board (in which small disks are flicked with a heavier disk to knock as many as possible into four corner pockets).

Photo 8 *Ocean View: Playing karrom board outside the flats*

Photo 9 *Maspihumelele: Shebeen*

Shebeens are often run from people's homes in Masiphumelele. Selling bottled and home-brewed alcohol, these businesses are also social centres where people gather to drink and relax. The music played in shebeens often attracts teenagers to them. To avoid this, Mdu (Photo 10) and his friends prioritised working and saving for equipment to play their own music so that they would not be tempted into shebeens and the violence and petty crime associated with them.

Photo 10 *Masiphumelele: Mdu listening to music*

Photo 11 *Fish Hoek: After school*

In Fish Hoek, children's activities are generally contained within the walls of 'safe' places. Thus Konrad is allowed to go to his friend's house for PlayStation games after school, but may not play outside in the street. Children are usually driven between school and other activities which ensures their safety but also means that their movements are confined by adult routines and decisions. To show where she loves spending her time, twelve-year-old Lara snapped Fish Hoek beach through the window of her grandmother's car whilst being driven to one of her after-school activities (Photo 12).

Photo 12 *Fish Hoek: Driving past the beach with Granny*

Our schools

Photo 13 *Ocean View Secondary School entrance*

Ocean View Secondary School offers basic amenities which include a computer room donated by the local Rotary Club. Although there are also sports facilities, maintenance costs are a continual challenge so they are not always in good condition.

Photo 14 *Ocean View Secondary School grounds*

Photo 15 *Masiphumelele High School*

Originally, Masiphumelele High School consisted of emergency classrooms and a makeshift staffroom erected on the primary school premises (Photo 15). In 2006 a new school was built (see insert). The new high school includes all the basic amenities, but maintenance costs and vandalism pose a serious challenge.

Photo 16 *In class at Masiphumelele High*

Photo 17 *Fish Hoek High School grounds*

Fish Hoek High School is set in large grounds with pristine sports fields. Facilities include an assembly hall, a comfortable staffroom, lockers for pupils, a computer centre, library, science laboratories and art rooms.

Photo 18 *Friends at Fish Hoek High*

Beyond our neighbourhoods

Map 5 *Fish Hoek and surrounds*

A group of 12-year-old Fish Hoek girls began this map by drawing a rough outline of the area, delineating this by the position of each of their homes, indicated by the pink circles on the map. Their everyday 'world' is bordered by Glencairn (bottom left), Muizenberg (bottom right), and Noordhoek (top), where they have horse-riding lessons and visit the Longbeach Mall (top left).

Although they fall within the boundaries of the map, Ocean View and Masiphumelele do not feature on the girls' map, because none of them go there, unless they happen to be in the car with their mother when she drops off a domestic worker.

It was difficult for the group to think of dangerous places to include in their map (red circles), because they do not go anywhere alone, and have to ask their parents to transport them anywhere they want to go. Their extramural activities, such as horse-riding, piano or dancing lessons, are regular and supervised. Social visits and visits to the mall are always in the company of parents. On the other hand, the girls had no difficulty in indicating important places, places where they have fun, and where they go to buy what they need (see the key on the right-hand side of the map).

Drawn by members of the Masiphumelele art club, Map 6 centres on Kommetjie Road, the main road linking them to the other areas in their immediate vicinity: Kommetjie, Simon's Town, Ocean View, Capri, Fish Hoek and Sunnydale, where the Longbeach Mall is. Through the use of colour coding, the children show the areas where they feel comfortable and the areas that make them feel ill at ease, as well as their perceptions about places that are important, places that are dangerous, and places where they can have fun.

Shaded in green, the areas where they feel welcome and comfortable are Masiphumelele, where they live, (bottom right), and the area around Longbeach Mall in Sunnydale (adjacent to the Masiphumelele Clinic on the map). Fish Hoek (bottom centre), Simon's Town (indicated by the green boats bottom left), and Kommetjie (top right) are also areas where the children feel at ease.

The areas shaded in pale brown are places where Masiphumelele art club members feel unwelcome. These places include the Fish Hoek sports fields (bottom right), and the middle-class area of Capri (centre left) even though, as indicated by the houses drawn in orange, some of them have relatives working there. Ocean View (top left) and an open wetland area next to Masiphumelele on the right are the other areas where the children feel uneasy.

Places important to them are drawn in blue and include the clinic and a community hall in Masiphumelele, as well as the schools, not only in their own neighbourhood, but in all the other areas, whether or not they feel comfortable there. Also important is Longbeach Mall because that is where they go shopping, but no doubt also because of its two fast food outlets which they associate with weekend treats: Mc Donald's (a very faint Mc on the map) and KFC (indicated by a large chicken burger).

The places drawn in 'red' (which in effect shows as dark maroon or purple on their map) are places the art club members perceive to be dangerous, where they feel unsafe. Thus in Capri, some of the houses are drawn in red, possibly because the properties house large dogs that bark and frighten them when they walk past to visit their relatives working in the area. The buildings drawn in red in Ocean View represent the 'flats', associated with drugs and violence and therefore perceived as dangerous. Fish Hoek Main Road (bottom centre) and the snake park (top right) are also drawn in red to indicate 'danger zones'.

'Fun places', drawn in yellow, include the sports amenities in Fish Hoek and Ocean View but are also placed in areas where these children feel unwelcome.

Map 6 *Masiphumelele neighbourhood and surrounds*

Fun place

Important places

Dangerous places

Where our relatives work

Where we feel welcome and comfortable

Where we do not feel welcome or comfortable

Map 7 shows the costs of travel by public transport for the residents in the Valley.

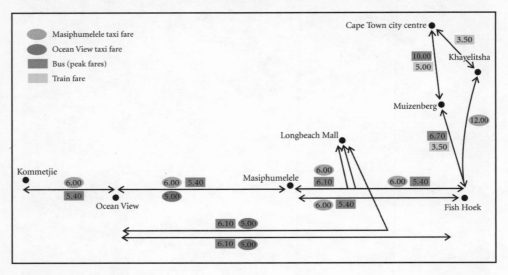

Map 7 *Transport routes and costs*

Notes: The map is not drawn to scale. All fares shown are for single trips, in ZAR, August 2009. Residents can also buy a bus pass for R51.00, which gives them 10 single trips between Ocean View or Masiphumelele, and Fish Hoek.

Map 8, drawn by children aged 11–13 years living in Masiphumelele, reveals that young people from this community travel further outside the Valley than many of their counterparts in Ocean View and even Fish Hoek. Masiphumelele features bottom centre, showing where they live, go to church and play sport. To the left, on the western side, is Noordhoek and Longbeach Mall where they shop for food. Numerous stars are drawn on the eastern side, in the Fish Hoek area, to show that this is where they go to swim and have fun. Central to the map are the main routes into and out of the Valley, which take them to (mid-right) Nyanga, a township where they visit family and go to church; Wynberg, a south peninsula suburb from where they would take the bus to the Transkei (Eastern Cape) to visit relatives; and, in the centre of the map, Cape Town central business district. Two very big stars show how much fun and entertainment is associated with Cape Town, where the children visit friends, shop for clothes, and may have visited the museum or St George's Cathedral on a school outing. The Huguenot Tunnel, which is 120 kilometres out of Cape Town, on the route to the Eastern Cape, forms the northern border of the map.

Map 8 *Places where we go in the Cape Peninsula*

Where we live 　　Where we visit friends 　V.F. Where we visit family members

Where we shop for clothes 　　Places we shop for food 　　Where we play sport

Where we go to have fun 　　Soccer field 　　Church 　　Museum

Where we take the bus to Transkei

Support circles

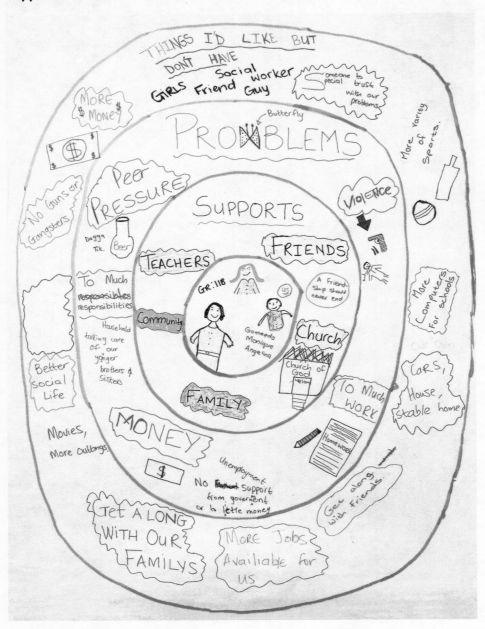

Map 9 *Challenges and support*

Drawn by a group of teenagers living in Ocean View, Map 9 shows what they consider to be sources of support, their challenges or problems, and suggestions for what would help them overcome their challenges.

1 Growing up in post-apartheid South Africa

There can be no keener revelation of a society's soul than the way in which it treats its children. We come from a past in which the lives of our children were assaulted and devastated in countless ways. It would be no exaggeration to speak of a national abuse of a generation by a society which it should have been able to trust. As we set about building a new South Africa, one of our highest priorities must therefore be our children. The vision of a new society that guides us should already be manifest in the steps we take to address the wrong done to our youth and to prepare for their future. Our actions and policies, and the institutions we create, should be eloquent with care, respect and love. (Mandela 1995)

Continuity and change in everyday life

Nelson Mandela, who, at the time of this speech, had recently become the first democratically elected president of South Africa, tells of how, driving back to the presidential house in Cape Town one wintry evening, he saw a group of street children. He stopped to talk to them. Later, he determined to establish a fund to assist children in need, and to change the way that society treats its children and young people. For Mandela, the struggle for democracy had been a struggle for opportunity. In his memorable speech from the dock in the Rivonia treason trial in 1964, he declared that he 'cherished the ideal of a democratic and free society in which all persons live together in harmony and with equal opportunities'. This, he continued, was an ideal that he hoped 'to live for and to achieve. But if needs be, it is an ideal for which I am prepared to die'. (He and his co-accused were facing a possible death penalty.)

South Africa's first democratic elections – in April 1994 – marked the achievement of a democratic and free society, but they did not usher in a golden age of equal opportunities for all children. Some South African children grow up amid extraordinary affluence and privilege. The boundaries of privilege have extended beyond whiteness to include considerable numbers of black children growing up within the fast-growing black elite and middle classes. In her novel *Coconut*, Kopano Matlwa (2007) describes her character, Ofilwe (or Fifi, as she prefers to be called), who lives with her newly wealthy family in a mock-Tuscan house in the 'Little Valley Country Estate' protected by 24-hour security guards; attends a Model C (or formerly 'white') school; and frequents the shopping mall. At the opposite extreme are highly impoverished rural children and urban street children, whose regular hunger and lack of access to basic services, healthcare or schooling serve as an enduring indictment of post-apartheid society. In between these extremes are the majority of South African children and adolescents – many still living in poverty

(Meintjes & Hall 2008) – for whom the transition from apartheid has engendered a mix of opportunities and disappointments, changes for the better and changes for the worse.

This book is about the realities of everyday life for children and adolescents in a democratic South Africa, after the end of apartheid. We examine the lives of young people at home, in the neighbourhoods where they live and at school. We examine their relationships with friends, close family and other kin and neighbours, and their anxieties about the threatening 'other', which shape the margins of their daily lives. We consider the diversity of experience, opportunity and risk facing young people as they navigate their way through the uncertain and complex post-apartheid landscape. We do not focus on those who are especially vulnerable or most in need, such as street children. Instead, we seek to understand the lives of ordinary urban children and adolescents, of young people facing many challenges in life, but, for the most part, dealing with them in ways that did *not* lead to the outcomes identified as social pathologies by the media, policy-makers and many commentators. The stories of most South African children and adolescents are not stories of 'failure' or of a 'descent' into marginality. They are the opposite: stories of creativity and at least partial success in tackling old and new challenges alike. As Nelson Mandela himself has often emphasised, young people 'are special not only because they are vulnerable, and are the first to suffer whenever we adults get things wrong, but also because of their remarkable spirit, their ability to heal not only themselves but their societies as well' (Mandela 2000).

Nelson Mandela, ever the optimist, points to the possibility of young people helping to heal South African society. After decades of apartheid – and before that, colonial conquest, dispossession and segregation – South African society was certainly in need of additional healing. For children and adolescents growing up in the late 1990s and early 2000s, post-apartheid society was unevenly *post*-apartheid. In some respects, apartheid had been buried: all adults had the vote; the government was led by black political leaders; legislation discriminating against black people had been abolished; the status of black people had changed; and their dignity was no longer impaired through the policies and practices of apartheid. There were no longer legal restrictions on which public schools black children could attend, or where they could get healthcare. The state had undertaken a massive reallocation of public funds from the schools, hospitals and municipal infrastructure serving the rich to those serving the poor. The welfare state was extended, most importantly through the expansion of child-support grants, which provided a small but significant cash income to poor parents. Racial restrictions on the jobs that someone could do, or how and where someone could set up a business, were removed. Also abolished were statutory racial restrictions on where people could live and the requirement that African people had to carry a pass showing where they were allowed to reside. No longer were people prohibited from having sex with or marrying someone from a different racial group. Unsurprisingly, large majorities of black South Africans tell pollsters that they think their lives have improved since the end of apartheid. White South Africans are more ambiguous, but few admit to regretting the passing of apartheid. There is a general view that what were once called 'race relations', i.e. relationships between black and white people, have changed for the better.

At the same time, however, many features of the apartheid era persist, as the legacy of apartheid shapes everyday life after apartheid itself has died. Material inequalities persist and the distribution of income has probably become even more unequal after apartheid than during it. Income poverty seems to have deepened in the late 1990s, before declining somewhat in the early 2000s. This does not mean, however, that all rich people are white, or all black people are poor. On the contrary, a fast-growing proportion of the wealthy in South Africa are black people who have taken advantage of new opportunities and moved up into the middle-class and elite echelons. Fifteen years after leaving law school, Patrice Motsepe had acquired the wealth (about R15 billion – equivalent to US$2 billion before the crash that began in 2008) that the Oppenheimers took three generations to acquire. Just as interracial inequality has declined, by many measures *intra*-racial inequality has increased. Massive unemployment sentences many to chronic poverty, mitigated only to the extent that people receive financial support from the state through old-age pensions, child-support grants or other social assistance programmes. In many respects, class has replaced race as the foundation of deep social cleavages in post-apartheid society (Leibbrandt et al. 2009; Seekings 2010; Seekings & Nattrass 2005).

Apartheid is also echoed in the continuing relationship between race, neighbourhood and class. Almost all white people are relatively rich, as they continue to reside in well-resourced areas and have succeeded in reproducing other privileges even after the demise of apartheid. Almost all poor people are black, or, more specifically, African, and live in areas with compromised infrastructure and services. For the poor however, the demise of apartheid might have brought dignity, but it has not brought real opportunity: poor African children typically attend compromised and struggling schools; acquire neither skills nor qualifications; enter a labour market that offers no prospects for unskilled workers; and struggle to access healthcare when they fall sick. South Africa remains a highly segregated society: most people reside in neighbourhoods whose populations are – in apartheid terminology – overwhelmingly either 'African', or 'coloured' or 'white', but not a mix of these; their children attend schools dominated by one 'race' group; and few adults or children have racially diverse friends. Race continues to be salient in this supposedly *post*-apartheid society (Seekings 2008).

The Valley

Our research was conducted in the periphery of Cape Town in the Fish Hoek valley, a place which, in some respects, is a microcosm of South Africa. The Fish Hoek valley (henceforth 'the Valley') straddles the Cape Peninsula to the south of the world-famous Table Mountain. (See Map 1, showing the Valley and its position within the Cape Peninsula.) As one approaches the Valley, it seems to be an affluent mix of middle-class suburbs and semi-rural smallholdings, with retirement villages, a brash, new shopping mall, riding stables, beautiful marshes and beaches and even a former farm where children can ride camels. This is an area that, under apartheid, and with the exception of one small corner, was declared a 'white group area', meaning that 'non-white' people could live there legally only as domestic workers or farm labourers. The exception was the 'coloured group area' of Ocean View, an isolated working-class housing estate built in the 1960s and 1970s, and to which most coloured people from the Cape Peninsula, south of Cape Town, were forcibly and traumatically resettled (see Jacobs 2003 on the experiences of one particular family). By 1990, approximately half of the population, occupying almost all of the Valley, was classified white; just under half, confined to Ocean View, was coloured; and a tiny number, living on employers' properties or squatting in the bush, were African.

In the 1980s and 1990s the Valley changed dramatically, becoming primarily a suburban extension of the city of Cape Town. The population doubled over 20 years. The town of Fish Hoek and the existing villages of Kommetjie and Noordhoek expanded, and new suburbs were built on old farms across the length of the Valley and the adjacent hillsides. By the early 2000s, middle-class immigration and suburban development had resulted in an almost contiguous line of suburbs crossing the peninsula, from the Atlantic on the west to False Bay on the east. In 1991, a semi-formal settlement, Masiphumelele, was established for African people. Initially intended for the small number of African people already living in the Valley, either legally or illegally, Masiphumelele grew quickly as people moved in from elsewhere in Cape Town or from the Eastern Cape. By 2001, Masiphumelele was home to about 20 per cent of the population of the Valley. Further population growth in Masiphumelele probably increased its share to about 25 per cent by 2004. Although the white population is now a minority in the Valley as a whole, this area still shows the spatial impress of apartheid: almost all of its coloured and African residents still live within the narrow confines of Ocean View and Masiphumelele, whilst richer, white residents live in the suburbs and smallholdings that stretch across the peninsula from one coast to the other. (See the introductory photographs [Photos 1–6], which depict the diverse infrastructure and landscapes of the three neighbourhoods in the Valley.)

The Valley shows many signs of change since the apartheid era. Almost everyone has access to electricity, a flush toilet and regular refuse collection – including those living in Masiphumelele. Municipal services are funded primarily through property taxes on the rich and, therefore, entail considerable redistribution to the poor. Fish Hoek, Ocean View and Masiphumelele all have at least one primary school and a high school. All three have at least one health facility. The clinic in Masiphumelele is home to a pioneering, world-class treatment programme for people with HIV/AIDS. In other respects, however, the legacy of apartheid is very clear. In Masiphumelele, people get water from taps in their yards, not inside their houses. Most live in very small shacks built of wood and metal sheeting. Only a few live in three-room brick homes recently built with government funds. Here – and in Ocean View – large families sometimes live in one small room and several families share a yard, flat or house designed for one.

Whereas Fish Hoek has tennis courts and lush sports fields with clubhouses, Ocean View has only bare soccer fields, and Masiphumelele a patch of ground filled with rubble, which until recently was covered with temporary classrooms for the high school. Fish Hoek has a wide range of supermarkets and shops; tea rooms and restaurants; and an 80-year-old department store. Ocean View has a handful of formal shops, including a small supermarket, butchery and video-hire store, as well as informal shops operating out of people's homes. Masiphumelele has only informal spaza shops run from shacks, roadside sellers and shebeens (bars). The particular characteristics of the buildings, streets and shops, as well as the way residents use them, make each neighbourhood look, sound and feel very different. Only the occasional dog-walker or school pupil can be spotted on Fish Hoek's pavements, whereas most streets serve as pavements in Ocean View, and Masiphumelele's narrow roads are bustling with activity. In both the latter neighbourhoods, children play games that straddle the entire street while adults chat on street corners and over fences. As evening falls the music from the shebeens in Masiphumelele gets louder while the streets of Fish Hoek get even quieter.

Differences in infrastructure correspond to economic differences between residents of the various parts of the Valley. Apartheid fostered not only racial residential segregation, but also racial economic inequalities. In the 1950s and 1960s, better-paying occupations were reserved for white people, whilst access to privileged education meant that from the 1970s, white people could dominate these occupations even when statutory job reservation was abolished. The Coloured Labour Preference Policy meant that employers were required to employ coloured workers in preference to African workers, whilst influx control (the pass laws) accentuated the vulnerability of African people and curtailed their mobility and access to even semi-skilled employment. This history was reflected in patterns of employment and unemployment in the early 2000s. In 2001, the unemployment rate stood at 8 per cent in Fish Hoek; in Ocean View it was 24 per cent; but in Masiphumelele it was a massive 61 per cent. Unemployment rates were highest among younger people, at 10 per cent, 31 per cent and an extraordinary 73 per cent respectively. Of the working population of the Valley, most managers, professionals, teachers and nurses live in Fish Hoek. White-collar workers are evenly divided between Fish Hoek and Ocean View. Most skilled or semi-skilled workers and some labourers live in Ocean View. In Masiphumelele, occupations are limited to domestic work or commercial cleaning (for women) and unskilled labour and security-guard work (for men).

A major reason why people living in the different areas of the Valley have different occupations – or indeed have jobs at all – is the variation in their education levels. It was perhaps the racial inequality in public education where apartheid left its most pernicious legacy. Four out of five adults (aged 20 or more) in Fish Hoek and its suburbs had matric or even post-matric qualifications in 2001; the equivalent proportion in Ocean View and Masiphumelele was just one in five. In both Ocean View and Masiphumelele, almost a quarter of the adult population completed less than grade-7 schooling. The big differences in schooling help to explain the differences in employment status and occupation between the middle-class suburbs, Ocean View and Masiphumelele. But education does not explain the differences between Ocean View and Masiphumelele. The education levels of the adult population are much the same, but the unemployment rate is much higher in Masiphumelele than in Ocean View, and Ocean View workers are in better-paid occupations than those in Masiphumelele.

The combination of unequal earnings and very different unemployment rates ensures that there are huge inequalities in household incomes across the Valley (see Figure 1.1). In 2001, the poorest fifth of households had incomes of less than R10 000 per year, whilst the richest fifth had incomes of (approximately) more than R150 000 per year. The poorest households are mostly in Masiphumelele, the middle-income ones in Ocean View and the higher-income households in the middle-class suburbs. The mean household income in Fish Hoek and its suburbs is approximately three times the mean household income in Ocean View and eight times that of Masiphumelele.

Its persistent residential segregation and material inequality along race-group lines renders the Valley both typical and atypical at the same time. It is typical in the sense that post-apartheid South Africa as a whole remains highly segregated residentially (Christopher 2001, 2005) and great disparities persist in employment

Figure 1.1 *Household incomes in the Valley*

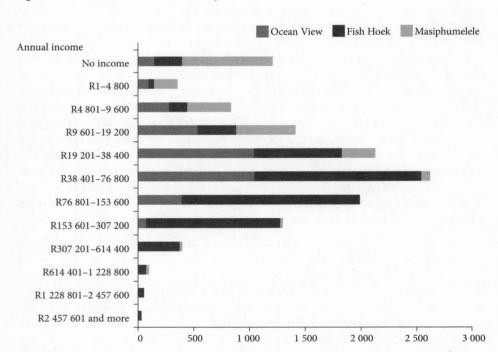

Source: Stats SA (2001)

and earnings between racial groups. But the Valley is atypical in other respects. Firstly, it is unusual in the major cities for white, coloured and African people to live in as close proximity as they do in the Valley. In Cape Town, the vast majority of people live in mono-racial neighbourhoods clustered in mono-racial parts of the city. In this respect, the Valley is much more like a small town than a part of a large South African city. Secondly, the tri-racial composition of the Valley is typical of Cape Town and the Western Cape, but not of South Africa as a whole. Most of South Africa comprises a massive African majority and a small white minority. Only in the Western Cape (and its much less populated neighbour, the Northern Cape) is there a large coloured population and an African minority. Moreover, a much higher proportion of the population of the Valley is white than that of Cape Town as a whole (45 per cent compared to 19 per cent). In terms of income and class, the Valley is also much more diverse than most urban areas of its size, for the same reasons that it is distinctive in residential terms. In this respect, the Valley is a microcosm of Cape Town, precisely because it is unlike other mono-class and mono-racial parts of the city. The distribution of household incomes in the Valley is broadly similar to that of Cape Town as a whole, except that in the city as a whole there are relatively more households that have a very low income.

Masiphumelele, Ocean View and Fish Hoek are all examples of a common category of race- and class-segregated neighbourhoods across South Africa. Masiphumelele is like many other post-1980, low-income settlements that started off as informal settlements, but have since been transformed through municipal infrastructural development, service provision and house construction – except that it is unusually small, feels more 'rural' (residents say) and has better job opportunities. It is not yet as formalised a settlement as places like New Crossroads (described by Henderson 1999 and Ramphele 2002), and it is certainly *not* like the older apartheid-era townships, such as Soweto (outside Johannesburg). Ocean View is perhaps typical of the working-class townships built to house coloured people removed under the Group Areas Act, such as Mannenberg (see Salo 2004), although it is unusually isolated geographically. Both the older and newer areas of Fish Hoek are much like 'white', middle-class residential areas across South Africa. In subsequent chapters we present survey data on adolescents in Cape Town that distinguish between 'poor African', 'medium-income African', 'poor coloured', 'medium-income coloured', 'rich coloured' and 'rich white' neighbourhoods. In these terms, Masiphumelele is a 'poor African' neighbourhood, although it includes a minority of households with a medium income. Ocean View is a largely 'medium-income coloured' neighbourhood, although it includes minorities of poor and rich households. Fish Hoek is a 'rich white' neighbourhood, although it includes a small minority of people who are not 'white' and some 'white' people whose incomes are low or medium (see Figure 1.1).

The study of ordinary young South Africans

So this book is about ordinary young people in reasonably ordinary South African neighbourhoods. The young people living in these areas whom we describe in this book are, we believe, not atypical of the 20-odd million ordinary young people who have spent most or all of their lives in a democratic, post-apartheid South Africa. These are tomorrow's voters, parents, workers and consumers. Yet astonishingly little has been written about this huge cohort of South Africans.

The predominant emphasis in literature on children, adolescents and youths in South Africa has been on atypical groups. As with most other social science research in South Africa, research on childhood and adolescence has been heavily reactive to the political environment. In the 1980s and into the 1990s, the primary focus of such research was on the participation of young people in political protest and violence (Marks 2001; Ntsebeza 1993; Seekings 1993; Straker 1992; Van Kessel 2000). Although it was sometimes assumed – or even asserted (e.g. Straker 1992) – that most young people participated in protests, this was never demonstrated, and no evidence was presented on the experiences of ordinary children and adolescents. Most research was conducted among an undoubtedly atypical sub-sample of activist youth. (A subsequent study by Dlamini [2005] explored how many young people tried to construct ordinary lives amid widespread violence and heightened politicisation.) In the early 1990s, during the transition from violent conflict to political negotiation, a 'moral panic' over the subversive 'lost generation' of youth first erupted and then evaporated (see, for example, CASE 1993; Van Zyl Slabbert et al. 1994). Adolescents in South Africa's townships who had boycotted and failed to complete school, who had fought with the security forces in township streets, who had challenged the authority of parents and teachers and who had used violence against other township residents in the name of 'the struggle' became the 'lost generation' of 'marginalised youth', undermining public safety and morality and perhaps even the stability of the political transition. Moral panic was fuelled by the media and legitimated by the fast-growing policy-studies industry (Seekings 1995, 1996). With the peaceful transition to democracy in 1994, policy-oriented research shifted its focus from the 'problem' posed by older youth to the problems facing younger children, especially specific groups of children, such as street children or AIDS orphans (Bray 2003a).

The study of the everyday lives of ordinary children and adolescents was not entirely neglected before and during the demise of apartheid. Burman and Reynolds's edited volume, *Growing up in a Divided Society: The Contexts of Childhood in South Africa* (1986), provided an important antecedent for our own study. In the mid-1980s, Reynolds (1989) conducted pioneering ethnographic work on the everyday lives and cognition of young children in New Crossroads, a poor Cape Town neighbourhood, whilst Jones (1993) studied children living with their families in the hostels built for male migrant workers. The end of apartheid meant that new space opened up for scholars to study the challenges facing children – especially poor children. Psychologists Dawes, Donald and Louw collaborated on edited volumes, *Childhood and Adversity: Psychological Perspectives from South African Research* (Dawes & Donald 1994) and *Addressing Childhood Adversity* (Donald et al. 2000). In the early 1990s, social anthropologists Ramphele and Henderson, worked with teenagers from New Crossroads. Henderson (1999) wrote of the extensive efforts by children and adults to maintain nurturing relationships and of the fragility of these ties in the face of apartheid and its consequences. Ramphele's *Steering by the Stars: Being Young in South Africa* (2002) provided a searing account of teenagers struggling to achieve their ambitions in the face of parental neglect, material hardship, dire schooling and destructive pressures from friends and neighbours. Barbarin and Richter's *Mandela's Children: Growing up in Post-apartheid South Africa* (2001) used data from the Birth to Ten study of a cohort of children born in 1990 in Greater Johannesburg to set out the behavioural, emotional and academic problems experienced by children faced with neighbourhood violence, household poverty and dysfunctional families. (The project was later extended into a Birth to Twenty study that examined the birth cohort through their teenage years.[1])

Our book builds on the foundations laid by these earlier studies. We follow in the footsteps of scholars such as Reynolds, Ramphele and Henderson in trying to understand the everyday lives of young people by talking to them and spending time with them. We follow the lead of the Birth to Ten project in making use of quantitative data. We pay particular attention to the choices that children and adolescents themselves make, i.e. to their agency, as they navigate their ways through the many challenges and more occasional opportunities of life after apartheid. Most importantly, perhaps, we do not confine our analysis to poor or African children, but extend our gaze across all of the neighbourhoods in our multiracial Valley. A series of excellent studies has focused on the experiences of children in racially mixed schools (Dawson 2003; Dolby 2001; McKinney 2007; Soudien 2007). We go further by examining not only the experiences of interaction in the exceptional spaces provided by relatively privileged schools, but also the experiences and consequences of non-interaction described by the majority of children and adolescents, even in a multiracial area like the Valley.

'Race' and definitions of race

Even in the space of the first few pages of this book we have been unable to avoid using the racial vocabulary that is deeply entrenched in both scholarship and everyday life in South Africa. Scholars routinely preface their work with an apology for using apartheid-era categories, but rarely reflect on precisely why and how they are using them. The South African state and Statistics South Africa claim that their reasons for retaining apartheid-era racial classifications are to target policies of 'redress' on the 'historically disadvantaged' and to monitor their progress in overcoming racialised patterns of inequality. Such arguments do not explain why social scientists use the same racialised terms, as if they have explanatory or causal value, namely explaining or causing important patterns and dynamics in social, economic or political life.

There are a number of possible reasons why race might seem to have some continuing causal effects. Insofar as racial discrimination persists in the new South Africa, race might denote vulnerability to advantage and disadvantage. In terms of health, race might be a proxy for distinctive genes rendering individuals more or less susceptible to particular illnesses. Given the relationship between race and class (whether class is defined in terms of what people do, what they get, or the opportunities open to them), race is often a proxy for class or class background – especially in Cape Town. It is, however, an increasingly less accurate proxy as the relationship between race and class erodes. The apartheid state's success in segregating residentially the population by race also means that race is often a proxy for neighbourhood, i.e. for the effects that living in particular neighbourhoods have on different aspects of life. Finally, race might denote distinctive cultures in terms of values, attitudes and beliefs. Originally distinct 'settler' and 'native' cultures have interacted with each other over several generations and both have been influenced by global cultures, with the result that both have been transformed repeatedly. But South Africa is clearly far from being a cultural melting pot. None of these effects are homogeneous or monolithic: racial discrimination, even when present, affects people differently; genes vary among even close kin; race and class are no longer coterminous, primarily because of an increasing diversity of class within the majority racial groups nationally and provincially in the Western Cape; neighbourhoods vary across short distances; and cultures are fluid and varied. Nonetheless, racialised identities are still salient in the lives of most South Africans – albeit often alongside other identities of class, religion and so on.

This book is in part about the ways that race continues to matter in the lives of young people, for any or all of the reasons above. As racial discourse is common and important in everyday life, it would be inappropriate to avoid examining it directly, and that can hardly be done without employing the discourse ourselves. Qualitative studies (e.g. Soudien 2007) suggest that racial categorisation remains salient for young people, but in *some* rather than *all* contexts. Survey data from Cape Town show that most young people readily employ apartheid-era racial terminology to describe themselves (Seekings 2008). Even within the 'coloured' population there is evidence of the salience of 'coloured' identity (Adhikari 2005).

To avoid erroneous causal inference or the impression of internal homogeneity, we try to avoid making racial distinctions except when we believe that race does have some meaning (according to one or other of the mechanisms identified above). Therefore, when we think that race is simply a proxy for class or neighbourhood, we identify individuals in terms of class or neighbourhood. But there are many cases where it is difficult and probably misleading to avoid racial vocabulary. There are some important differences between poor 'coloured' and poor 'African' neighbourhoods, for example. These may be due to lingering cultural diversity, variations in economic opportunities, differences in the organisation of social life or other reasons. Whatever the reason, we distinguish by race between neighbourhoods and, occasionally, households or individuals. In so doing, we use the vocabulary 'African', 'coloured' and 'white'. Some young people describe themselves as 'black' or 'black African'. We use 'African' because 'black' is also often used to encompass all those previously disadvantaged, including the 'coloured' population. This usage of African raises an additional difficulty: many people who would in the past have been classified as 'white' or 'coloured' now have an 'African' identity in that they identify with the continent of Africa rather than other continents. This African identity can and often does coexist with racialised identities such as 'white' or 'coloured', and many may see themselves in these terms. We are not including these individuals in our usage of 'African'.

Researching the everyday lives of children and adolescents

Our choice of research methodologies reflected our goals. First, we were concerned to break out of the racial segregation that characterises so much of what is written about South Africa. Rather than write only about African children and adolescents, we sought to conduct an integrated and comparative analysis of young lives across physical and social space, and especially across racial boundaries. Comparing and contrasting experiences across the social and geographical boundaries of race and class is crucial also for an assessment of the extent to which and manner in which the new political dispensation has made a difference to the lives of ordinary South African children. Secondly, we were concerned to focus primarily on the lives of 'ordinary children'. Whilst we knew that ordinary children are part of a highly heterogeneous group and many face major challenges and obstacles in life, we did not want to focus only on those children who are deemed (invariably by adults, and usually by the elite) to constitute a social problem. Thirdly, we sought to engage with, and make connections between, the various social arenas and relational spheres in which children operate, especially the home, neighbourhood and school. Studies that simultaneously explore several domains of South African children's lives are rare, but valuable because they illuminate the importance of ordinary social settings and the many dimensions of resilience and vulnerability (Ward et al. 2007). Finally, we wanted to understand the experiences of young people across a range of ages comprising both childhood and adolescence in order to comment on what is important to each age group in the present day and to reflect on the influence of childhood experience on the perceptions and decisions of adolescents. Overall, our aim was to explore the everyday interactions of ordinary children, and to build an understanding of the manner in which their actions, relationships and well-being are influenced by their social worlds, as well as by the nature and extent of their agency in shaping these worlds.

We therefore employed two very different but complementary approaches. The first was an in-depth qualitative study of children and adolescents living in the different neighbourhoods of the Valley. The second entailed the analysis of quantitative data from a study of a large sample of adolescents across Greater Cape Town. By combining qualitative and quantitative research, we sought to overcome the weaknesses or limits inherent in each. Surveys are unable to pursue the links between meaning and experience, while qualitative studies are limited in their ability to generalise findings beyond the small sample investigated.

Most of the quantitative data used in this book come from the Cape Area Panel Study (CAPS) conducted by the Centre for Social Science Research at the University of Cape Town.[2] CAPS is a panel study that, starting in 2002, followed the lives of a large, representative sample of adolescents in Cape Town as they underwent the multiple transitions from adolescence to adulthood. During 2002, a representative sample of almost 5 000 young people between the ages of 14 and 22 was interviewed. Since 2002, most of these young participants have been re-interviewed several times, although little of the data from these re-interviews are used in this book. CAPS covers a range of aspects of adolescence, including schooling; entry into the labour market (i.e. employment, unemployment and job search); sexual and reproductive health; and experiences within families and households. Most data are collected from the young people themselves, but also from parents and other older household members, and data on individuals and households have been combined with community- and school-level data. CAPS is not simply a study of adolescents or adolescence. Because the patterns of inequality in society as a whole are rooted in the differentiation evident or generated in this age span, CAPS is also a study of transition – and the lack of change – in 'new' South African society as a whole. The objective was in part to assess and understand how the opportunities for South Africans have – or have not – changed since the end of apartheid.

The CAPS sample was drawn through a two-stage process in which initially neighbourhoods and then households within neighbourhoods were selected (Lam, Seekings & Sparks 2006). The response rate was lower in rich neighbourhoods with mostly white respondents than in poorer, African or coloured areas. Attrition between the waves of the study differed similarly, although 75 per cent of the initial panel were re-interviewed in the third wave (in 2005). Non-response and attrition set some limits to the representativity of CAPS data, especially among older white adolescents. However, the CAPS data are the best available, and attrition rates are well within the bounds of what is accepted internationally. Weighting the data helps to deal with some of the more obvious problems. The CAPS sample includes some young people from the Valley, but the number is small and the sampling design means that they cannot be considered as representative of the local population. We do not report, therefore, separate results from CAPS for the Valley. Instead, we use CAPS data to analyse aspects of childhood and adolescence in Cape Town generally.

Panel studies such as CAPS that conduct very highly structured, short interviews with large numbers of respondents enable us to identify social patterns that point to the challenges and opportunities for young people. Quantitative methods and analysis alone are of limited use, however, in understanding the motivations and constraints that underlie these patterns or the ways in which they are experienced. The strength of ethnography is its ability to investigate the way the world appears in the eyes of those whose lives are the focus of study. The central purpose of our extensive ethnographic research in the Valley was to make connections between the perceptions and actions of young people (and of the adults with whom they interact), and between their experiences and features of the wider environment in which they live.

The core of the qualitative research was conducted by three of the authors of this volume (Rachel Bray, Imke Gooskens and Susan Moses) in 2004 and 2005 (with some research continuing into 2006). Initially, we spent most time with children and adolescents on school premises, observing interaction during tuition hours in the classroom and in after-school activities. We then began using local schools and community centres for weekly art and discussion groups (described below). These centres were more spacious and neutral in the sense that they were not associated with hierarchical teacher–pupil relationships. The fact that the only relationships at play in these settings were those between the young people present and the researchers gave us insight into peer relationships. Time was also spent in their home environments. Only after having built trusting relationships with the young participants (and securing parental consent) did we conduct in-depth interviews with them.

Our approach could be described as an iterative process consisting of a mosaic of methods designed to build rapport with, enable observation of and elicit conversation with young people and the adults whom they defined as significant, in a variety of everyday settings. It was not one of total immersion traditionally used by anthropologists because none of us lived within the neighbourhoods we were studying. All of us – the authors of this book – live in Cape Town; one of us just outside the Valley and some in neighbouring areas of Cape Town that share many similarities with the higher-income parts of the Valley. Like Reynolds (1989), Jones (1993), Henderson (1999) and Ramphele (1993, 2002), we spent many long days and occasional evenings in the neighbourhoods we were studying. While confident that our multiple strands of enquiry illuminate the diverse facets of young people's lives, we are aware that observation of the kind possible through long periods of residence would have deepened our insights.

We are also aware that our own linguistic abilities and cultural heritage posed challenges to interpretation. As Ramphele (2002: 22) reflects in relation to her research in a primarily isiXhosa-speaking neighbourhood: 'Knowledge of language, idioms, customs and traditions and their distortions is an essential tool in tackling social questions, which leaves white social scientists, generally unfamiliar with black South African languages, at a disadvantage.' None of us speak isiXhosa fluently and not all of us speak Afrikaans well. Two isiXhosa speakers, one a mother living in Masiphumelele, collected data with us (particularly from younger children), interpreting both language and cultural nuance between researcher and participants. Adolescents spoke in both their home tongues and English, the combination providing opportunities to probe idiom and meaning.

By extending the research over 15 months we were able to observe the impact of events on young people's lives and thinking. Observation over a period of time gave us some insight into the character and strength of social norms influencing individual behaviour, and into the differences between what children and adolescents said they would do should certain events arise and what they actually did. Another benefit to the long duration of fieldwork was the ability to reflect on changes in young people's perspectives and actions as they mature. It was particularly instructive to witness our participants anticipating moving through their educational careers, making expected or unexpected transitions and then reflecting on these changes.

At the outset, we elected to work with three age cohorts of young people, spanning late childhood to late adolescence, in order to attain a better understanding of age-related differences and the process of growing up. The age cohorts selected were 10–13, 14–16 and 17+. We sought to work with pupils in specific grades at school. Permission was given by the Western Cape Department of Education and the respective principals. Owing to a large variation in the age of children in each class in some schools, our samples were not exactly the same in different areas. In Masiphumelele, for example, our older age cohort included some young people up to the age of 22. We spent time in classrooms and school grounds observing and talking to young people about our study and the after-school activity clubs that we planned to run. Young people responded positively – although with more enthusiasm in Ocean View and Masiphumelele than in Fish Hoek, probably because of the relative paucity of extracurricular activities on offer in these first two settings. The possibilities afforded by visual media for explorative data collection with children (Christensen & James 1999; Johnson & Ivan-Smith 1998) impelled us to establish weekly art clubs for the younger age cohort in each community. The older teenagers expressed a preference for a regular discussion group, diary writing and drama workshops as ways of generating information, and were happy to make use of visual methods within these more informal sessions. Teachers also helped recruit participants, taking into account our goal of forming groups of mixed gender, socio-economic background and individual ability. Participation in these groups was entirely voluntary: the method of recruitment into the project entailed self-selection.

The participants included very few young people who had left (or 'dropped out' of) school, or perhaps entered into the world of gangs. Our focus on ordinary children and adolescents comes at the price of paying scant attention to the minority of children and adolescents who reject the schooling system. Our participants may also be unrepresentative even of the ordinary majority in that they are individuals who exhibited initiative and greater enthusiasm than their peers to join the study.

In each study site (i.e. Fish Hoek, Masiphumelele and Ocean View) and each age cohort, we collected some data from a large group of more than 30 young people and then worked more intensively with a smaller group of between 5 and 15 people (see Table 1.1). The smaller sample generated most of the in-depth material drawn on in this book, whilst the broader sample provided data to contextualise these findings within a wider spectrum of experience and opinion. Some fieldwork was also conducted with younger children in Masiphumelele and Ocean View. This focused on care-giving relationships, developmental stages and work roles in the home in Masiphumelele (see Brandt et al. 2005; Bray 2003b; Bray & Brandt 2006, 2007) and on community mapping and issues relating to support and challenge in Ocean View (see Moses 2006).

The participants in the smaller sample provided basic socio-demographic information, including household composition, place of residence and parental employment. This exercise suggested that our samples were broadly representative of the wider population. It is possible that by working with young people who were not involved in crime or other socially proscribed activities, we may have generated an overly

Table 1.1 *Details of participants in ethnographic research*

Neighbourhood	Young children	Pre-/early teens (10–13)	Mid-teens (14–16)	Late teens (17+)
Fish Hoek				
Larger sample			70 grade-9 students in the classroom	47 grade-11 students in the classroom
Smaller core		15 grade-6 students	10 grade-9 students	6 grade-11 students
Masiphumelele				
Larger sample		40 grade-6 students (classroom observation)	55 grade-10 students in the classroom	
Smaller core	5 children < 5 years; 12 children in grades 1–3	15 grade-6 students	12 grade-10 students in workshops	13 grade-10 students who wrote diaries
Ocean View				
Larger sample		24 students in grades 4–7	120 grade-8 students in classrooms	120 grade-11 students in classrooms
Smaller core	19 children in grades 1–3	15 students in grades 4–7	12 grade-8 students	8 grade-11 students

rosy picture. However, the fact that several young participants had direct or indirect experience of so-called antisocial activities, while others attended school irregularly (or even left school, temporarily or permanently) during the 15 months of our research, shed light on the social processes underlying these actions. As we will discuss in Chapter 5, the nature of school attendance and mobility served to question the utility of defining young people neatly into 'school-going' or 'non-school-going/drop-out' categories.

Our approach to the ethics of research (see further Bray & Gooskens 2006) was based on standard ethical guidelines for social research with minors, and paid special attention to the need to protect them from any possible harm associated with their participation (see, for example, Boyden & Ennew 1997; Greig & Taylor 1999; Schenk & Williamson 2005). This entailed, but was not limited to, careful attention to informed consent. Information sheets and consent forms were designed for young children, teenagers and adults; colourful cartoon-style drawings were used to enhance the accessibility of the material designed for the youngest age group. Written in each of the three predominant local languages (Afrikaans, English and isiXhosa), these documents set out the right *not* to participate and explained how we would ensure confidentiality. They were used as resources within conversations about the study and the implications of being part of it, not as replacements for verbal explanation and discussion. We were especially concerned that young people understood what their participation entailed, and used the documents as the basis for continuing discussion in the course of our research. The few who stopped attending sessions were not put under pressure to return, but were informed that they were welcome should they wish to return. The children and adolescents themselves chose the day, time and (where possible) the location of our meetings. In general, we sought to allow the young participants in our study to participate in making decisions about how we conducted our research. Their comments on our findings and interpretations were gleaned during a day-long feedback gathering that involved the core samples of young people from all three neighbourhoods. Opportunities to write stories for the media (see Chapter 4), contribute to a graffiti wall, debate core findings and give consent to artwork being used in media and scholarly publications entailed efforts on our part to fulfil our obligations to the young people with whom we worked.

Six teenagers from the Valley became part-time researchers with us and exercised some control of the design and implementation of fieldwork. The 'Tri' group, as they dubbed themselves, consisted of two teenagers from each of Fish Hoek, Masiphumelele and Ocean View, aged 17 or 18 and studying in grade 11 at the outset of the study. (Keen to establish a group identity, the young researchers chose the name 'Tri' because it reflects the interaction and work of people from three neighbourhoods.) We sought to provide an opportunity, not usually available to teenagers in the Valley, to meet weekly to discuss a range of personal, social, political and historical issues. Our rationale for inviting teenagers to be research partners was political and social, as well as empirical. Their motivation for joining the research team complemented our intentions in that they wanted to gain skills in social research as well as to find out about, as one of them described, 'what is going on in the lives and minds of young people living in the Valley'.

Heedful of the lively international analysis of so-called participatory research with children (Boyden & Ennew 1997; James 2007), we aimed to go beyond the tokenistic or even exploitative involvement of young people found in many studies. Close, long-standing relationships between the six young researchers and three adult researchers were built over the research period (and continued after). After careful preparation, the young researchers conducted interviews, which we then discussed extensively. The data produced by young researchers were cross-checked in a similar manner to all our material: they were not assumed, therefore, to be accurate or authentic merely because they were generated by children or adolescents. Our weekly meetings facilitated regular opportunities for young researchers' feedback on substantive or ethical issues. Not only did we learn a lot from their research, but the partnership itself became an important learning process, for us as well as for the young researchers.

Our research on friendship, dating and sexual behaviour involved material from an additional source as well as from the main ethnographic project and CAPS. One of us (Kahn) was separately conducting research among 20 grade-12 girls from the different parts of the Valley, some of whom were already participants in the main ethnographic project. Intimate relationships and sexuality are recognised as sensitive topics of research, particularly when conducted with young people. However, we found that after building rapport over time, young people were comfortable – and enthusiastic – about discussing these issues. Many of them told us that there are few spaces available in which they are able to talk about such matters and welcomed the opportunity to discuss them. Chapter 7 is based on information that was shared with us by young people whom we came to know well, most of whom were female and in their late teens. We have less information from boys or from younger children. We also have little information on young people's experiences within homosexual relationships.

Our research in the Valley was designed to give young people the space to raise and pursue issues that they considered important, relatively unconstrained by preconceived academic – and, therefore, adult – categories. We used a range of methods, some of which were purposely open-ended and others that were designed specifically to elicit information complementary to, but unavailable within, studies such as CAPS. We kept journals of our observations and conversations with and about children and adolescents. We combined one-to-one interviews with participatory group activities, including art and drama, which enabled young people to express themselves. Our methodology was iterative (see Reynolds 1989), allowing us to respond to young people's own priorities and understandings. Among the participatory methods we employed were exercises in which young people mapped their neighbourhoods (see Chapters 3 and 4) or their support networks and challenges (see Chapters 3 and 8), and a modified version of the 'hero book' (see Morgan 2007), whereby children write and illustrate their life-stories with themselves as the heroes. Older adolescents who were hesitant to discuss their more personal everyday relationships kept diaries and were given disposable cameras to take photographs illustrating their diaries. These pictures stimulated valuable discussions about relationships. Together with the drama company Jungle Theatre, we also ran drama workshops with older teenagers.

Whilst our focus was very much on working with children and adolescents, we also spoke to a range of adults relevant to the project. These included the participants' relatives, neighbours, teachers, social workers; church and NGO (non-governmental organisation) leaders; and police officers.

Rights, agency and transition

South Africa is no island. Just as young South Africans are exposed to the international world of fashion and consumption, listen to imported music and wear – or aspire to wear – imported clothing brands, so we, as social scientists, have been influenced by the changing study of childhood and adolescence internationally.

In both our methods and our analysis we have been influenced by the growing recognition worldwide of the rights of children. Such rights require that children are not simply treated as the subjects of public policy to promote their well-being, but that they should also have a say in the decisions affecting their lives. In South Africa, a rights-based approach underlies the work of the Children's Institute at the University of Cape Town; the Child, Youth, Family and Social Development Programme at the Human Sciences Research Council (Dawes, Bray & Van der Merwe 2007); and individual studies of, for example, child labour (Budlender & Bosch 2002; Levine 1999, 2002; Streak et al. 2007), social security for children

(Leatt 2007), service responses in areas where AIDS rates are very high (Giese et al. 2003; Meintjes et al. 2007), and the quality of pre-school education (Dawes & Biersteker 2009). Both locally and internationally, the popularity of participatory research with children within scholarly and policy spheres has meant that precedence, authority and authenticity have been given to children's voices, without the appropriate critical reflection on how these 'voices' are being produced and interpreted.

A second important influence on us was the emergence of a new paradigm in childhood research within anthropology and other social sciences initiated by European scholars (James & Prout 1997; Jenks 1996; Qvortrup et al. 1994), as well as more recent reflective interrogation of the achievements of work conducted in this paradigm. This new paradigm is now the common starting point for social research involving children in South Africa and internationally. Typically, it recognises both the historical and cultural variations in notions of ideal childhoods; moves away from studying children simply as members of families or communities undergoing processes of socialisation into adulthood; and focuses instead on their everyday experiences as social actors navigating through socio-economic, cultural and political environments (see, for example, Boyden & Holden 1991; Hecht 1998; Nieuwenhuys 1994).

The focus of scholarship on childhood has shifted away from identifying what children lack to understanding the particularities of their daily lives, the meanings associated with their actions, and their relationships (Matthews & Limb 1999; see also Stephens 1995). Affording children agency has become popular even with the World Bank, which endorsed seeing and treating children and adolescents as 'decision-making agents' in its *World Development Report 2007* (World Bank 2006: 53) and which emphasises its own efforts in listening to young people (through focus groups in developing countries). But, as James (2007) points out, opening up conceptual and practical space in which children can speak as research participants and researchers, does not ensure per se that children's views are heard at the level in which they contribute to our understanding of and theorising about the social world.

In South Africa, development psychologists working cross-culturally have recognised the centrality of children's perceptions in their relationship with the social and physical world around them, asserting that 'the way [children] perceive their circumstances will influence the way they respond to their human and physical contexts' (Donald, Dawes & Louw 2000: 4). Studies such as Henderson's (1999), Reynolds's (1989, 1995) and Ramphele's (2002) revolve around the real choices that young people make, albeit rarely in contexts of their choosing, and the immense consequences of their choices on their unfolding lives. In other words, the significance of children's understanding of the world in directing their actions, the consequences of which affect these individuals and those of all ages around them alike, is well understood. Perhaps less well interrogated is the recognition of children as cultural producers, an analytical stance that requires understanding children from the perspective of their own 'multiple life-worlds' (Stephens 1995).

Viewing children and adolescents as actors, decision-makers and shapers of the wider social world, however constrained, raises difficult questions about the appropriate age bounds for a study such as ours. The problems with setting a lower bound are practical and ethical: the conduct of ethical research with younger children requires a different approach and methodology to those used with older children (Dockett & Perry 2007). Our research was conducted with children from about the age of nine, for practical, more than theoretical, reasons. The problems with setting an upper bound are more conceptual. If we move away from viewing adolescence simply as an episode of transition to adulthood, during which some adolescents deviate and constitute social problems, then how do we demarcate the experience of adolescence, i.e. of 'growing up', as we declare in our title? The American National Research Council's project Transitions to Adulthood in Developing Countries confronted this directly by considering the preparation of young people for five key adult roles: as adult workers; voters and community participants; spouses; parents; and household managers. The project defined a 'successful' transition to adulthood not in terms of traditional rites of passage or becoming a productive worker, but instead in terms of (quoting Amartya Sen) the acquisition of the capabilities that allow young people 'to lead lives they have reason to value and to enhance the substantive choices they have' (quoted in Lloyd 2005: 24; Lloyd et al. 2005).

Whilst the general form of a successful transition might be common to all developing countries, the precise form will vary, for example in terms of the balance between individual autonomy and embeddedness in larger households and communities. In addition, the transition was becoming more extended in many settings:

> In the past, young men and women tended to move directly from childhood to adult roles. But today the interval between childhood and the assumption of adult roles is lengthening. Compared to the situation twenty years ago, young people are entering adolescence earlier and healthier, more likely to spend their adolescence in school, more likely to postpone entry into the labor force, and more likely to delay marriage and childbearing. (Lloyd 2005: 2)

An emphasis on transitions into adulthood lends itself to empirical measurement, as is evident in the Transitions to Adulthood in Developing Countries project and the World Bank's *World Development Report 2007* (World Bank 2006). Using CAPS data relating to young people's first experiences of sex, pregnancy and birth; leaving school; and marriage or cohabitation, Biddecom and Bakilana (2003: 15) found that 'the pathways taken through adolescence are characterized by more disorder than order in terms of the variety of combinations and chronological sequences of important social and family formation transitions'. Table 1.2 presents data from Cape Town – also mostly from CAPS – on the five transitions identified in the 'Transitions' study. What is immediately striking is how long several of the transitions are delayed. By or at the age of 22, most, but not all, young people have some experience of work, and one-third of young women have children. But marriage and cohabitation are very rare, and few young men admit to paternity. Most young people at the age of 22 are still living with parents or other older non-sibling adults. Only a minority of young people vote; even fewer attend civic meetings.

Table 1.2 *Markers or indicators of the transitions to adulthood*

Dimensions of adulthood	Marker or indicator	Percentage of young people in Cape Town who have made the transition by or at the age of:		
		18	20	22
Workers	Ever worked*	42	65	72
	Working now*	18	43	46
Spouses	Ever married*	1	1	8
	Ever cohabited without ever being married*	1	6	6
Parents	Men who are fathers	2	3	11
	Women who are mothers	9	24	34
	Men who live with their children	0	1	3
	Women who live with their children	8	20	31
Independent household managers	Not living with mother, father or other older generation kin	12	21	33
	Self or spouse is head of household	3	7	16
Citizens and community participants (public responsibility)	Registered to vote	The IEC estimates that 58.5% of young people aged 18–25 registered to vote in the last elections.**		
	Vote	58% of people aged 18–29 at the time of the 2004 elections later claimed that they had voted.***		
	Attend community meetings or participate in community organisation (excluding age-specific)	21% of people aged 18–29 say that they have attended a community meeting in the past 12 months; another 25% say they would do so if they had a chance.***		

Sources of data:
* Cape Area Panel Study wave 1 (2002)
** Nyc.gov.za. Note that this is for South Africa as a whole.
*** Cape Area Study 2005
Note: IEC = Independent Electoral Commission

In post-apartheid South Africa, 'transitions' are rarely neat moments of permanent and irreversible change from one state (characteristic of adolescence or youth) to another (associated with adulthood). This is most clearly the case with respect to employment. Among 22-year-olds, three-quarters have worked at some time in the past, but fewer than half are currently working. In Cape Town, one in three young people aged 20–22 are studying and another third are not studying but working, mostly full-time. The final third are neither studying nor working. Of these, just over half have never worked, whilst many of those who have worked in the past have only done temporary or part-time work. This is because unemployment is so widespread in South Africa, even in urban areas such as Cape Town. High rates of unemployment in turn constrain both marriage (or cohabitation) and the establishment of independent households. There are few men aged 22 who admit to having children, but even among the minority who do, few are actually living with their children.

Young people leave school, then return. Some have children, but typically remain living with older kin. Some do form independent households, but even this is not necessarily a permanent shift. Reality in societies like South Africa is very different to the clear transitions that characterised northern European and North American societies in the mid-twentieth century. There is no neat movement from school to work, from financial dependence to independence or from living with parents to marriage and parenthood of one's own. Childhood, adolescence and adulthood are not neat, sequential phases, but experienced and ascribed in various ways at various points in an individual's maturation. Therefore, the question is as much about investigating changes in social status experienced by young people and the blurring of boundaries between these changes as it is about considering age differences. Moreover, in South Africa, children themselves appear to be primary agents in the design and timing of their own complex 'transitions'.

Given the complexity of transitions and ascribed status, the choice of any age bounds for the study of adolescence is ultimately arbitrary. This book discusses young people of a variety of ages and without any fixed end point, but we say little about men and women after the age of 22. Our labelling might be arbitrary, but we have endeavoured to be consistent. We use the terms 'children' to refer to young people aged 13 and under; 'adolescents' to refer to young people between the ages of 14 and 17; and 'young adults' to refer to young people between 18 and 22 years of age. The term 'young people' describes members of all these age groups. Our focus in this book is on what we are calling children and adolescents, namely people younger than 18.

Outline of the book

Family and home are of crucial importance to young people, both objectively and subjectively, and are the focus of Chapter 2. One of the most invidious aspects of apartheid was the system of migrant labour, regulated through the pass laws, which separated husbands from their wives, and fathers from their children for long stretches of time (see, for example, Ramphele 1993; Wilson & Ramphele 1989). People classified as coloured were not subject to pass laws, but suffered from discriminatory public-housing policies (relative to white people), with the result that people in places like Ocean View lived in grossly overcrowded houses. The pass laws might have been abolished and new housing projects reduced overcrowding in many places, but domestic arrangements remain complex and 'fluid', and the stable, discrete, nuclear-family household is far from standard.

In Chapter 2, we show that most children and adolescents hold to an ideal in which they live with both biological parents, and both parents provide not just material support, but also emotional intimacy and reciprocal respect. We find that there are striking similarities between the norms and ideals attached to family life among children and adolescents in all parts of the Valley. They prioritise sharing time and tasks with adult family members above material provision. They identify active engagement and interest on the part of family members as critical to building their own self-esteem, especially given that the peer environment is often challenging. Young people emphasise the importance of open communication, trust and respect, and experience relationships to be most fulfilling and supportive when trust and respect are reciprocated between adults and children. In the cases of children and adolescents who do live with both biological parents, these ideals are sometimes achieved. For others, however, the experience of living with both parents is less rosy. Whilst generally reluctant to discuss parental shortcomings and aware of the difficulties posed by long work hours, domestic conflict and other factors, young people are critical of adults' failures to meet their ideals, and many adolescents become especially critical of mothers who are seen to *choose* to neglect their children. Fathers, especially, can be abusive, to the extent that some teenagers opt to leave home and move in with other relatives. This is much easier to do in certain parts of the Valley – Ocean View and Masiphumelele – where the model of a nuclear-family household is more of an imagined ideal than a lived reality. In Fish Hoek, adolescents face few easy alternatives to living with their biological parents; any other arrangement is stigmatised in terms of a 'broken home'. For them, the nuclear-family household can serve as an inhibiting constraint.

The experiences of children and adolescents who do *not* live with both biological parents are also examined in Chapter 2. A few live apart from their mothers, and typically turn to other kin as mother figures. But it is difficult for other kin to perform all of the roles played by most co-resident mothers. More children live apart from their fathers, sometimes because their fathers have died, but more often because they have left (or never lived with) the mothers. Paternal absence need not entail the disruption of relationships between children and their fathers. Young people often represent their fathers in terms of financial and material provision, but we found that fathers often perform significant acts of social and emotional care and that even material provision is valuable to their children as a symbol of emotional attachment and care. Grandparents, 'aunts' and others often provide continuity in caring relationships and domestic routines, even when children and adolescents physically move between households. Neighbours, too, can perform important quasi-parental roles. Overall, we conclude that it is not the particular composition of the domestic group per se that matters to young people, but the quality of relationships therein. Moreover, the qualities of relationships sought and nurtured by children and adolescents align with the principles of South Africa's new democracy and, at least in theory, honour the duties and entitlements of younger and older generations.

Chapters 3 and 4 extend our gaze beyond the home to the neighbourhood. As noted already, the Valley comprises discrete and largely mono-racial neighbourhoods. Even when the notion and language of a new integrated South Africa is familiar to all, the local neighbourhood remains critically important. Young people construct a sense of community from, and draw support through, regular interaction with people and in spaces they use often and know well. Chapter 3 examines where children and adolescents play, relax or hang out; their friendships; and how these contribute to identities and a sense of belonging, and, therefore, how young people define self and other in the everyday local context. Chapter 3 examines security and the ways in which children and adolescents try to protect themselves. Widespread concern about safety, among all generations, sets limits on young people's mobility, especially for girls and young children. Middle-class children and adolescents spend a larger proportion of their time at home, and their interactions in their immediate neighbourhoods are both limited and structured by adults. They often feel constrained and disempowered by their restricted independent mobility. By comparison, their poorer peers spend a large proportion of time in the space around their homes playing and socialising, despite concerns about safety. Because they are mobile independently of adults, they have considerable control over the manner and extent to which they draw on neighbours for material and emotional support. Poor young people's much greater participation in the public life of the neighbourhood has a downside, in that it exposes them to public scrutiny and makes them more vulnerable to rumour and gossip. These characteristics of neighbourly interaction deeply affect children and adolescents because they resonate with the gulf between the aspirations associated with a new democracy and the realities of persistent challenges in realising personal goals.

Chapter 4 considers the ways in which the boundaries of community are drawn and sometimes crossed. Persistent residential segregation means that most children and adolescents in the Valley have little direct knowledge of their peers in other neighbourhoods; readily reproduce stereotypes about them; and often feel both curious about and threatened by these 'others'. They attend schools, socialise and engage in organised or informal recreational activities within their immediate, mono-racial neighbourhoods. The limited mobility between neighbourhoods and interracial contact that does occur is typically in one direction, from poorer neighbourhoods into richer ones, and involves individuals from each neighbourhood who are relatively wealthy in terms of family income or social networks. Thus, some young people from Masiphumelele have some direct knowledge of Ocean View, but not vice versa, and some young people from both neighbourhoods have some direct knowledge of Fish Hoek, but, again, not vice versa. The primary spaces of interracial interaction are, therefore, generally linked primarily to the middle class: Fish Hoek High School, which has a significant minority of African and coloured pupils; the Longbeach shopping mall; some churches; and a youth-focused NGO. Pupils attending Fish Hoek High School display an apparent disregard for race in some respects, including personal identity and friendship patterns, at the same time as they construct a cultural world that is highly racialised in terms of the labelling of taste and fashion. The shopping mall provides an unusual, interracial and even cross-class space for young people, but even in the mall young people tend to remain in neighbourhood-based, and hence mono-racial, social groups, interacting with each other across racial lines as groups, but not as individuals.

Schools are popularly considered to be the arena in which social change consistent with democracy can operate most directly and realise its potential. Chapters 5 and 6 examine schools, first as educational institutions, then as social arenas. Chapter 5 begins with a summary of the general character of schooling in post-apartheid South Africa, demonstrating that policy reforms (including the redistribution of resources to schools in poorer areas) have not resulted in substantial improvements in the quality of schooling. Schooling outcomes remain very unequal. Even in Cape Town, which has unusually good schools by South African standards, good pupils in poor neighbourhoods fail to acquire the skills of even the weaker pupils in rich neighbourhoods. Chapter 5 proceeds to draw on ethnographic research in the Valley in order to go beyond survey data and probe the reality of the classroom. In schools in poorer neighbourhoods, many (but not all) classrooms are not looked after, teachers are poorly motivated and do not explain material, and there is a high level of indiscipline during classes. Teachers' frustration and lack of interest fuels – and is fuelled by – rebellion among pupils. Teachers fall behind the requirements of the curriculum and then race ahead, leaving weaker pupils stranded far behind. Pupils who are struggling with the material rarely get the individual attention that they need. Many speak positively about those teachers who encourage them and who are approachable about problems at home and with school work. But few comment on the educational commitment of their teachers. As a result of the poor teaching they receive, many adolescents have little understanding of what pupils need to do in order to achieve educationally. Adults in the neighbourhood, including their parents, are no better informed, having been part of the apartheid state's highly compromised and inequitable education programme. And because of this history, they expect the state to deliver to their children the proper education they were denied.

Schools in richer neighbourhoods display a very different and virtuous cycle of teachers who are (generally) motivated and capable and pupils who are (generally) disciplined and industrious. There are some dedicated and successful teachers in schools in poorer neighbourhoods, just as there are some ineffective teachers at schools in richer neighbourhoods. In general, however, pupils in different schools have very different experiences of and at school, and these differences explain much of the divergence in their later lives.

Chapter 6 explores how the real worlds of public schooling are shaped heavily by the social location of schools in the neighbourhood, by pupils' home backgrounds and by the meaning of education for young people and the older generation. It begins by exploring the economic, social and cultural factors that lie behind the decisions of most parents and children in poor neighbourhoods to attend poorly performing local schools. Unfamiliarity, marginalisation and illiteracy among adults at home and local norms surrounding the respective roles of schools and parents are found to be major barriers not only in selecting better schools, but in supporting their children in their efforts to keep up with their school work. For these pupils, access to someone in or near home who is able, available and willing to help with homework and talk about challenges at school has a greater impact on their motivation and performance than the (sometimes considerable) obstacles posed by material poverty in the home. Shaped by apartheid-era inequalities, these factors also explain the gulf between the very high educational expectations of adolescents and parents, and the difficulties young people in poor neighbourhoods face in achieving these. Adolescents in different parts of the Valley enter secondary school with similar aspirations: they want to pass 'matric' (the grade-12 school-leaving examination), go on to higher education, and secure a well-paid and respectable job. Most parents make real sacrifices to enable their children to attend better schools. But most adolescents in poor neighbourhoods fail to achieve their own and their parents' aspirations, partly because they do not understand what is required to do so.

Chapter 6 also considers what else young people do at school besides learning, and what the identity of 'school pupil' means. Young people in all schools expend a great deal of time and energy on cultivating peer relationships, but these take on a greater significance to children and adolescents in schools where the teaching is inconsistent and educational rewards are uncertain. Adolescents are under pressure from peers to engage in activities that are often experienced – and always described – to be incompatible with study. Their use of a morally imbued discourse to categorise each other as being on the 'right' track (e.g. investing time in school work) or the 'wrong' track (e.g. prioritising peer relationships) speaks of an attempt by the young to maintain personal control and integrity with respect to familial and neighbourhood expectations in what is a highly challenging environment. A close look at young people's decisions regarding attendance at different points of the school career sheds light on subtle but significant differences in the value attached to education between neighbourhoods, as well as the knowledge underpinning these values. Both real and perceived understandings of future opportunity in a post-apartheid setting explain why in Fish Hoek and Masiphumelele education is seen as *the* route to success by adolescents and their parents, whereas in Ocean View it is seen as *a* route to success for the small minority.

Chapter 7 turns to the private and intimate realm of young people's sexual lives and entry into the world of parenthood. At first glance, these seem to be arenas in which broader, sociopolitical change would have little direct influence. But historical influences on the contours of gender roles, the formation of intimate relationships and the manner in which knowledge is contained and shared all have a bearing on the decisions young people make today. So too do their perceptions of social identity and personal opportunity – or otherwise – that are associated with being the first generation to grow up after the demise of apartheid. In their teenage years, adolescents in all parts of the Valley enter into relationships in which sex plays a big part. They either enter into intimate and sexual relationships with other boys or girls, or they decide not to do so. Many, but not all, discuss sex and relationships with their friends. Sex hangs over their relationships with their parents, changing the relationships, even when – as is usually the case – it is rarely discussed. Parental silence about sex is generally broken only by directives to daughters to avoid sex so that they might avoid the 'disasters' of pregnancy or 'disease'. Parental attitudes towards sex seem to be gendered in all parts of the Valley: daughters are to be protected and remain chaste, but sons can do much as they like. Few adolescents learn about sex from their parents, and some remain ignorant – and anxious – because of a lack of constructive discussion within the peer group. In all parts of the Valley there is peer pressure on adolescents – especially on boys, but also on girls – to have relationships and to have sex. Sex is bound up with a rebellion against parental authority and with style and status. Girls expect to receive gifts from the boys or men with whom they have sex, and they seem to have similar consumerist aspirations in different parts of the Valley. But the consequences are different in the richer and poorer areas. In the wealthier neighbourhoods, girls often receive financial support from their parents, and do not need to rely on boyfriends for new clothing or other markers of style and success. This means that girls in poorer areas are more vulnerable to the brutality and violence that often seem to accompany transactional sex. Adolescents are mistrustful of each other – for good reason, as friends try to 'steal' boyfriends or girlfriends. Knowledge of HIV plays almost no role in shaping sexual behaviour: it is pregnancy that girls fear, and which attracts stigma (but is also sometimes a marker of rebellion). Some adolescents seem to exercise agency by embracing sex, but this generally comes at the cost of their studies; others resist pressures to have sex, but it is not easy to resist peer pressure and the status associated with having a sexual partner. Overall, whilst there are some differences between rich and poor neighbourhoods, teenagers in different parts of the Valley think and behave in broadly similar ways.

Chapter 8 asks the fundamental questions of where and how, in a society still riven with inequalities and restricted opportunities, children and adolescents are able to make decisions and act in ways that bolster their own well-being. In this way, it considers young people's agency in their interaction with adults and peers around them, firstly through their own definition of such agency. Adolescent perceptions of their own self-efficacy are influenced by neighbourhood poverty, the relationship between historical disadvantage and perceived current opportunity and culturally validated norms shaping child rearing. Also central to children's and adolescents' sense of control of self and of their life paths is the quality of their everyday interpersonal relationships through which they achieve support, encouragement and a sense of self-efficacy when such relationships are characterised by reciprocity and trust. Information and the knowledge required to make positive decisions are described by many poor young people as critical gaps in what is offered even within very positive interpersonal interactions. Faith in God and participation in religious activities bolster young people's self-efficacy, particularly within the peer group. So too does the individual decision – often publicly asserted – to live by certain codes that are consistent with culturally validated goals and life paths, such as passing exams and pursuing formal education. Decisions like these tend to provide young people with only a short-term sense of control over self and the world around them, primarily because they rely on the myth that success is guaranteed by investment in certain institutions (such as school) and their associated practices. A range of structural, economic and sociocultural factors act to facilitate or limit young people's self-efficacy within the home, local neighbourhood, school and peer environment. The middle section of this chapter draws together findings presented in detail in previous chapters that explain variations within and between neighbourhoods in young people's control over self and their achievement of personal goals and socially ascribed markers of status. Finally, we look at the narratives of a young person entering adulthood in each of the neighbourhoods studied and describe the implications of our study for further research on the social, cultural, economic and intrapersonal dimensions to the transition to adulthood in contemporary Cape Town.

The book's conclusion draws together our analysis of the spectrum of experiences and possibilities of ordinary children growing up in post-apartheid Cape Town. It illuminates the achievements of the young in building and sustaining relationships across physical, social and emotional distances created during, and in response to, apartheid. In this way, young people are able to engender intimacy and nurture, thereby protecting themselves and others in ways consistent with Nelson Mandela's assertions of their power to heal not only themselves, but also society. That said, however, contemporary society places a range of restrictions on young people in pursuing the opportunities theoretically available to them, in accessing knowledge and in creating identities that are dissociated from former racialised categorisations. Moreover, our evidence raises the possibility that some children and adolescents are doing too much to care for themselves and others, and may risk long-term costs to their well-being. In the second decade of South Africa's democracy, the immediate neighbourhood in which young people live remains the most critical factor in defining their everyday experiences and opportunities. As yet, there is little movement of people, ideas and resources between neighbourhoods. And broad community institutions that encompass all class, neighbourhood and race groups are scarce and fledgling in nature. Children and adolescents enjoy engaging in these when given space to do so. But few (if any) provide a forum in which they can bring issues for debate and action, and in so doing share the information urgently needed to fill knowledge gaps, develop new vocabularies for understanding difference, and build a collective sense of identity in which local 'othering' is overlaid by legitimate claims on the state and civil society for basic human rights and the creation of a social world that better matches the rhetoric of the post-apartheid era.

2 Discourses and realities of family life

I was at home with my family making supper and talking about my day. We shared hugs and kisses. I felt *happy* because I know that my family loves me. (Diary entry by Nonkululo, girl, aged 15, Masiphumelele, living in a one-room shack with her mother, stepfather and two younger sisters.)

Sat on couch and ate supper while having a conversation with my mom. Spoke of morals and values, attributes, family, brother, dad, future, exams. I felt happy; I enjoy talking to my mom about anything...Lying in bed before going to school, I thought of how privileged I am to have the family I do. (Diary entries by Justin, boy, aged 18, Fish Hoek, living with his mother and siblings.)

We don't even sit and eat supper together because we are not a happy family. They [her parents and brother] eat together in my mother's bedroom and I eat in my room...I choose not to join them because they pretend to be a happy family, but they are not and I don't like the falseness of it all. (Interview with Veronique, girl, aged 17, Ocean View, living with her parents and younger brother.)

Apartheid had devastating effects on many families, reproducing in family life the divisive hierarchies and separated living imposed on society by the state. Privileged South Africans enjoyed relatively comfortable lives, and were strongly encouraged to live in stable nuclear families, in part through state-validated Christian ethics. A larger number of disenfranchised families were wrenched apart: wives and children were prevented from living with husbands and fathers, and extended families forcefully scattered. Unsurprisingly, family life and home for children of the current generation comprise very diverse experiences. Neither Nonkululo nor Justin lives with their fathers, but they paint positive pictures of their families. Veronique lives with both parents, but expresses her alienation from her family. Neighbourhoods and their associated sociopolitical histories have some bearing here. But children's experiences of family life vary widely *within* neighbourhoods, whereas their ideals and challenges are strikingly similar *across* the Valley.

The contours of family membership for children in contemporary Cape Town are shaped by, but cannot be reduced to, the effects of apartheid, for at least three reasons. Firstly, and most obviously, the end of apartheid meant the abolition of many policies that structured families in different ways. Secondly, whilst the past has left its legacy in the present in terms of the *form* of many families and households, the complex meanings and everyday undertakings of being a family member and sharing a home are not the consequences of only the form of families and households. Thirdly, the children and adolescents growing up in post-apartheid South Africa have themselves shaped and reshaped the terrain of family life through their ideals, actions and aspirations. This chapter explores children's everyday realities in the home and family. It illuminates where and how they succeed or fail to protect and bolster their well-being through their domestic interactions and kin relationships.

The impact of apartheid on family life

> When if I think of Ocean View and the family unit, for me the main factor [that impacts on young people emotionally], I think it's the absent father. We have loads and loads of single parents. We do actually have quite a fair amount of fathers who are raising their children single-handedly, but…most of the families have the absent father. (Social worker and mother, Ocean View)

> Many children at school [in Fish Hoek] are from 'broken homes' and are largely unsupervised…I see parents and families coming in for kids who are in real trouble. You do what you can [as a teacher] but it's hard; the parents don't have it together enough to provide what the kids need. (Teachers in Fish Hoek)

Apartheid affected all South Africans, but did so in very different ways. The most pernicious effects on the family were experienced by people classified as 'African', for whom the physical and psychological integrity of family life was undermined through the apartheid state's policies of 'separate development', 'influx control' and underinvestment in rural areas. Influx control (i.e. the control of immigration into towns) by means of the pass laws and restrictions on housing separated many African parents from each other as men moved to urban areas for work, leaving women and children in rural homes. Restrictions on African people were especially severe in the Western Cape because it was declared a Coloured Labour Preference Area, meaning that employers were required to show preference to coloured workers over African workers. As recently as 1970, African people comprised only 10 per cent of the total population of Cape Town. In the late 1970s and 1980s, many women began to subvert the system of influx control, migrating to the cities themselves, but leaving children in the care of grandparents or other kin in rural areas. Many grandmothers received old-age pensions, which underpinned this pattern of childcare, with many children physically separated from their fathers and even their mothers. Low wages – and from the 1970s, rising unemployment rates – further impeded men from fulfilling their role as providers accorded them by cultural ideals, and risked alienating them from the familial care nexus (Jones 1993; Ramphele 1993; Wilson & Ramphele 1989).

Coloured people may have been privileged compared to African people, but their family life also suffered under apartheid. Forced removals under the Group Areas Act (No. 41 of 1950) uprooted families to new neighbourhoods – such as Ocean View – far from their workplaces. Such removals disrupted established relationships of support between kin and neighbours. Poverty was widespread and housing scarce, so that houses were often severely overcrowded, with married children living with their parents and grandparents. The position of men within the family was further undermined by preferences for women as permanent employees in the Western Cape's dominant canning and textile industries, and national welfare and housing legislation that paid cash grants to women (for child welfare) and favoured women as 'heads of household' in state housing allocations (Salo 2004).

Policy reforms at the end of apartheid changed some, but not all, aspects of the environment. The repeal of influx control legislation allowed further rapid urbanisation among African people. The African population of Cape Town doubled in the 1980s and again in the 1990s, rising from only 10 per cent to more than 30 per cent of the city's total population. The state provided large areas of land for settlement and subsidised the construction of new housing. The consequence for African people in Cape Town as a whole was a sharp reduction in overcrowding, although this was much less apparent in Masiphumelele than elsewhere. Some African women chose to leave their children in the rural areas (Henderson 1999; Jones 1993; Lee 2002; Ramphele 1993; Reynolds 1995; Spiegel & Mehlwana 1997), but many brought their children to Cape Town, and – for the first time – many African children were born in Cape Town. The rapid increase in the population of children required a massive school-building programme. Relatively few resources were invested in housing for coloured people, so that by the early 2000s, coloured households in Cape Town were generally larger than African ones.

Whilst policy reforms have made it easier for children to live with their parents, high unemployment and persistent poverty have continued to undermine family life. Economic factors probably explain a large part of the decline in marriage and the rising rates of parental separation and illegitimacy. The expansion of the public welfare system, in particular through the rising value of old-age pensions for most elderly people at the end of the apartheid era and the expansion of child-support grants to poor mothers in the 2000s, has given African women more economic independence (although reforms have disadvantaged coloured women). Older women living in extended-family households continue to play a major role in the care of children in both coloured and African neighbourhoods. Men have been excluded from the public welfare system; often rely on ad hoc, infrequent, daily labour (whilst women have relatively stable domestic work); often participate in gangs or take drugs when young and drink heavily when older. The result, according to Ramphele, has been that the 'family' is in 'crisis', with men (and paternal kin) playing ever smaller roles in their children's lives, whilst women are forced to bear ever more diverse responsibilities (Ramphele 2002; Ross 1995; Salo 2004).

Scholarly attention has understandably been directed primarily towards those who suffered under apartheid. Little social scientific work has been done on the white families privileged by apartheid. However, an abundance of fictional and autobiographical literary works offers insights into the economic, social and moral environments of these families (Behr 1995; Coetzee 1998; Courtenay 1989; Heyns 2008; Trapido 2003; Van der Merwe 2006). State policies that gave precedence to white male employment bolstered the strongly gendered roles of male breadwinner and female homemaker that were upheld within the dominant, traditional Christian churches (Van der Merwe 2006). Alongside job and income security came the expectation of a stable, contented, nuclear family life, an ideal that was often consciously preserved in order to mask oppression and conflict within the home (Behr 1995; Coetzee 1998). Many white children had full-time African or coloured nannies, who, from their infancy, provided food, company and care. A normative and economic system that supported the employment of nannies and other domestic staff in effect shifted a large portion of the intimate, caring role away from mothers (Courtenay 1989). It also provided the only point of interpersonal contact between race groups. While the parameters of this relationship were often restricted, strong friendships were formed between young white children and those of their parents' African and coloured employees – only to be disallowed as they grew older.

Differences and similarities in the *form* of families and households after apartheid can be identified using data from surveys like the Cape Area Panel Study (CAPS). The most striking feature of households in Cape Town in the early 2000s is the extent of parental absence. Fewer than half of all adolescents and only just over half of children in Cape Town live with both of their biological parents (see Tables 2.1 and 2.2). This, together with the presence of non-nuclear kin, means that the two-parent, nuclear-family household is the exception rather than the rule (see Figure 2.1).

Table 2.1 *Whereabouts of (biological) mothers and fathers of children aged 0–13 in Cape Town (% of total)*

		Father is…			
		In household	In other household	Deceased	Total
Mother is…	In household	56	28	4	88
	In other household	2	7	1	10
	Deceased	1	1	1	2
	Total	59	36	5	100

Source: Cape Area Panel Study 2002
Note: Figures are rounded off and therefore do not always add up to the reported total.

Table 2.2 *Whereabouts of (biological) mothers and fathers of adolescents aged 14–17 in Cape Town (% of total)*

		Father is…			
		In household	In other household	Deceased	Total
Mother is…	In household	46	24	9	80
	In other household	4	10	2	16
	Deceased	1	2	1	5
	Total	50	36	13	100

Source: Cape Area Panel Study 2002
Note: Figures are rounded off and therefore do not always add up to the reported total.

Figure 2.1 *Family-based household types, adolescents aged 14–17*

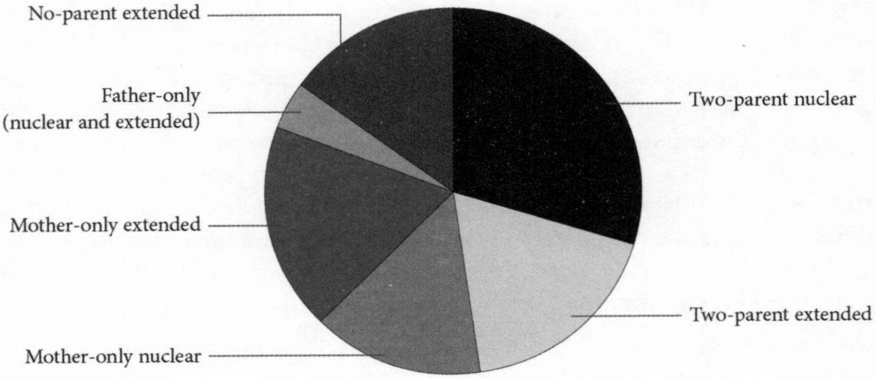

No-parent extended

Father-only
(nuclear and extended)

Mother-only extended

Mother-only nuclear

Two-parent nuclear

Two-parent extended

Source: Cape Area Panel Study 2002

Parental co-residence and absence do vary significantly by race, but they also vary by class, and the differences between racial groups are perhaps less pronounced than we might have expected. Figure 2.2 shows the proportions of children in Cape Town living with either or both parents, disaggregated by the kind of neighbourhood. Neighbourhoods are identified by race and household income. Race is included because its effect on household structure is probably not limited to the effects of apartheid policies of racial segregation and discrimination. It is likely that household structure is also shaped by cultural diversity. Whilst elsewhere in this volume we analyse differences by neighbourhood rather than race per se, in this chapter we discuss the effects of race as encompassing both neighbourhood and cultural effects and differences.

Levels of household income have a stronger influence than race group on parental residence, indicating that the post-apartheid economic landscape exerts a stronger influence on family composition than former state policies. Children living in poorer households are much less likely to live with both parents and more likely to live with neither parent (see Figure 2.2). In total, only 32 per cent of children under 13 in low-income households live with both parents, compared to 46 per cent of their age cohort in medium-income households and 69 per cent in high-income households. This relationship is very clear within the coloured population, but is somewhat muted in the African population. Because there are so few white children in low- or even medium-income households, it is difficult to detect any relationship within the white population. Race makes a difference in that African children in low-income households are less likely to live with one or both parents than coloured children in low-income households, but there are negligible differences between white and coloured children in households with high incomes. The pattern is essentially the same among adolescents aged 14 to 17.

Figure 2.2 *Proportion of children aged 0–13 in Cape Town co-resident with parents, by race and household income*

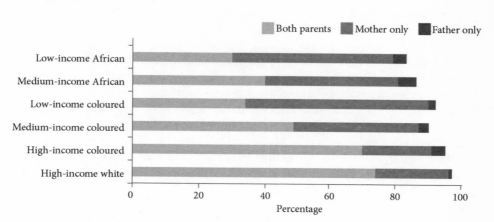

Source: Cape Area Panel Study 2002

Of those young people who do not live with both parents, the majority live apart from their father. Maternal absence is much less common than paternal absence: only about 12 per cent of children and 20 per cent of adolescents do not live with their mother (see Tables 2.1 and 2.2). Therefore, while it is generally the case that young people live with their mothers, it is *not* the norm that they live with both of their parents. In low-income households, it is far more common for children to live apart from their fathers than with them. Even in high-income white households, just under one-third of children live with only one parent. As children and adolescents grow older, they are more likely to live apart from their mothers. This is true also for fathers, but primarily because a rising proportion of the fathers of young people have died and less because of parental separation.

Anthropologists have pointed to the prevalence of what is termed 'domestic fluidity' among African people in Cape Town, as adults and children move between households (Ross 1996; Spiegel 1996). Fluidity is not limited to African children, however. There are also coloured and white children who currently live with one or both parents, but have not always done so; similarly, some do not currently live with one or other parent, but have done so in the past. Figure 2.3 shows the proportions of their lives that adolescents have spent living with their mothers and fathers. In total, only half of adolescents have always lived with their fathers, and three-quarters have always lived with their mothers. The proportions of adolescents living with both parents are almost identical to those who have lived with their fathers, across all race and income groups.

In summary, the majority of young people growing up in post-apartheid Cape Town have spent some part of their childhood living apart from one or both parents. Less than half have always lived with both parents. Just over a quarter of adolescents have *never* lived with both parents, i.e. at the same time (almost always because of chronic paternal absence), and almost none have never lived with their mothers. These patterns have been noted in previous studies on African families (Barbarin & Richter 2001; Richter & Morrell 2006; Russell 1995; Spiegel & Mehlwana 1997), but they are not limited to them. Parental absence is less common in richer coloured and white households: almost two-thirds of children in these households have always lived with both parents; four-fifths have done so for at least half of their lives; and only one in ten have never lived with both parents. Even in these social groups, however, parental absence is far from unusual. Parental absence is also very common in poorer coloured households. There are both similarities and differences between African adolescents and coloured adolescents in poor- or medium-income households. Among both African and coloured adolescents, about half have lived with both parents for more than half (or all) of their lives. There is a striking difference, however, in that only a quarter of African adolescents have *always* lived with their mothers, whilst three-quarters of coloured adolescents in low-income households have done so.

The survey data show that racial and class differences persist in structuring children's experiences of sharing a home with their parents. African children are still much less likely to live with their mothers for large portions of their lives than their coloured or white peers. And low-income coloured and African children are much less likely to live with their fathers than high-income coloured and white children. Part of the correlation between parental co-residence and income might be that the departure of a father from a household reduces household income substantially. Two-parent households are likely to be better off, on average, than single-parent households. The correlation is also likely to reflect the effects of unemployment itself. Unemployment delays the age at which men marry, if they ever do so.

Figure 2.3 *Proportion of life spent with parents, by race and income, adolescents aged 14–17*

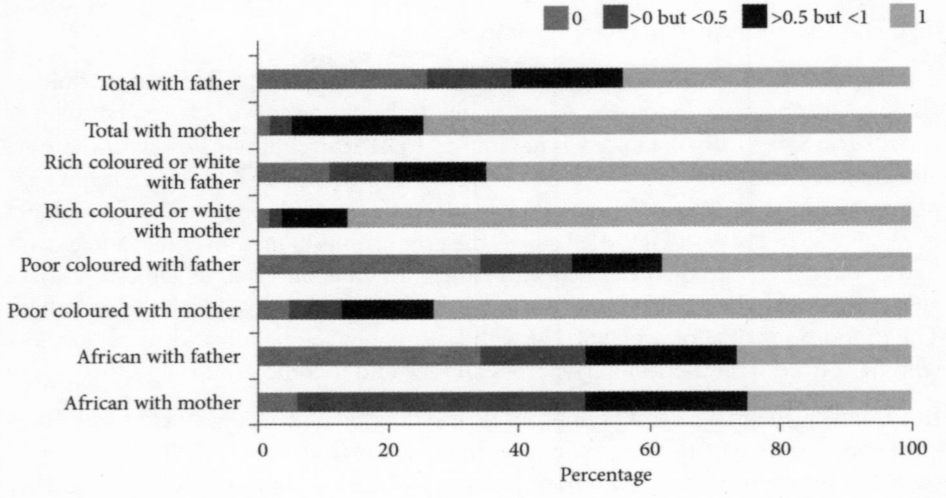

Source: Cape Area Panel Study 2002

The physical absence of one or both biological parents is a common experience for children in historically disadvantaged neighbourhoods like Ocean View and Masiphumelele, and is certainly not unusual in relatively privileged areas like Fish Hoek. These similarities are not obvious to people in these neighbourhoods. Apartheid-engineered residential separation and values of social hierarchy work together to prevent any sense of shared experiences among families. People of different racial categories have little knowledge of everyday life among the other racial groups (except, perhaps, through the relationship between domestic employers and their employees). Few people have the opportunity to recognise that many of the changes in gender relations, marriage, childcare strategies and parenting that characterise their own racial group might be shared by members of other racial groups. Physical and social isolation make difficult any sense of mutual empathy with the frustrations of maintaining family life across different neighbourhoods, or questioning the state's oppression across the demographic spectrum.

What do periods of living apart from one's biological mother or father mean for children in each of these sociocultural environments? In order to understand the significance of actual or potential change in family composition, we return to our ethnographic material to look carefully at the kinds of relationships children have with their parents, the nature of their investments in familial relationships and their responses to shortfalls in care or other risks to their well-being. Such a picture is critical to an accurate understanding of the contemporary meanings and consequences of previous and current parental absence for children. And it provides the necessary backdrop for comprehending the possibilities for children to achieve, and thrive within, a different kind of family life to that imposed by apartheid.

Heroes and providers: Children assert the parenting role

> My mom is my hero because if you don't have your mother then your life is not going to be the same again because she is always there for you. She takes me to the hospital if my arm is broken, makes me food if I come home, and gives me money if I ask her. (Robert, boy, aged 12, Ocean View)

> My parents do everything with me; they help me with homework and when I want something. They buy clothes for me to wear at Christmas. I am very proud of my mother and father. (Primrose, girl, aged 12, Masiphumelele)

When children were asked to draw or describe their heroes in the early stages of this project's fieldwork, those living in Masiphumelele and Ocean View invariably depicted their parents as reliable, unconditional providers. This image was sustained even by children who, we later learnt, had had ambivalent or negative experiences of being parented. In contrast, children in the Fish Hoek art club hesitated when asked to draw their heroes. Some eventually chose sports or movie stars, but spoke of them in only remote aspirational terms rather than as everyday heroes.

How should we interpret these differences? What is most striking is that the children who consistently position parents as all-providing sources of unconditional love and support are those living in neighbourhoods where many parents have struggled to fulfil these roles for several generations. These children appear to regard growing up without biological parents – or parent-figures ascribed the same role – as entailing extreme vulnerability, even in late adolescence. One young researcher asked Bonani, his soccer teammate, which age group he thought was most vulnerable in Masiphumelele, and why:

> I think that teenagers are most vulnerable because there are so many here who live without parents…Like for me, it's my parents who make me vulnerable 'cause they are still alive both of them, but they are not together any more. And neither of them wants to support me. I'm still young and I really need the support of parents. I dropped out of school because no one was supporting me and I really want to go back to school. My mother sometimes comes to visit me and if I ask her for something like money she refuses to give me, saying, 'I don't have money on me, I will send it to you some time' and it ends like that. (Bonani, boy, aged 17, Masiphumelele)

Two 15-year-old girls living in Fish Hoek were asked the same question by another young researcher and agreed that street children, who they thought come from Masiphumelele or Ocean View, are the most vulnerable and gave the following reasons:

> Helena: …they are kids who don't have a responsible adult around. They don't have the security. Kids need security. And they don't have a place where they are loved…

> Clare: They actually need their parents, who love and support them.

> Helena: Any child that is abandoned by their parents will feel worthless.

All three children assert that the physical presence of parents is important, as is their desire to, and demonstration of, support. As we shall show, context is very important in interpreting children's assertions of what is critical. For example, high death rates among adult males in poor neighbourhoods partly explain why paternal presence cannot be guaranteed for Bonani and his peers in Masiphumelele and Ocean View.

Understanding what is probable within a particular historical and social setting helped us understand why Bonani and his peers assert that parents should be all-providing, always reliable and unconditional in their provision. At this early stage, a number of interpretations were available. One was wishful thinking on the part of individual children who have little or no other means to achieve the kind of parenting they desire than to portray parents as fulfilling all their ideals. A second was that these assertions reflect a strong cultural interdict against talking to others about problems in the home, and the child's efforts to mask these from public scrutiny. Finally, the absence of parents from Fish Hoek children's portrayals of heroes suggested an unquestioned given, namely that middle-class children have no need to assert parental provision in a context where parents were, or were assumed to be, fulfilling all their children's needs. Ongoing ethnographic work produced strong evidence that these mechanisms work simultaneously, and revealed a more complex picture of young people's expectations of their parents and relationship ideals in the home.

Over time, we were able to observe the domestic and familial experiences of individual children in all three neighbourhoods – including the departure of a parent – and then analyse the children's perspectives on family life in the light of these. It was apparent in this process that children's portrayal of the parent-provider is the most readily vocalised of a range of strategies used by children to negotiate the realities of contemporary family life. Other strategies include the clear prioritisation of qualities within the parent–child relationship that bolster their well-being; an active engagement with the cultural rubrics guiding intimate domestic relationships in particular neighbourhood contexts; and a tacit acknowledgement of the socio-economic challenges faced by parents and adults more generally. While there were striking and unexpected consistencies in some children's responses across the Valley, others varied in form and in the children's ability to achieve the level of care and nurture they desired.

Eleven-year-old Mandisa is unusual among her peers in Masiphumelele in that she has always lived with both her biological parents. Her experiences of, and insights into, family life are, therefore, those of a young person growing up in relative stability in terms of her parents' presence. They provide a useful context against which to consider children's responses to parental mobility or their inability to fulfil aspects of the parenting role.

Mandisa recalls the movements of her family and individual family members as follows:

> I was born in Nyanga, another suburb of Cape Town, and lived there for three or four years. We then moved to Masi; I'm not sure why. My eldest sister stayed in Nyanga for a few years, as she was attending school there. My mother's cousin looked after her during that period, but then my mother said she must come here to live with us.

Her mother's decision is consistent with the strong opinion she voiced to us regarding living with her children, and reflective of a departure by some from traditional practices of raising children with grandparents in rural areas that is captured in other research among urban Xhosa-speaking families (Lee 2002; Spiegel & Mehlwana 1997). According to Mandisa's mother:

> The Eastern Cape is a good place to raise children, but there is no work so we have to be here. In this situation, I think it is better to bring up children here with us so that we can be together as a family, eat our meals together and such, rather than them staying in the Eastern Cape while we live here.

Unlike many of her peers, Mandisa has not visited the Eastern Cape since she was a toddler. Her drawings of a three-legged cooking pot and thatched rondavels suggest that she retains an important symbolic connection to Tsomo, the village in the Eastern Cape where both her parents grew up and her grandparents still reside. Mandisa regards Masiphumelele as her home, but is proud of her rural heritage. She and her parents share a sense of belonging to the urban world, while at the same time retaining a strong identification with their rural origins. Expressions of an urban-focused but rural-rooted identity are common among children and parents who have lived in Masiphumelele for a decade or more. Russell's (2003) comparative analysis of rural and urban African adults' ideas pertaining to appropriate familial behaviour found evidence of rejection of the rural tradition of multigenerational domestic groups, but points out how divided these respondents were in their views. For children and their parents in Masiphumelele, villages of origin and kin therein remain important for their ancestral heritage and because they offer a potential future resource base (Bray 2009).

Mandisa's parents are in their late 40s, married and attended high school, but did not matriculate. Her father runs a business from home, spraying and mending cars. Her mother used to work in a nearby company that supplied wood for housing construction, but now assists her husband in his car-repair business. Our visits to Mandisa and her family indicated a demand for their business and a level of economic stability: their spacious shack is well furnished and there was always food in the fridge.

Mandisa describes a strong caring environment within her immediate family and in her circle of local friends. She is a self-assured girl, popular with her friends in the art club, who described her as kind, loyal and fun-loving. She was invariably relaxed and contented during art club and when we visited her at home. Her drawings are done with a firm hand, are colourful and the people she depicts have smiles on their faces. Her teachers describe her as one of the most diligent and competent in the class.

Our interactions in her home and conversations with Mandisa over an 18-month period showed how much she valued spending time with her parents in ways in which they were actively engaged together or assisted each other in mundane domestic tasks, homework activities or something unusual. The fact that her parents were interested and involved in aspects of her life, and that she had an active role in the domestic economy, were critical to the quality of their relationships and Mandisa's experience of care. Her peers in the art club applied similar criteria to their assessments of their relative enjoyment of domestic tasks. According to 14-year-old Babalwa, 'the best job is washing clothes, as my mom and I do this together'. Arriving at their home, we often found mother and daughter jointly tackling a pile of laundry.

Her parents' steady income from their home-based business is a likely contributor to Mandisa's positive domestic experiences and general well-being. That said, the family is by no means wealthy and their relative economic security is not in itself a defining feature of family life in Mandisa's eyes, or as far as we were able to observe. Instead, it is the qualities of the relationships that she enjoys at home, and with her parents in particular. Explaining why she enjoys homework, Mandisa said: 'Doing homework involves my parents. They help me if it is too difficult for me, and so does my big sister. We do it together, and they are there to correct my mistakes if I have done it wrong.' Her parents left school before they completed grade 9 in a rural high school at least 20 years ago. The level of education they received will have given them some grounding in the subject matter that Mandisa is learning as a grade-6 student in Masiphumelele. However, as is clear from the fact that Mandisa's elder sister often assists, it is not their educational capacities alone that make a difference to Mandisa. Just as significant are their availability (made easier by their home-based business) and their willingness to devote time and mental energy to her school tasks.

Mandisa expects her parents to provide financially, socially and emotionally, and in return she puts time and effort into her allotted tasks at home, namely sweeping, washing up and making the beds. The inherent intergenerational reciprocity within this relationship is tempered with mutual respect and understanding that enables Mandisa's preferences to be acknowledged: 'I enjoy doing these [things], but I hate washing clothes. My mother knows of and respects my dislike, so she does not ask me to wash clothes.'

Earlier research in Masiphumelele showed that both girls and boys contribute to the domestic economy through their everyday chores (Bray 2003b). Girls work indoors, cleaning, cooking, doing laundry and caring for younger children, whereas boys are usually expected to do outdoor jobs, such as sweeping the yard, and may wash their own clothes. Girls tend to spend more time on domestic chores than boys.

Other girls and boys of Mandisa's age spoke of the conditions under which they are happy to do various domestic chores. They said that they objected to tasks that cut heavily into time needed to socialise with friends or do homework, and the underlying message was of a willingness to participate, but in a manner that did not involve being forced to do chores or being taken for granted.

Whether children were able to achieve these ideals in their domestic relationships depended in part on demographic and economic parameters that are largely out of their hands, and in part on their successful use of culturally validated discourses guiding intergenerational relationships. The former include children's gender and birth position, their mother's age and the household's composition and work arrangements at a given time. As the second of four children, all of whom are daughters, Mandisa enjoys some scope for negotiation when it comes to domestic tasks. Her older sister takes on a large share of the cooking and laundry. The fact that her parents are fairly young, in good health and work in or near home also allows for some flexibility in household chores. For many others, the consequences of apartheid-instigated underemployment continue to circumscribe their options. First-born or eldest resident teenage girls (and occasionally boys) whose mothers worked long hours often had little choice but to cook, clean and care for younger siblings before and after school. And whether willingly or begrudgingly, some learn the skills needed to work in the businesses their mothers run from the home, such as hairdressing or running a shop.

Patterns of movement that have a long-standing historical precedent, but are driven by current poverty and inequality, brought advantages to some: very light domestic tasks were given to children living in homes that included a female relative, usually in her early 20s, who had recently arrived from the Eastern Cape. These women were often responsible for the day-to-day domestic duties while older urban-based mothers worked, an arrangement usually made in lieu of charging rent and as a stepping stone towards the young immigrant finding employment and establishing a home (Bray 2003b).

In vocalising their wishes regarding domestic roles, children in Masiphumelele are making reference to, and to some degree challenging, actions by older kin and adults that derive from culturally sanctioned notions linking power with age and particularly generational difference. The isiXhosa word *ukuhlonipha* (to respect) is widely used by children and adults alike to describe what is considered an essential element of interpersonal relationships, especially those between generations. We heard it used frequently in conversations about the values that adults should inculcate in children, and about how children should behave towards their elders. IsiXhosa- and isiZulu-speaking parents participating in the study of child development markers used the term 'respect' to frame their descriptions of their child-rearing goals and practices (Dawes, Bray et al. 2004: 60). In her recent book on youth and identity politics in South Africa, Sibusisiwe Nombuso Dlamini (2005) points to the significance of *ukuhlonipha abadala* (respect for adults) in raising Zulu children. Importantly, these cultural scripts apply to anyone older, meaning that children are expected to show respect to children older than themselves. Dlamini observes that the practical demonstration of respect involves deference, polite speech and behaviour, and the use of non-confrontational ways of disagreement. Popular usage of the term by adults and children in Masiphumelele seemed at first to substantiate the picture painted in the literature, namely of a community value entailing deference by the young to adult authority (for example, Shelmerdine 2005). Testimonies such as Mandisa's point very clearly to the way in which children acknowledge dependence on adult kin for their everyday needs and a respect for their seniority and authority. Yet at the same time, they convey a degree of reciprocity and space for negotiation between children and adults that exist in everyday interpersonal relationships. This more open interaction suggests that *ukuhlonipha abadala*, as played out in contemporary Masiphumelele, is not as restrictive of children's abilities to influence adult decisions as it first appears. The question then arises as to where the limits of adult preparedness to reciprocate respect and decision-making power lie. The true test to reciprocity in these relationship qualities must lie in parental responses when children moot or embark upon risky or adult-like activities, such as going out late at night or bringing a boyfriend or girlfriend home.

During a drama workshop in Masiphumelele,[1] 15- to 17-year-olds who cast themselves in the role of parent wagged their fingers threateningly or beat their teenage children for staying out later than permitted. Before beating their children, several 'mothers' probed them for full explanations of who they were with, what they were doing, whether they were aware of the time and asked whether they were seeking punishment. In none of these scenes did young people challenge the decisions of their parents, or the methods used to exert authority. The message conveyed was of just desserts for their misdemeanours and of tacit deference to the older generation. These attitudes were also reflected in the sudden and non-consultative decisions of parents to move teenagers to relatives in the Eastern Cape when they suspected truancy or distraction from their studies.

Yet peppered within accounts of parent–child interactions are opinions and actions that oppose what many residents of Masiphumelele referred to as 'traditional' views. Teenagers reported parents' seeking their advice as to whether or not the family should move to a different yard or neighbourhood, and how to support members of the extended family. And mothers and fathers directly affected by HIV spoke of a growing proportion of adults who, like them, are being prompted to reconsider gender roles in the home and their assumptions regarding children's capacities by what they see happening locally (Bray & Brandt 2006). These parents not only demonstrated the nurturing role of men in the home, but spoke about its value in attempting to meet children's emotional and social needs when maternal physical and mental health are compromised. And they recalled their surprise that children aged between four and nine had understood the implications of their serious illness, and that those approaching adolescence could shoulder certain emotional and practical responsibilities. On the basis of such observations, they recommended talking to children about illness from a much earlier age than was ordinarily thought appropriate (Bray & Brandt 2006).

A degree of reciprocity in practical inputs, and subsequently respect, enables children and parents to sustain a tacit agreement between generations and, as illustrated in Peliswa's diary excerpt on page 68, is often articulated with regard to educational aspirations (see also Chapter 7). Thus, a strong thread of negotiable reciprocities between children and the parental, and even grandparental, generations is evident within the broader discourse of respect in Masiphumelele. Its presence and growing salience appears to relate to the ways in which democracy, modernity and contemporary threats to the integrity of the family are understood and experienced in this neighbourhood.

Further insights into the social and cultural landscape upon which children engage with their immediate families emerge when we compare Mandisa's experiences and perspectives with those of Charney, a teenage girl from Ocean View, and Sharon from Fish Hoek, both of whom also live with both their married and working parents.

In her recent diary work, 17-year-old Charney wrote about sharing dinner with her family every evening and using this time to chat about the day's events for each member. Like Mandisa, she actively participated in and thereby facilitated shared family time and frequent communication. Sitting with her at home, we soon became aware that Charney's parents know a great deal about her day-to-day life and the challenges she faces. For example, when talking about a fallout she had had with a female friend, she asked her father how long ago they had fought. She also spoke of going to her parents with problems she was having with members of her church youth club. Spending time with her family is clearly important to Charney and she ensures that she has regular opportunities to do so. She speaks about spending time with her mother in the evenings, just 'lying on her bed, chatting and having a *jol* (party)'. The closeness of the mother–daughter relationship is articulated by Charney in terms of her trust and their shared confidences: 'My mother is my best friend; I can tell her my deepest secrets, talk to her about everything, including sex.'

As much as her mother is a friend, she is also an appreciated authority figure in Charney's life. She explains that her mother is quite strict, sets clear boundaries for her behaviour and challenges her to use her talents and be the best she can be. At times, Charney finds this frustrating because she does not always feel she is able to achieve what her mother expects. But in the context of their friendship, Charney ultimately experiences these demands as encouraging and loving. Her mother also actively tries to build Charney's confidence and instil certain values in her, one of the most important being establishing an independent spirit in Charney by teaching her that she does not need other people, like friends or boyfriends, to define who she is.

Charney's references to the value of intimate friendship accompanied by authority in her experiences of being parented have particular social and cultural salience in Ocean View, and are in some ways equivalent to Mandisa's references to 'respect' within intergenerational relationships in Masiphumelele. Residents of Ocean View frequently spoke about the damaging effects of gossip, and of the tendency for adults to compare children to rare examples of 'successful' young people, thereby undermining both their current achievements and their future potential. Being able to *jol* with one's parent and at the same time receive constructive guidance is a rare and valued combination, expressed in terms consistent with social realities and cultural norms in Ocean View. It denotes some similar qualities in intergenerational relationships to those articulated through *ukuhlonipha* in Masiphumelele. For example, Charney reports that although her parents are strict and she is primarily responsible for the cooking and cleaning, she enjoys a similar flexibility in the domestic arrangements as Mandisa described because her parents are willing to listen and negotiate. Her father works an early shift so is at home in the afternoons. If she needs to go to the library or to a meeting she is able to ask him to continue the supper preparations. During the period of fieldwork, when she was working hard in her final year at school, Charney became frustrated with the fact that her younger brother never helped around the house. She was able to speak to her parents about this; they discussed her brother's contributions to the running of the home and he did more.

Like Mandisa, Charney stands out among her peers as being articulate, unusually successful at school and popular among her friends. Children in Ocean View recognise this to be a rare combination of characteristics in their neighbourhood. In Charney's eyes, the nature of the advice and support given by her mother has been critical to her achievements in recent years. She described some early experiences of succumbing to peer pressure, saying that she now takes a strong stand against being persuaded to do things she does not wish to. She does, however, mention that she has had difficulties maintaining some of her close friendships, indicating an awareness of the social costs to her taking this stance.

> Even if they not 24/7 with you, right enough, they are not with you 24/7, but if you as a parent know what your child does and you and your child have an open and honest relationship, then your parents won't have to judge you and assume things. (Charney, girl, aged 17, Ocean View)

Charney's emphasis on openness and honesty as mitigating parental assumptions or negative judgements has particular salience in the context of her neighbourhood's history and associated sociocultural norms. The term *skelling*, literally meaning scolding, appeared very frequently in young Ocean View residents' accounts of their domestic and peer-group interaction. Its meaning is more general than just being reprimanded for doing wrong. *Skelling* is a widespread means of venting frustration – rather like kicking the cat – and young people portray themselves as being unable to put a foot right and feeling consistently in the firing line of criticism. They also pointed out adults' deliberate withholding of affirmation or encouragement, and how this fuels poor decision-making:

> My mom has this thing where she loves to talk proudly about her children to others, like my aunt, granny or the neighbours, but she never tells us directly that she is proud of us. This makes me think that my mommy doesn't honour me, so I may as well do things that fit in with this, that are not honouring of her. (Ronaldo, boy, aged 17, Ocean View)

A paucity of positive emotional language and a tendency towards the negative socialisation of children through gossip and verbal denigration (such as *skelling*) have been noted by anthropologists working in poor communities with similar social and political histories (Ross 2009; Salo 2004). These parallels suggest that past racial classification as 'coloured' and state actions towards this sector of the population have shaped a social environment and a spectrum of cultural norms that threaten the coherence of family life. Resident mothers, social workers and a pastor were quick to identify specific aspects of parental attitudes and behaviour that they attributed to the neighbourhood's particular history of disempowerment. They indicate that poor decision-making and inadequate nurturing by parents arise from a focus on economic well-being, pressures on single mothers, and a sociopolitical identity that bears the legacy of ascribed and internalised inferiority. None of these trends are unique to Ocean View or other coloured neighbourhoods. Margo Russell (2003) notes that black and white participants living in urban and rural areas experience similar social pressures to command two incomes in order to pay for basic subsistence and follow consumer trends (e.g. owning cars and electronic equipment and wearing designer labels). But what Ocean View's residents consider to be a specific threat to familial relationships are the combined effects of socio-economic pressures and the neighbourhood's sociopolitical identity. These are evident in one woman's explanation of why parents spend their meagre incomes on designer clothing, while at the same time asserting vociferously to teachers and social workers that they cannot afford their child's school uniform:

> I think it has a lot to do with where we come from…we've been made
> to feel 'less than' so we dress 'more than'. The value system that we have,
> ok, say, I might not have money, but if I dress as if I have money, ok,
> and if the deco of my house tells you this cookie has got money then
> that is ok, never mind if every second day I get a red letter of demand.
> You know what I'm saying? So it's that whole culture, it's almost like an
> inborn culture, I almost want to say, with our people. (Social worker and
> mother, Ocean View)

When viewed in relation to their peers, Charney and Mandisa stand out as having particularly supportive and close relationships with their parents. The relationship characteristics that they identify bear testimony to what some adults and children are able to achieve in spite of the ongoing impacts of apartheid-generated violence on family life and contemporary social and economic pressures. The quality of their relationships is sustained in part by reference to and use of cultural norms guiding social interaction that have emerged from particular community histories. Their parents' employment and the resulting economic security at home is another factor in bolstering the quality of their domestic relationships.

The relationship characteristics that Mandisa and Charney identify and enjoy represent ideals to which others in the neighbourhood aspire but rarely achieve, for reasons that we illuminate later in the chapter. Notably, the same ideals pertaining to parent–child relationships are held by young people growing up in middle-class Fish Hoek. Sharon has lived with her biological parents and siblings in the same house all her life. Her father has worked as a teacher for as long as she can remember and her mother recently started part-time secretarial work. Sharon's analysis of relationships in her home reveals that economic means are not a guarantee that children will experience relationships with parents of the quality they desire:

> I get support from Mom and Dad, but only for certain things – for other
> things I look to my friends or I manage on my own. I wish that my
> family could be more open with me and give me an opportunity to be
> open. All I want is for my family to be there more for me. They are there
> for me financially – they give me a room, food and things – but they are
> not there personally. (Sharon, girl, aged 17, Fish Hoek)

Parents in Fish Hoek use a number of the same phrases to describe their approach to raising children as their counterparts in Ocean View. One of these was the assertion of responsibility for one's children until they reach the age of 18, when they consider them old enough to do as they like. The parents of 12-year-old Vanessa made this point in relation to their strict house rules and their perceived need to make decisions for their children. Both parental authority and distinct gender roles guide domestic interaction in Vanessa's home. Her father makes most of the rules and decisions, attempting to control what his children are exposed to by prohibiting television in the house and deciding what his children are and are not allowed to do. Vanessa speaks appreciatively of her father's efforts to protect the family, makes no protest at home against the role she is ascribed and only hints to us of her resultant sense of exclusion:

> Whenever my parents have friends over I have to run around and bring tea…but I am not allowed to join into adults' conversation. (Vanessa, girl, aged 12, Fish Hoek)

The assertion of exclusive responsibility for one's children is further evidence of the persistence of the nuclear-family model in middle-class Fish Hoek. Norms, of course, are undermined or bolstered by everyday realities and perceptions of reality. Although of a different nature and scale to those facing children in Ocean View and Masiphumelele, the types of risks to children's safety and well-being perceived by parents in Fish Hoek seem to contribute to a parenting approach that places firm boundaries on their children's behaviour.[2] Parents position themselves as the agents of their children's acquisition of the personal development, skills and autonomy that they most desire for their children – a point also made by Shelmerdine (2005) in her psychological analysis of a small set of interviews in the Valley. From this perspective, children are positioned as reactive to their parents rather than as able and active in exerting their own influence on their well-being and development.

Most children residing in Fish Hoek reported happy and effective relationships in homes in which an ethic of parent-agent and child-respondent prevails. As elsewhere in the Valley, there was little evidence of a discourse of children's rights that in any way challenged these notions. And while a few said they feel stifled by what they describe as the conservative attitudes of their parents, none of the children we worked with questioned the basis of these rules. Twelve-year-old Annie, who comes across as mature and expressive, was one of several children living in Fish Hoek who reported a very different approach by their parents. Paraphrasing her parents, she said, a little mockingly, 'We are an open family! Anyone who has an opinion can talk.' Time in her home revealed that her parents encourage their children to think about things, negotiate and be independent. Their less authoritative approach to parenting was achieving communication between generations and a sense of mutual respect. However, the presence of conflict and competition suggests that both generations are struggling to manage notions of equality while at the same time fulfilling the roles of parent and child. Annie spoke of frequent arguments with her mother, saying, 'It's because we are both stubborn people', and expressed some ambivalence towards her. She sometimes listed her mother as one of the most important people in her life and at other times said that she hated her.

Despite divergent sociopolitical histories and normative environments, young people's analyses of their interactions with parents are strikingly similar in terms of the qualities of relationship they identify as critical to harmony in the home and their own well-being. The differences lie, firstly, in the modes of expression of these qualities – for often these are tied to reference points within a particular cultural discourse – and, secondly, in the kinds of obstacles to children and adults achieving relationships of this nature, for example when faced with absence, neglect or abuse.

Silence and resistance: Responses to neglect and abuse

Sharing a home with their parents does not guarantee children the quality of care and interpersonal relationships described by Mandisa and Charney. Young people respond to shortfalls of care common in post-apartheid family life by attempting to protect their own well-being and that of their family members. Their strategies include the tacit acknowledgement of particular challenges facing adults in the family; silence; strategic communication; residential moves; and the reassertion of the parental role of provider even when it is weak or absent. Some, like Lindiwe, succeed in protecting the social integrity of the family, but compromise their physical safety and emotional nurture. Others, like Veronique, take decisive actions to alter their domestic sphere, but sustain costs to their psychological well-being. A child-centred understanding of neglect and abuse in post-apartheid Cape Town necessitates exploring the interface between threats currently imposed on children through familial relationships and the actions of children to avoid or mitigate these threats.

Thirteen-year-old Lindiwe lives in Masiphumelele with her biological parents, younger siblings, an uncle and a cousin (whom she refers to as 'sister'). The presence of Lindiwe's parents, and because both they and her uncle work, would suggest that she, like Mandisa, is in a relatively secure position. However, it was soon apparent that Lindiwe was, on the basis of her own and others' judgement, one of the most vulnerable children we worked with. Moreover, we witnessed her peers in the art club and at school and her teachers interacting with Lindiwe in ways that suggested their sense of her as both different and disadvantaged. She often worked on her own during art club and was the object of gentle teasing. Although provoked, and often sharp in her responses, Lindiwe was liked by her peers and her marginality was partly self-directed. When asked about her friendships, she stated bluntly: 'I do not have friends…Even close friends are liars, they are not confidential, I can't trust anyone, I can't even trust you.' And in response to our observation of the apparent efforts of another girl in art club to befriend her, she said: 'Babalwa is good to me – we go to Student Christian Meeting together, but she is not a friend.'

Lindiwe's mother works until late and her father 'comes and goes all the time, as he drinks in the local taverns'. Lindiwe and her siblings are often at home without an adult for up to five hours of the day, extending into the evening. Speaking of these periods, Lindiwe explained: 'We sometimes go next door – I eat breakfast with my neighbour, Phiwe, there, but usually we stay at home on our own at night as well as during the day. We look after ourselves.' The neighbours also regarded these children as vulnerable. They were quick to criticise Lindiwe's parents for leaving the children alone to look after each other, including the four-week-old baby, while her mother attended a 24-hour gathering of *iigqirhakazi* (female traditional healers).

Although Lindiwe never stated that she felt neglected at home, she admitted to feeling unsafe there. Her fears have a tangible basis: during the research period, Lindiwe spilt boiling oil on her legs while cooking for her family. The seriousness of the burns meant three days in hospital, three weeks off school and eight weeks in heavy bandages, requiring regular hospital visits. Six months before we met Lindiwe, her eight-year-old cousin was allegedly raped at home during the day by a relative.

Lindiwe's parents are clearly failing to protect the children in their care from severe long-term physical and emotional harm. Nevertheless, she describes her mother as her hero 'because she keeps me safe in her life, that is why I am a big girl now'; draws attention to what she does provide; and positions her as ultimately dependable, at least in terms of her presence:

> My father comes back from work then goes straight to get a drink, and he shows no interest in what happens at home. My mother at least puts food on the table and provides clothes for her children…When my days are dark, my mother is there for me.

The words 'at least' in the above quotation hint at Lindiwe's awareness of the limitations to her mother's care. Moreover, there is something missing from Lindiwe's drawings and descriptions of her interaction with her mother when compared to those of her peers. They lack the nuance and detailed communication that convey emotional attachment or reciprocity of emotional care. The relationship between mother and daughter is not as close or effective in its caring capacities as Lindiwe presents it to be. The discrepancy between description and reality raises the question of why children remain silent about inadequate care, neglect and even abuse in the home.

However conscious Lindiwe is of the level of her parents' neglect, she observes others in her neighbourhood who have similar experiences and in this light may not judge her own circumstances as worth reporting. Then there is the question of who she might tell. Speaking about abuse within the family or neighbourhood has serious ramifications for an individual child, including, for example, reactions of disbelief or rejection by relatives, and the risk of discrediting the family among neighbours or friends. There is even more at stake for very poor children: by exposing an abuser, they may lose a breadwinner and place their whole family at economic risk (Townsend & Dawes 2004). Reporting neglect or abuse to social workers theoretically entails the real danger of being taken into custodial care and removed from the familiar environment for an unknown period of time (a reason for children's silence found in other impoverished settlements in Cape Town – see Henderson 1999; Ross 2009). But our evidence suggests that very few children in Masiphumelele are taken into custody, at least in a manner that removes them from everything familiar. Young residents of Ocean View are more likely to fear this outcome because they witness it more frequently. In more than 20 case files of social workers relating to domestic neglect or abuse in Masiphumelele, only two recorded removing a child from the home, and in both cases this was to a foster mother who was local and already well known to them. (See Chapter 3 for a full description of this informal foster-care arrangement.) Of the same number of social-work cases open in Ocean View, three recorded removing children, two to unknown custody and one to an aunt.

The context of a particular neighbourhood appears to inform children's decisions to remain silent. When domestic disputes arise in Masiphumelele, young people tend to make their point by curtailing communication, either by refusing to speak or walking out, rather than contributing to an argument:

> My mother didn't buy me anything [on my birthday[3]], not even a chocolate. I was so angry that I didn't even talk to her, or my sister. So she asked me why I'm not talking to her and I told her. She replied that she is fixing money for me to have a better education and saving for me to attend the OIL camp[4] in June, for which I'll need money to buy clothes and other stuff. So I understand her and she gives me a big hug and thanks me for understanding. (Diary entry by Peliswa, girl, aged 15, Masiphumelele)

Silence on the part of young people is consistent with respectful behaviour towards one's seniors, and, therefore, ensures the continuing possibility of reciprocity between generations. In the above case, the problem is resolved by mother and daughter's reaffirmations of their commitments to their respective responsibilities:

> When my mother explained that she could not afford to throw a party, I was not cheeky to her. I gave her a big hug and she told me that she has many plans for me because I am the last born and she will make sure that my dream comes true if I keep doing my school work.

While such strategies of communication are often successful in managing lack and its resulting disappointment or conflict, their efficacy is limited by the economic possibilities available to parents. When parents are consistently unable to produce the money or resources consistent with good care and can no longer bring themselves to promise to do so, this intergenerational bargain is no longer sustainable. In Lindiwe's case, chronic impoverishment and scant parental provision act to undermine the power of culturally validated discourse to sustain a sense of well-being. Her choice to retain a positive image and remain silent about problems is also driven by individual-level influences, which are also consistent with social norms. Psychologists would argue that by presenting an image of being in a caring family environment through strategic, and perhaps culturally validated, silence, children are protecting themselves by avoiding having to confront reality (Wallerstein & Kelly 1980). In addition, maintaining silence and choosing not to criticise parental care are ways of conveying respect that are consistent with the cultural norms guiding child–adult relationships in Masiphumelele. Thus, by shielding their parents (or mothers at least) from scrutiny, children are protecting the reputation of their parents and ultimately their own. They are ashamed of their parents and simultaneously anxious that parental actions may reflect badly on the family and on them as individuals within the peer group. As will become evident in chapters to follow, such steps matter to children in Masiphumelele and Ocean View because those who are known in the neighbourhood to be very poor are likely to be teased and excluded by their peers.

But maintaining impressions of a healthy family may come at a huge cost to children in terms of their investment in social relationships that stand to support them now and in the future. Lindiwe's reticence to invest emotionally in her relationship with her mother resonates with her stated decision not to have close friends. We did not conduct the psychological assessments to know whether she was depressed, but in order to manage the absence of care and possibilities of abuse at home, she is actively cutting herself off from those who are physically and socially closest to her. It is telling that when chatting about her future plans, Lindiwe speaks of joining and depending on relatives and others with whom she has much more tenuous connections. One is a paternal great-aunt working for Telkom in Gauteng, who has apparently suggested that Lindiwe accompany her to America. The second is her mother's employer, who, says Lindiwe, plans to take her and her siblings to Germany. Lindiwe's vivacity and determination are persuasive, but all other indications suggest that she is clutching at straws.

The case of 17-year-old Veronique of Ocean View sheds light on other ways in which children respond to neglectful or abusive parenting. When we first met Veronique, she was living with her parents and 10-year-old brother. Constructive communication within Veronique's family is clearly very limited and occurs within an atmosphere of mistrust and anger. Moreover, they spend very little time together and do not engage in each other's lives. Veronique tries to avoid being at home when her parents are there:

> If my mom or her husband are here then I'll be out all day and come home at night. Other times I'll be here till 7 and then go out till like 9 or 10. It's pointless being here because they exclude me. They watch TV and I don't like that.

Since the age of 12, Veronique has spent several long periods living with other relatives on her mother's side in Ocean View:

> It was my decision to move in with my aunt in grade 9. It was not an official move, but gradually I spent more and more time there and because they didn't object and I liked it there, I started moving my stuff across bit by bit. I decided to leave home because of the stress with my father. I warned my mother I would move out if she didn't get a divorce, but she didn't believe me. This house was very full though; there were 11 of us there. So my aunt told me I must move back home and I shouldn't run from my problems. Then I decided to move in with my other aunt. That was at the beginning of grade 10.

Veronique made frequent reference to her long-running conflict with her father, whom she refers to as 'my mother's husband'. (Children often referred to their mother's partners as *'my ma se man'* [my mother's man], but in this case we know that Veronique's father is indeed her biological father.) She also referred to her efforts to persuade her mother to divorce her father, and of the level of anger and emotional distance she experiences in this relationship. She reported being shouted at and insulted by her father, recalling an occasion when he threatened to throw the kettle at her 'for being rude'. And she is infuriated by what she perceives as his occasional attempts at pretending to like her and care for her. Veronique described her fruitless efforts to communicate with her mother about how she feels about her father, and to motivate her mother to act on her behalf. When her strategy to pressure her mother into a divorce failed, Veronique went alone to Simon's Town court to apply for a restraining order against her father and informed her mother several weeks later. At the close of our fieldwork she was anticipating that her father would discover this and expecting a combative response to her actions.

Veronique's request that her parents divorce, her repeated decisions to move out of her home and the manner in which she refers to her father are assertive and confrontational actions, and ones that fly in the face of notions of respect for one's seniors (*ukuhlonipha*) spoken about in Masiphumelele. In Ocean View, fewer references are made to respect in everyday conversation about intergenerational relationships. This is not to say that notions of respect between generations have no currency in Ocean View, but that they are more readily interpreted and enacted in terms of deference and even subservience, as can be seen in the strict boundaries on behaviour imposed by Charney's parents. In Veronique's case, violence is used to overcome forms of resistance from a child who should be respectful: her father threatens to throw the kettle at her 'for being rude'.

Veronique's father and his contemporaries grew up in a state-controlled social hierarchy in which those at the top wielded their power by commanding the respect (or, in other words, demanding the subservience) of workers, migrants and even ordinary residents through regular, intentional, physical violence and by the restrictions to freedom imposed by pass laws and forced removals. Fiona Ross (2009) writes of adult male informants who reported learning *ordentlikheid* (proper behaviour) through frequent beatings with a sjambok (cowhide whip) on the farm where their fathers were employed. Beatings were given when younger or 'inferior' people (those placed lower in the racial hierarchy) failed to show respect, or, in other words, subservience.

It is, therefore, unsurprising that older people, and men in particular (for there are gender as well as age dimensions to notions of propriety and the conveyance of respect), expect to hold positions of respect and maintain their authority in ways familiar to them. The highly confrontational nature of Veronique's efforts to improve her home environment illustrate the way dominance and subservience are forcefully expressed within adults' and children's attempts to resolve conflicts.

Younger children are especially vulnerable to the psychosocial effects of conflict in the home. Ten-year-old Jumat's father is rarely at home. He lives elsewhere in Ocean View and visits occasionally. Jumat drew a picture of his father shouting and punching his mother, who was also shouting, but had her head down to protect her face from the blows. He drew himself in the corner of the picture, screaming 'No!' Underneath the picture Jumat wrote: 'This is when my dad is hitting my mother.' He told us that he felt 'like a lion' and reacted by 'walking away'.

Witnessing emotional and physical violence between parents forces children to make a choice between getting involved – even by remaining an observer – or walking away. Jumat may recognise that removing himself is safer than getting involved, or his response may be only an instinctive wish to blot out the horror. Either way, one consequence of his parents' actions and Jumat's choice to alienate himself from the situation is to render impossible the kind of open and respectful communication between parents and children that we have seen to be highly valued by children across the Valley.

While a precise account of the particular psychological impacts of growing up in a conflictual family environment are beyond the scope of our study, Veronique's own analysis throws some light on how these relationships have affected other aspects of her life, including her emotional well-being and education. She reports that although she has never been seriously physically hurt by her father, he has wounded her emotionally and this has made her more angry and hateful. She has given up trying to speak to her mother about this and other issues that she is grappling with because she is tired of her efforts only to find that she is wasting her time, as her mother pays no attention. When we talked to Veronique about how she copes with the resulting emotional burden, she explained that she is able to talk to her close friend and this friend's mother, who live a few doors away. Tellingly, however, the defences she has mounted appear to obstruct these friends' attempts to assist her:

> I'll tell them about stuff, but I don't like to be comforted because it makes me feel weak – I don't like the hugging thing or the 'everything's going to be ok' talk.

Indeed, Veronique recognised that frank discussion about her difficulties made her vulnerable. When talking about her father, she would often shut down the conversation as soon as she came close to tears, almost as if allowing herself to express her vulnerabilities would prevent her retrieving the internal strength upon which she relies. Veronique is intelligent and a quick thinker: she was selected to represent the school at the Mathematics Olympiad in 2004. However, her performance at school does not reflect her abilities. She consistently gets D grades and does only the very minimum of homework: 'I won't sit with my books unless I absolutely have to. I sit in my room on my own and do it, as there is no one I can ask for help.' Both her parents completed high school (although her mother did not matriculate) and, therefore, have sufficient education to engage with their daughter's school tasks. In the light of the conflicts described above, Veronique's parents may have refused to engage in her schooling and she may have rejected any such efforts on their part. Whatever the reasons, Veronique, her parents and sibling do not spend time together, communicate effectively or show interest in each other's lives. Veronique, like her peers in all three neighbourhoods, described these practices as critical to positive relationships in the home and to good care. Their absence in Veronique's violent home environment is particularly stark and raises questions we explore later in the chapter, namely whether young people feel able to attain relationships with these qualities outside the home, and how the particular characteristics of neighbourhood social interaction may influence their sense of the potential inherent in these wider relationships.

Knowledge of the extent, nature and causes of various forms of abuse of South African children is very scanty. It is widely recognised that incidence figures of physical or sexual abuse collected by the police and social services are inaccurate owing to significant under-reporting (Dawes, Borel-Saladin & Parker 2004). The reasons why children choose not to report abuse to family members or the authorities are likely to include those mentioned above. A recent study in the Western Cape found that perpetrators of physical and sexual abuse resulting in traumatic injury or hospitalisation were typically men known to the child, and that most assaults occurred in the home (Dawes, Long et al. 2006). The scant evidence also shows that the majority of reported violent acts against pre-pubertal children are perpetrated by adults with whom they share intimate relationships, including parents, relatives, friends, lodgers, neighbours and others entrusted with the care of children (Richter & Higson-Smith 2004). The younger the child, the more likely that this is the case, and that the abuse is repeated over time (Richter & Higson-Smith 2004). Local research also shows that adolescents are largely responsible for the sexual abuse of younger children between five and twelve years (Wood et al. 2000, cited in Townsend & Dawes 2004: 56). These findings remind us of the way in which older children can use their relative power to exploit younger ones, and for this to take place within what is often assumed to be the safe space of the home. Children's exposure to high levels of violence and conflict in the home has been detected in recent regional and national surveys. In a Western Cape study, 16 per cent of parents surveyed reported that they were in violent relationships (Dawes, Long et al. 2006: 50), whilst nationally, one in five young people reported witnessing disputes between family members, and the use of physical violence as a way to resolve disputes was described as 'common' (Leoschut & Burton 2006: xi).

In posing questions to adolescents about their experiences of physical and verbal abuse in the home, the CAPS survey offers us a window onto the prevalence and severity of various types of violence as defined by young people themselves. In this instance, surveys are more helpful than ethnography because respondents are much more likely to speak of abuse to a relatively anonymous interviewer who does not stay in the vicinity, than to someone who mingles with their family, friends and teachers. An alarming 5 per cent of adolescents in the CAPS sample reported being 'sometimes', 'often' or 'very often' hit so hard that they had marks or were injured. Just under 20 per cent experienced lower levels of physical violence (pushing, grabbing or slapping) and a similar proportion lived with adults who made them afraid they would be hurt (a definition that could encompass sexual abuse). Rates of very frequent verbal and physical abuse were similar in predominantly African and white neighbourhoods (1–5 per cent), but higher in predominantly coloured areas (2–11 per cent) and especially in low-income coloured neighbourhoods. Adolescents in African areas were less likely to report actual physical abuse than adolescents in similarly poor coloured areas, but they were more likely to report that they had occasionally been *afraid* of being hurt. These figures indicate that neither socio-economic nor cultural factors alone can be considered causal of intimate domestic violence against children.

Little attention has been devoted to investigating the individual and contextual factors that contribute to the physical, and particularly sexual, abuse of children within South African homes (Townsend & Dawes 2004). Young people's own observations of the social dynamics within their homes and neighbourhoods are, therefore, as credible a starting point as any in trying to identify some underlying causes. Children in Ocean View linked their peers' safety in the home with the sale and use of drugs and alcohol therein and the various types of neglect or abuse by parents or other adult relatives that could result from these activities. They and their peers in Masiphumelele also made direct and indirect references to the everyday implications of unemployment and poverty for both adults and children:

> Some children from Ocean View are living on the streets in Fish Hoek because their parents don't look after them – this is because they don't have money or jobs or because they drink too much. (Boys and girls aged 10–12 years, Ocean View)

There is an increasingly recognised link between acts of violence by men and their disempowerment resulting from unemployment and chronic poverty (Hunter 2006; Ramphele & Richter 2006). Patriarchy and a widely accepted gendered social division are common features of South African communities across the spectra of wealth, language and culture (Guma & Henda 2004), but are expressed in rather different ways within and across different communities. Feminist scholars have argued that through wider ideological influences and socialisation processes within patriarchal societies, men come to believe that they have the right to exert the power endorsed to them through control over those less powerful (in other words, women and children), as well as to be sexually and emotionally sustained by women (Calder 1999; Magwaza 1997, cited in Townsend & Dawes 2004). There is some South African evidence that patriarchal ideology directly influences behaviour – male farm-workers justified violence against their partners on the basis of their household headship (Paranzee & Smythe 2003, cited in Dawes, De Sas Kropiwnicki et al. 2006) – and that a large portion of women consider it sometimes or always acceptable for one adult to hit another adult (Jewkes et al. 2002, cited in Dawes, De Sas Kropiwnicki et al. 2006).

Patriarchal social norms can act either to protect or endanger children. By conferring responsibilities on men to protect members of their own family such norms may forestall abuse or act to reduce children's sense that they owe something to a male relative. On the other hand, they may place children at greater risk by subjugating and silencing them. Magwaza (1997, cited in Townsend & Dawes 2004) draws attention to these two possibilities within the predominately patriarchal Nguni culture (incorporating isiXhosa speakers of Masiphumelele), which expects unquestioning obedience and subservience to adults, particularly men.[5] Research in southern Zimbabwe found that abusive acts towards children in the home persisted because cultural scripts emphasising respect and obedience heavily discourage children from speaking out against their elders and legitimise their punishment for doing so (Meursing et al. 1995, cited in Townsend & Dawes 2004).

Caution is required in using these findings to interpret the relative vulnerability of children in contemporary Cape Town. There is a danger of assuming that cultural influence is far less prevalent, or even absent, among non-African populations, or of assuming that culture must be an explanation. These assumptions can persist because there is so little research on the dynamics of interpersonal relationships involving children in non-African components of South African society.

Our data suggest that cultural traits cannot explain children's differential vulnerability to abuse and their impotence to address it. For example, responses in CAPS suggest that rates of frequent and serious harm are as high or higher for white and coloured adolescents as for African adolescents. Ethnographic data gathered in the Valley show that cultural scripts based on intergenerational respect render middle-class white children vulnerable to abuse. Sylvia, a 17-year-old who lives in Fish Hoek, was sexually abused by an older male cousin when she was 9 years old. She said that she 'allowed it to happen' and felt unable to confide in her family about it because he was an older relative:

> It's very funny, because in my family it works that you respect your elders.
> What your elders say is right, type thing; that's how my family works.
> They're like a more old, traditional type…And that's what I believed when
> I was like young. And he was older, so…

The particular workings of kinship and seniority within Sylvia's wider social relationships not only put her at risk, but also discouraged her from seeking help at home: 'My parents don't even know about it to this day. I kept it a secret because of the family; I don't think it's worth upsetting the family.' Her response indicates a sense of responsibility for holding the family together and avoiding raising an issue that would undermine its integrity. This sense of duty and perhaps accompanying fears of punishment explain why so many children choose not to report their abusive experiences. Sylvia said that she dealt with the problem in her 'own way' by confiding in two close friends and the mother of one these, who is a lay counsellor and someone Sylvia describes as her 'guide'.

Sylvia's experiences illustrate the possibility of a more frightening and dangerous aspect of patriarchal norms that are expressed in everyday discourse in the enactment of so-called 'respectful' relationships between children and adults. Her case perhaps illustrates the more ubiquitous use of subservience by older people, particularly men, and that this occurs especially in contexts where they feel vulnerable and seek a means of exerting power. Our suggestion notwithstanding, the fact remains that the majority of adults do not abuse children in their care. It would appear that patriarchal norms usually act to protect children rather than endanger them, and that social and economic factors (such as unemployment, low wages and substance abuse) contribute significantly to conditions and relationships in homes where children suffer violence.

The meanings and implications of parental absence

> When my mother returned from working in Cape Town she greeted everyone and then came to me saying 'hello my boy'. I ran to my mom (who is my granny) and sat next to her. My [biological] mother asked 'why are you scared?' and I said 'why are you saying "my boy"? I am not your boy', and she laughed. (Gift, boy, aged 17, at school in Masiphumelele and living in Ocean View)

> When we were young [my dad] wouldn't phone and say 'do you guys want to go to a movie or something?'...But we always had a dad-connection. (Justin, boy, aged 18, Fish Hoek)

> It wasn't easy when I started high school because I was doing all the shopping, cooking and cleaning at home – as well as looking after my granny, who was sick at the time. My elder brothers were at work, my dad wasn't around and my mum was in and out. She has never been a mum to us. When my granny got better, she took over these jobs so that I could focus on my school work. She did so much for us. (Brian, boy, aged 17, Ocean View)

Gift, Justin and Brian, all boys in their late teens, convey something of the diversity in young people's experiences of parental absence that we observed across and within neighbourhoods in the Valley. On the one hand, the kinds of absences and circumstances that drive them differ. On the other, the meaning of 'absence' (as recorded in the survey) varies in relation to social norms and to children's power to sustain connections and ensure their own nurture. In this section we grapple with the nature and implications of parental absence as one of many facets of contemporary family life. We ask how young people's analyses compare with lay and scholarly perceptions of large compromises to family integrity and to the care of children that accompany parental mobility. Historical patterns of movement are an important backdrop to the decisions made by parents in a post-apartheid context and to the normative setting to children's expectations of care and parent-like relationships in the context of mobility.

The period leading into and following South Africa's transition to democracy saw large numbers of people move into Cape Town who had been born elsewhere in the country; it also witnessed high mobility within the city. Just under a quarter of 13- to 20-year-olds in the city as a whole in 2002 were born outside Cape Town (according to CAPS). In the Valley specifically, a similar proportion of the adult population had not lived in the same place five years before (according to the 2001 Census). Whilst the media portray the typical immigrant into the Valley (or Cape Town in general) as African and coming from the Eastern Cape, the Census and CAPS both show that there are at least two kinds of immigrants: African people (including children and adolescents) into low-income neighbourhoods (such as Masiphumelele) *and* white families into high-income neighbourhoods (such as the expanding suburbia of Fish Hoek).

Historical explanations for such high rates of immigration among Africans are well understood: the pass laws that curtailed the movements of residents of the impoverished bantustans (such as the Transkei and Ciskei in the Eastern Cape) were lifted in the late 1980s, making it easier for adults – many with children – to move to the city and seek work. Moreover, vastly inferior education in rural areas prompted parents, and often children themselves, to move to Cape Town for secondary schooling. Why such high numbers of white middle-class adults and children moved into or within Cape Town in the last two decades is less clear. Perceptions of good employment prospects, high educational standards and a more liberal and safer environment than in other parts of the country are likely motivators.

The mobility statistics indicate that this generation of African and white children have either themselves moved to the city, or experienced parental mobility with a historical precedent in the neighbourhood. CAPS data indicate that the difference here is in the tendency for white children to move with their parents, and African children and adults to move both independently and together. In contrast, coloured children primarily live in the neighbourhood they were born in and witness very little adult movement in or out of the area. While their parents' childhoods were marked by state-enforced evictions and relocation, their own experiences are of a largely sedentary community and a socio-economic climate that restricts movement beyond the neighbourhood (see Chapters 3 and 4).

Death, divorce and departure: Persistent post-apartheid trends

The figures presented in the section 'The impact of apartheid on family life' indicate that the majority of parental absence across Cape Town's demographic spectrum results from changes in marital or partnership arrangements: more than a third of children and adolescents in Cape Town have fathers living elsewhere, in different households – and this proportion is even higher in neighbourhoods like Ocean View and Masiphumelele. The likelihood that a child's parent has died is also higher in these neighbourhoods. The historical shapers to these inter-neighbourhood differences have contributed to diverse sociocultural norms and practices that surround parental separation and movement. Some make it easier than others for children to navigate the process and outcomes of parental departure. That said, there are certain ways in which parents may move out of their children's lives that are inconsistent with their experience or normative framework.

Premature, unanticipated or violent death is one such scenario. Fertility patterns matter here, in that the longer period over which men father children in Masiphumelele and Ocean View raises the rates of age- and illness-related deaths above those in Fish Hoek. But persistently high rates of violent crime remain more significant in killing fathers and leaving children and their mothers bereft. With about 19 000 murders, 55 000 rapes and about half a million cases of assault or attempted murder per year, it is no surprise that Altbeker (2007: 37–38) describes South Africa as 'a country at war with itself'. Violence is etched into the lives of many young people in the Valley.

The father of one art club member was stabbed following a fight over money. The stepfather of another was robbed and stabbed by *tsotsis* (gangsters) near his work elsewhere in Cape Town. Fourteen-year-old Thandi explained that she misses the presence at home of her murdered 'father' (who was in fact her stepfather), and worries about the family's future financial security. Thandi has reasons to worry: she has a five-year-old disabled brother, her pregnant mother's high alcohol consumption compromises her ability to sustain work and to mother effectively, and their home is impoverished and chaotic. The suddenness of Thandi's stepfather's death and her sense of impotence in the face of its consequences for the family speak of the material, social, emotional and psychological dimensions to the pain of this sort of parental absence.

In middle-class Fish Hoek, parents tend to 'separate' or 'divorce', and the departure of one parent is part of a formalised and often public process. Children had often witnessed conversations at home or correspondence with lawyers that gave them some anticipation of the event, and often some form of explanation. Justin paints a rosy picture of a conflict-free divorce that he considers to have benefited him and his siblings:

> That's the thing about my parents, if they fought they didn't fight in front of my brother and I; if I look at it now I see [the divorce] as a good thing because my parents they cannot live together, but they are good friends. I have never seen [the divorce] as a problem. My brother was about 11, he also says it was for the better, he didn't say they were fighting… (Justin, boy, aged 18, living with his mother and siblings in Fish Hoek)

Justin's positive perspective appears to result both from hindsight and effective communication within his family. We were told by children, parents and teachers in Fish Hoek that parental separation or divorce is one of the most traumatic events in young people's lives. Conflict at home and the ensuing distress were often major players, but so too were the assumptions that surrounded changes in family composition and that rendered any non-nuclear arrangement inferior and problematic. Associations were frequently made between so-called broken homes and children's antisocial behaviour:

> Many children at school are from broken homes and are largely unsupervised. The grade nines are the most difficult because they are in between childhood and adulthood. (School staff member, Fish Hoek)

We are not suggesting that there is no link between the departure of a parent and compromises to children's care that are manifest in their behaviour. What is evident, however, is that there is little latitude for children, or adults, to shape a different and positive family form when popular discourse still validates – and even prescribes – the nuclear family as the correct environment for children. Such norms are not unusual in contemporary Europe: John Borneman (1992) detects a similar persistent ideological commitment to the nuclear-family model based on consanguinity in Germany, despite the existence of a much wider range of actual domestic arrangements and relationships.

Some changes have occurred since the demise of apartheid: the state no longer exerts as much pressure on white middle-class families to uphold these forms – although there was a recent attempt to encourage 'proper' family form alongside a fight against moral malaise and crime across the whole population in the government's high-profile, but short-lived, Moral Regeneration Movement (Rauch 2005). A strong, Christian-based moral ethos to preserve 'the family unit' is still promulgated within Fish Hoek's numerous churches, and filters into social discourse.

Formal divorce is relatively unusual in Masiphumelele and Ocean View, partly because marriage is less common. CAPS data show that about 30 per cent of adolescents in low- and medium-income coloured and African households report that their parents were *never* married to each other. It is also relatively unusual partly because partnerships can dissolve and later re-form. The most common formal expression of separation that we witnessed is the legal process instigated by mothers and social workers to ensure that fathers pay child maintenance. Strong local kinship and neighbourly networks ensure that news of changes in consanguinal relationships spreads quickly and parental departures thereby become publicly acknowledged. The limited recourse to official procedures and a historical precedent of 'protecting' children by withholding difficult information can mean that children are not warned by adults about any impending parental departure. And although they will doubtless have observed certain clues, they are left desperately anxious and powerless by the absence of direct communication (recall Jumat's drawing of his desire to flee the scene of his father hitting his mother).

Children in Masiphumelele often described a parent's departure as being associated with their search for work, a very common scenario in the rural Eastern Cape. Many recalled a parent moving in and out of the home over a period of months or years, and did not interpret the moves as indicative of problems between their parents. The distress they experienced at the time related more to the suddenness of a departure and being lied to about the details, than to potential fissures in their parents' relationship:

> I was born in the Transkei. My mother left when I was eight years old. She told me she is going to Umtata where she worked on a project, then my cousin told me mother is in Cape Town looking for work and I cried that day…For a long time I was not sleeping right in my aunt's house…I used to cry all night. You see when I was small I used to sleep with my mother in the same bed. (Babalwa, girl, aged 12, Masiphumelele)

Two years later, Babalwa's mother brought her to Cape Town to share her urban home, a move that Babalwa initially said was driven by her mother's success in finding work. Subsequently, she framed it as a response to her father's violent behaviour towards her mother:

> I saw my father last at the time I moved from the Transkei. At that time my parents weren't getting on so well; my father used to drink and beat my mother, and tell her to go out of the house. So she did and I went with her. My father is working in Butterworth in the Transkei – I'm not

sure what his job is, but he sends money regularly. My mother has asked him to come to visit, but he doesn't want to come to Cape Town. And I've never been back to the Transkei.

For children who grew up in the diaspora from the Eastern Cape to Masiphumelele, the search for work has long been a feasible explanation for adult male mobility – and subsequently for adult female movement too. A cultural precedent of extended family households means that the reintegration of parents, siblings or other relatives is not inherently problematic. Therefore, historical patterns of movement and the meanings accompanying these enable African adults and children to interpret and reinterpret the meanings of parental departures, and thereby protect themselves from an element of potential distress. At the same time, they, like all children in our study, struggled when parental departures were sudden, violent or clouded with unclarity.

Recent trends have shifted the terrain of adult mobility in white middle-class households: real and perceived restrictions on employment imposed by the government's Black Economic Empowerment (BEE) policy lie behind increasing work-related mobility among adults in Fish Hoek. Several teenagers reported that one or both parents had moved to another province, or even overseas, in search of work. And in some cases these parents subsequently divorced. The stretching of intimate relationships is clearly not confined to poor or African people, as is often assumed. Leanne, a Fish Hoek resident, describes her long but temporary periods of separation from a parent and sibling and co-residence with extended family members – experiences not dissimilar to Babalwa's. In both cases, the movements of people are consistent with being a family and do not foreclose emotional and social connectedness:

> I was born in Boksburg, Johannesburg…When I was 15, my family decided to move to Cape Town. My mom and I moved first because my dad had to carry on working till the end of 2002…It was difficult because my brother and I are very close and my family had been split up. We were staying with my gran, who has a strong personality, and so do I, so we kind of clashed. Also, I was on the receiving end of my mom's depression. My mom and I decided we were going home because we missed our family unit too much. We were just about to go back to Johannesburg with not much money in our pockets when some friends we had made persuaded us to stay. My mom and I had a big fight with my gran, and after that we went looking for a room we could stay in. We found a small room and moved in, and it was much better, but it was still hard without my dad and brother. Eventually, about two years after mom and I had moved, my dad and brother joined us in Cape Town. (Leanne, girl, aged 18, Fish Hoek [extract from life history])

By comparison, few adults leave Ocean View to seek work or set up home elsewhere, and children can only interpret a parent's departure as resulting from a breakdown in their relationship. Social discourse tends to idealise the nuclear family as the answer to more wholesome child rearing, yet at the same time explicitly values extended and multigenerational households. The net effect is a less prescriptive picture of what could be termed the proper environment for children than that created by popular discourse in Fish Hoek, but it does not offer alternative or flexible interpretations of parental absence.

The effects of the past are evident in these persistent inter-neighbourhood differences in the frames of reference available to children for understanding parental departures and for negotiating the implications of physical absence. But we are now aware that a large proportion of children in all neighbourhoods will encounter parental absence, even when the underlying historical drivers vary. The question of how robust normative frameworks are in their ability to sustain children's nurture in the face of prevalent parental mobility, therefore, becomes pertinent across the whole cultural and economic spectra. Research on this topic during the late 1980s and early 1990s focused specifically on African neighbourhoods and resulted in two views on the impact of what was termed 'domestic fluidity' on the care of children. The first asserted that children become accustomed to culturally validated fluid, non-exclusive family relationships such that they experience an 'almost seamless continuity…between the various households within which they are housed' (Spiegel & Mehlwana 1997: 30). The second, bleaker, view was that children's well-being was severely compromised not so much by adult departures but by the lack of consistent parenting (Jones 1993; Ramphele 2002). Mamphela Ramphele (2002) wrote of the costs of emotional nourishment incurred when parents made the difficult choice to move to the city to find work. Patricia Henderson (1999) found that the ruptures in children's intimate relationships over time had contributed to the fragility in their subsequent bonds with family members and their emotional well-being. And Pamela Reynolds, also working in impoverished, isiXhosa-speaking areas of Cape Town, suggested 'an undoing of obligations towards certain children – a decomposition of nurturance' that occurred when adults failed to play their conventional providing roles (Reynolds 2000: 143). Such conclusions prompted us to ask how children now experience the long-term effects of parental departure. Are they and their absent parents able to sustain relationships across physical distance any more successfully now than in the past? Do children respond to a mother's absence in similar ways to a father's? What roles do others in the family and neighbourhood play to ensure continuities of care for children?

What happens next? Retaining connections with absent parents

CAPS offers the opportunity of quantifying contact between adolescents and their absent parents, and shows that living apart does not necessarily mean a loss of all contact. Just over half (56 per cent) of adolescents whose mothers live elsewhere report spending time with them, whilst a third of adolescents whose fathers live elsewhere report spending time with them (see Figure 2.4 and Table 2.3). Physically absent fathers appear to play less of a role in their children's lives than physically absent mothers. Twice as many adolescents regularly visit and converse with absent

Figure 2.4 *Frequency that adolescents spend time with absent parents*

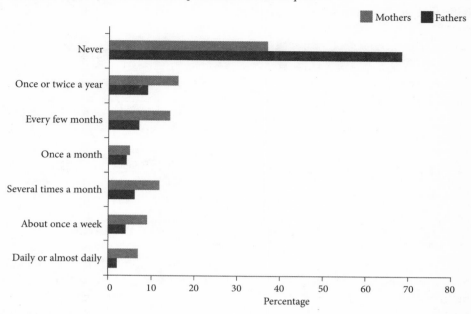

Source: Cape Area Panel Study 2002

mothers compared to those who do so with absent fathers. It should be noted that the wording of the question was quite demanding, in that it specified spending time together, 'just the two of you'. If an adolescent spent a lot of time with a parent, but always with others and never on their own, the response would be recorded as 'never'. Consequently, some of these responses may mask the persistence of a relationship between an adolescent and an absent parent which is not particularly intimate, or in which intimacy is experienced in the presence of others.

The possibility that culturally inflected notions of whether or not it is appropriate for older children to spend time with fathers may affect responses to questions relating to parental intimacy. However, in neither Ocean View nor Fish Hoek did we encounter norms discouraging teenagers and men from spending time alone together. Our data suggest that notions of impropriety pertaining to men and adolescent girls spending time together exist in a portion of the older generation of isiXhosa-speaking residents of Masiphumelele, but have little currency in most contemporary households. Mothers of teenagers said that in the past, adolescent girls and older men – including fathers – would not have spent time alone, and that in a minority of homes with older mothers this may still be discouraged. But they reported a shift in these norms that influenced their own behaviour, stating that in most homes now teenagers of either sex spend time alone with their fathers. Their explanation lay in teenagers' efforts

Table 2.3 *Proportions of adolescents aged 14–17 who report spending time with mother, father or both parents, according to parental whereabouts (%)*

		Father is...			
		In household	In other household	Deceased	Total
Mother is...	In household	Mother: 93 Father: 87 Both: 86	Mother: 90 Father: 29 Both: 28	Mother: 88	Mother: 91 Father: 58 Both: 58
	In other household	Mother: 61 Father: 85 Both: 54	Mother: 63 Father: 39 Both: 35	n is too small	Mother: 62 Father: 44 Both: 34
	Deceased	n is too small	n is too small	n is too small	Father: 34
	Total	Mother: 89 Father: 86 Both: 81	Mother: 78 Father: 32 Both: 29	Mother: 74	Mother: 83 Father: 55 Both: 51

Source: Cape Area Panel Study 2002
Note: The question asked: 'Over the past 12 months, how often has he/she spent time with you, just the two of you?' Figures above aggregate responses varying from 'daily' or 'almost daily' to 'once or twice a year'.

to secure their own emotional needs and their responses to the new demands on mothers to be both breadwinners and the nurturing hearts of the home. Adolescent girls sometimes gravitate towards fathers because they consider them more discreet than mothers, who 'talk too much' with kinswomen and neighbours. And mothers say they are comfortable with this level of intimacy because they themselves are always busy at home, often juggling long work hours with heavy domestic responsibilities, whereas fathers are better able to 'keep a good eye on children'.

The survey results indicate that while a third of young people spend some time with their absent fathers, many more have fathers who appear both physically and emotionally absent. These trends contrast sharply with children's ideals of parental presence and involvement. Might there be other ways in which children connect with absent parents, and, if so, what are the limitations placed upon their efforts to do so? Are we witnessing changes in the parameters of child–parent relationships emerging in the post-apartheid landscape?

As more and more children own their own cellular phones, so the possibilities for keeping in touch with absent parents in ways most desirable to children have increased. Some enjoyed regular conversations, whereas others used the phone primarily to arrange when next to meet or to conduct financial transactions with a parent. A large proportion of children we worked with in Ocean View and Masiphumelele spoke about needing to contact their fathers to ask for money, under duress from their mothers in some cases. Women and children draw on deeply rooted patriarchal norms that hold men primarily responsible for material provision to assist their cause in encouraging absent men to bolster the fragile household economy. Chronic and debilitating poverty puts pressure on children to sustain a financial bridge between their parents, a role that can entail repeated rejection. This was especially true for children in Ocean View whose absent fathers lived nearby, often with a new partner or offspring also exerting claims on his resources or actively alienating his older children:

> My stepmother makes me wait outside when I go to my father's house to get money. I don't like to go there 'cause I don't feel welcome. I have a half-sister living there who is 16 years old. She just miscarried twins last month and I only heard about it at school. (Brian)

Many children were able to sustain an active, positive relationship with their absent father because both parents invested large portions of their meagre incomes in travel expenses:

> My father left our home here in Masi when I was seven years old because he was always fighting with my mother. But I like to see him still. Sometimes he comes here, sometimes I go there. He is a kind person. He works on construction sites. He has a wife in Steenberg but no children. I used to call him quite a lot then I lost his phone number and he doesn't phone my mum's phone. But if I want to go and see him, I ask my mother for money and take the train from Fish Hoek and then a taxi. It costs R25 for the whole journey and I go for the day only. (Thulani, boy, aged 11, Masiphumelele)

Steenberg is only 20 kilometres from Masiphumelele, but the return journey involves four taxi rides and two train rides, costing the equivalent of one-third of Thulani's mother's daily wage as a domestic worker. Reasons for her investment in Thulani's visits to his father are likely to include her sense that he is a good father who can exert a positive influence on Thulani, and her aspiration that Thulani will be incorporated into his father's clan through his initiation ritual. These roles are perhaps more salient given that Thulani's mother runs a shebeen (a bar and liquor shop, usually unlicensed) from their home and the men with whom Thulani otherwise interacts are usually drunk from early in the morning.

Children's efforts to sustain connections with absent fathers through phone calls and visits can bear tangible fruits in the long term. A number of teenagers in Masiphumelele whose mothers have AIDS planned and executed their own move to their father's or paternal grandparents' homes in distant cities or villages. Some returned after a few weeks, but others enrolled in schools near their father's home. And several young Fish Hoek residents spoke of plans to join their fathers elsewhere in the country, or overseas, once they had completed school and wished to travel, work or study further. A portion of children whose fathers are technically absent clearly regard their bonds with these men and the duties they entail to remain strong regardless of the amount of time they have spent together in childhood.

Absent mothers are more of an anomaly than absent fathers, and children's responses more demanding of the maternal role. Nearly three-quarters of adolescents in Cape Town reported having lived their entire lives with their biological mothers, although only a quarter of African adolescents have done so. And the greater frequency with which adolescents report visiting and conversing with absent mothers than with absent fathers suggests a stronger social and emotional connectivity over time and distance. These patterns are consistent with the pivotal role of provider, protector and mentor accorded to mothers – and mother figures – by teenagers in the Valley, and are supported elsewhere in the survey. Powerful poems praising and thanking mothers for their dedication lie alongside compositions about freedom, love and identity in an anthology by high-school pupils in Soweto (Newfield & Maungedzo 2005). Fathers are conspicuous by their absence.

Adolescents who spent most or all of their childhood with their mothers generally identify their mothers as their most important influence (according to data collected in the third wave of CAPS in 2005). Among adolescents who spent less than half of their childhood with their mothers, only about half identified their mothers as their most important influence, with about one-fifth identifying a grandparent, and the remainder various other kin and occasionally even non-kin. We are by no means the first to observe the tendency for children to name a grandmother or aunty 'mother', and their biological mother 'sister' or 'aunty', thus reflecting what they have known since infancy (Lee 2002). Questions in CAPS were designed to try and prevent this kin-naming obscuring results but it remains likely that the data overestimate the reported influence of biological mothers on adolescents' lives. A consistent picture emerges of the centrality of mothers – biological and ascribed – in children's perceptions of their nurture and well-being. How then do children cope when a mother departs, and to what extent can mother figures provide a substitute for biological mothers?

Like many adolescents raised in the Eastern Cape by a maternal relative, Gift did not experience the absence of his biological mother as traumatic because at that point he did not know her as his mother:

> When I first heard that my 'aunty' was my mom, I was shocked and didn't believe them – I think I was about nine years old. Then I started picking it up in the way people were talking at home, so I began to believe them. It all began by the time my mother came back to the Eastern Cape on holiday at the end of the year. And I started hearing my mother's sisters saying 'Gift's mother is coming home tomorrow'. She was working here in Cape Town you see. When she arrived the following day, she greeted everyone and at the end she came to me and said, 'Hello, my boy'. Then I ran to my mom (who is my granny) and sat next to her. My mother asked, 'Why are you scared?' and I said, 'Why are you saying "my boy"? I am not your boy' and she laughed. The days went on and every single day I heard people when they came to see her they always say 'mama ka Gift', which is 'Gift's mother'. That's when I started to believe she was my mom, and my granny also told me it is so. I started spending more time with my mother and I was happy to have two moms around me at the same time.

Gift's recollection is of confusion and distress at the point when his mother returned home and he was first told of their true relationship. His mother's frequent visits enabled Gift to adjust to this new reality. He credits the periods of time that he was able to spend in the company of both his 'mom' (grandmother) and his mother with his relatively smooth adjustment.

Many young residents of Masiphumelele told similar stories of a profound reconfiguring of their intimate maternal relationships in early childhood. Some were still struggling to achieve a positive relationship with their mothers. At the age of seven, Victoria moved from the rural home she had always shared with her grandmother (whom she calls 'mother') to Masiphumelele in order to attend a 'good' school. She moved in with the woman she knew as her sister and was informed then that in fact she was her mother. Victoria was immediately thrown into a new environment in which she had major responsibilities for the housework, including cooking for the family and caring for her younger siblings. She spoke of her intense frustration and anger at home that resulted in her rude behaviour towards her mother, and her desire to retrieve the care she had received from her grandmother:

> I ask where my food is [that I saved from breakfast] and they don't answer me, so I am shouting that I have decided that I don't want to stay here next year, that I am going to go to the Transkei to my 'mother' [her grandmother]. Every day they eat my food and when I come home from school I am supposed to cook. This is my solution: my 'mother' comes from the Transkei and then I am happy. She buys beautiful clothes and uniform for me. That's all. (Victoria, girl, aged 14, Masiphumelele)

Victoria struggles with the maternal authority imposed by the woman she has always known as 'sister' and her inability to achieve her proposed solution, namely to bring her grandmother into the home. And, unlike Gift, she had not spent periods of time with both her mother figure (grandmother) and biological mother, which would have offered continuity in her care and the building of emotional bonds with her mother. Popular discourse tends to link problems children face adjusting to changes in roles and relationships with parental separation or the arrival of a step-parent. The fact that they occur in situations of parental presence challenges assumptions that children fare better on all accounts when they live with a biological parent.

As we saw earlier, maternal absence is much more likely to occur during the childhoods of African youth than among their coloured and white counterparts. But grandmothers, aunts and even neighbours frequently act as mother figures in Ocean View. Here, few mothers move away for work, but many suffer mental health problems associated with drug or alcohol addiction. It was only after several months of working together closely that Brian felt able to express to us his feelings about his mother:

> I don't actually speak to my mother any more. The doctors have said that there is something wrong with her brain, psychologically I mean, but I don't actually care. When she comes to my aunt's I just go to my room. I think my granny may kick her out because she is never there and so she might as well stay wherever it is that she sleeps…My mother isn't actually a mother to her children, I rather see my granny as my mother. (Brian)

Teenagers in all three communities whose mothers live close by (but not with them) express a combination of hurt, regret and blame towards mothers who do not fulfil their definition of the mothering role. Lara has lived with her grandmother in Fish Hoek since she was three months old. Her mother lives in a flat a few streets away and they see each other regularly:

> Lara: She is my mother, but she has never been my mother. I don't know how to describe it…being a mother…being there for me, caring, just understanding, looking after me, watch my back…

> Interviewer: So who does that for you?

> Lara: My dad's wife and my gran. My dad's new wife has helped me through a lot, I mean she is more of a mother to me than my own mother has ever been and that has really helped me out.

Lara's descriptions of her own mother's failures (and this applies in the manner in which other adult relatives fall short of providing maternal input) suggest that she sees something unique in what a biological mother should provide. Is this only because she does not have recourse to the kinds of historical precedents and cultural rubrics that appoint and validate 'mother figures' in Ocean View and Masiphumelele? Our data suggest not, for even those who enjoy intimate bonds with their mother figures, scrutinise the failures of their biological mothers in ways that imply their unique status and symbolic importance. Although Chloe has been lovingly mothered by her grandmother since her infancy, she regrets that her biological mother is unable to mother her properly and holds her at least partly responsible:

> Long ago, my mum used to work in a fruit shop in Alexandria [outskirts of Johannesburg] where my dad lived at the time. He is from Swaziland and speaks Swati. They met there – my dad had a tavern and my mum started to drink there. My mum and dad never got married, and they split up about the time I was born. I lived with my dad and stepmother for a few years, and since then I've been living with my granny…I don't get along with my mother at all. When she's in a bad phase with her drinking, it's worse. My granny ignores it, she doesn't like talking about it…We, my granny, sister and I think that there might be something wrong in her head as she does things that are very stupid, that even my little brother wouldn't do. Once she was forced to give up drinking by one of her boyfriends in Jo'burg, but when she came here she started again. I think it's a family thing as my granny says my grandfather was also an alcoholic. But I blame her for not sorting it out and being a mother to us. (Chloe, girl, aged 17, Masiphumelele)

Our data suggest that children are tacitly, but powerfully, weighting the care responsibilities of mothers and fathers differently. Perhaps in response to paternal mobility, children are casting mothers as ultimately dependable, thereby placing a moral imperative on the individual and then the family to ensure 'maternal' care. CAPS data suggest that they are largely successful, at least in late childhood. When adolescents live with one parent only, the parent in question rarely moves out (CAPS panel data from waves 1 and 3). The vast majority of single-resident parents are mothers and most children living apart from fathers are in low-income neighbourhoods. Thus the mother–child relationship appears to be the focal point around which a domestic group often coheres and there is a degree of residential stability in mother–child bonds for many adolescents, including some who experienced maternal absence during childhood (see Figure 2.2).

Young people's greater onus on mothering helps explain why mother figures can and do provide a maternal relationship, but young people struggle immensely to live with the understanding that their biological mother was in a position to have fulfilled such a role and did not do so. Brian, Lara and Chloe all describe their awareness of the wider social and economic influences that have contributed to their biological mother's inability to mother. Yet at the same time, they suggest that their mothers have, at one level at least, chosen not to fulfil the mothering role. Physically or emotionally absent fathers are not scrutinised in the same way, indicating that children's idealised notions of care involving both parents are counterbalanced by norms that position women as sources of nurture and by the practical reality of more mobile and transient fathers.

Who else cares at home?

Thus far our data have shown how effectively parent-figures – particularly grandmothers and stepfathers – can provide parent-like care for many children whose biological parents are absent. But the dedicated nurture of a parent-figure is not guaranteed, especially in middle and late childhood. Who else do children turn to for various kinds of care, and how available and effective are these sources? Are we witnessing any changes in the concepts and practices of 'family' or the circle of care extended to children?

It is possible that children seek care from members of their own household, relatives living elsewhere and friends or neighbours. In theory, there are more people available to offer care in the homes of adolescents in low-income than in high-income neighbourhoods. The average adolescent in a low-income household lives with 5.6 other people, whereas his or her counterpart in a high-income household lives with only 3.7 other people (according to CAPS). In any household income category, coloured adolescents live in larger households than African adolescents (although the average for all coloured adolescents is lower than for all African adolescents because a higher proportion of the former live in higher-income households). Larger households in medium- and low-income coloured and African areas are explained by larger numbers of brothers and sisters, as well as the presence of the extended family, particularly uncles, aunts, cousins, nephews and nieces. A significant minority (between 13 and 25 per cent) of these adolescents share a home with one or two grandparents. The higher percentage relates to coloured adolescents because a large portion of African grandparents reside in the distant Eastern Cape, only making occasional visits to Cape Town for healthcare. Co-residence with grandparents is unusual for white adolescents, reflecting the tendency for elderly people to remain independent or move into retirement homes when they become frail.

CAPS also showed that one-parent households are much more likely to be extended than two-parent households (see Figure 2.1). Therefore, children with an absent parent have at least one other related adult in the home who, in theory, may provide care. The more distant but co-resident kin are almost always *maternal* kin. An adolescent was between four and five times more likely to have co-resident maternal kin (grandparents, uncles, aunts and others) than co-resident paternal kin. In Cape Town, co-residence with paternal kin is exceptional, whilst co-residence with maternal kin is widespread. This pattern was almost identical among white, coloured and African adolescents.

Analysis of CAPS data also showed that most of the fluidity in young people's homes is accounted for by the entry and exit of extended-family members (uncles, aunts and cousins) rather than of parents and siblings. The pattern among African adolescents' homes is similar to the general pattern. In other words, contemporary household fluidity is not characterised by high levels of parental mobility for children in low-income African neighbourhoods and 'stable' households elsewhere, as is often assumed.

Stepfathers feature prominently in a context where children commonly live with their mothers, but not their biological fathers. CAPS asked adolescents to rate the quality of their relationships with resident and absent biological parents, resident step-parents and other resident adults. The majority (58%) described their relationships with resident step-parents (the majority of whom we know to be stepfathers) as 'good'; 23% said they were 'excellent'; and 19% reported them as 'not good' or 'bad'. The survey data support our ethnographic findings in demonstrating that a step-parent is parent-like for a large portion of adolescents, providing social, emotional and material care roles: more than two-thirds of adolescents with co-resident step-parents report that they spend time together alone with their step-parents. Roughly half reported having personal conversations with their step-parents, and the same portion said that step-parents spend money on their schooling and clothing, and have given them presents and money.

Second to mothers, siblings were the most common co-resident kin, with three-quarters of 14–17-year-olds in Cape Town living with one or more siblings. The significance of sibling companionship and relationships is poorly understood in South Africa (except for Niehaus 1994 and brief commentaries in Henderson 1999; Reynolds 1993; and Ross 1995). Adolescents may not live with all of their siblings, especially in poorer neighbourhoods, and there is some flux in co-residence between siblings. Nonetheless, most adolescents co-reside for long periods of time with particular siblings. Young people across the Valley who had resident siblings of a similar age spoke about being 'alongside each other' in relation to adults or infants in the home, and in light of the fact that they had always spent time in one another's company, playing, laughing and squabbling. Conflict over resources and space in the home was presented as a challenging, but expected, part of living with siblings that did not necessarily undermine relationships in the long term. This was particularly evident in Fish Hoek where young people spend larger amounts of time at home with their siblings compared to their peers in Ocean View and Masiphumelele:

> My brother plays Metallica too loud and gives me headaches. (Annie, girl, aged 12, Fish Hoek)

> I don't really hang out upstairs with my family. It's boring. My brother and sister, they get on my nerves…If I come down here I can sit here in my lounge and do my own thing. I am always in my room. (Lara, girl, aged 17, Fish Hoek)

Young people who had moved around with their siblings spoke of the importance of having a companion with a shared set of experiences and who was notionally equal (despite small age differences) within the family and in relation to the new environment. Leanne, quoted earlier in this chapter, wrote of how much she missed her brother when she and her mother moved to Cape Town, leaving her father and brother temporarily in Johannesburg. Chloe, recalling her move to Cape Town with her mother figure (her grandmother) and her younger sister, describes a close, highly supportive, but almost exclusive, relationship between the two sisters. She attributes their slow acquisition of the local language to their tight bond, suggesting that this may have hindered their integration into their new neighbourhood. But the emotional benefits at the time, and those that persist, outweigh these earlier social costs:

> When we moved here, Anele [younger sister] and I could only speak Sotho, so we could not even talk to the cousins we'd moved in with. We always used to sit together because there was no point sitting with others who we didn't understand and who we feared might be laughing at us. At that time Anele and I were best friends. We still are, even now. We did everything together. We were trapped in this language thing. It took us about three years to understand isiXhosa very well, and to make good friends. Perhaps it might have been shorter if we hadn't spent so much time together as the two of us. What made a difference was me starting primary school and leaving Anele in the pre-school. Then we had to speak with other children. (Chloe)

Children in Masiphumelele and Ocean View with siblings more than three years older often described them in terms that initially suggested a strong overlap with the parenting role: an unsurprising characteristic given the frequent large age gaps and periods when elder siblings ran the daily domestic routine. However, upon closer inspection, the role of much older siblings differed from that of parents in that it included an expectation of practical response and involvement in a young person's concerns, rather than a more remote advisory stance taken by some parents. Older brothers were described as sources of protection, particularly by boys, who drew pictures of 'my older brother' in trendy, macho clothing retrieving a soccer ball taken by friends or fighting their corner in a dispute with peers. Even for those with another mother figure, older sisters were described as sources of social and emotional care, and even material support when they were earning and contributing to school fees. The flip side of this senior, and ostensibly protective, role of older siblings is the potential for using their relative power to exploit their younger siblings. Dynamics of this nature may result in relatively benign outcomes for younger children, such as being asked to run errands, but could equally involve compromising their relationships with adults by being asked to lie or steal for the gain of an older sibling.

In adolescence, across all neighbourhoods, siblings can become valued routes into wider social circles and exert an influence on teenagers' attitudes and social interaction. Virginia, who talked about her relationship with her sister using the words 'love', 'fight', 'advisor', 'fun', values her elder sister for introducing her to a social world outside Fish Hoek:

> My sister influenced me…She mixed with coloured people and she came here and said you should mix with them…She is my older sister I look up to, so ever since then I just hang out with them [coloured people], like sleeping at their houses, being with them most of the time. (Virginia, girl, aged 17, Fish Hoek)

At the same time, siblings confide in one another, particularly (but not exclusively) when they are the same sex and not more than three years different in age. Advice on topics such as dating, sex, school- or career-related decisions that are not discussed with parents or other adults in the home is often sought from siblings (including co-resident cousins who are considered siblings).

> Tracey: I miss her [older sister] a lot because she used to help me with my homework, I used to go to her to talk to her, to go out together, for money, and just to be with her.
>
> Interviewer: What did you used to talk to her about?
>
> Tracey: We talked about things that happened, and make jokes about them. I could go to her if I had a problem or was sad.
>
> Interviewer: Who do you go to now if you feel sad or have a problem?
>
> Tracey: I keep it for me alone. My mom is too busy and sometimes I am nervous to go to her. (Tracey, girl, aged 12, Ocean View)

Tracey and her sister had lived with both parents in the same house in Ocean View all their lives, but her elder sister moved to be nearer to her long-term boyfriend and improve her chances of finding work. Tracey's reflections on the impact of her elder sister's recent move to another suburb of Cape Town suggest that a sibling's departure from the home, even when planned and anticipated, can have immediate social and emotional consequences for children, which, if others do not fill the gap in support, may lead to young people making uninformed decisions that shape their longer-term well-being.

Scant attention was paid to the separation of siblings in the body of childhood ethnography conducted in the early 1990s, which detailed the movement of parents and adult kin and the consequences so attentively (Henderson 1999; Jones 1993; Ramphele 2002; Reynolds 2000). Sean Jones (1993) flags the issue by pointing out that parents were forced by circumstances to choose which children to take with them and which to leave in others' care. Only in certain specific contexts has the role of sibling relationships been given recent attention by social scientists. Studies of the impact of AIDS-related mortality and migration in southern and central Africa have revealed that being separated from a sibling is experienced by children as one of the most traumatic consequences of household rearrangements (Mann 2003; Young & Ansell 2003). Our findings strengthen the case for further research into sibling relationships (including those between cousins), their effectiveness in providing psychosocial support within a generation and the degree to which older siblings provide a mentor figure or influence of a different nature in children's everyday decision-making, especially when a mother or father is absent. Are children who have had a consistent sibling companion through residential movement and alterations in the domestic environment – for example, the coming and going of parents – more resilient than their peers who have not? If so, what aspects of the sibling's presence count?

CAPS data show that adolescents living with one parent or neither parent at the outset, regardless of neighbourhood, were much more likely to acquire new co-residents (especially siblings and cousins, nephews and nieces) than adolescents residing with both parents. Greater flux in the households of young people with one or two absent parents raises questions about the quality of care that can be provided when people are frequently moving in and out, and flags the potential for abuse.

The risks of abuse posed to children by transient relatives or kin and neighbours living close by is much greater when their own domestic environment is economically and socially impoverished. Earlier we saw how the sudden and violent death of her stepfather placed Thandi, her young disabled brother and their mother in a perilous financial position. An uncle living in a nearby shack began to contribute some of his income to their household, and we often encountered him drunk in the vicinity of Thandi's home. At no point did she report abuse or state directly her fears of this man, but she made several allusions to his unpredictable, sometimes threatening, behaviour and to her sense of dependence:

> I only love my uncle when he brings us nice things. Because sometimes
> he shouts at us, saying that he is not working for us and that he decided
> to resign from work because he does not want to support anyone else.
> (Thandi, girl, aged 14, Masiphumelele)

Economic impoverishment renders it almost impossible for adults and children to refuse assistance from a relative and creates a relationship of indebtedness. Thandi has little immediate familial protection because her mother works until late and she has no elder siblings or cousins in the vicinity. The risks she faces are underscored by gender- and age-related hierarchies operating across the financial means and cultural spectra, as well as by powerful norms that link the appearance of economic sufficiency with respectability in low-income neighbourhoods (discussed further in the next chapter). But these risks are raised considerably by her mother's alcohol consumption, long working hours and the household's meagre income, all of which have been exacerbated since her stepfather's sudden death.

'I'm like a daughter in that house': The reaches of communal care

The extent to which children seek care from their wider non-resident family depends on their accessibility to them, social norms and the quality of relationships they enjoy. Patterns in the geographical proximity of children's wider family members can be linked to the migration histories of particular neighbourhoods described earlier. The extended families of the vast majority of young Ocean View residents live in the neighbourhood, and a portion live in other low- to middle-income suburbs of Cape Town, designated 'coloured' by the apartheid state (including Manenberg, Grassy Park and Lavender Hill). Their peers in Fish Hoek and Masiphumelele live close to a smaller portion of their wider family and frequently have relatives in very distant provinces and other parts of Greater Cape Town.

Our ethnography points to the very targeted nature of children's efforts to secure care from non-resident relatives and dramatic variation between neighbourhoods. Eleven-year-old Thulani, whose weekly bus journeys from Masiphumelele over the mountain to see his father were described earlier, has a clear strategy to compensate for his mother's preoccupation with the shebeen run from their home, and the noise created there:

> It is so busy at home that I can't do my homework. So I take my books to my aunt's place, just two plots away. It is much quieter there. And if I get stuck I ask my sister, who is in grade 10…When I feel bad, my other aunt and uncle are the ones who make me feel better. They live in a shack on the same plot as ours. I trust my aunt and can tell her anything. In this way, she is a bit like a mother to me.

The support roles played by Thulani's aunts, uncle and sister are specific, and each provides an essential input in the context of his needs. His actions are typical of children in Masiphumelele and Ocean View, where movement between extended family and neighbours' homes is intrinsic to sociality among adults and children. Voting with their feet, some children in these areas moved in with relatives or friends for periods of weeks or months. Young Ocean View residents often explicitly sought the company and parent-like support of neighbours, who were experienced as less partisan than relatives. Recalling Veronique's highly conflictual home environment, it is revealing to read the way she recreates her ideal of a family in her best friend's home down the road:

> I am always there [at Marianca's house]. They are like family. I eat there, sleep there, they are like a second family to me…If I haven't been round

their house Marianca's mom asks me where I've been and says that she has missed me…I'm quite close to her. She likes teasing me and Marianca about our relationships with boys. We also do stuff together. We go walking, go to the mall and to Fish Hoek. We chat about TV and our days. She will make me coffee or I will make coffee for her, at her house. I'm like another daughter in that house. (Excerpts from interviews and diary, Veronique, girl, aged 17, Ocean View)

Tellingly, Veronique experiences her relationships with this family as emotionally supportive because they contain some of the qualities of openness and reciprocity that children value in relation to their own well-being (see Chapter 3). But neighbourly relationships like this do not carry the same density of obligation as those within families (Bray 2009). We observed that relationships with non-kin were often very intense during a certain period of time, but fragile in the sense that they could quickly turn bitter or conflictual.

Fewer young Fish Hoek residents cultivated relationships of this kind with local relatives, neighbours and friends. Local grandparents are the most frequent sources of intimate care, especially when parents are ill or have long working hours. Those who see their grandparents frequently report a close, supportive and reciprocal relationship, similar to those described by children elsewhere in the Valley:

Really I know I am spoilt, I can go to my gran or anywhere and ask for something. But I also always help out…I will cook for her, do dishes, spend time…not because it's expected, but I want to do it. Why shouldn't I? They have always been there for me. It's just a natural thing. I always have family to go to if I need a lift…anything I need. (Justin, boy, aged 18, Fish Hoek)

Justin describes himself as 'spoilt' on the basis that he has ready access to grandparents who are willing to help him in any way that they can. He sees himself as both unusual and privileged, an indication that everyday mutually supportive relationships with grandparents are rare in middle-class Fish Hoek. His analysis also holds in the context of the whole Valley: he has always had high-quality care from his resident mother and receives regular emotional care and financial support from his grandparents.

A handful of young people in Fish Hoek spoke about a local family with whom their own immediate family is very friendly: sharing lifts to school; playing in each other's homes regularly; and going on family holidays together. But very few reported the level of self-motivated familiarity and even dependence on neighbours and friends that we saw in Ocean View and Masiphumelele. Domestic workers employed by most middle-class households often monitor children playing at home and prepare food until parents return from work, thereby reducing the need to turn to neighbouring friends. Restrictions on young Fish Hoek residents' independent mobility are a major constraint on their opportunities to draw support from outside the home (discussed in the next chapter). Cultural preferences for childcare to be contained within a nuclear-family arrangement further discourage children from seeking or receiving care from elsewhere, and serve to undermine the significance of any such support that children succeed in securing.

Conclusion

One of the legacies of apartheid is a high rate of physical fragmentation in the families of children and adolescents. But patterns of co-residence do not accord neatly with the racial divisions of apartheid. It is true that many African children and adolescents live apart from their fathers, have little contact with them or with paternal kin, and some also live apart from their mothers. However, patterns are not dissimilar among poorer coloured children, and a significant minority of historically privileged white children face similar challenges. The differences that persist seem to reflect class as much as race, in that children in poorer households spend more of their childhood with their parents than their peers in richer households. Income is now a more accurate predictor of family form than race group.

Extended family households are also widespread. In terms of their form, households in contemporary Cape Town have not converged around the two-parent, nuclear-family model. Instead, they have converged on a range of models that include these, as well as households comprising mothers and no other adults and households comprising a wider or extended range of kin, mostly maternal. South African households are converging around a diversity of household forms, and not around any one of the specific forms that characterised racial groups under apartheid.

In the face of actual or at least possible flux in household composition, children and their intimate adults across Cape Town seek to build good relationships in a variety of ways. Absence need not entail bad relationships, any more than presence entails good relationships. Children consistently assert the roles and obligations of their parents as providers – especially their mothers – looking for reciprocity between generations and protecting parents from the unwelcome scrutiny of shortfalls in their care. Their methods and the extent of their success differ according to neighbourhood. The variations we observed reflect the material and social possibilities of adults to meet children's expectations, and the scope of cultural norms to respond to children's efforts to mould the character of intimate relationships in the home. And both these variables are profoundly influenced by the persistence of past injustice and impoverishment, as well as present-day opportunities for change – both real and perceived.

Positive investments in family dynamics are much easier for children in Masiphumelele than in Ocean View. They are less often demanded of children in Fish Hoek, although when they are, they are equally difficult. Correspondingly, children tend to negotiate challenges in the domestic arena more successfully in Masiphumelele than in the other two neighbourhoods. This seems to reflect the resilience of more flexible ways of 'doing family' within South Africa's African population. African children can draw on long-standing social and cultural resources concerning collective care for children, codes of respect towards older people, the designation of care responsibilities to senior women and investment in a rural home of origin. These cultural resources are not unchanging, however. African children add to this palette some recently legitimised values and aspirations consistent with their new sociopolitical status. Parents (especially mothers) now consider it beneficial to raise their children with them in the city (in living arrangements that sometimes seem somewhat nuclear). The expectation that schooling is a passport to success means that children have more bargaining power in the family or household. There are also indications that adult vulnerability to AIDS is prompting the re-evaluation of gendered roles in the home and of the capacities of young children in directions consistent with children's relationship ideals. These possibilities are supported by a sense of permanence and urban identity shared by this generation of children and parents whose symbolic connections to their rural origins are still able to solidify their African identity and offer a potential future resource base.

Apartheid's disenfranchisement had different implications for children growing up in coloured neighbourhoods two decades ago, the effects of which are apparent today. Children's ready recourse to confrontation and the high levels of interpersonal violence in Ocean View mirror the methods of repression and forced dislocation used by the state. A small minority of families have become relatively wealthy, but the majority perceive themselves as 'stuck' in socio-economic terms and do not envisage a better future for their children. In this context, a coherent, positive, normative framework attached to community history and identity is much more elusive.

In neighbourhoods like Fish Hoek with a history of privilege and economic security, the gender and age hierarchies upheld by apartheid's ruling elite continue to restrict what is possible for children and adults at home. When parents encourage debate and negotiation, children are drawn to these ideals of reciprocity and equality, but find that they sit uneasily alongside long-held notions of directive parent and responsive child. Family mobility and separation from parents is not unusual, given the real and perceived narrowing of employment opportunities resulting from the post-apartheid state's policies of BEE. Neither children nor their parents have the social or cultural resources to negotiate these transitions smoothly. Communal care within or outside the wider kin group is rarely expected or valued. And children and their intimate adults are effectively forced to prove that they can retain social and emotional coherence in the home when one or both parents are elsewhere.

The restrictions of the past are by no means deterministic in any neighbourhood: young people remain positive about their familial environment and creative in their efforts to secure nurture within and beyond the boundaries of 'home'. It is perhaps particularly remarkable that neither the overt oppression nor apartheid's insidious undermining of individual worth has filtered into the way in which children in poor African and coloured neighbourhoods experience and conduct familial relationships. The scarce mention of children's rights indicated that young people do not draw explicitly on this international policy discourse to frame their aspirations and actions.

But this generation of children – especially young Africans – is taking advantage of a greater latitude in the structures and norms governing family dynamics to nurture relationships that contain certain qualities, for example trust, open communication, reciprocity and mutual respect. If given the opportunity, young people are quick to assert their desire for these. And these qualities typify an approach to family life that is didactic rather than confrontational, and more akin to the principles of democracy than to those employed by the apartheid state. If we follow young people's priorities, family coherence would be judged on the basis of relationship quality and shared values rather than its biological integrity. Children's efforts towards such coherence in all three neighbourhoods suggest a re-forming of the family alongside social change, which, theoretically at least, enables entitlement and honours duty.

The brakes countering this process are strong in all neighbourhoods, but especially limiting in homes with very low incomes. Economic shocks mean that parents can suddenly fail in their provider role. Children are usually powerless to bolster their family financially, but tenaciously uphold the parental role. They do so to the extent of creating a kind of parental protection that barely exists and exposing themselves to neglect or serious harm. Violence against women and children in the home is persistently condoned through patriarchal values playing out in an increasingly matrifocal context.

Children struggle to communicate with parent-figures in ways they consider effective and feel impotent because neither party has the interpersonal tools or vocabulary to ease this process. And when opportunities to debate such challenges across neighbourhoods remain so scarce, young people are unable to recognise the common obstacles they face in 'doing family'. Consequently, they resort to explanations that ultimately imply a 'failure of my neighbourhood' and of 'us' as a race group, to address what are often common contemporary predicaments.

3 The familiar world of the neighbourhood

In her diary, 14-year-old Samantha records that she spends most of her time with a group of close female friends who, like her, live in one particular block of flats in Ocean View. She writes about hanging out 'around the corner' from their flats, having a braai (barbecue) in the mountains, playing table football at the game shop across the road or just walking around Ocean View together. Because they do most things together, they have given themselves a 'gang' name, 'The Young Little Bastards'. Their camaraderie is summed up by Samantha:

> The other day one girl's mom sent her to the shops to buy electricity and eggs. So we all went along. We were walking the road closed [walking in a line to block the road]. (Samantha, girl, aged 14, Ocean View)

Jake, a 12-year-old, spends most of his time at home in a navy compound just outside Fish Hoek:

> I play a lot of computer games, watch a lot of TV and read at the weekends because there is nothing else to do. I am not allowed to play outside the garden gate, but I often go to my friend next door. I don't see friends much during the week and I can't go out by myself. (Jake, boy, aged 12, Fish Hoek)

Apartheid kept so-called 'racial groups' geographically separate – except when cheap labour was required in 'white' residential or industrial areas – and discriminated racially in public spending. These policies resulted in the Valley comprising starkly contrasting neighbourhoods, as we saw in Chapter 1. They also rendered movement and interaction between the neighbourhoods very difficult. For most children and adolescents, most of the time, the familiar world in which they live their everyday lives is limited to the neighbourhoods formerly allocated to particular 'race' groups and now characterised by significant class differences.

The long and pernicious legacy of apartheid is reflected in deep-rooted differences in physical infrastructure, socio-economic possibilities and forms of sociality between neighbourhoods in the Valley. Evident in the quotes above and reflected in the numerous maps drawn by young participants are the striking differences we found in the way children use the spaces that surround their homes and experience neighbourly interaction. Alongside these differences there are some similarities in young people's ideals and priorities regarding the character of a neighbourhood or, more importantly, a community. Parallels also exist in the significance of independent mobility and of local social resources available to the young in poor neighbourhoods, which, in turn, shape the manner in which they understand and use space in an effort to protect themselves from physical and social danger. Thus Map 2, drawn by a group of grade-9 boys in Ocean View, illustrates places they perceive as dangerous: an area of informal housing named Mountain View, where they say a lot of gangsters live and where you might be robbed or stabbed; Soetwater, where people go drag racing; the open and unlit space used for dumping rubbish; the flats, where drinking and drug-taking cause fighting and people sometimes get stabbed; and a shebeen, which exposes them to drinking, drug-taking and violence.

This and the following chapter explore how children and adolescents use and understand space. The focus of this chapter is the everyday, familiar worlds of the immediate neighbourhood. In Chapter 4 we examine young people's more limited access to, and perceptions of, places beyond the local neighbourhood and pay particular attention to the nature of relationships formed therein. Both aim to extend our empirical understanding of children's social worlds in the second decade of South African democracy. On a conceptual level, they offer insight into the precise ways in which the neighbourhoods as physical, cultural and social spaces with specific local histories exert influences on children's well-being – a relationship that is little-investigated and poorly understood (Ward 2007a).

Ecological models developed by social psychologists to further understanding of the mutually interactive relationship between children and their social and physical worlds recognise the role of neighbourhood in influencing well-being at various levels (see, for example, Bronfenbrenner 1979, 1986). But much less scholarly enquiry has focused on the nature and impact of children's local residential and social spaces in comparison to attention paid to the family, school or wider policy environment (Ward 2007a). Pockets of research in the United States and United Kingdom have demonstrated that neighbourhood characteristics exert influences independently of individual- and family-level variables, and indirectly through the home setting (Brooks-Gunn et al. 1993; Huston 2002; Leventhal & Brooks-Gunn 2000). For example, child outcomes are directly affected by the quality, quantity, diversity and accessibility of local institutional resources targeted at children's learning, recreation, education, social support, health and employment (Leventhal & Brooks-Gunn 2003). The limited level of enquiry in this area in South Africa has centred on the local social dynamics underlying children's recruitment into gangs (Kinnes 1995; Pinnock 1982a, 1982b; Salo 2004; Scharf 1990; Ward 2007b; Western 1981) and the effects of politically motivated, criminal and domestic violence on children and their families (Henderson 1999; Ramphele 2002; Straker 1992). Such studies demonstrated the corrosive impact of forced removals and state repression during the late apartheid era on the social fabric of communities, as well as the protective effects of supportive familial relationships and an easy temperament during infancy for children exposed to high levels of violence.

Aimed understandably at exposing the impacts of the state's actions, the starting point of these early studies was usually one of an adult-defined social pathology requiring investigation. One consequence of this vein of enquiry is the notion of the neighbourhood as a homogeneous entity, its labelling as either a high- or low-risk area for children and the unintended perpetuation of popular negative stereotypes.

Work done during and after the transition is more child-centred in its attempts to understand and describe the physical space and its complex, often contradictory, social dynamics by observing what young people do within their immediate environments and how they perceive them. The Growing Up in Cities project showed how both real and perceived dangers to children in impoverished local neighbourhoods on Johannesburg's periphery continue to severely constrain their lives even after the demise of apartheid (Swart-Kruger 2000, 2001; Swart-Kruger & Chawla 2002). Salo (2004) looked carefully at familial and neighbourly influences on girls' socialisation into femininity in Manenberg, a poor neighbourhood of Cape Town zoned 'coloured' during apartheid. The new and racially mixed neighbourhood of Summer Greens in northern Cape Town was studied by Broadbridge (2002), although she has little to say about young people in particular. Most recently, several studies have observed children and sought their views on their strategies for managing violence (Parkes 2007) and gang involvement (Ward & Bakhuis 2009) in suburbs of Cape Town that, like Manenberg, were created for coloured people four decades ago and have remained economically and socially impoverished. Each of these studies is area-specific and neither encounters, nor explores, diversity by race group or class. Our analysis offers a uniquely comparative perspective in the different areas of the Valley on the way that children engage with their neighbourhoods; how they define and experience 'community'; and their understanding of how sociopolitical and spatially local histories have shaped their own worldviews and those of the adults close to them.

Whilst the terms 'neighbourhood' and 'community' are often used synonymously or interchangeably in social research, we distinguish between the two by treating the former as purely a spatial referent, namely the geographically defined residential area in which children live, and the spaces and places that they go to on a regular basis. Thus, neighbourhoods have physical and social characteristics of significance to children's lives, which are, in turn, shaped by historical, geographical, political and cultural influences. The term 'community', on the other hand, is used to refer to the social nexus with which children identify and derive a sense of belonging. Community *might* be understood in terms of physical neighbourhood, but in our research we did not assume that children's communities would necessarily fall within a geographically, racially or otherwise bounded neighbourhood. The mapping activities and subsequent discussion were structured in such a way that individual children themselves were able to illustrate the boundaries of their neighbourhoods and communities.

Immediate neighbourhoods

Children of all ages relished the opportunity to create maps of their local worlds within the Valley and beyond the mountains that bound it. Their collaborative and individual drawings were the springboard for discussion about mobility, commerce, leisure, safety, local sociability and the perceived characteristics of other neighbourhoods in the Valley.

The immediate space around the home has particular practical and social relevance to children living in Masiphumelele and Ocean View. Like Samantha, quoted at the beginning of the chapter, children typically spend large portions of time with friends of their own age and their families who live very close by. Young children play cricket, soccer and various other games in the communal yards in blocks of flats in Ocean View and those containing a cluster of shacks in Masiphumelele. The immediate neighbourhood space is, therefore, an important environment in terms of peer-group relationships. For example, see Map 3, a painting by 12-year-old Praise from Masiphumelele, showing her own shack, neighbouring shacks where her friends live, and the communal toilet, shower and tap shared with other families. Much of what children do with neighbouring friends and the adult family members of these friends is domestic and everyday in nature: their application of kinship terms to neighbours demonstrates children's familiarity with and emotional connectedness to these people, and recognises their fulfilment of at least some of the providing role normally ascribed to parent-figures (see Chapter 2).

Describing their yard paintings, like the one shown in Map 3, Praise and her friends spoke of neighbouring 'aunts' and 'uncles' (whether biologically related or not) as being 'like a mother/father to me'. Seventeen-year-old Veronique, whose conflictual relationships with her parents are described in Chapter 2, relies heavily on her neighbour living opposite and her best friend's family, who live a few houses away in Ocean View. She regularly chats about her personal goals with 'Aunty Annie', the mother of the family living opposite, and spends time at their house when she does not want to be at home. This woman is not only a source of encouragement and comfort, but also provides practical support, such as giving her information about how to realise her aim to become an au pair overseas when she finishes school and helping her get holiday work. The nature of what they do together and what they discuss means that Veronique and others around her experience this kind of relationship as akin to a mother–child one:

> I go out with Aunty Annie to the shop or if she is going out then I might ask to go with. I also went 'charring' [doing domestic cleaning work] with her in the last holidays. People think that I am Aunty Annie's daughter.

Ronaldo, a 17-year-old who shares a shack in Ocean View with his mother and siblings, goes to his maternal aunt who lives next door if he needs to talk about a problem, if he is hungry or needs help with homework. As these cases demonstrate, households providing practical, social and emotional support to children are often located in the immediate vicinity of their own homes. Children and adults in both Masiphumelele and Ocean View move around on foot because most families do not have cars. Moreover, particularly in Masiphumelele, distances to friends' or relatives' homes or to the local shop or amenity are short because the neighbourhood covers an area of less than two square kilometres. Ocean View is larger and we observed that extended-family members and friends who live in the same road or block of flats are more regular and significant sources of support to children than those who live elsewhere in the neighbourhood.

The nurturing role played by children's neighbours, whether they are related or not, in Masiphumelele and Ocean View illustrates the permeable nature of the boundary between 'home' and the broader community alluded to in the previous chapter. Henderson's study of childhood in New Crossroads, a community not dissimilar to Masiphumelele in terms of ethnic composition and poverty levels, points to the blurring of boundaries between the home and other places (Henderson 1999). Importantly, this porosity derives not only from connections with distant rural homes, but from neighbourly interaction. Evidence of communal responsibility for children in these and other poor African neighbourhoods is often given a romantic gloss by those living outside them. Attention is drawn to the strength of the African community spirit, or *ubuntu*, the absence of which in their own neighbourhoods is discussed below. Such representations are usually based on scanty knowledge of the actual characteristics of neighbourhood relationships and of children's experiences of them. The possibility that children living in communities with different social and cultural histories, such as Ocean View, may also experience intimate and supportive neighbourly relationships is rarely considered. Moreover, the positive picture of neighbourliness in African communities tends to overlook the fact that one of the factors underlying this neighbourhood porosity is children's experiences of inadequacy or conflict within the home. Unsurprisingly, when familial resources are stretched or relationships tense, children look to others whom they know and trust to plug the gaps. Evidence that in many cases children receive from neighbours at least a portion of the support they are seeking does not mean that their input is a complete substitute for insufficiencies at home or ameliorates the impact of conflictual relationships. The romantic view of *ubuntu* also sits uneasily with the reality that violence and jealousy are evident in all neighbourhoods disenfranchised by apartheid policies. As we shall shortly demonstrate, the variation lies in the social and cultural mechanisms through which these are articulated and managed, which include ridicule, gossip and witchcraft.

In wealthier Fish Hoek, where almost all families have a garden or small yard outside their home, children experience their neighbourhood in a very different way. Our observations and conversations with children supply little evidence of frequent contact with, or reciprocal relationships between, neighbours, nor the expectation that neighbours could or would take on any form of care of one's children. Fences, walls and gates, although low, separate houses from each other and constrain neighbourly sociability. Such physical barriers are much higher in middle- and upper-class suburbs nearer the centre of Cape Town, rendering interaction with neighbours very rare. Seventeen-year-old Leanne lives in Silverglades, a small suburb of identical whitewashed houses built around cul-de-sacs. Although seemingly a safe environment for children, this neighbourhood houses a fairly high percentage of elderly people. Leanne does not feel particularly at home there and notices an absence of contact between neighbours. She commented that she would not even go next door 'to borrow an egg'. The age profile of localities within Fish Hoek is significant in children's neighbourly interaction. While very few children had any contact with elderly neighbours, some reported a close friendship and daily contact with a child of their own age next door:

> I just jump the wall. In weekends I sometimes stay over there. I really like going there because I get different food, and I like being in another house. (Melissa, girl, aged 12, Fish Hoek)

Neighbourly contact is usually restricted to those living next door and only rarely extends to groups of children from a certain neighbourhood playing in the streets together, or residents of a street feeling responsible for each other's children. Children in their late teens recalled playing cricket and skateboarding in the streets when they were younger, sometimes using this recollection to draw attention to the increased popularity of computer games and the conservative attitudes of adults, particularly their grandparents' generation, which today restrict their neighbourhood interaction (see Photo 11).

Variations in children's independent mobility

The sight of children of different ages playing on the streets and in public places in Masiphumelele and Ocean View creates an initial impression of their extensive access to, and use of, the local neighbourhood. Upon investigation, age was found to be critical in shaping children's mobility and the kinds of interaction they engage in outside the family or home. So, too, is the nature of the built environment, including the size of their home and whether it is part of a private space (such as a yard) or not. The immediate neighbourhood around the home is especially important for children under 11 years old. In Masiphumelele, we observed groups of children aged between four and eight playing in the small spaces between shacks that shared one plot or yard. Adults or older siblings charged with monitoring them were expected to ensure that they did not leave the yard, particularly in the direction of the road (see Bray & Brandt 2007). Children roamed more freely across the sandy spaces between shacks in Masiphumelele's informal settlement in the wetlands because there are no plots or yards – or any equivalent physical or social boundary. Poorer children, therefore, play more remotely from those tasked with watching them owing to the physical nature of their immediate neighbourhoods. The particular risks to younger children associated with neighbourhood play are discussed below.

Similarly, poorer children living in Ocean View's flats were allowed to play in the communal yard, street or play-park areas that are visible from their homes. The absence of a private yard, however small, makes it more difficult for adults to restrict children's play to safer areas nearer the home. Children participating in our study saw this as posing a threat to very young children:

> In the flats you see small babies walking around by themselves while the mothers are watching 'Days' [a soap opera] or cooking or something because they don't have their own outside areas like houses. (Grade-8 girls' explanation as to why they drew the flats in red – the colour they chose to denote danger – on their map of Ocean View.)

During group discussions, pre-teenage children in Ocean View informed us that, having reached the age of about nine, they were allowed to walk alone to nearby places, such as friends' houses or a play park, to meet up with friends. Should they wish to go further afield, for example to a game shop, parent-figures insisted that they go with older siblings or cousins. Diary work by teenagers supported our observation that once children reach their early teens they socialise independently of older people, spending time 'hanging out' in public spaces in the flats, mountains, graveyard, streets, local game and video shops, and the multi-purpose centre and adjacent soccer field (see Photos 7 and 8). At the same time, the immediate neighbourhood remains important in that teenagers often walk around Ocean View with friends and cousins who live close by. Gender becomes an important consideration in teenagers' own decisions about mobility in Ocean View (and to a lesser extent in Masiphumelele), as well as in the wishes and actions of parent-figures wishing to restrict their movement, as evident below.

Maps drawn by 12-year-olds living in Fish Hoek showed that, unlike their peers in Ocean View and Masiphumelele, their movements are largely determined by the routines and (often safety-related) decisions of parents, and the use of a car as the main mode of transport. See Map 4, drawn by a 13-year-old girl living in Fish Hoek, showing places she goes to frequently and her 'community', which stretches beyond the Valley. Her map depicts several friends' houses, all between a five- and 20-minute drive away, and Fish Hoek Beach (a five-minute drive away from her home); a nearby shop she sometimes walks to with her mother; her school (a ten-minute drive); her dad's workplace in Constantia (a 20-minute drive); and the Longbeach Mall, where she goes shopping with her parents (a ten-minute drive). A large proportion of young Fish Hoek residents take the school bus, but other forms of public transport are generally considered unsafe and 'not cool'. Again, age is critical to perceived vulnerability. Children in primary school fear to make the short journey on foot:

> Dad drives me to school, and sometimes I walk with a friend. I am a little afraid someone will snatch me…I heard this on the news and it's a small fear inside of me. (Sarah, girl, aged 12, who lives a few streets from her primary school in Fish Hoek)

> I walk just two blocks, but I sometimes feel uncomfortable, especially when I am walking alone. (Melissa)

Mapping exercises with teenagers suggest that once they are 14 or 15 years old, most feel able to walk through their neighbouring streets alone. At the same time, parental caution persisted and permission to walk around alone depended upon the distance, the parents' perceptions of risk within a particular neighbourhood and gender.

> Interviewer: Have you always been allowed to go out by yourself?

> I usually tell my parents where I am going so they know where I am and I don't usually come home late. They only drive me to my girlfriend, that's a bit further away. But I don't mind taking a walk. My parents were kind of strict when we were younger…my mother was always…how do you say it, protective. I'm fine, it's my sister she is more worried with. I

can handle myself and my brother, and we usually go together wherever we go. (Konrad, boy, aged 19, Fish Hoek)

I used to go to my gran after [primary] school because my mom didn't like me to go home alone. I used to walk to my gran's house, which was quite close, and in middle school I would catch the bus. [When we moved to Marina da Gama] she used to bring me to school, but there were a few days a week I would take the train and she would pick me up from the station. She wouldn't want me to walk home alone from there. (Justin, boy, aged 18, Fish Hoek)

As a result of such mobility patterns, children in Fish Hoek tended to have little or no sense of social connectedness to residents of the streets surrounding their homes. Instead, they were linked into a collection of places within and beyond the Valley separated by distance and requiring car journeys. A further consequence of very limited interaction with neighbours or in the nearby streets is that middle-class children in Fish Hoek have much fewer opportunities to cultivate relationships within, and derive support from, their immediate neighbourhoods. Twelve-year-old Annie, who lives in a neighbourhood with very little neighbourly contact, tries to avoid staying at home alone: 'I got a bit scared after I saw a TV show on kidnapping, so I usually go out with my parents.' The flip side to adults' efforts to provide appropriate activities for children and protect them from harm outside the home is that they constrain children's social networks and their ability to cultivate support networks. Few children – and even fewer parents – made this link because involving children in sporting, musical and social activities, plus ensuring their safe transport between them, is culturally normative in middle-class Fish Hoek (see Photo 12).

Beyond the instances of defiance against parental rules found across the research site and considered to be 'normal' teenage behaviour, we found teenagers in Fish Hoek to be highly compliant with adult guidelines. They considered such advice appropriate to the environment and its inherent risks (see the later section on children's efforts to avoid danger in their neighbourhoods, 'Physical dangers in the local neighbourhood'). A reflective analysis of these behaviours was, however, voiced by members of the young research team, whose experience of everyday sociability in neighbouring Masiphumelele and Ocean View grew as the study progressed. The significance of bodily knowledge – or the awareness gained by being in and moving around in previously unfamiliar spaces – to young people's understandings of their own and other communities is explored in the next chapter.

Conversations about the maps drawn by young people revealed that their decisions about where to go and when, and their responses to parental restrictions, related to their perceptions of danger in the neighbourhood. The Cape Area Panel Study (CAPS) shows that adolescents' sense of personal safety in both the neighbourhood and the home varies inversely with levels of wealth in the neighbourhood. Figure 3.1 shows that very poor and poor African neighbourhoods are judged to be unsafe at night by over half of adolescents, whilst approximately one-third of poor and middle-income coloured young people made the same judgement about their own areas. These data indicate higher levels of violence in poorer, and particularly African, neighbourhoods. In interpreting these findings we should also recall our earlier evidence that adolescents living in poor neighbourhoods are much more independently mobile than their wealthier peers, and are, therefore, more likely to witness situations that make them feel vulnerable. Their mobility decisions are therefore based on more accurate knowledge than those of their middle-class peers whose movements are restricted and supervised. But very few have access to cars as safe alternatives to walking. Younger adolescents and children – especially girls – in the Valley have more negative perceptions of neighbourhood safety and a greater exposure to risk than the older adolescents surveyed in CAPS.

For younger children, the limits placed by parent-figures on children's mobility are spatial. For older teenagers, they are based on time and imposed more vigorously on girls than on boys: two 17-year-old girls in Masiphumelele said '...there are no rules, we just have to be home by nine'. Interviews with parents there and in Ocean View soon showed that while they too worried about the safety of their young children and older daughters, they were constrained in their abilities to monitor and curtail their movement by socio-economic factors. Many parents in all three neighbourhoods were out at work all day and sometimes in the evenings too. Children residing in Fish Hoek in this position are known as 'latchkey kids' and they tend to spend their

Figure 3.1 *Safety in the neighbourhood as reported by young people aged 17–20*

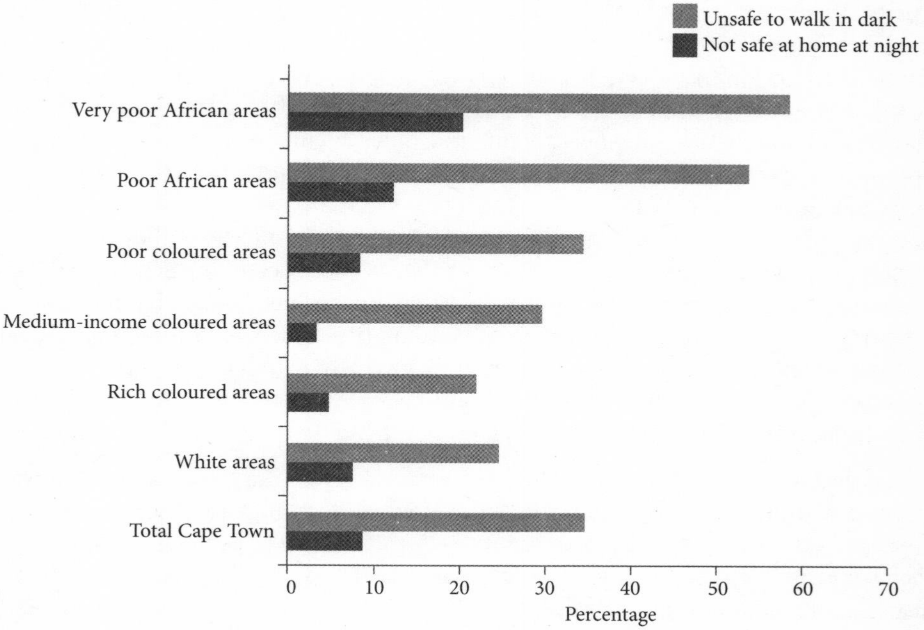

Source: Cape Area Panel Study wave 3 (2005)
Note: Limited to people who were living in the same area in 2005 as at the time of the original CAPS interviews in 2002.

time at home alone watching television. Some of their peers in Ocean View do the same, but a proportion of these and the majority of young people in Masiphumelele whose parents are out spend their time with others in or near their homes. The low incomes of many households in these neighbourhoods mean that there were times when parent-figures could not provide children with food, pocket money and other goods. Such implications pose a difficult dilemma for parents: their decision to forbid children from moving around with friends would deny them access to social networks through which they stand to be fed, provided with companionship, leisure and assistance with their homework. Therefore, parental efforts to protect children may in fact run counter to the fundamental role and duty of parents as providers, described in the previous chapter.

Children's experiences of neighbourhood sociability

The mapping activities elicited spontaneous comments from children about what they appreciated in their neighbourhoods:

> Because Ocean View is small, everyone knows you and so people will look out for you. (Nicola, girl, aged 17, Ocean View)

> People are definitely willing to help each other. You can borrow a cup of sugar or bread from your neighbours, and people have braais together. And ok, it doesn't happen as much as I'd like, but sometimes people clean the area up together. (Charney, girl, aged 17, Ocean View)

The positive character of local social interaction was often foregrounded by children in Ocean View. They spoke about people supporting fund-raising functions at the school, such as karaoke evenings, and watching sports events at the multi-purpose centre or even spontaneous soccer games in the streets. Being involved in formal and informal activities with neighbours and other members of the community is not only valued by children as a source of fun and entertainment, but as providing a sense of belonging and of a shared vested interest in the area where they live. Similar observations and opinions were expressed in Masiphumelele, although not as forcefully: young people's emphasis on positive aspects of neighbourhood sociability in Ocean View must be understood in light of the various destructive patterns of interaction that emerged in other conversations (described in the section 'Social dangers in the immediate neighbourhood' below). By expressing positive feelings about the place where they live, these young people are able to counter powerful negative norms and practices and to retain their belief in a collective efficacy.

When discussing their future plans, older teenagers across the Valley said that it was important to them to live in an area where people do things together and 'things happen in the street and the community' – something they perceive as lacking in 'rich suburbs'. Teenagers living in middle-class Fish Hoek, even those who had spent just a small amount of time in Masiphumelele and Ocean View, spoke positively and enviously of the vibrant street life and neighbourly interaction they observed there:

> There's always so much happening – people walking about, talking to each other, just hanging out, even at night. Fish Hoek is so quiet and completely dead at night. (Leanne, girl, aged 17, Fish Hoek)

Neighbourliness in Fish Hoek is equally vibrant, but much less visible because it occurs within networks of people who are related or connected to institutions such as sports clubs, schools and churches. Distinguishing the precise reasons why forms of sociability vary between neighbourhoods requires delving into histories of movement, the constraints imposed by housing quality and income poverty and the contours of a neighbourhood's sociopolitical identity.

In South Africa, for obvious historical reasons, much store is given to cultural differences between so-called 'race' groups. Just about everyone in the Valley perceives African people as having different values and social practices, based on notions of communality and shared ancestry, compared to white and coloured people. These perceptions often extend to a connection made between the levels of poverty and strength of community – or *ubuntu* – in African communities. This link is, in part, associated with notions of 'simple' rural living where material goods are few and shared, and an assumption that these values and practices are transposed by migrants to the urban setting. In Masiphumelele, observation showed a significant sharing of resources. For example, all those living on the same plot use the single tap to collect water for drinking and bathing, as well as for washing dishes and clothes. Children, particularly girls, assist their older female relatives and neighbours in communal laundry sessions. Similarly, while most dwellings have at least one light bulb, fewer have a working fridge or television. Owners of these goods tend to share their use with others living in and near the yard. A home with a television will often attract a large gathering of kin and neighbours of all ages. Close residential proximity, a serious shortage of facilities and poor infrastructure do seem to necessitate more communal domestic and leisure activities, and children grow up observing and enacting these forms of sociability. However, they offer only a partial explanation for the form of neighbourliness that children describe.

Another major contributor to the character of social interaction is the particular demographic characteristics of immigration and residential settlement. Masiphumelele's physical expansion has not matched its high rate of population growth, so a large proportion of newcomers have been accommodated on existing plots. Newcomers tend to join relatives or friends from their rural birthplace; residential space is extended by adding on rooms or creating separate dwellings in the same yard. Therefore, neighbours often share rural origins or clanship, both of which resonate with kinship in the sense of creating a sense of unity and belonging. Though large in scale, Masiphumelele's growth has been incremental and responsive to individual or kin-group residential and employment demands. Consequently, existing social relationships have been maintained and strengthened, and new connections between neighbours forged. But these relationships are put under enormous strain by inadequate space, poor sanitation and overstretched household budgets. Supporting one's neighbours is highly exacting for established residents and newcomers, and the demands continue with time and increasing familiarity. There is no doubt that neighbourliness entails a very high degree of assistance and support in Masiphumelele and Ocean View (where fewer people move in, but the pressure on housing remains great). But, as we shall shortly see, there are limits to the informal resourcing of neighbours in these localities expressed in the form of jealousy, accusations and gossip, as found by others in neighbourhoods with similar histories and contemporary socio-economic profiles (Henderson 1999; Ramphele 2002; Ross, 2009; Salo 2004).

Similar rates of immigration exist in Fish Hoek, although people rarely move into the house next door to extended family members or long-term friends. They do, however, remain in close contact with kin, and children often go to relatives' homes after school. Some parents return to Fish Hoek from other parts of the country, often following separation or divorce, and re-enter networks formed in the past. There are also strong networks linking those who have moved to Fish Hoek from Zimbabwe, but these are commonly centred on a church rather than a particular small section of the neighbourhood. The population of Ocean View is much more stable than either Masiphumelele or Fish Hoek and has been so since the neighbourhood was constructed during the 1950s.

Figure 3.2 *Perceptions of friendliness and helpfulness of neighbours*

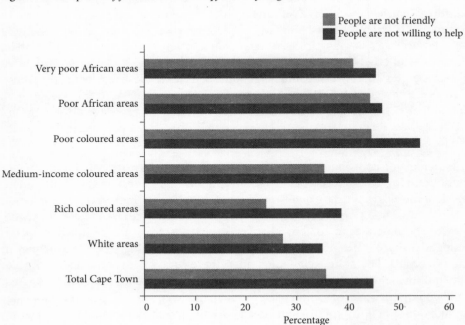

Source: Cape Area Panel Study wave 3 (2005)
Note: Limited to people who were living in the same area in 2005 as at the time of the original CAPS interviews in 2002.

The qualitative data suggest that the variation in forms of neighbourhood sociability perceived by children across the Valley can be explained by mobility demographics and their impact on age profile, proximity of kin, differences in household income and the extent or provision offered by local infrastructure, as well as by culturally informed notions of kinship and of the associated social and emotional obligations to adults and children connected through kin or neighbourhood. At first glance, there appear to be some contradictions between these findings and responses by older adolescent participants in CAPS regarding the helpfulness and friendliness of neighbours.

Figure 3.2 suggests that older adolescents in wealthy white and coloured areas judge their neighbours to be more friendly and helpful than do their peers in poor African and coloured areas. But the qualitative component of our work highlights two important considerations in interpreting these data. The first is that the nature of 'willingness to help' or 'friendliness', and their frequency, vary between neighbourhoods. Being 'friendly' to one's neighbour in Fish Hoek, for example, might entail chatting over the fence every few weeks and keeping the noise down. In Ocean View or Masiphumelele it might entail sharing a tap and bathroom amicably, looking after someone's children several times a week and sharing food, often unexpectedly. Therefore, adolescents may have used very different criteria to judge 'unfriendliness' or an 'unwillingness to help' among neighbours. The fact that over half of adolescents in poor African and coloured neighbourhoods did *not* regard their neighbours as unfriendly despite the very demanding nature of neighbourliness is consistent with the picture of highly supportive, but volatile and limited, neighbourliness emerging from the qualitative data. The second related consideration pertains to the frequency with which adolescents engage with those living very close by and encounter the limits of neighbourly interaction. Young residents of areas like Ocean View and Masiphumelele engage more frequently with their neighbours than their counterparts in wealthy areas, often under conditions of need. So the fact that adolescents in wealthy coloured and white neighbourhoods reported least unfriendliness may reflect their scarce interaction with neighbours and a sense that although not experienced as unfriendly or unhelpful, neighbours are not necessarily known to be friendly or helpful.

The 'adult' worlds of local neighbourhoods

The common assumption that commerce is an adult activity can mean that children's engagement in local business activities and informal recreation is overlooked in research, or that it is approached as inherently negative in its impact on children's lives. For example, the limited body of neighbourhood research related to children and adolescents often focuses solely on socially unacceptable activities and their problematic implications to child well-being, such as drug use, petty crime and violence. Similarly, discussion with adults across the research site focused on young children's susceptibility to being socialised into 'bad ways', like drinking and taking drugs. Their concerns are not unfounded given children's and adolescents' reports of excessive drinking at weekend parties, with the result that they struggle to concentrate at school and engage in risky sexual behaviour. Importantly, however, this is only part of the story. Our concern is to illuminate the multiple dimensions of young people's involvement in neighbourhood commerce, leisure and service provision by probing the nature and extent of interaction with these social arenas. We also analyse the opportunities and challenges for young people at the neighbourhood level that have accompanied the new democratic era.

Children's participation in local commerce

Some aspects of local commerce are immediately obvious when walking through Masiphumelele. The streets are peppered with small grocery shops known as 'spaza stores' run from shacks or containers often adjacent to people's homes. Children, like adults, find it convenient to shop locally for basic provisions and cheap snacks, and knowing a shop owner means that purchases can be made on credit. Interestingly, children engage in a similar form of local commerce in Ocean View, but it is far less evident to the casual observer. The striking scarcity of formal shops in the community gives the impression of little commercial activity within the neighbourhood and a reliance on larger shops and businesses several kilometres away. Yet in conversation with children, we learnt that throughout Ocean View there are houses in which the front room or garage has been converted into a shop. Many families rely on their local 'house shop' for everyday household items and it is usually children who are sent on errands to buy these goods. During map work children pointed out both the convenience of these small businesses and the important economic role they play to the families that run them and those who use them. 'House shops' permit known customers in the neighbourhood to buy on credit – a critical facility given that many families run out of money before receiving their monthly pay or grant. In contexts where children are independently mobile in their neighbourhoods, the informal nature and local position of the 'house shops' and 'spaza stores' mean that children are aware of and engage in an economic relationship between their households and these local businesses. While it was unusual to find children under 14 bearing significant responsibilities for the household economy, they were aware nonetheless of what was available locally and the costs. By contrast, children living in Fish Hoek tended to have little engagement in local shops or businesses independently of their parents, and were not involved in buying for their households. The only exception was for children living very close to either the Main Road shops or Valyland (a small shopping centre in the residential suburb), who were allowed to walk to these shops on their own.

There was evidence of strong similarities throughout the Valley in the manner in which children derive incomes within the neighbourhood, but differences in earning potential that become more marked with age. Children in all three neighbourhoods reported receiving money from their parents for doing chores at home, and those in Masiphumelele and Ocean View earned small amounts by doing odd jobs for relatives or neighbours, such as babysitting, washing cars, tending gardens and running errands.

She was later sent to buy electricity for her neighbour. This is not just out of obligation, as she does get some money (50c/R1), money which she used to use to buy cigarettes. (Interview notes with Samantha)

Mina: My cousin and sister had gone to the mall to watch a movie. I was supposed to get R20 from a boy, but he didn't pay me [because] he was still at work, so I couldn't go with.

Interviewer: What was the R20 for?

Mina: I washed, blow-dried and plaited his hair. If there is no blow-dry then I only charge R10.

Interviewer: Do you do any other people's hair?

Mina: No, only him.

Interviewer: Who is this boy?

Mina: He lives in our road. His parents are friends with my parents. (Mina, girl, aged 14, diary interview, Ocean View)

Children may find odd jobs quite easily in poor neighbourhoods, but they generally earn only a few rands. Rates for equivalent work for teenagers in the Valley remain very different. Teenagers in Fish Hoek charge R20 per hour for babysitting, whereas their peers in Masiphumelele and Ocean View earn approximately this figure for a day's childcare. And a much larger proportion of adolescents in Fish Hoek than their counterparts in poor neighbourhoods have jobs in local shops or restaurants that pay reasonably well (see also Chapter 4).

Our data point to the importance of neighbouring households and recognised commercial activities to children both in the sense of what they derive towards meeting their everyday practical needs and in what they gain in terms of knowledge and social connectedness. Being able to shop, earn or take a loan enhances basic economic skills and boosts children's sense of self-efficacy. Moreover, participation in the local economy and neighbourhood leisure pursuits contributes to children's sense of belonging in a wider social arena than the family. But just how much wider is this arena? It is quickly evident that children do not have the same freedom of movement, commercial know-how or spending power outside their own neighbourhoods. Pertinently, income-poor children in Masiphumelele move relatively easily in and out of social and commercial spheres in the Cape Flats, such as Gugulethu and Khayelitsha. Their peers from Fish Hoek, who have more cash, do so in the shopping centres, cinemas and clubs in the city's wealthiest suburbs. But the restrictions of the immediate neighbourhood most obvious for young residents of Ocean View speak volumes about the persistent force of apartheid-instated boundaries.

Taverns or shebeens run within people's homes – sometimes in conjunction with a spaza store – are also evident in Masiphumelele (see Photo 9). Selling bottled and home-brewed alcohol, these businesses are also social centres where people gather to drink and relax. In the late afternoons and over the weekend the music coming from shebeens gets louder, reflecting their increasing prominence in neighbourly interaction at these times. The majority of teenagers spend time in shebeens and consider them important gathering points for groups of male and female friends, and therefore for dating. Yet when compared to the open conversation we had with teenagers about parties in friends' homes or the community centre, our discussion dwelt only scantily on shebeen life. We know little about which they prefer and why, or about their commercial or other relationships with shebeen proprietors. They tended to avoid speaking in detail about shebeen life, partly because of their own antipathy towards these places (see Photo 10). Many have witnessed or taken part in fights in or just outside shebeens, some of which have ended in bodily violence and even fatalities. (We discuss children's experiences of, and responses to, local dangers later in this chapter.) A second reason why little was said about shebeens relates to their consistently negative portrayal within adult discourse. Parents and local service providers described shebeens as places of physical danger due to alcohol-induced violence and associated them with vice and risks to moral integrity, particularly for young children and girls.

Teenagers reported noticing that children are starting to spend time in shebeens at a much younger age than they did, and that girls aged only 12 or 13 are 'hanging out' and drinking there in the evenings. They point out that these girls dress provocatively, an indication that they are propositioning older boys in the shebeen. The trend towards younger participation in shebeen life was also noticed by adults, who blamed the proprietors for attracting children from an early age.

> Health worker 1: The shebeens here attract children by having pool tables and playing music all the time.

> Interviewer: What age children are you talking about?

> Health worker 2: Oh, my dear, here in Site 5 [Masiphumelele] you will find children aged five to six years in the shebeens. OK, they are not drinking alcohol, but they want to be there for the games and music, and to be with the older ones. At that age they are very affected by things; yes, they are impressionable.

We have no reason to doubt the commercial motivation of shebeen owners in supplying electronic games and music, especially during the day when they have fewer adult customers. Young children enjoy these distractions and being part of an informal neighbourly gathering. The important question not raised by the health workers is whether there are alternative places for children to play and socialise. While play parks are readily accessible to, and much used by, young children, interest in the activities available there dwindled with age. By early teens, the role of more organised social and leisure pursuits increased.

Illegality and, consequently, secrecy, make precise information on the recreational, commercial and, for some, survival roles that drugs play in the lives of young residents in the Valley difficult to obtain. Teenage boys in Masiphumelele and Ocean View spoke of the pressure to use and take part in the trading of hard drugs: coming off the soccer pitch, for instance, one might find a small bag of white powder stuffed inside one's shoe – an unsolicited 'gift' designed to pull one into drug-using circles. They explained that young boys see older team members whom they look up to using drugs, and wish to be included. Children living in Ocean View remarked on the extreme difficulty of avoiding drugs when both friends and family are open users and traders, a trend with a historical precedent that has heightened considerably in the last five years and was confirmed by local social workers and the police. But the role and even centrality of drugs in young people's lives is certainly not confined to the poorer neighbourhoods of the Valley. Young teenagers in all three neighbourhoods reported knowing where one could buy drugs locally, and social workers across the Valley reported the increased incidence of drug-related mental and physical health problems and the strain on social relationships at home and in school that arise from these (discussed below).

Leisure and recreational activities

Some insights into the extent and demographic dynamics of teenage participation in structured social activities are provided by CAPS survey data. In 2002, adolescents were asked whether they belong to a sports group or team, a study group, a religious group, or a dancing/singing, music or choir group. The results show that almost two-thirds of 14–17 year-olds in Cape Town do and a third do not. Participation in these groups is slightly higher among adolescent boys than girls, primarily because of high rates of participation in sports clubs by boys.

Figure 3.3 shows only a very slight variation in participation in religious groups between neighbourhoods, but a large variation in adolescent involvement in sports and music or dancing groups (including church choirs). Residents of white middle-class areas participate most frequently in these and their peers in coloured areas are much less involved. This pattern may reflect the relative lack of recreational resources in poor coloured communities compared to wealthy white communities and to poor African communities.

The ethnography illuminates these figures by showing how children's involvement in structured recreational activities is shaped by differences in sociocultural norms surrounding child rearing and forms of sociability, as well as by the way that communities understand apartheid to have shaped their own and other community histories.

As mentioned earlier, young people in Fish Hoek socialise and learn skills within a series of organised activities scattered across the Valley and other parts of Cape Town, including sports teams, swimming lessons, dance classes and horse-riding. The focus of such activities is very much on achieving sporting prowess and learning life skills considered important in middle-class culture. Consequently, with these activities there is limited opportunity for social interaction and the development of peer relationships. The one notable exception is young people's involvement in church-run activities and youth groups, for although these are also considered by adults to be 'safe' and 'appropriate' to children's development (especially for girls), they are often more frequent and less structured, thereby offering greater scope for socialising.

Figure 3.3 *Participation in sports or religious or music/dancing groups among adolescents aged 14–17*

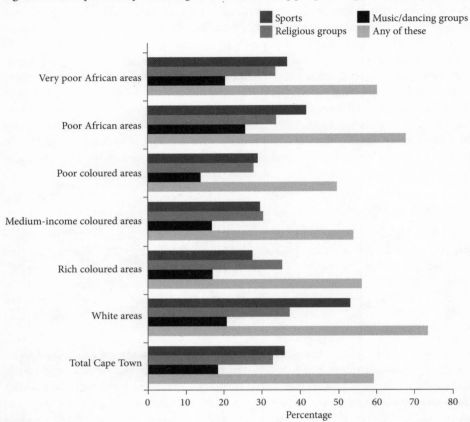

Source: Cape Area Panel Study 2002

Young residents of Masiphumelele participating in our study were typically involved in one or more after-school activity, sports team or youth club. We were immediately struck by the much greater number and range of clubs and social activities available to children in Masiphumelele compared to in Ocean View. The majority of these are free or charge only a token joining fee. Many of the activities offered outside the school context focus on imparting particular educational and life skills of which their instigators were deprived through the legacy of past disadvantage. Examples include computer classes at the local library and the AIDS prevention and education group at the clinic, loveLife. While these were clearly of value to children, the social aspect of belonging to a group and having a physical and social space in which to interact with peers and develop friendships or dating relationships seemed to count for more – particularly among teenagers.

Rates of alcohol consumption are very high in the public shebeens and private home spaces within Masiphumelele and Ocean View. Children frequently drew shebeens on their maps in red to denote danger, and the evening parties that evolve in them and spill out onto the streets draw scores of teenagers and adults of all ages. Their attraction is unsurprising given the lack of alternatives. If young people wish to spend time with friends beyond the gaze of family members, they have few options other than shebeens, unsupervised friends' homes, outdoors on the soccer pitches or in the 'bush' on the outskirts of the neighbourhood. As we shall shortly show, there are dangers in these places, particularly for girls. But what was also abundantly clear was that children in Ocean View are more likely to experience drunkenness and alcohol- or drug-induced violence in their own homes – and had fewer options for leisure, social or sports pursuits – than their peers in Masiphumelele.

Across the Valley, children and adolescents who are involved in sports, the majority of whom are boys, see their sporting activities as very important aspects of their routine, identity and personal resource base. Sport provides a space for interacting with peers and adults. In a discussion with grade-11 learners in Ocean View, sport was identified as a source of self-esteem because it provides children with encouragement and rewards for doing well. Encouragement can come not only from a coach, but also from teammates. Playing soccer (even though informally) is definitely a boost to Samantha's self-esteem, as the boys she plays with in a local Ocean View team encourage her and tell her that she is talented and will 'make it'. Patrick, who attends school in Ocean View and lives in Hillside Farm near Masiphumelele, was persuaded not to leave his Fish Hoek soccer team and has been recruited for a team in Masiphumelele. He explains that being in demand makes him feel good about himself and his talent, and having younger boys look up to him and wanting to be like him encourages him to do well. By bringing older and younger boys together, sports clubs facilitate the creation of role models, benefiting both younger and older boys, who have the responsibility of setting a good example. Sport also provides role models and heroes on a national level, and identifying as a sportsman allows boys to develop goals to be like their heroes, and, therefore, to have a future orientation. Many of the 'art club' boys in both poor neighbourhoods identified themselves as cricket and soccer players and spoke of wanting to be like national and international stars. Children recognise that having such goals helps sustain their personal motivation to succeed in the particular activity, such as soccer, as well as in other areas of their lives. Boys in Ocean View spoke of the way their involvement in sports bolsters their personal coping mechanisms because the physical activity helps them deal with the everyday stress encountered at home and at school. Sport also provides potential support structures. Coaches and members of the team were described as people one can turn to about problems at school, home or with friends. Bonani, having explained that his parents no longer live with him or support him financially, describes how his soccer team fulfils his needs in ways that other local services fail to:

> Interviewer: Are there people or services who take care of vulnerable teenagers in Masiphumelele? If so, what do they do for them? Do they meet all their needs?

> Bonani: I will say no coz there are no people who supports me except the team which I play for; they all give me that hope and they always encourage me to do things that I can get something from it at the end of the day. My team is the best place for me. I always feel comfortable when team members are around. Cape Town Visitors are my home. (Bonani, boy, aged 18, Masiphumelele)

Adolescents in Ocean View were as aware of the very limited organised recreational facilities available to them as we were, and spoke also of their lack of interest in various attempts by organisations to provide 'something for the youth to do'. The one notable exception to their complaints was Art Vibrations, a club run by a local volunteer, which is open every evening and offers training in a range of performing arts, including break-dancing, singing and drama. The reasons why this organisation is so popular and meets a range of young people's needs are, say teenagers, quite simple. First, Art Vibrations offers a range of different activities, so children are likely to find one art form that they enjoy and learn that there are a number of alternative career routes in life. Second, they put on shows and enter competitions, which provides adolescents with social rewards for their efforts and public recognition of talents, both of which young people consider to contribute to the positive self-esteem necessary for coping with the denigrating attitudes of the older generation and persuasion by their friends to use drugs or drink heavily on a regular basis. Third, the adult volunteers who run Art Vibrations show an interest in children's lives and problems, and believe in the value of young people's contributions:

> Going to Art Vibrations helps build self-esteem because it supports your talents in music, art, poetry, dancing or whatever they may be. Kevin [the adult founder of the organisation] provides the youth with discipline and encouragement. Not only for art, but for school as well. Like, if you are not coping at school he will encourage you to prioritise school over arts. He also gives advice and encouragement not to use drugs. (Notes from grade-11 discussion on self-esteem)

Finally, the structure of the organisation allows adults and children alike to play mutually supportive roles. Adults are available for private chats and facilitate 'open meetings' in which children are encouraged to talk about whatever is on their minds and support each other. The value placed on children's contributions is mirrored in their explicitly participatory approach: children are given a decision-making role in the club's activities, which strengthens their sense of control over self and their contributions to positive social relationships within the group.

> Kevin is big on children's participation in the programme and appoints kids who have been around a while and have commitment as junior co-ordinators for the various divisions. We find that the kids step up to the responsibilities when they are given them. The kids also make up their own sequences and are encouraged to use their own creativity, and Kevin mainly overseas what they do…The kids themselves have a high standard of professionalism and are proud of their work and so

will not tolerate lack of discipline or dedication from each other. (Adult co-ordinator, informal interview)

In short, this particular independent and entirely voluntary club in Ocean View works for children so much better than any others we came across in our study because it is structured in a way that enables adults to be available and responsive, because adult staff value children's contributions and collectively these provide an appropriate context for building high-quality, respectful relationships across the generations and within the peer group.

Children's use of local services

Kin and neighbours are the first port of call in times of crisis for most children in the Valley. Nevertheless, the strain on social relationships exerted by poverty, ill health or unemployment means that familiar adults are not always available or effective in what they offer. Some are reticent about discussing illness, sexuality and other aspects of young people's well-being. There are cultural proscriptions against sharing knowledge about these topics with children across the Valley, bolstered in Masiphumelele by so-called traditional ideas and in all three neighbourhoods by conservative Christian ideals of innocence and chastity in childhood. And in both Ocean View and Masiphumelele, a legacy of poor education and discrepancies in opportunities between the generations mean that some adults simply do not have the information that the young are searching for or a bank of relevant personal experience from which to draw.

The inequality of service provision characteristic of apartheid times persists in the Valley. Children in Fish Hoek frequently seek assistance or information from school guidance teachers or counsellors, and speak highly of their support. Schools elsewhere in the Valley cannot afford to hire such staff, and the single state social worker allocated to the entire area was hopelessly overburdened. Voluntary organisations offering social services to children in Masiphumelele and Ocean View are respected and trusted, but struggle with large caseloads, high staff turnover and slow bureaucratic processes. Our analysis of social worker case notes in both Masiphumelele and Ocean View showed that formal intervention for many children at risk had been inadequate and ineffective, a problem well documented among social services directed at children in South Africa (Meintjes et al. 2007).

Remarkably, however, even vastly overstretched services proved highly effective in protecting very vulnerable children in Ocean View and Masiphumelele. Their success derives from how the formal input of a voluntary organisation and the informal systems of care operating in the neighbourhood complement one another – planned or otherwise. For example, a feeding scheme for children considered at particular risk in Masiphumelele was designed to meet a nutritional need, but in reality served a broad spectrum of social and emotional needs. This is because a strong relationship developed between the children and three local women employed to cook and serve the food. These women keep an eye on the overall well-being of the 40 or so children and report absenteeism or other concerns to the social worker, who interacts with family members accordingly. In turn, the children choose to play near the kitchen before and after their meals, and have built up a level of trust with the cooks that enables them to stay overnight with them when conflicts erupt or care is absent in their own homes. A highly effective informal fostering system has emerged that is able to safeguard children until alternative arrangements can be made.

One of the promises of the new government was to improve the distribution and quality of core services. Certain services considered critical by children are, in their view, too far away. The absence of a police station or fire service in Masiphumelele worries many young people because crime rates are high and runaway fires very frequent, often resulting in fatalities. During 2006 the fire service responded to 35 large-scale fires in Masiphumelele in which two people were killed and no fewer than 1 681 made homeless (DC Okkers, City of Cape Town Fire and Rescue Service, December 2007). Many of those whose shacks burnt down lost not only their homes, but all their possessions, including identity documents, school uniforms and school books. As a result, families stand to lose access to state grants, which may have been their only source of income, and children are at risk of missing periods of school. It is, therefore, no surprise that children perceive fire to be the greatest threat to life and well-being in their neighbourhood.

Of greater concern to adolescents in poor neighbourhoods is the inaccessibility of health and social services to their age cohort, and the resulting opinion within the peer group that these services cannot meet their needs. Clinic staff in Masiphumelele acknowledge that, for various historical and organisational reasons, their services are structured in ways that obstruct adolescents' access. Girls do use the clinic to obtain hormonal contraceptives, but staff report that they themselves are embarrassed to discuss condom use, indicating an inability on the part of the clinic to support girls in protecting themselves against sexually transmitted disease. The few teenage boys who attend the clinic are extremely sick, and very rarely do boys seek either treatment for sexually transmitted infections or voluntary HIV testing. Staff are aware that some young residents regard attending the clinic as carrying a social risk and assume they go elsewhere for treatment. Indeed, adolescents reported that being observed in the queue can lead to rumours of positive HIV status. In Ocean View these social risks are perceived to be even greater: the young people with whom we worked said that they stayed away from the clinic for fear that rumours of pregnancy and AIDS would be spread. Records kept by a voluntary organisation providing counselling services suggest that a few teenagers consult clinics outside their neighbourhoods. The majority, however, appear to let things lie and do not get access to the services they require.

Fish Hoek, by contrast, has a plethora of different social, psychological and health professionals. Most of these are private and accessible to those families who can afford the consultation fees or medical aid. Such costs prohibit most young residents from having direct access to these services. Teachers and youth workers in churches and non-governmental organisations (NGOs) are highly valued because parental permission or knowledge is not needed. Adolescents who have, or wish to build, close, trusting relationships with these individuals enjoy direct, confidential access to advice and encouragement. However, such figures are attentive to the rights of parents to know what is happening in their children's lives. In serious cases, parents are informed and involved, meaning that assistance is likely. This process means that, compared to their peers in poorer neighbourhoods, young people are less able to control independently how their problems are defined and responded to.

Like the recreational facilities discussed above, much of the success or failure of services for children and adolescents can be put down to the extent to which the organisational structure and ethic enables a trusting rapport between staff and young people, whether the staff are attuned to and have the resources to respond to young people's concerns, and whether their approach to their mandate is one of problem solving *for* young people or *with* them. Most state services and NGOs operating in the Valley work within a traditional welfare approach in which adults, usually living outside the neighbourhood, design and implement services to meet children's needs. OIL, an NGO aiming to equip adolescents with the knowledge and skills to act as resources to their peers, is rare in that it premises its work on young people's rights and capabilities. OIL offers young participants opportunities to build skills, do community service and share leisure time with peers from nearby neighbourhoods. The impact of this for social integration in the Valley is discussed in Chapter 4.

Physical dangers in the local neighbourhood

> People get raped and stabbed at these discos. Even if you are with a group of girls or with boys people will still cause trouble with you. They may take a gun or knife and tell you to take everything off. People drink inside and when they come out they walk in circles. (Teenage girls in Ocean View explain why they labelled the disco at the multi-purpose centre 'dangerous' on their map.)

> We try to avoid walking past the shebeens at night when people are drunk and start fighting, sometimes with knives. But it's hard because there are so many shebeens everywhere. (Thandi, girl, aged 14, Masiphumelele)

> I usually walk home from my gran's house, which is two blocks away. It's OK, but sometimes I do get scared. (Melissa, girl, aged 12, Fish Hoek)

Sharp differences still exist in what young people living in different areas in the Valley encounter in their neighbourhoods: weapons are visible in the evenings in Ocean View and Masiphumelele, but rarely in Fish Hoek. But there are also important commonalities: young people across the board see the post-apartheid neighbourhoods in which they live as containing some level of physical danger, although the magnitude of this danger varies by class and race group. More than a fifth of all young men and women (aged 17–20) perceive themselves to be unsafe at night, this proportion rising to between a third and a half in poor and very poor African neighbourhoods (see Figure 3.1). Other similarities lie in the association between a child's gender or the relative economic and social fragility of his or her household and their level of risk and the options they have for avoiding or reducing personal risk associated with these dangers.

Police data on the nature and incidence of crime in the Valley concur in showing that young people have reason to fear for their safety, and that levels of risk vary both within and across neighbourhoods. Incidents of assault with and without weapons recorded by Ocean View police station (also serving Masiphumelele) stand at between 300 and 450 per year between 2001 and 2006. The figures are three times higher than those recorded each year by Fish Hoek police station over this period. Officers working in Ocean View report that about 70 per cent of all the assault cases they handle occur in Ocean View, and 30 per cent in Masiphumelele. Figures on assault are not disaggregated by gender or age, but reported rape figures suggest much greater vulnerability of girls and women in Ocean View and Masiphumelele. While rates of reported rape in South Africa are widely understood to be much lower than actual incidence (see Chapter 2), differences between neighbourhoods indicate varying degrees of vulnerability in the Valley. There were 35 cases of rape reported in 2004/05 at Ocean View police station and only three at Fish Hoek police station. Murder rates are very high in Ocean View and Masiphumelele (between 17 and 21 per year in each from 2001 to 2006, compared to between two and four per year in Fish Hoek), and murders predominately affect men. Therefore, while we have seen that parents and children in Fish Hoek curtail their movements significantly owing to worries about safety, the reality is that they are in fact much less likely to be victims of violent crime than their counterparts in Ocean View and Masiphumelele.[1]

Correspondingly, most young participants residing in Ocean View experience their neighbourhood as unsafe and spoke of frequent fighting, muggings, rape and stabbings. Their accounts convey their sense that young people are often directly involved in violent acts, and that danger lurks nearby at all times. Children blame the widespread overcrowding in homes, as well as unlit open spaces and roads, which make it easy for attacks and muggings to take place. And when driving through Masiphumelele with the research team, two young residents of Ocean View quickly remarked upon 'the many dark alleyways between shacks where people may attack you'. Their inaccurate assumption that young residents consider these alleys dangerous is a clue to the different, and more extreme, social pressures that underlie high rates of interpersonal violence in Ocean View (discussed below).

Similarly, most young participants living in Masiphumelele have witnessed violence of various kinds, including muggings and drunken attacks. They report feeling most threatened when passing drunken crowds outside shebeens. However, towards the end of our research, residents of all ages were reporting an increase in targeted violent crime, including theft and rape, and asserting that teenagers and young adults are the primary perpetrators. Their observations are consistent with findings of the 2005 National Youth Victimisation Survey, which shows that male youth and young adults are the primary perpetrators of violence in poor neighbourhoods, and points out the large proportions of this cohort who have witnessed, or been victims of, personal assault (Leoschut & Burton 2006).

In Masiphumelele, there are clear age and gender differences in young people's sense of vulnerability to physical danger in the neighbourhood. Younger children and girls of all ages spoke of the possibility of encountering drunken violence or of being mugged when walking around at night, pointing out that only recently had rates of muggings of children increased, which, therefore, made them worried. Conversations with social workers, children and adults suggest that, although few in number, acts of extreme violence to young children (such as rape) are of concern to parents and children alike. The picture presented is that they are perceived to occur too frequently in other poor suburbs of the city with which residents have kinship connections, and that the incidence of such acts is increasing in Masiphumelele. In Chapter 4, we discuss children's understandings of how similar or dissimilar their own neighbourhoods are to others in the Cape Town environs.

By contrast, none of our participants living in Fish Hoek had direct experiences of violence in their neighbourhood or of witnessing such acts. The vast majority of crime committed in Fish Hoek consists of house burglary, theft of or from vehicles and malicious damage to property. Yet, as pointed out above, the everyday lives of children in Fish Hoek are structured around activities and transport arrangements designed to protect them from possible dangers in the neighbourhood. Parents reported that there are few public spaces that are suitable and safe for their children to play, and refer to the danger of letting their children outside alone for fear of road accidents, kidnapping and other crimes. Children spoke about being afraid and their fears were real despite their not having any direct experience to base them on. They largely adhered to parental cautions, rarely venturing out by themselves without parental permission. Reasons why children are complicit in these perceptions and related actions are explored in Chapter 4.

According to a police officer who has worked in the Ocean View station since 1997, about 80 per cent of burglary, theft and damage to property in the Valley occurs in Ocean View and the remainder in Masiphumelele.[2] Much of this is allegedly motivated by the need to raise money to fund drug addiction.

Young people consider the sale and consumption of alcohol and drugs to increase their exposure to danger. Children and adolescents in Masiphumelele said that they are familiar with the possibility of encountering alcohol-induced violence outside shebeens, and try to avoid these if they observe trouble. Police officers informed us that most cases of assault, robbery and rape in Masiphumelele (that they were aware of) occur in shebeens. Their recent patrols to close down shebeens at 10 p.m. were intended to address this problem, as well as that of unlicensed alcohol outlets. The greatest risk that children associated with alcohol consumption, either within or outside a shebeen, was fire. Some named particular neighbours who they knew to be frequently intoxicated, fearing that they would start a large-scale fire by not attending to their stove. And for the few children we worked with who live with adults addicted to alcohol, shebeens are associated with intense anxiety affecting their well-being and tense relationships within the home.

Highest on children's lists of unsafe areas within Ocean View are those connected to physical spaces used for selling and consuming alcohol and drugs. These include a variety of places meant to be recreational spaces for children, including the soccer field, the play park and the underage disco held at the multi-purpose centre. Other places highlighted were shebeens, certain flats, and open and unlit spaces, such as the various open fields, the graveyard and the bush surrounding Ocean View, which tend to be unpopulated and, therefore, ideal for illicit activities.

> I feel unhappy in the bush because I never know who is there. (Fatima, girl, aged 12, Ocean View, explaining her drawing of places where she feels uncomfortable)

Children also see vandalised and dilapidated buildings, such as those next to the multi-purpose centre, as unsafe spaces because they attract people who engage in these behaviours.

> At night people sit in the building and they can hurt you. (Clarisa, girl, aged 10, Ocean View)

Substance abuse aggravates the effect of severe overcrowding in the council blocks of flats, increasing conflict and violence, especially at night and at weekends. In this way, physical and economic factors in the environment interact to heighten children's experiences of extreme social difficulties with direct negative implications on their own well-being.

> You won't understand; you must live there [in the flats]. They're really dirty and there is a lot of drinking. (Grade-9 girls' explanation for drawing flats as dangerous on their map)

> They [the flats] are dangerous. People drink and get drunk and then fight and can stab you. Once it is dark you must stay in. Sometimes gangsters come and sit on the stoep [porch] and smoke dagga [marijuana] and make a noise. Then they don't want to leave. Sometimes adults come and chase them away, otherwise we shoot them with stones and marbles or throw hot water on them. (Grade-9 boys' explanation for drawing the flats as dangerous on their map – see Map 2)

Drinking and drug-taking affect both the accessibility and quality of public spaces for children. Being drunk or high leads to fighting over what often seem to be quite trivial things, such as someone swearing at a person. This violence erupts among children who themselves are consuming drugs and alcohol and is also perpetrated against children who come across adults doing these things. Discussions with children and adults pointed to the easy accessibility of drugs and alcohol in Ocean View, because of the concentration of shebeens and drug merchants' frequent use of public space.

> The problem here [in Ocean View] is children being rude and people sitting on the corners smoking slow boats [mandrax smoked with marijuana in bottlenecks], tik [crystal methamphetamine] and then they are rude to people. And if it's a pension day they wait for the old ladies

to come past and then they grab their bags and run away. (Suraiya, girl, aged 12, Ocean View)

Children in Ocean View are aware that many of their peers at school and adults in the community sell drugs in order to earn a living and that this factor makes it very difficult for the authorities to eliminate drugs from circulation. They are also aware of the history of inequalities, discrimination and economic hardship that has contributed to individuals taking solace in drugs. Such awareness offers children little protection against domestic violence prompted by drug or alcohol abuse, or from the economic hardships that follow when household members siphon off large sums of the domestic budget to support their habit. However, knowledge of this nature can enable children to sustain a positive attitude towards and relationship with adults who drink heavily or use drugs. At the same time, young people whose everyday domestic sphere includes the consumption of drugs or alcohol may be attracted to consume or to sell these products. Several teenagers in Ocean View alluded to the predictability of their friends acquiring their own drug habits on the basis that their parents were using them openly in the home.

Having considerable control over their own mobility enables poor children to avoid some of the drug- or alcohol-induced violence and pressures to conform that arise in the neighbourhood. Map work revealed children's detailed knowledge of dangerous spaces in the locality, particularly around their own homes – knowledge that they used to decide where to play or walk, and whether they should seek an adult to accompany them for a particular journey. Fourteen-year-old Samantha and her female friends make sure they stay close to the road when they braai in the bush opposite their block of flats, because they know that people go deeper in the bush to smoke drugs and drink alcohol. In a study conducted in four poor urban areas of Johannesburg, children were found to be similarly resourceful in creating safe social spaces for themselves (Swart-Kruger & Chawla 2002). Here too, real and perceived danger on the streets, linked to public drinking and drunkenness, which leads to fights, was found to lead to the restriction of children's mobility (Swart-Kruger & Chawla 2002). Research by Parkes (2007) in a Cape Town suburb with a similar demography to Ocean View also showed children relying on avoidance of dangerous areas and on peer support as means of staying safe amid community violence. Adult protection and retaliation were other strategies used by children in this context.

There are limits to the efficacy of children's efforts to protect themselves by restricting their mobility. Some young residents of Masiphumelele and Ocean View live close to a shebeen or known drug merchants and even playing close to home puts them in what they regard as a dangerous space. Moreover, adult expectations of children's participation in the domestic economy can undermine these safety strategies:

> Jumat: I do not like bars because there are people who hit you when you walk past.
>
> Interviewer: Do you ever have to walk past a bar?

> Jumat: When I get sent to get bread and the one shop doesn't have then I have to walk to the other shop. Then I have to walk past a bar.

Adolescents in Ocean View commented with irony that the only way to keep safe is to 'just stay in your house 24 hours', which, of course, they do not. Self-imposed restrictions on mobility have social consequences for young people because they entail avoiding certain places, such as the community multi-purpose centre where various leisure and sports activities are held. The discos held in this centre (disturbingly nicknamed *'messteek jols'*, or stabbing parties) and informal shebeens are reputed to be particularly dangerous, partly because they are largely evening activities. Restricting mobility is not considered a practical option by adolescents in Ocean View for avoiding contact with drugs because they are so pervasive. Instead, these teenagers emphasised individual self-determination and wisdom in the cultivation of friendships:

> The merchants are everywhere – you cannot avoid them. All you can do is say 'no'…You can't run away from your problems. You must watch who you associate with and have friends who will cover for you if you are in trouble. (Girls in grade 9, Ocean View)

Social dangers in the immediate neighbourhood

Perhaps surprisingly, young people consider that particular patterns and features of social interaction in their neighbourhood pose a greater challenge to their nurturing of high-quality relationships – and, therefore, their long-term well-being – than the physical threats described in the sections above. Socialisation plays a powerful role here: at times, children and adolescents resisted the negative patterns of behaviour arising from these dynamics; at others, they perpetuated them.

The everyday presence of drugs and alcohol

The prevalence and easy availability of alcohol and drugs are seen by young residents of Ocean View to exacerbate peer pressure to drink, smoke and inhale. Consequently, the task of managing and resisting this peer pressure is a constant and demanding challenge. Consuming drugs and alcohol was seen to incur negative effects on school performance and, indeed, to determine whether or not one managed to stay in school at all. Children also make links between the use of alcohol and drugs and young people's engagement in sexual activity, implicating substance abuse as one of the reasons for the high rate of teenage pregnancy in Ocean View (see also Chapter 7). Many had teenage sisters or cousins who had babies or who were pregnant. Adults point out that this is not a new phenomenon in Ocean View, but that it is becoming more common. Teenage girls blamed it on drug and alcohol use; the desire of pre-teens to experience what they see on television; peer pressure; and a lack of information about, and inadequate evidence of, the consequences of pregnancy. Some pointed out that teenage mothers usually give their baby to their mother to look after, and avoid the everyday tasks of parenting. Children in our study also made a clear connection between the consumption of drugs and alcohol and the neglect or abuse of young children.

Drug use is considered one – if not the main – 'problem' facing youth in the Valley and one that appears to transcend class and neighbourhood. During our fieldwork period, the local papers regularly featured drugs and their destructive effects on young people and although generally sensationalist on any topic, these reports display particular moral outrage and powerlessness against a trend. One front-page headline, 'Drugs: the dirt beneath the beauty', was set underneath an aerial photograph of Fish Hoek beach with a rainbow touching the shoreline. The article began:

> The drug problem that has been simmering in the Fish Hoek valley over the past few years has now exploded into an outright pandemic, with children as young as eight and nine using highly addictive, highly destructive drugs. This is according to John Stewart of the Fish Hoek Drug Crisis Centre, who says that the drug problem in the valley is not merely one of Rizla-rolled dagga joints over weekends – 'South Africa's national pastime' – but of seriously dirty chemicals. And even more worrying is that the age group of users is dropping. 'Six months ago, I was getting older users. In the past two months there hasn't been anyone over the age of 21. And I've been consulted by children as young as 13, and even 8 and 9. Drug use has really blown the banks in the last six months...' Of the 250 individual assessments he has conducted in the past two years, 46 per cent were for people under the age of 21. (*People's Post*, 12 October 2004)

As mentioned above, most children in their pre- and early teens living in Masiphumelele and Ocean View – and a large proportion of those in Fish Hoek – are aware of where drugs are being sold locally. Most know of individuals their own age or older who use drugs regularly and of those struggling with addiction. The perception of Valley residents – both young and old – that rates of drug use and related interpersonal violence have increased sharply within the last decade is mirrored in empirical data and popular opinion across the city. In 2006, the Provincial Education Department's free call centre received double the number of calls from learners reporting abuse – drug abuse, as well as physical or sexual abuse – than it had in 2002 (Dawes, Long et al. 2006: 32). The novelty of the call centre system is a likely contributor to this trend, but the figures indicate a dramatic increase in the presence of drugs and of abuse as boundaries between neighbourhoods have become more permeable. Unfortunately, the relative proportions of drug abuse and physical or sexual abuse are unknown because the call centre captures all these in one category of 'abuse'.

These general trends require interrogation at a local level. Our data suggest that drugs are part and parcel of everyday life for a much smaller portion of young people in Masiphumelele and Fish Hoek than in Ocean View, and that consumption in these two neighbourhoods is predominately of dagga (marijuana) rather than tik (crystal methamphetamine) or heroin. In 2005, the acting head of Ocean View Secondary School reported to the *Cape Times* that about 60 per cent of pupils, namely more than 700 young people, were tik addicts, saying that 'the drug is everywhere…it's scary and out of control. Teachers complain daily. Pupils are often absent. The drug makes them aggressive, so we have four or five fights breaking out every day, some in class.'[3] While teenagers and adults alike expressed worries about an observed increase in drug use among younger children, their assessments of the associated dangers and moral consequences reflect strongly gendered norms. Teenage boys explain that smoking dagga or using tik earns them a degree of respect among other men of all ages, whereas girls who do the same are maligned and shunned. But the dynamics of drug use and dependence are the same for both boys and girls. Friends commonly offer a free hit to newcomers. Once accustomed or addicted, young people are easily drawn into criminal activities organised by older youth because they need money to fund their habit.

Rumour and gossip

> I think ['community' is] about people standing together. They mustn't put each other down. Here in Ocean View people talk of each other. (Byron, boy, grade 11, Ocean View)

Many young residents of Ocean View struggle to form a positive notion of community because they perceive the social dynamics in their neighbourhood to be the antithesis of the social factors required to create a 'community'. They feel confident in their ability to navigate potential physical dangers because they know their environment so well. But avoiding gossip and the judgement of those around them is seen as much more difficult. Adolescent girls, and indeed some boys, spoke of staying indoors and 'doing nothing' in order to minimise such risks. Their rationale helps to explain why formal youth activities are poorly attended and quickly lose momentum.

Very high levels of gossiping are considered by children to be the flip side of the dense – and often supportive – social ties within their neighbourhood. They attribute serious disruption to personal and familial integrity to the ease with which false rumours are spread and the impossibility of quelling these. Seventeen-year-old Nicola and her mother were living with a woman from their church who became unhappy with these living arrangements. Instead of speaking directly to Nicola's mother, she spread rumours at their church, saying that they thought they were too good for her home. After denying that anything was wrong when confronted by Nicola's mother, this woman asked them to move out of her flat. Nicola and her mother also had to leave their church as they felt that the gossip had made people see them in a different light, making them uncomfortable in that space. Resorting to gossip rather than confronting the problem directly caused Nicola to lose her home (albeit an open-ended, temporary arrangement) *and* her church. She valued church as a setting in which to express her faith and for its social networks. Boys and girls alike of all ages experience gossiping as a major cause of conflict among friends. The fear of being the subject of rumour and its inherent negativity shapes young people's use of space (see also Ross, 2009).

Earlier we noted how these anxieties translate into great reluctance by children and adolescents in Ocean View to use the local clinic, and a lesser but still significant hesitation by their peers in Masiphumelele to do so. Such fears also curtail the extent to which young people dare draw on everyday social relationships with neighbours, friends, teachers and even extended family for advice or support, particularly when it comes to personal matters. The risks of a hasty and negative judgement of character being quickly circulated are very high.

> Nicola: I think that's why sometimes people don't want other people's help because they say, 'no, just now they talk about it' or whatever.

> Charney: It's not so much that people don't want them to know their business; they're just scared that it might leak out. (Grade 11, group discussion on 'community')

Children, especially those who see themselves as, and are seen by others as, 'high achievers', struggle with the fact that people in Ocean View tend to denigrate rather than encourage. Some described Ocean View as a community of 'vision killers' who respond to a young person's achievements and dreams with jealousy and attempts to undermine them.

> Cheryl, she's also from Ocean View and people, 'cause she was one day on e-TV, and somebody actually said that '*ja, nou that she's op die TV, nou dink sy, sy's all that*' ['yes, now that she's on TV, now she thinks she's all that'], and that's not fair because if you have the guts to go somewhere in life then other people always want to put you down. (Nicola, grade 11, group discussion on 'community')

The very real possibility that friends could undermine one's personal efforts and achievements features large in the minds of young people in their selection of close friends and in the cultivation of intimate relationships:

> Never try to impress a next person 'cause the next person won't encourage you to do that – they will press you down until you down in the gutters and they'll laugh you out and that's not a real friend. (Sean, boy, aged 17, Ocean View)

The use of gossip and negative labelling are not experiences that are exclusive to young residents of Ocean View, but they are most problematic for children in that neighbourhood. One or two children living in Masiphumelele spoke of neighbours who scold them when their parents are out, who do not care for those living near them, or who like to spread bad rumours about nearby families. The manner in which these few incidents were reported suggests that children generally receive support from neighbours, but are aware of the potential for relationships to involve jealousy or conflict and for the expression of these sentiments through witchcraft. Thirteen-year-old Babalwa, a member of the art club, spoke of her intention to study hard in the final years of high school with her aim of becoming a doctor, and identified the main threat to her career success as follows:

> Babalwa: A witch will be jealous; they will kill me.
>
> Interviewer: Can you explain a bit more about this, what could happen?
>
> Babalwa: I mean that I could be cursed by a friend and their family who are jealous because I am doing better than their child.

Beliefs and practices that are often labelled 'traditional' or as belonging to the older generations clearly retain some currency with the young. Witchcraft is understood to work against the success of one individual over another. Like the denigration of personal efforts expressed in Ocean View, it can be seen as an expression of a powerful social sanction, the particularities of which are shaped by neighbourhood sociopolitical and cultural histories (see also Ashforth 2005; Ramphele 2002). The difference is that young residents of Masiphumelele do not regard witchcraft actions and accusations as always directed at them, whereas their peers in Ocean View feel targeted by the older generation's 'vision-killing' discourse.

Children in Fish Hoek often find attitudes and norms in their own neighbourhood oppressive and overly prescriptive in terms of what young people should do, or even look like. Seventeen-year-old Lara reported being branded a satanist by local neighbours because of the clothes she wore and the colour of her hair. Virginia, whose father is a priest, attributed labelling like this and the extreme pressure she was under from family to behave well, to the pervasive conservative Christian ethos within the neighbourhood. Gossip can prompt middle-class children to change church or to stop socialising with those who are disapproved of (including friends from Ocean View or Masiphumelele), and consequently has a significant impact on their social networks and identities. For most children in Fish Hoek, 'neighbourhood' and 'community' overlap but do not comprise entirely the same set of social relationships. Consequently, they are able to protect themselves from neighbourhood-specific social sanctions while at the same time sustaining social relationships within and outside the neighbourhood. The majority of children in Ocean View and Masiphumelele are unable to do so because 'neighbourhood' and 'community' are experienced as one and the same. Only those who are able to travel to other parts of the city or country on a regular basis are able to build a broader set of relationships and a social identity that is not neighbourhood-specific. As we shall see in the next chapter, social denigration has a particularly severe impact on the young in Ocean View. Reasons include their limited mobility in and out of the neighbourhood and their accompanying sense of restricted opportunity in contemporary society. The latter arises from chronic social and income poverty, geographical isolation and a perceived marginal sociopolitical position.

Intergenerational dynamics

> Children in Ocean View is very *onbeskof* [rude] – they don't say 'aunty' and 'uncle' and they just shout '*d'jy*' ['you']. (Samantha)

Young people attribute a number of their most significant social challenges to a lack of respect between the generations. These include their own sense of being negatively judged and labelled by adults; adults setting a bad example by fighting, drinking and taking drugs in front of children; ineffective communication across the generations; and the tendency of adults to discount young people's engagement in social relationships and contributions to decision-making.

Across the Valley, children complained that adults tend to speculate and jump to conclusions about their behaviour instead of speaking frankly with them. They expressed frustration and hurt at adults' willingness to believe the stories circulating in the neighbourhood. In Ocean View, some reported responding by buying into these 'deviant identities' in order to spite accusing adults. This form of negotiating and resisting externally imposed identities clearly incurs potentially serious costs to an individual's physical and mental health, as well as their career, and, ironically, serves to reinforce adult perceptions of deviance in the young.

> Mandy: No, if you lose weight, they say you have AIDS.
>
> Byron: My mother always tells my grandmother, and I used to be a chubby guy, and I'm growing and I'm tall and I'm thin, and my mommy asks me 'Byron, wat goed doen jy? Lyk my jy druk tik.' En ek sê, 'Ja, lyk ek so maer, ek doen tik.' ['Byron, what stuff are you doing? Looks to me like you are smoking tik.' And I say, 'Yes, I look so thin, I'm doing tik.'] I don't like my mom accuse me of stuff, because then I'm really going to do it. I don't like it; then I'll show her I'm really going to do it.
>
> Veronique: Is ja [It is, yes].
>
> Nicola: Then you'll be like my cousins as well. They always try and prove their parents they were right about them, ja.
>
> Byron: No, I really don't like that.
>
> Mandy: And if you get fat, you're pregnant. (Grade 11 students, Ocean View)

Children warn that adults who fail to recognise children's competence risk alienating them and heightening the conflict between the generations.

> And even if you 18 [years old] people still treat you like a child and that's not fair on you as a person, I mean you've come a long way…sometimes people don't recognise you and they think 'Ag, you younger than me why should I listen to you?' and sometimes you might even be right… sometimes when you are, when you excel in something, sometimes the older people don't recognise it and say, 'Ag, you young, what have you got to offer or what do you know?' (Nicola, 'community' focus group)

It is often the hypocrisy of adult judgements that most infuriates young people, alienating them from adult norms and rules, and prompting a disrespectful response:

Byron: Ok, if I'm doing something wrong, I'll admit I did it wrong, but don't accuse me and don't blame me and don't tell me to do stuff and I know you doing the same thing.

Charney: You know what bugs me the most, hey, if people see you doing something wrong but they don't see their own children doing something wrong... (Grade 11 students, Ocean View)

Elements of this tension between generations are familiar manifestations of parental anxiety regarding adolescence and a greater detachment from elders in this generation of young people, both of which are found across the modern world. Working alongside these trends are habits specific to South Africa's history, including the tendency to categorise people into groups with certain attributes, rank these and behave pejoratively towards them regardless of the particular 'rights' and 'wrongs' in any given interaction. Their role in shaping contemporary intergenerational relationships cannot be measured, but it is highly plausible that the ready negative or suspicious labelling of the young by the older generations is an aspect of apartheid's legacy that remains unrecognised.

Neighbourly antipathy and othering

Ocean View is not the homogeneous community it is often portrayed to be. Conversations with children revealed that colour, class and language all operate divisively within the area. Their own experience of discrimination often centred on the lightness and darkness of their skin, indicating a complexity in how they understand being 'coloured'. Charney attributes the fact that her grandmother gave her R400 less than she gave her other grandchildren to her 'not being dark enough'. Nicola reported that her father used to favour her younger sister because she was fair and Nicola was not. Colour still matters within Ocean View, but it is not a simple matter of being 'white', 'coloured' or 'black'. Among 'coloured' children in Ocean View, notions of 'whiteness' and 'blackness' operate divisively.

In a similar manner, language is still used to create divisions that draw on apartheid notions of hierarchy. Although the vast majority of children are competent in both languages, they report ongoing rivalry between members of the English and Afrikaans classes at the secondary school. Parents assured us that little had changed in this regard since they were at school 25 years ago. In Ocean View, language signifies claims to, and rejection of, an ascribed social status because of the historical positioning of English speakers above Afrikaans speakers in the hierarchy of apartheid society. In the past, English-speaking school pupils were afforded certain privileges, such as being allowed to board the school buses first. Such practices are no longer officially sanctioned, but English speakers tend to have a higher income than many Afrikaans speakers.

Map-making exercises in Ocean View revealed children's experiences of class-based othering and exclusion. Residential areas within Ocean View and types of housing are both considered indicators of poverty or wealth. Children living in council blocks of flats call those living in houses 'sturvies' (stuck up), and feel that these children think they are better than them because they have 'kwaai [cool] clothes' and other material goods. Children who live in houses often make derogatory comments about children from the flats, labelling them as rude. As Giddens (1984, in Henderson 1999) pointed out, geographical locales are invested with contested and conflicting values, meanings and activities, which make them sites of shifting power relations. Residence in a particular locale within Ocean View matters to children because it affects their inclusion and position within the peer group.

One way that adults can contest labels of relative poverty is to buy the latest televisions or DVD players for the household and brand-label clothing or new models of cellular phones for their children. Girls in the Ocean View art club commented that 'some people waste money and then become poor', identifying this as a common response that may mean that there is little money left to meet children's basic needs. In Masiphumelele, one's residential area and type of housing are seen by children as indicators of financial status, but are not used as reference points for class-based othering. Living in a shack or in the informal 'Wetlands' area does not currently attract negative comment in the way that lacking a school uniform does, probably because the former are the experiences of such large proportions of the community. Teenagers discussing the anticipated increase in brick houses in the neighbourhood raised the possibility that types of housing could become a reference point for social inclusion and exclusion.

Young people in Fish Hoek experience subtle but powerful othering when they are less wealthy than their peers. Some of this is masked within institutional practices – for example, the school's provision of sandwiches for certain undisclosed children. And some is overt through discourse and action within the peer group. Sam spoke of the surprised and disparaging comments she received when she brought friends to her sparsely furnished, rented home. Several pupils pretended to have a cellular phone in order to avoid ridicule and exclusion. Jake, whose parents come from a 'coloured' area near the city centre, distinguishes himself from other coloured pupils who live in Ocean View by referring to the latter as 'lower-class' children. And like their peers elsewhere in the Valley, young people in Fish Hoek usually regarded wearing brand clothing as the most certain way of ensuring inclusion and popularity.

Most young participants residing in Masiphumelele know, and enjoy interacting with, children of different backgrounds who live very close by. Although isiXhosa speakers are the majority, Masiphumelele is a more diverse community than most Valley residents assume and is still growing fast. Children and adults are forming new neighbourly relationships with incomers, who speak isiZulu, Afrikaans, Sesotho, Setswana, Shona, isiNdebele and Portuguese and who have roots elsewhere in the country or in Mozambique, Zimbabwe, Malawi or Somalia. Children's experiences of neighbourly relations involving different languages and cultures vary: some said that such diversity made no difference, whereas others stated that it can cause tension. In May 2008, a spate of violence against immigrants that was labelled as xenophobic erupted in poor urban neighbourhoods across the country. Subsequent interpretations of the motivations underlying this extreme othering point to the mounting frustrations of impoverished South Africans attempting to find work and feed their families, and their consequent resentment against foreigners among them who have set up businesses and appear to be better off (Cooper 2009).

The open economy and media of democratic South Africa places internal and external class differences firmly within a global consumer culture. The pressure to obtain the symbols and markers of wealth is felt strongly by poor children, and is understood to have important educational, social and emotional consequences. Overspending on consumer items can mean that households are unable to finance school transport or uniforms. In a drama workshop in Ocean View, grade-8 girls acted out a scene where a girl was dumped by her boyfriend because she went to shop at Pep instead of Edgars. Pep, whose slogan is 'low prices for everyone', is one of the cheapest high-street clothes retailers in South Africa. Edgars is a department store that stocks brand-name clothing and is significantly more expensive. Brian told us about a friend he was very close to who suddenly changed and became 'uppity' when she became rich. He says they are not friends any more because she now thinks she is 'too popular' for him.

Young people in Masiphumelele and Ocean View consistently remarked on the irony of their spending very high proportions of their scarce cash on clothes that are expensive purely because they have brand labels, and of their resultant inability to invest money in education, goods or services for their future or their children's. Their capitulation to this vicious circle is not lost on the young. But having the right clothes is also a means of resisting the burden of being working class and poor. Wearing designer clothing is a way of asserting inclusion among both local and global peers. One can, quite literally, label oneself as an equal in a society that, in most other respects, is increasingly divided and divisive.

Conclusion

The purpose of this chapter was to identify what matters most about neighbourhood spaces as far as young residents of Cape Town are concerned. The built environment is important in so far as poor housing and limited space contribute to high levels of independent mobility in late childhood and adolescence. Considerable freedom to move around is enjoyed by the young in poor neighbourhoods, often because they have some choice in whom they turn to for material or emotional support when these are unavailable at home. But densely situated, overcrowded homes and unsupervised social spaces are also regarded as physically threatening: children in Masiphumelele fear rampant shack fires and speak of the possibility of abuse or even abduction. The social dangers of moving around pose a greater threat than physical dangers to adolescents in poor neighbourhoods. Where rumour and gossip are widespread, and the resulting negative labelling and exclusion take a strong hold, young people must face these dangers or greatly restrict their movements (even remaining indoors) and risk isolation from the peer group, kin and neighbourly networks.

By comparison, adequate housing and established recreational facilities mean that children in middle-class neighbourhoods spend their time at home or in organised leisure pursuits and have very little control over their own mobility or interaction with those who live close by. Children living in Fish Hoek rely more heavily on institutional networks and supports, such as those provided through schools and churches, than do their peers in poor neighbourhoods. State policies to redistribute resources and the efforts of voluntary organisations to counter previous institutional disadvantage in 'coloured' and 'African' areas are proving slow in bearing fruit. Accessible and appropriate support to young people is still more readily available in Fish Hoek than in Masiphumelele or Ocean View. That said, it often comes at the cost of dependence on parents or teachers and is experienced by adolescents as disempowering.

Like adults, children across the wealth and cultural spectrum of the Valley set limits on their mobility and carefully plan their journeys and where they play in an attempt to protect themselves. For those in middle-class Fish Hoek, success in this regard stems from the fact that adults rarely permit them to make their own mobility-related decisions. Young residents of Masiphumelele and Ocean View choose their routes, timings and companions carefully. They recognise that their accurate knowledge and efforts in this regard afford them a degree of self-protection. At the same time, they acknowledge that aspects of neighbourhood commerce and social interaction (such as the ubiquitous use of drugs or alcohol in homes and public spaces) pose unpredictable and often unavoidable dangers because violence spills out onto the streets and into homes. Observation within the Valley corroborates data from Greater Cape Town, which show that drugs of various types have become increasingly available across all neighbourhoods in the last decade. The movement of drugs appears to have been facilitated by the extension of social and economic networks that were previously constrained by apartheid's legally enforced neighbourhood boundaries.

The nature of neighbourhood interaction and sociability matters greatly to young people, but is seldom a topic for research or policy discussion. Middle-class children struggle with a sense of being contained and controlled by a conservative religious ethic and relationships between generations. Children in poor areas, who enjoy greater participation in the public life of the neighbourhood than their middle-class counterparts, are more exposed to public scrutiny and more vulnerable to rumour and gossip. Not only are false rumours spread quickly which can precipitate fractures in personal and family integrity, but adult expectations of children are also a prominent part of neighbourhood discourse. In Ocean View, for example, public discourse often undermines personal achievement and is dominated by the notion that only a handful of young people will succeed, while the majority succumb to social pressures, fail to complete their education and stand little chance of finding a good job. Young people in Masiphumelele express the threatening dimension to neighbourliness in terms of jealousy and malevolent wishes or actions (through witchcraft, for example).

Young people find the affirming and supportive facets of neighbourhood sociability in the informality of 'looking out for each other', and by means of certain services and recreational activities run by voluntary organisations. Their use and enjoyment of, and investment in, these institutions increases dramatically when the approach to provision enables the formation of trusting, respectful relationships with adults, and encourages children's input in the design of activities. But existing recreational facilities and services are found to meet only a small portion of the needs of a fraction of the Valley's young population. Middle-class Fish Hoek is comparatively well resourced in this regard. And greater financial and human investment is being made by state and voluntary organisations in Masiphumelele than in Ocean View – a trend that its young residents are acutely aware of. But in both poor neighbourhoods, there are too few local resources, and even fewer that provide accessible, high-quality services for children and adolescents.

Emerging in this chapter is a picture of young Capetonians' intense daily interaction with the material and social characters of their neighbourhoods. It has demonstrated that the local infrastructure, commerce, institutional resources and the character of social relationships have a direct influence on children, in addition to shaping what is possible for their families. Threats to children's physical safety that stem from alcohol and drug use by older youths or adults have their roots in apartheid's disenfranchisement of African and coloured people, and the associated disempowerment of men. The corrosive nature of neighbourly sociability also has its antecedents in the ideas and mechanisms used by the state to organise society. But influences cannot be reduced to historical 'hangovers': rates of alcohol and drug consumption appear to be rising, as are the frustrations caused by unemployment and lack of basic services, especially the government's failure to deliver long-promised housing. The inability of adults and children to communicate in ways that can identify and respond to the needs of the young is partly symptomatic of the post-apartheid intergenerational conundrum. Adults running services tend to underestimate the knowledge and competence of children, and parents have misaligned expectations of what is possible for their offspring. In Ocean View, they continue to undermine their children's efforts to have a respectable career because of their sense that 'coloured' people are still excluded from opportunity. The realities of post-apartheid Cape Town are that most young people spend most of their time in their immediate neighbourhoods, and that adults at home are struggling not only with their own ghosts of apartheid, but with how to understand and engage with the realities of contemporary society. In such a context, recreational, social and health services designed for and with young people stand to make a significant difference to their safety, self-esteem, access to dependable relationships and projections of what is possible in the future.

4 Segregated and integrated spaces: Mobility and identity beyond the neighbourhood

Michael, a blond, blue-eyed, 15-year-old boy, takes the bus to school every day. The bus drives from Kommetjie ('white') through Ocean View ('coloured'), past Masiphumelele ('black') to Fish Hoek ('white'), picking up schoolchildren. He told me he had never really been to Ocean View even though he travels through it every day. 'They are racist towards whites, even the small children in Ocean View already act like little gangsters, using gang symbols and rude gestures, and shouting at me, "hey whitey".' He then said with a wide grin: 'I got out of the bus only once, just to be able to say that I have been to Ocean View.' This provoked some laughter from the rest of the discussion group, who showed an ambiguous reaction to the depiction of the dangers of Ocean View and its people. None of the participants in this discussion group live in Ocean View, and only one of the boys (who is white) actually goes there regularly: 'I go to church youth meetings, and I visit my friends there', he said, shrugging his shoulders before continuing, 'and it's not dangerous at all!' (Notes from grade-9 discussion group, Fish Hoek Middle School, November 2004)

This conversation encapsulates critical features of young Valley residents' knowledge and understanding of the world beyond their immediate neighbourhoods: inexperience, prejudice and surprising discoveries about those living a few kilometres down the road abound. Like the overwhelming majority of their peers across the country, the participants in our research have grown up in neighbourhoods that have changed little in their demography since the formal end of apartheid. Central to South Africans' expectations of the new democratic era is greater integration, the imagined vehicles for which include previously prohibited physical and social mobility, and desegregated schooling. To what extent, we ask, does this generation of children live in a more integrated society than that of their parents' childhood?

In this chapter we examine the movements of children and adolescents living in the Valley, their sense of community and its boundedness and their understandings of social diversity. The formation of identity and the nature of othering are consistent threads in our analysis, particularly given their salience in adolescent development. We look carefully at the character of interaction that occurs in the few physical spaces where young people from a variety of neighbourhoods, class and 'race' backgrounds are able to meet and socialise. We find that children and adolescents make new and creative use of racial terminology, and succeed in building strong friendships across old neighbourhood boundaries. However, they are restricted in such endeavours by the absence of a vocabulary for grappling with class and other lines of difference or similarity that exist in their peer group and in contemporary South African society more broadly.

Mapping the Valley

Maps drawn by children and adolescents themselves provide an invaluable starting point for our analysis.

> A group of 12-year-old girls at Fish Hoek Primary School began their map (see Map 5) with a rough outline of the area they wished to depict, delineating this by the position of each of their homes and a few places in the Valley they visit regularly for surfing, horse-riding lessons, shopping and school. I noticed that they had not marked Ocean View or Masiphumelele, even though both neighbourhoods fell within the boundaries of their map. My query as to their location on their map was met with silence and then an explanation: 'We have never been to those places, so we don't really know.' (Extract from field notes, Fish Hoek)

> Over here is Kommetjie where my aunt and her mother work as domestics (see Map 6). We've been once or twice to visit and the houses are nice. Then a bit closer is Ocean View. It's marked in red because it's a scary place where there are gangs and lots of drugs. The coloureds can sometimes rob you so we don't go. On that side is Fish Hoek. We go there once in a while to shop or to visit the beach with our families. (Members of the Masiphumelele art club, aged 11–14, explaining their map of the Kommetjie Road and surrounding areas)

The interactive construction of maps of the southern Cape Peninsula, Greater Cape Town and beyond proved to be a fascinating process. Children quickly and vividly depicted what was most familiar in their everyday journeying. The unknown spaces in between were sometimes quickly labelled on the basis of their reputation, and sometimes overlooked. The language young people used to explain these places was very revealing of their sense of the broader locality and the boundaries that they either experience or perceive. The maps and accompanying explanations reveal not only why young people *do* go outside of their immediate neighbourhoods, but also why they *don't* do so more often.

Map work quickly conveyed the wide variety of destinations within and beyond the southern peninsula visited by most middle-class children several times a week. Their families have cars and enough money to pay for regular leisure pursuits, such as swimming lessons and dance classes that are very much part of a middle-class upbringing. Interestingly, however, their reliance on cars driven by parents means that they make very few spontaneous journeys initiated by themselves or their peers, and their options are tightly circumscribed by adult perceptions of necessary, appropriate and safe destinations. As is evident in the words of the Fish Hoek girls quoted at the beginning of this section, middle-class children and adolescents rarely, if ever, travel to Masiphumelele or Ocean View. Those who do accompany a parent to drop off a domestic worker and do not get out of the car. The absence of any lived experience in these neighbourhoods means that children know very little about them. These neighbourhoods were usually depicted on maps as red blobs to signify danger. And sometimes, when children were adding detail, these areas 'fell off' and were replaced by large, colourful drawings of the nearby Longbeach Mall where they enjoy shopping and 'hanging out'. The mall is clearly a social arena that parents frequent and children, therefore, have access to it. They are less able to access the sought-after shops, clubs and party venues 'over the mountain' or 'up the [railway] line' (i.e. in suburbs closer to the centre of Cape Town) because parents are not always able or willing to make a special trip. Teenagers actively sought other means of travelling to these venues in order to be part of a larger and more vibrant social community:

> You need to find someone older with a car to make friends with and then you can use them to go out…Over the mountain it's like a whole different world! We go clubbing in Claremont and meet lots of people. (Boys in grade 9 at Fish Hoek Middle School)

Pupils in Fish Hoek said that they preferred not to go to local areas they are unfamiliar with, thus apparently endorsing adult codes relating to safety and danger (discussed in the previous chapter) rather than challenging them. For example, four girlfriends drew their neighbourhoods, shaded everything in red and wrote: 'Everywhere u go is dangerous, but most of the time, in our areas, it is safe.' The fact that two of these girls live in Masiphumelele is an illustration of the fact that girls across the research site worry about their safety when moving around, and that unknown places are feared and avoided. Teenage boys report walking home alone from social events within local middle-class suburbs, but girls are more cautious about being alone anywhere, particularly in unknown places. This is one example of parallel gender-related experience that emerges from our analysis, but is not identified or experienced by young people themselves. For a number of reasons to be explored later in the chapter, only very rarely do young people seem able to make connections as young women or young men through church or school that go beyond their physical and social boundaries.

Young Fish Hoek residents describe networks of friends and support based in their peer groups at school, sports teams and church youth clubs. The way in which such networks are bounded by class and physical space is unsurprising given the constraints on mobility described above. These networks provided a sense of inclusion and a source of self-esteem, but – with the exception of some churches – did not afford the possibility of extending young people's social interaction beyond the structural boundaries of these institutions. Evident in young people's narratives is a sense of claustrophobia and frustration associated with frequent references to Fish Hoek as boring, staid and 'old-fashioned':

> Fish Hoek is like 'Grannyville', a boring place where you have to be quiet and behave. Fish Hoek grannies get upset about everything! It's because they grew up in a different time. We read complaints in the *Echo* all the time; people write in and stereotype middle-school students, exaggerate about graffiti, vandalism, and say 'they all do drugs'. (Notes from grade-9 discussion group, November 2004)

Children, and more particularly adolescents, perceive and react against a conservative ethic in the community that restricts their social activities and, more seriously, judges them negatively. In letters to the editor of *The People's Post*, a local newspaper, elderly writers regularly complain of 'hooligans' skateboarding on the streets and pavements, and how 'the youth of today' have no respect and misbehave in public. This experience of being categorised and labelled by the older generation dominates the way young people represent Fish Hoek and seems to undermine their sense of belonging to a neighbourhood community. While many consider Fish Hoek a satisfactory place to live, not once did we hear young people express positive identification with the place itself or its residents. Nor did we hear about a desire to live there in the future. Instead, their orientation in terms of social activities was towards middle- and upper-middle-class (largely white) communities nearer the centre of Cape Town, and for some towards relatives and friends living overseas:

> There's no nightlife in Fish Hoek, like in Claremont there's the mall and lots of places around to hang out, so you don't need alcohol to have fun. Here people do drugs because it's boring. So you go out of Fish Hoek whenever possible! (Notes from grade-9 discussion group, November 2004)

Recalling that a large proportion of young residents of Fish Hoek have moved around the country or even internationally, it is unsurprising that these places feature in conversations about their networks and future aspirations. What becomes clear is that they feel more connected to the cohort of young people with a similar socio-economic position in other parts of the city, country or even globe, than they do to their peers who live a few kilometres along the road. Young Fish Hoek residents whose parents grew up in poorer areas zoned coloured or African during apartheid held similar aspirations and attitudes to those from long-established families. Class, it would appear, plays an equal if not greater role in shaping young people's sense of affiliation than a shared economic and racialised history.

Maps created by young residents of Masiphumelele and Ocean View show that few make daily journeys beyond their neighbourhoods for social and leisure reasons, primarily because of the distances involved and the prohibitive cost of public transport and leisure activities more readily available to middle-class children. A very small number of children from both poor neighbourhoods travel to school in Fish Hoek. Despite these restrictions on regular mobility, young residents drew elaborate pictures of several sites outside their neighbourhood, including Longbeach Mall (the largest local shopping complex), the shops on Fish Hoek Main Road, False Bay Hospital (in Fish Hoek) and Fish Hoek beach. Although some have visited these places only a couple of times, they all have personal experience of journeying to them and spending time there. Often drawn in bright colours, these are the few areas in the southern peninsula that children feel familiar with and comfortable in (see Map 6). The particular nature of social interaction in these areas and their associated potential for increased integration between the three neighbourhoods is discussed later in the chapter.

In contrast to the detailed and multicoloured drawings of the local mall, poor neighbourhoods just a few kilometres away were depicted with little detail and almost always coloured red to signify danger. One boy in the Ocean View art club commented that 'there are only shebeens in Masi', while another used a red crayon to draw a bar and games shops that 'get violent', as well as homes in which 'people keep guns and there is shooting'. Their counterparts in Masiphumelele spoke of Ocean View as 'a place full of gangsters and drugs'. It soon transpired that these perceptions were based on local rumour and stories they read in newspapers, and that poor children living in Masiphumelele and Ocean View are almost as unfamiliar with each other's neighbourhoods as middle-class children are of both areas. A small proportion of young residents of Masiphumelele attend school in Ocean View or visit relatives or friends living there. And with the exception of the few (African) isiXhosa speakers, it is very rare indeed for young residents of Ocean View to visit Masiphumelele.

Somewhat surprisingly in the context of higher household incomes in Ocean View, we found that children and adolescents living in Masiphumelele travel further and more frequently to places outside the Valley than their counterparts in Ocean View. A vivid map of Greater Cape Town drawn by Masiphumelele art club members includes places where they shop in distant suburbs and the city centre; several large 'townships' on the edge of the city that they visit regularly; bus stations in these areas where one catches a bus to the Eastern Cape; and the Huguenot Tunnel 120 kilometres outside the city on the road to the Eastern Cape (see Map 8). Our conversations revealed that children in Masiphumelele make more frequent visits to Longbeach Mall and Fish Hoek than many of their (slightly wealthier) peers in Ocean View. Moreover, they travel to see family and friends in other parts of Cape Town and in the Eastern Cape, sometimes on their own in their teenage years. Adolescents' diaries and life-stories recount journeys to parties in other parts of the city and the reciprocal hosting of friends living elsewhere through parties held in Masiphumelele. Common destinations for weekends or evening parties are Westlake (8 km away), Gugulethu, Langa and Khayelitsha (between 40 km and 65 km away). This level of mobility and the ability to socialise elsewhere were not evident in Ocean View where very few young people travel outside the neighbourhood on a regular basis.

Explanations for these differences lie partly in the combined effect of spatial location, resulting perceptions of distance and sense of social isolation. Longbeach Mall is 3 kilometres by accessible road from Masiphumelele and, therefore, within walking distance, although most residents prefer to go by taxi. The additional 4 kilometres to Ocean View makes paying for a taxi or bus necessary. However, despite the greater distances involved, the costs of public transport from Ocean View to Longbeach Mall, Fish Hoek and thence to the rest of Cape Town are no higher than from Masiphumelele. (Refer to Map 7, which shows public-transport routes and costs.)

Given that household incomes are substantially higher in Ocean View than in Masiphumelele (see Figure 1.1 in Chapter 1), there must be other reasons besides cost why children in Ocean View do not move around the Valley as much as their peers living down the road. Children reported that transport costs restricted visits to family members living outside Ocean View to special occasions, such as births, weddings and funerals. These remarks suggest that adults do not regard paying for children to travel locally for social, sports or skill-development purposes as essential or even a priority in relation to other household expenses. By contrast, the costs of moving around are higher in relative terms in Masiphumelele, but are met more readily by children and adults alike. This difference raises the question of habit in relation to moving around for social and economic reasons, and the role of history in defining the distinct characteristics of these communities and shaping such habits. Ocean View was created by the apartheid state to house people who were unwillingly removed from the nearby coastal communities that provided a livelihood and ancestral home. Masiphumelele was first settled by labourers and their families moved off local farms, and was then formally established by a post-apartheid government in response to this housing need and to the desire of immigrants to settle in the southern peninsula and at the same time maintain ancestral homes in the distant Eastern Cape. Differences in habits and expectations surrounding mobility are but one consequence of the contrasting social and psychological processes underlying the formation of these communities. As we saw in Chapter 2, many young residents of Masiphumelele have either themselves moved around since infancy or have witnessed those around them doing so. Journeying over short and long distances is familiar to the young, and all generations are accustomed to rallying the required resources and energy, as Loyiso verifies:

> This is a picture of my best friend, who lives in Simon's Town. I met him when I lived there too, and I see him when we go and visit my cousin's family, who live in the navy flats. He doesn't come here, but on weekends when I'm not playing soccer I cycle to Simon's Town. It takes one hour but I enjoy the journey...I love cycling and I am a member of a club here in Masi. We wear vests saying 'Pick n Pay' [a supermarket chain], and older guys from Fish Hoek Cycling Club sometimes take us on training rides. (Loyiso, boy, aged 16, Masiphumelele)

Map work revealed the myriad connections young people in Masiphumelele have with other parts of the city, and in conversation a number said that they consider Cape Town as a whole to be their community. Like young people in Fish Hoek, their connections are to areas of similar socio-economic and language profiles where relatives and friends from previous homes live. Therefore, they maintain regular connections and experience certain affinities with large townships on the outskirts of the city (including Langa, Gugulethu and Khayelitsha), while at the same time asserting the distinctiveness of Masiphumelele. Even in the context of rising crime, adult and child residents alike assert that Masiphumelele is much quieter and safer than the larger townships where going out after dark is to risk being a victim to violence. These differences give residents of Masiphumelele the reputation of 'farmers' and 'simple people'. In Masiphumelele the advantages of physical and emotional well-being are pitted against a sense of marginalisation and even social inferiority. Young residents, and particularly girls, said that they feel safe walking around with friends in the evening, but would not do the same in the other suburbs. The flip side to this is that they perceive themselves as living in a semi-rural backwater, rather removed from the 'cool and happening' young people's scene elsewhere in the city.

As was evident in the map work described above, children in Masiphumelele are also actively connected to places considerable distances from Cape Town, including villages and townships in the Eastern Cape and poor suburbs of Johannesburg. Their sense of 'community' encompasses, therefore, wide geographical horizons, very different to those of their peers in Ocean View and more akin to those of young people in Fish Hoek. Yet, although high levels of people moving home and daily mobility generate a sense of belonging to a broader geographical and social community, they generally do not involve interaction with people and social institutions in stronger economic and political positions. As noted in Chapter 2, children in Masiphumelele refer to relatives in distant cities or even outside South Africa as potential sources of upward mobility, but there was little evidence of these ideas translating into reality. Middle-class young people in Fish Hoek, on the other hand, often had ready access to a relative elsewhere in the country or abroad who could accommodate them during periods of study, travel or work experience, thereby facilitating their access to wider social and economic networks.

In summary, when we assess the combined effects of mobility trends we see that the limited everyday movement of young residents of Cape Town's southern peninsula either occurs within networks that share a common socio-economic, linguistic and historical profile, or in one class direction only, namely from poor to middle-class neighbourhoods. School attendance, discussed in the next two chapters, also follows this pattern. A small number of Masiphumelele residents visit Ocean View, but there is no movement in the other direction. Middle-class children who enter these poor neighbourhoods usually do so in the confines of a car, and only a few have direct experience in the form of a school sports or charity outing, or through reciprocal church services. In the absence of practical knowledge of everyday life beyond their own local areas, children have little basis on which to build social identities or notions of community that stretch beyond the physical boundaries of neighbourhood spaces that are, in contemporary Cape Town, linked to the socially constructed and politically imposed 'racial' boundaries of the apartheid past. In this context, and particularly for the less mobile young people in Ocean View, lines of inclusion and exclusion at work within the neighbourhood, the character of community spirit, and the manner in which others perceive their neighbourhood become very important in the formation of young people's social identities. In short, their place of residence occupies a dominant position in the hierarchy of factors from which young people draw to make and shape their social identities.

Why go beyond the neighbourhood?

Children and adolescents occasionally pass through or visit other neighbourhoods in the Valley. But when they do so, their interaction is limited and often perceived to be difficult. A small minority regularly spend large chunks of time in a neighbourhood close by because they attend school there (reasons for which are discussed at length in Chapter 6). Only rarely did we hear about these pupils' regular visits to friends' homes in the vicinity. The minority of young people with family in other neighbourhoods tend to travel directly to and from their home by car or taxi, often saying they were afraid to walk elsewhere in the area. A very small proportion of adolescents have paid work outside their immediate neighbourhoods. Cape Area Panel Study (CAPS) data show that waged labour among adolescents in Cape Town is the preserve of the middle classes. Children and adolescents in low-income neighbourhoods might look after young siblings or help with household chores, but rarely for money. In areas like Fish Hoek, however, adolescents earn money from babysitting, delivering newspapers and serving in restaurants. Middle-class adolescents get jobs in middle-class neighbourhoods, probably by using their middle-class networks. Adolescents in poorer neighbourhoods lack both employment opportunities in their own neighbourhood and contacts with employers in middle-class neighbourhoods. Consequently, employment does not provide a mechanism for adolescents to experience other parts of the Valley.

Shopping and sport are two major motivators for young people to travel outside the neighbourhoods in which they live. Shops in the immediate vicinity are generally more expensive and much smaller than those in the Longbeach Mall, on Fish Hoek Main Road or 'over the mountain' near Cape Town's centre. Children from across the Valley – particularly girls – accompany their mothers on shopping trips to these destinations and teenagers enjoy window-shopping there with friends. Soccer is very popular in Masiphumelele, and boys from the age of 10 regularly travel to pitches behind Longbeach Mall or in Noordhoek (5 km north). Members of the cycle clubs (described above by Loyiso) tour the peninsula during training. Far fewer young people living in Ocean View move outside the neighbourhood for leisure or sport: a similar cycle club was set up in Ocean View, but when its leaders moved on members were asked to buy the bikes (rather than being donated to them, as was the case in Masiphumelele). The majority of young members could not afford to and the club folded. This series of events further illustrates the differing perceptions of need in Ocean View and Masiphumelele by those living outside these neighbourhoods and wishing to resource them in some way, and demonstrates the negative consequences of these perceptions.

Many – but, importantly, not all – young people perceive and experience their local neighbourhood as their source of facilities and services. What is present or absent therein (as described in Chapters 1 and 3) often underlies their sense of what is available to them. Their ignorance of alternatives in part arises from the economic and parental restrictions placed on their travel within the Valley and beyond. That said, we met a number of young residents of Ocean View and Masiphumelele who attend churches elsewhere in the Valley, even though there are many churches of different denominations and styles much nearer home. Some of these reported cultivating friendships outside their neighbourhoods by visiting one another's homes (see below).

Under apartheid, the state discriminated racially in its provision of facilities, and these inherited inequalities had not been abolished by the time we did our fieldwork. But the map work discussed above was a starting point for our growing awareness of how many children in the least advantaged neighbourhood – Masiphumelele – succeeded in accessing sports, leisure and life-skills activities outside of their neighbourhood. Loyiso, quoted above, has learnt to cycle with a local, externally resourced club and his ability to borrow a bicycle from the club enables him to visit his friend living 15 kilometres away in Simon's Town. His peers in the art club also attend weekly computer classes, a local youth club, loveLife activities and sports practice. Adolescents sing in church choirs, attend church youth clubs, learn ballroom dancing and go to regular meetings and camps run by the OIL peer education network (described in Chapter 3). While some are local initiatives run on a shoestring, a large proportion are funded by charities or churches located in parts of the Valley formerly zoned 'white' and include free or subsidised transport where necessary.

In stark contrast, young people in Ocean View consistently complained of being bored and having nothing to do because of the very limited range of sports, leisure and development-orientated activities on offer:

> Byron: The only thing that I think will bring Ocean View right, that will bring any community right, is sports.
>
> Charney: *Ja*, they looking into doing that as well.
>
> Byron: Just to keep like youngsters active. I've got nothing to do at home…
>
> Veronique: I've also got nothing to do at home.
>
> Nicola: If you not interested in soccer…
>
> Byron: Why don't they make a soccer club, a rugby team, table tennis…?
>
> Veronique: *Is ja*. Extramural activities by the multi-purpose or at the Civic.
>
> Charney: That's what they were supposed to do with the multi-purpose centre, but that hasn't happened.

Very rarely do young residents of Ocean View cycle outside their neighbourhood to take part in activities run elsewhere in the Valley.[1] They said that they feared their bicycles would be stolen en route along the Kommetjie Road (which passes by Masiphumelele). As we observed the numbers of short- and long-term 'development' activities multiplying in Masiphumelele, the dearth of these in Ocean View became more obvious. Teachers regularly referred to this disparity in facilities, as did the minority of young people who had personal experience of the activities available in Masiphumelele. They perceived a lack of interest in their community and the narrow and contrasting ways in which Ocean View and Masiphumelele are portrayed by the press. Such depictions were identified by young people as problematic labels of 'community' and, therefore, significant in shaping their social identities and status in relation to those living outside Ocean View.

Identity, othering and the inhibition of mobility

The mobility of young people across the Valley is curtailed by a widespread othering – stereotyping of other neighbourhoods. Those living outside them have perceptions of particular physical and social characteristics about all three neighbourhoods. But young people's interaction with and participation in neighbourly othering – and, therefore, the implications of these processes to their sense of identity and well-being – differ markedly between the areas studied.

Young residents of Ocean View pointed to a tendency for the local media to perpetuate stereotyped and negative images of their neighbourhood, often with the complicity of local adults. Their observations were substantiated by our own content analysis of the local press. Gangsterism, drugs and sexual promiscuity are the characteristics most frequently attached to the place and people of Ocean View in the Cape Town press.[2] Children explained how these negative and one-sided perceptions discourage visitors and heighten the sense of isolation among residents, who already struggle with Ocean View's peripheral location at the far end of the Kommetjie Road.

> It creates a negative impact on the community because they're not looking at what the community is good at, they just looking at what the community is bad at, all the bad points. And I mean you cannot judge a community by what it does badly. I mean there is a balance between the two…But they just continue on running bad press releases over and over and over again. And it's such a negative vibe because no one wants to come into the community, and then there's no interaction, it's like you isolated, you an island, nobody wants to go there. (Charney, girl, aged 17, grade-11 discussion group on 'community')

Their predictions were substantiated by the fact that the four young researchers living in Fish Hoek and Masiphumelele said that prior to their involvement in this research project they had been too scared to enter the neighbourhood. Conversations about reasons for their fear revealed largely stereotyped perceptions of Ocean View that only began to shift when we held meetings in the homes of their colleagues who lived there.

Young people in Ocean View are frustrated by the prevalent negative images of their community, not only because they reflect a skewed picture of reality, but because they have serious consequences for individual behaviour. One teenager explained how images that focus on problematic aspects of neighbourhood life lead to community apathy in the face of problems:

> And one of the things, I can compare the community to a person; if you always concentrate on the negative of the person then they will actually break down because nobody's actually recognising their potential or highlighting their good points. And the same thing with the community, if you every time you hear bad news you going to say, '*Ag*, I might as well just leave and stop trying to do good' or whatever, and the people might just start collapsing and that's why I think the majority of the people lose hope in actually trying to become a community together because of what they read in the newspaper. (Nicola, girl, aged 17, grade-11 discussion group on 'community')

Interestingly, however, inaccurate and solely negative representations of the community can provoke the opposite reaction in young people, namely to resist the identity by contesting it fiercely and, in some cases, working hard to prove it wrong:

> I don't want people thinking I am a 'tik monster' just because I go to this school. (Charney, individual interview)

> Being at Ocean View it's very hard because there is that stigma that says that Ocean View children are going nowhere and that actually motivates me more because if no one believes in you, you become stronger by showing them that you can do it, I can prove you wrong. That motivates me a lot. (Lenore, girl, aged 16, 'Tri' interview)

As will be seen in chapters to follow, verbal protests against imposed identities do not always translate into positive decision-making and the ability to achieve different realities. We noted in the previous chapter that some young people buy into deviant identities to spite adults who think badly of them. Children's choices and actions in the face of difficulties are influenced by a range of factors, including individual personality and the specific challenges, opportunities and supports operating in their lives at any given time. We develop our analysis of the relative roles of these internal factors and external contingencies, as well as the efficacy of children's choices, in Chapter 8.

As fieldwork progressed it became increasingly evident that, like Nicola (quoted above), young people in Ocean View feel particularly frustrated and disempowered in terms of their community identity compared to their counterparts in other neighbourhoods. They also drew greater attention to divisions within the community on the basis of colour, language and class, often recounting personal experiences of discrimination. We suggest that these internal lines of inclusion and exclusion contribute significantly to young people's ambivalence and negativity in their experiences of 'community' and their own identities in relation to these. As we will now demonstrate, these internal dynamics are highly influential precisely because they resonate with both old racialised hierarchies and contemporary markers of identity, and because they operate alongside negative labelling by outsiders.

The reader will recall from Chapter 1 differences in house sizes, incomes and types of employment that point to a greater diversity of wealth within Ocean View than is popularly assumed, and greater than that found in other parts of the Valley. Children's maps of Ocean View show that their experiences of class differences and symbols of wealth are used to discriminate against their peers (see Chapter 3).

A comparison of the media coverage of Ocean View and Masiphumelele quickly reveals two different sets of discourses. Most reporting on Masiphumelele is a consistent account of the problems experienced there (such as crime) and efforts to address these (normally involving middle-class whites living in other parts of the Valley), while a minority of coverage is a conscious effort to recognise the vibrancy of community life and local enterprise in the face of poverty. Thus, unlike Ocean View, Masiphumelele is presented as a needy and deserving community owing to its political and economic disadvantage in South Africa's history and ongoing poverty. Few children we worked with confronted this representation, and those who did so reinforced notions of the community as needy and deserving, while rejecting labels of antisocial behaviour and criminality as being specific to their neighbourhood. For example, one 13-year-old girl living in Masiphumelele and attending school in Fish Hoek wrote the following piece in the style of a news article about a topic of importance to young people in the Valley:

Site 5 (Masiphumelele): is it really that bad?

Masiphumelele is said by most to be the cruellest place in the Cape, but I live there and I know much more than some people. Anyway, Site 5 (or Masiphumelele) is not that bad a place because it is poor and dirty and has had a few rapes. I've been living there for 12 years since I was one year old. Yes, people get out of control on weekends, but that happens in Fish Hoek and anywhere else, just it sometimes doesn't show. In the last few years, people from Fish Hoek and Simon's Town have started going to Masi to buy drugs and alcohol. Anyway, Site 5, or Masiphumelele, needs to be recognised and needs attention just like any other place. We get help from Fish Hoek Middle School, but it is not enough.

There are plenty of good things going on in Masiphumelele: we now have a library, a clinic and Hokisa [Homes for Kids in South Africa] – an organisation for children and families affected by AIDS.

Thank you. Plz help and support us – we need your help.

Young residents of Masiphumelele refer less frequently to labels given to their neighbourhood than their peers in Ocean View. In conversations involving people living in all three neighbourhoods, we often heard the words 'in our culture…' or 'in Xhosa culture, we…'. A marked consciousness of cultural distinctiveness has been noted among adult African people (Ashforth 2005), related to the continuation of beliefs in ancestors and witchcraft, distinct languages and particular church affiliation. Variations of these markers of social identity are pertinent to young people in Masiphumelele: drawings by teenage art club members revealed a strong sense of identification with rural origins and their associated people, lifestyle practices and language. These drawings typically included thatched rondavels, three-legged cooking pots containing tasty 'village food' and grandparents. Their experience of a shared culture is firmly rooted in the sense of a common history and ancestry and of the persistent role of a set of traditions and practices that originate from outside Masiphumelele. The significance of a sense of shared origins is evident in the way one adolescent described his feelings following his move from Ocean View Secondary School to Masiphumelele High School:

> I didn't play any sport in Ocean View 'cause I was afraid to do so…But in Masi I felt like I was at home in the Eastern Cape because many students were coming from my part of the world…I had people who knew me, Mr M [a teacher] is from the same place [in the Eastern Cape] and he said, 'You must run', as he knew I did it in primary school there. When I said, 'No I don't do it any more' and he just said, 'You can, I know you can.'
> (Gift, boy, aged 17, living in Ocean View and at school in Masiphumelele)

Notions of a common cultural identity are often articulated with reference to the older generations and, therefore, serve to adhere young people to their elders. Yet at the same time, young people assert a social identity constructed around an unfamiliarity with traditional ways and rural living, and instead appeal to ideas of modernity and youth.

> Gift: It [gender difference] is even more so in Eastern Cape, coz like in our culture, boys must be outside going to bushes to look for cows…They think that only girls can work inside as they think that boys are stronger than girls, as they don't think girls can do outside work.
>
> Chloe: It goes back to what we said in the car that parents are overprotective of girls, so boys can go outside, but girls must stay inside.
>
> Interviewer: Is this still the same now in the modern urban setting?
>
> Gift: No, it's not like this now. They don't obey it like they did before.
>
> Interviewer: So are boys sometimes working in the home?
>
> Gift: Yes, like me if I go to the Eastern Cape I don't go out with the cattle, as I'm too scared. I don't know what's in the bush – it's not familiar to me.
> (17-year-old residents of Masiphumelele in a discussion of gender roles with peers from across the Valley)

Here we note Gift's assertion of unfamiliarity with the rural practices of the older generations that draws attention to a difference in outlook between the generations. While teenagers assert their distance from traditional ways, they also present the older generations as being removed from the world of fashion, music and styles of cellular phones. These important shapers of young people's identities exist in a space associated with modernity and youth as defined in national and global consumer culture. Interestingly, young people made very few direct references to being young Africans or attempts to separate themselves from older generations on the basis of being in tune with a larger and more economically and politically powerful younger generation. Instead, the significance of fashionable clothing, hairstyles and cell phones lay in the social status conferred among their peers.

Like their counterparts in Ocean View and Fish Hoek, children in Masiphumelele employ and experience class-related inclusion and exclusion. While housing size or quality is not used in this way, clothing is strongly symbolic of wealth in the sense of having money, or coping adequately with its shortage. Young children spoke of their fear of being without a school uniform because of the insults this would attract. Being without a uniform, they explained, is symbolic of coming from a home where people are struggling to provide even the basics. Children and adolescents placed great importance on having new outfits, especially at Christmas, and preferably those from the 'right' (fashionable) shops. While these markers of identity are undoubtedly about wealth and require access to at least some cash, they appear to be more easily acquired (owing to less emphasis on designer labels) or circumvented (through borrowing or acquiring second-hand uniforms) than those that are de rigueur in Ocean View.

Similarly, while language differences exist in Masiphumelele, they do not confer social status or shape identities with nearly the intensity that they do in Ocean View. While all our participants spoke isiXhosa and some English, a number have a different first language and recall a steep learning curve to learn isiXhosa when they arrived in Masiphumelele. As was explained in the previous chapter, all know local children or families from other countries in southern Africa who cannot speak isiXhosa and they communicate in English. Few spoke of their own or others' antipathy towards foreigners, many of whom had joined, and were forming families with, South African isiXhosa speakers. The violent, so-called xenophobic attacks described in the previous chapter illustrate the tendency of some residents (or incomers from larger townships, as many people from Masiphumelele believe – and many of them teenagers and young adults) to vent their frustrations on a group of foreign 'others'.

Imagining community

In an area where historically structured neighbourhoods remain physically and, to a large extent, socially separated, the question arises as to what children consider to be their community. Our findings reveal some interesting differences between the three research sites that relate directly to young people's mobility patterns and to the persistence of negative assumptions about 'other' communities. In turn, we see the effects of this valley's political and economic history in shaping both children's and adults' decisions regarding mobility and the attitudes that underlie them. These include the manner in which neighbourhoods were formed, their geographical position, the legacy of very unequal resource allocation and current efforts to redress the balance in resources.

Middle-class children living in Fish Hoek do not express a strong affiliation with their neighbourhood as a space in which they belong. By contrast, being from Ocean View is very important in young residents' social identities and one that is largely problematic owing to negative stereotyping in popular opinion and the media. This label becomes more significant because children in Ocean View rarely travel outside the neighbourhood, do not assert a positive identification with communities elsewhere in Cape Town or beyond, and perceive themselves to be isolated in the context of local leisure opportunities and development efforts. By comparison, children in poorer Masiphumelele express a positive affiliation with their local neighbourhood and strong ties with townships on the other side of the city as well as villages of ancestral origin in the distant Eastern Cape. These connections foster a sense of belonging to a common Xhosa culture that distinguishes them from others in the Valley. And although young people associated certain cultural practices and attitudes with the traditions of the older generation, they did not reject these as invalid, but held them in balance with sometimes contradictory ideas about youth and modernity derived from broader, often global, cultural influences. The more numerous and positive assertions of identity based on membership of a sports team, youth club or church choir among children in Masiphumelele are linked to the wider range of activities available there than in Ocean View, and to their minimal but still greater inclusion in organisations based in Fish Hoek. These trends notwithstanding, a proportion of children and teenagers in Masiphumelele do not participate in such activities or groups because of, for example, extreme household poverty or early childbearing.

Subsumed within young people's assertions of community identity that seem to reaffirm neighbourhood boundaries are some important common features. These may be easily overlooked owing to the fact that they are rarely identified and, therefore, articulated by children. One of these is the simple familiarity that develops in a context of shared heritage, language, normative cultural practice and the everyday participation in social relationships – a sense of feeling 'at home' that remains tied to local geography, given the immobility of both children and adults in the Valley. A second common feature is the experience of being labelled in a way that draws an association between colour, place and behavioural characteristics – though the label is more negative and has greater potential to undermine self-esteem for children in Ocean View and Masiphumelele than for those living in Fish Hoek. Children living in Ocean View experience division and exclusion articulated around colour, language and class particularly acutely; in part because these labels are applied in the course of everyday life within the neighbourhood as well as in their relationships outside it. We highlight this case because exclusion of this nature undermines children's self-esteem, and thereby reduces their confidence to develop alternative identities by joining clubs and organisations. A third common component to young people's social identities is their faith and membership of a church. Christian beliefs and their associated moral codes are important in connecting children within neighbourhoods and young people feel a sense of affiliation with Christians elsewhere in the Valley. We discuss the role of churches in inter-neighbourhood integration later in the chapter.

149

Importantly, we draw attention to the fact that children participate in and reinforce this labelling process by virtue of the fact that they have little or no direct experience of everyday life in other neighbourhoods. The factors that contribute to this picture include residential isolation; constraints on independent transport; journeying habits; class-affiliated lifestyle and leisure choices; and language differences. When routes are opened up for children and adolescents to socialise in other communities then they are eager to do so, and tend to build a very different picture of the community they witness. Our data point firmly to the importance of young people's physical presence and conducting social relationships in a given neighbourhood space. Occupying and exploring previously unfamiliar places in this way is critical to altering children's perceptions of difference.

Our ethnographic enquiry reveals a number of constraints on children's ability to extend their sense of belonging to areas beyond their own neighbourhoods, which are common across the three research sites. Importantly, these became evident in our analysis, but are not articulated as such by children. As yet, there is little evidence that these shared experiences contribute to new lines of connectedness across the old boundaries, probably because only a small minority of children have had the opportunity of in-depth social interaction in residentially mixed settings. One common constraint is the perception that all neighbourhoods other than their own are 'dangerous' – and the constraints this imposes on movement for girls in particular. The second is a sense of being cut off from mainstream social interaction with Cape Town's youth, which arises from their geographical distance from the city centre and other residential suburbs, as well as the social distance created by the factors preventing them from travelling 'up the line' more regularly. This sense of isolation and backwardness generates a range of responses in young people, including an appeal to wider social networks as a means to move out of their neighbourhood. Thirdly, young people in Fish Hoek and Masiphumelele identify themselves as thinking and acting in rather different ways from the older generation they live among. This juxtaposition was less evident in Ocean View, perhaps owing to a reduced sense of the possibility for upward and outward mobility compared to their peers, whose neighbourhoods are historically more advantaged and more disadvantaged in turn. As will become evident in the chapters to follow, the sense of social and political centrality related to being seen as a black African (rather than being 'black' and from any other previously disadvantaged group) is associated with optimism, but acts as a thin veneer over complex and harsh circumstances that rarely enable the translation of aspirations into reality.

Global cultures, shared spaces and crossing boundaries

Social scientists have long believed that contact across group boundaries is conducive to the erosion of prejudice. As Jenkins (1996: 118) writes, 'the more people have to do with each other in everyday life, the more likely they will be to identify each other as fellow individuals'. There are also many studies, however, that suggest that the contact hypothesis is naïve. A careful review of the evidence from

South Africa suggests that contact in hierarchical relationships does not seem to have benign effects (Finchilescu & Tredoux 2007). Under apartheid, many white people employed African domestic workers and gardeners without any obviously positive, disruptive effect on their racist attitudes. Contact outside of hierarchical relationships is generally more conducive to reduced prejudice. The problem is that there is little such contact in a society where neighbourhoods largely conform to old racial categories – as do the Valley, Cape Town, and much of South Africa.

In light of the very limited mobility between neighbourhoods enjoyed by children in our study, the few sites where they do meet and interact become particularly significant to the process of identity formation. In the paragraphs that follow we look at what happens in these spaces and the nature of the social interaction among children. We look at young people's experiences of crossing so-called 'race' boundaries and the factors that enable them to do so. We also comment on the potential of communal spaces in terms of enabling young people to construct understandings of 'others' based on experience rather than hearsay and to manipulate established social boundaries to achieve coherence with their own everyday experiences.

The shopping mall, high street and beach

The vivid colouring and attention to detail given to children's pictures of Longbeach Mall on their maps of the southern peninsula speak of the significance of this space to children across the research site. The shops were often named and painted in colours appropriate to their branding. A large chicken burger labelled 'KFC' was drawn in the middle of the map made by Masiphumelele art club members, who associate this fast-food outlet with an occasional, or for some an inaccessible, treat (see Map 6). Conversations about these drawings suggested a shared enjoyment of spending time at the mall, whether shopping, window-shopping or just 'hanging out' with friends. Substantiated by our own observation, these conversations also revealed distinct patterns in the way young people use the spaces that act as barriers to social interaction.

Children in Masiphumelele and Ocean View visit the mall and Fish Hoek Main Road with relatives, usually adult women, to buy groceries. Trips to the mall with their peers are often made with the expressed intention of a financial errand for a relative, such as checking their bank account, repaying a loan in a department store or buying a Lotto ticket. Some teenagers visit to monitor and withdraw cash from their own bank accounts. The main attraction of these trips is the opportunity to wander around with friends. Notably, young people travel to the mall with family or friends from their neighbourhood and on no occasion did we observe a mixed-race gathering of young people, even among groups of school friends wearing the same uniform. That said, testimony from our participants of trips to the mall with friends from other neighbourhoods shows that mixed interaction does occur, albeit very minimally. Middle-class children are generally not permitted by their parents to 'hang out' in public spaces without adult company, a constraint that hinders any desired efforts to build friendships with other young people. Yet the mall seems to be an exception to this general rule: many middle-class teenagers go there with friends and some work there too.

Teenagers across the research sites had clear ideas about which clothes shops were to be avoided because they carry a certain class stigma, and in which ones they aspired to shop. There were strong similarities in the brands and shops favoured by all young people, suggesting a shared link with the broader world beyond of modern urban youth. Yet this relationship with a wider consumer culture is largely played out within existing peer networks from each community, and independently of their peers from other neighbourhoods (although there are some exceptions regarding tastes in fashion or music that arise in the context of a mixed school environment; see below). Young people's abilities to fulfil aspirations to buy and wear these goods are, of course, tied to economic means. Unsurprisingly, middle-class children shopped much more frequently and extensively with their parents and on their own. The fact that a number of very poor children alluded to their discomfort at being among attractive goods that they could not afford suggests that consumption habits served to reinforce boundaries between children from different neighbourhoods. On Fish Hoek Main Road, patterns of consumption separate the spaces that young people use. Young residents of Masiphumelele and Ocean View tend to frequent the supermarket and games shops at one end of the high street, whereas middle-class children are to be found in the banks, boutiques and cafes at the other end. In sharp contrast, middle-class youths in malls in Johannesburg exhibit a consumerist and very explicitly non-racial culture (Nkuna 2006). This discrepancy is an indicator of differences between Cape Town and Johannesburg in the degree of integration between former race groups, and of the growing significance of class as a social marker that transcends 'race' in the latter city.

The beach is a popular destination for children across the research site, and the frequency with which they visited related more to the cost and availability of transport than to differences in their desire to spend time there. Young residents of Ocean View and Masiphumelele visit Fish Hoek beach at weekends, either with family or friends. Children in Fish Hoek who live much closer may visit more frequently, usually in the company of family until they reach their teens. Observing social interaction on the sand, in the play park and in the local cafe, it is quickly evident that the majority of young people socialised with those they came with or others from their own neighbourhoods.

Children from Ocean View or Masiphumelele who attend school in Fish Hoek usually meet their friends from other neighbourhoods in the mall or on the beach. There are few other options. Two girls who live in Ocean View said that their Fish Hoek friends never come to visit them at home, but they brushed this off as unproblematic because they enjoy spending time elsewhere, and 'there is nothing to do in Ocean View'.

In summary, all children spoke positively about being able to spend time in and use these spaces, in part because they offer interesting shopping and leisure potential, but also because they offer a different and more diverse social environment than their respective neighbourhoods. For the small minority of children who have established friendships with those living in other neighbourhoods through school or church (see below), these places provide a venue for meeting and strengthening relationships. However, the majority of children in the Valley walk, shop, play and 'hang out' alongside their peers from other neighbourhoods, but experience little, if any, conversation or interaction of a quality necessary to form relationships and alter stereotypes. There is some evidence that this changes for adolescents who find work in shops at the mall. We turn now to consider institutions that offer the potential for a deeper level of social interaction due to their particular nature and objectives.

Churches and development organisations

Churches play an important part in the lives of many young people in every neighbourhood across the Valley – as is the case across South Africa as a whole. Nationally, one survey conducted in 2003 found that just under half of young adults aged 18–35 reported attending a religious ceremony at least once a week; one-third do so occasionally; and one-fifth never do so (Emmett et al. 2003: 202). One decade earlier, more than half of women aged 16–30 reported attending church at least once a week, compared to just over one-third of men of the same age (Everatt & Orkin 1993: 8). Then, only a tiny proportion said that they never attended church. These findings indicate that church and other religious institutions remain a key feature of the majority of young adults' lives, but are becoming less central over time for a minority (and perhaps especially so for those in their early 30s). Our analysis of the 2005 Cape Area Study showed that approximately a quarter of adults in Cape Town said that, of all the groups and organisations in which they participated, their church was the most important to them. Of this quarter, most said that their church brought together people not only from different neighbourhoods and levels of income or education, but also from different racial groups. Surveys can shed light on reported attendance, but ethnography illuminates the nature of interaction that occurs in churches with a mixed membership.

A large proportion of our participants across the Valley attend church on a regular basis for Sunday services and youth activities in the evenings. They often referred to the importance of God, the church, and their faith in their everyday lives. While most are members of a very local church, some children from all three neighbourhoods travel to other neighbourhoods weekly or sporadically for special events. There they participate in services and youth activities with people from a range of class and 'race' backgrounds. Portia, a 12-year-old resident of Masiphumelele, attends an independent church on Fish Hoek Main Road whenever she has money for the taxi and enjoys the music and activities laid on for young people. On Saturdays she often goes to Sun Valley to see her (white middle-class) friend, whom she met at church. Lindiwe, a 14-year-old, uses the free taxi provided to residents of Masiphumelele by a church in Fish Hoek and during the research period was attending three times a week. She spoke about feeling content and 'big' at church, but made no mention of particular friendships developed there. By contrast, very few of the young people living in Fish Hoek and its environs attend churches in Masiphumelele or Ocean View. A number of churches in the Fish Hoek neighbourhood actively seek to involve young people from throughout the Valley, such as Portia and Lindiwe, bringing them together for events and outings. Such efforts are greeted positively by middle-class teenagers because they appreciate the rare opportunity to meet peers from other neighbourhoods:

> I go to the New Apostolic Church in Sun Valley, and we often have
> events and outings with youth groups from churches in Ocean View and
> Masiphumelele, as well as churches from other areas in Cape Town. I
> really enjoy this, because I really like meeting new people from different
> places. (Virginia, girl, aged 17, Fish Hoek resident)

We point out that these efforts towards integration involve the movement of poor residents of Masiphumelele and Ocean View into the middle-class neighbourhoods and social spaces. Much less frequently did we encounter movement in the opposite direction. Even camps and outings elsewhere are held in areas much less familiar to poor children than their middle-class peers and are, therefore, not the neutral spaces that the adult organisers may assume them to be. While churches are clearly able to bolster the depth and quality of social interaction among young people from different neighbourhoods, they are repeating the existing one-way trend in children's movements from poor to middle-class areas and reinforcing perceptions of status and identity that accompany these.

Other churches have attempted to play a role in integration, but were discouraged by problems they attributed to so-called cultural differences. One youth worker explained the difficulties in organising events that would appeal to young people across the Valley:

> The things that the youth do there [Ocean View] are very different. It's a
> total cultural thing. Some of their kids came along to one of our worship
> evenings and they hated it; they don't like the music – it's not their style…
> then they want our kids to come to a fashion show in Ocean View and
> our kids are like, 'fashion show?' They don't enjoy the same things.
> It's a cultural thing: if you don't enjoy the same music it doesn't work.
> (Interview with two church youth workers in Fish Hoek)

Discussed in more detail below, young people also draw attention to the variation in music tastes and styles of social interaction between neighbourhoods and the way these can create obstacles to feeling comfortable in each other's social spaces. In addition, certain habits and perceptions that derive from racially and spatially segregated thinking limit possibilities for social integration in churches. Later on in the conversation quoted above, one youth worker alluded to these by noting that each neighbourhood had its 'own' church and pointing to the barriers to travel – economic in the case of poor communities, and normative for all and perhaps especially middle-class ones (as evident from the youth worker's expression 'trek out there' in the following interview):

> Interviewer: And in your church, do you have people from other areas?

> Very few, I mean we are the Baptist Church of Fish Hoek and they have their own Baptist Church in Ocean View and Masi. We are affiliated slightly, but don't really get together. They have their own churches in the area they can walk to so they don't bother coming here and we are not going to trek out there… (Interview with two church youth workers in Fish Hoek)

Like many churches, one of the major goals of the local youth-oriented organisation OIL (mentioned in the preceding chapters) is to promote connections across neighbourhoods. It is interesting to look carefully at what this organisation has tried to achieve precisely because there is no equivalent institution for adults. Moreover, the organisation is explicit in its aim to empower young people with the ability to make positive choices, which would presumably include the ability to construct alternative social identities. OIL's core activity is to train teenagers attending four high schools in the southern peninsula to be 'peer educators' and get involved in local development, advocacy for young people and service facilitation. Every three months, OIL organises 'LubeLounge', an evening of workshops and celebrity presentations on youth issues involving all trainees. Held in the Simon's Town navy base and with free transport for all attending, this event is warmly received by teenagers for its unusual qualities:

> It is so nice to be in a place where we don't even think of the colour of our skin and hug our friends from different communities. (Brian, boy, aged 17, Ocean View)

The relative success of OIL's activities in enabling young people to build friendships and create social networks across the Valley appears to stem from regular inclusive events, like LubeLounge, and the sustained involvement of young people over time. That said, during the period we conducted fieldwork, events involving children from diverse neighbourhhoods were always held in predominantly middle-class Fish Hoek (or in Simon's Town, where OIL also worked), and never in Masiphumelele or Ocean View. The fact that there are large community halls in both these neighbourhoods suggests a persistent hierarchy in people's minds about the accessibility or appropriateness of certain places for community events. Another limiting factor in young people's eyes was the tendency for OIL and other NGOs to structure activities along educational or community-development lines. Such an approach provided interesting topics for debate, but allowed little time for 'hanging out' with those from elsewhere in the Valley, or for the organic, adolescent-initiated growth of activities evident in Art Vibrations in Ocean View (described in Chapter 3). It may also have inadvertently reinforced white middle-class notions of how young people should spend their time, thereby devaluing forms of socialising common in Masiphumelele and Ocean View. In these ways, even the most well-intentioned initiatives inadvertently reinforce social boundaries within the Valley.

Crossing boundaries

As we have seen, the Valley contains a few large public spaces, such as the mall and the beach, that are shared by large numbers of residents from all neighbourhoods, as well as the smaller forums of mixed churches and development organisations frequented by a smaller number of young people. Evidence suggesting that these shared spaces appear to have made minimal difference to perceptions of 'other' neighbourhoods and the interaction between them raises the question of what happens when young people cross these boundaries. Upon being questioned, young people pointed to the significance of prior knowledge and familiarity based on shared neighbourhoods, and of individual attitudes that arise from experiences of interaction with those from other backgrounds in their early childhood or recent past:

> Interviewer: If you were here in the mall and you walked up to a group of teenagers of another 'colour' group, and started chatting, what do you think would happen?

> Ronaldo and Chloe: You would only do that if you knew someone in that group, and then you'd go up to that person and say 'hi', and perhaps they'd introduce you to some of the others. If it was a group from your neighbourhood, then you'd just go on up, but not if they are all strangers. They'd look at you weirdly if you did that.

> Ronaldo: But I never have a problem introducing myself to people I don't know, as I mix easily in all groups and always have done [our observations confirm this aspect of his personality]. So I'd be very comfortable no matter where they are from.

> Interviewer: Why do you think this is so?

> Ronaldo: I've been interacting with white people for a long time, and I know lots of people who live around the Valley from OIL. Remember that I went to pre-school in Fish Hoek with the daughter of my mum's employer – she and my mommy were very close and still are. So I used to come to Fish Hoek after school – almost every day, usually with my sister, to spend time with her daughter and all the other friends used to come round as well. We still keep up. She is now in matric year at Fish Hoek Senior High.

> Chloe: It's very different here in the mall as compared to say an OIL camp where you are in a particular area living with these people and you *have* to mix. Once you're there, you just get on with it and it's easy, and nice.

> Ronaldo: And for teenagers who go to a multicultural church it's like that too, you know individual people on the one hand and because you're familiar with a mixed environment you don't feel shy of other races.

The young researchers, Chloe from Masiphumelele and Ronaldo from Ocean View, remind us of what is an obvious compass to social interaction in public spaces within the Valley, namely the fact that young people know or at least recognise those from their own neighbourhoods. The fact that each neighbourhood is fairly small and has one high school means that personal recognition is a primary guide to initiating interaction rather than a notion of shared 'race'. Ronaldo attributes his comfort among residents of all neighbourhoods to his early childhood experiences of attending pre-school in Fish Hoek where the majority of children were white and middle class, and to the long-standing, close friendship between his mother and her white middle-class employer. Chloe, by contrast, had negative early experiences of those she grew to understand as 'white' and 'coloured' – even though she lived in a largely 'white' neighbourhood for some years. Chloe reported her nervousness about joining OIL and our 'mixed' research team, and went on to explain why in the following interview.

> Chloe: Remember that my uncle was fighting with Umkhonto we Sizwe[3] and he'd indoctrinated us with all this 'whites are evil' stuff, so that's the way I thought. Also, when we were living in Kommetjie the white kids used to be really nasty to us, calling us horrible names, saying about my little brother 'look at that little monkey'. And the white lady who my granny worked for, and with whom we lived…she used to treat us pretty bad, getting us to do all her dirty work like taking all the bugs out of the house. But we didn't mind her because she was old, and also getting sick. She had a brain tumour.

> Interviewer: And what about coloured people?

> Chloe: Well I was scared of them, as I just knew that they are corrupt and nasty. The little children in Ocean View used to chase us on our bicycles when we were walking from Masi to Kommetjie.

Chloe's confidence grew as a result of attending OIL camps and having the opportunity to learn counselling with two OIL female staff who encouraged her to be open about her own feelings. She recalls her initial reluctance to talk to the 'white lady' and the shift that occurred once she had voiced the above experiences and perceptions to this woman's colleague, who was African. The experiences of these two teenagers indicates that young people are better equipped to cross boundaries of various types when they have had informal or formal opportunities for in-depth social interaction of the kind through which friendship and trust can be established, and which involves both adults and children.

Schooling and social integration

Schools are widely reputed to be potential frontiers for social change in South Africa because they offer the opportunity for regular and sustained interaction between children from different neighbourhoods – and, therefore, 'race' and class groups. Such a reputation has prompted research into this potential. Crain Soudien (2001, 2004, 2007) undertook surveys, observations and interviews among high-school children attending 'mixed' schools in Cape Town, and worked in schools in the Eastern Cape and KwaZulu-Natal over a 10-year period. Nadine Dolby (2001) conducted an ethnographic study of social relationships following racial desegregation of a Durban high school in 1996. Subsequently, Marcelle Dawson (2003) looked at youth identities in a school in Pretoria and Carolyn McKinney (2007) explored the role of language – specifically different kinds of English – in identity formation in desegregated high schools in Johannesburg. This body of work showed race was still a primary marker of social identities in these schools, and that young people use and reinforce these categories while at the same time resisting and negotiating racial identities. Soudien (2001: 314) finds that 'the identities young people develop are internally divided…Their identities are…of their apartheid past, but simultaneously against it'. He concludes that despite the official government ideology of non-racialism, racial tensions have not disappeared, and that students struggle to evade the racialising structures in which they find themselves.

A notable limitation of Soudien's early work is that he paid little attention to other aspects of identity than race and considers only the racial categories used by the apartheid state. The possible roles of class, language, religion and values relating to work or education in identity formation were thereby obscured, making it difficult to understand whether 'race' was acting as a trope to mark other social differences. In a recent synthesis of his own and others' findings, Soudien (2007) looks at the roles of class, national identity, gender, schooling and race in shaping youth identities.

Dolby's research interrogated the meaning of 'race' in young people's social interaction at a deeper level. Working for one year in a formerly 'white' school in which two-thirds of the students were African or coloured and the majority of teachers white, she examined young people's construction of racial identities and the social dynamics among pupils and in pupil–teacher interaction. She found that a discourse of race remains prominent in the assertion of identity, but that young people draw on a different set of references than those of biology, 'culture' and history used by the apartheid state and among the adult generation. The references used in this environment are those of style and taste, for example music, clothing and clubs. African (or 'black') pupils define 'blackness' not in terms of Zulu tradition ('This is the [19]90s,' one girl protests to a white teacher, who anachronistically imagines that isiZulu-speaking girls attend the 'traditional' Zulu reed dance), but in terms of global African-American culture (and icons such as Michael Jackson, Michael Jordan, Whitney Houston and top rap artists). The use of style and symbols of popular culture means that a 'racial' identity does not necessarily correlate with skin colour: a girl can be seen to be 'black' because of her clothing style, even though her skin is 'white'. This allows individuals to manipulate the identity they wish to present and shows a certain transience to a 'racial' identity. At the same time, the fact that those who do so risk being scorned and ostracised points to young people's continued use of 'race', as defined by their own cultural markers of style, to police social interaction in the peer group. They also persistently associate certain music genres with each 'race' group (Dawson 2003; Dolby 2001). Consequently, argue Dolby and Dawson, these students are themselves actively reproducing racial difference and division.

A small minority of pupils attending schools in Ocean View and Fish Hoek live outside the neighbourhood and/or are from different 'race' groups. Schools in Masiphumelele are similarly officially racially desegregated, but the pupil body comprises only local residents and a few isiXhosa-speaking children living in Ocean View or Red Hill (an informal settlement near Simon's Town). In Ocean View, the majority of teachers are 'coloured' and speak either Afrikaans, English or both. At secondary-school level, students are divided into two classes and are taught in one of these languages, meaning that first-language isiXhosa speakers from Masiphumelele are put in the English-medium class. In Fish Hoek, the majority of teachers are white English and Afrikaans speakers and although there are a few 'coloured' and African members of the staff body, the sole language used for instruction and administration is English. Like the Durban school that Dolby studied, schools in Fish Hoek strive to maintain aspects of their former 'white' or 'model C' identities through the sports they offer and the network of schools with which they organise sports matches and other competitions.

Schools at a distance of 40 kilometres from Fish Hoek are part of this network, yet the nearby Ocean View and Masiphumelele schools are not. These historically initiated, but actively sustained, associations speak volumes about the official identities schools wish to preserve. Ocean View schools compete against other 'coloured' schools across Cape Town, whereas Masiphumelele High School organises fixtures with counterparts in the large townships of Khayelitsha, Gugulethu and Langa.

The way that schools are run reinforces ideas of difference based on 'race'. In both Ocean View and Fish Hoek, pupils whose first language was not the one used by the school administration were told that they should not speak to each other using their mother tongue. Reasons of school policy were often given, but these children felt that teachers and fellow pupils were uncomfortable because they could not understand and, therefore, feared that they were being talked about.

Anyone entering the grounds of Fish Hoek Middle and Senior High schools or Ocean View Secondary School would soon observe that children in the playground tend to be with others of the same 'race'. The initial impression, therefore, is that 'race' is critical to these learners' identities and delineates certain boundaries in their formation of social relationships. Here the value of an ethnographic approach is affirmed, for it is only once one gains insight into individual lives and the nature of friendships among these young people that a more accurate understanding of the place of 'race' in school and in youth interaction more broadly emerges.

In getting to know teenagers attending school in Fish Hoek whose skin colour would have placed them in different racial categories, it soon became clear that in terms of their sense of self and their everyday social interaction with peers, race is not the only, or even the strongest, determinant of identity. Francis, aged 19 and at school in Fish Hoek, considers herself 'African' – not in the sense of a colour or racial category, but owing to her Tanzanian and South African heritage. For Francis, language has been a source of inclusion and exclusion. She speaks fluent English at school and with her friends outside school, but speaks both Swahili and isiXhosa at home (her mother's and father's languages). Francis commented:

> I do not really identify with being Xhosa. Most people in Masiphumelele, where my father now lives, consider me an outsider because of my English accent. (Francis, girl, aged 19, Fish Hoek)

In the same way, skin colour and any notions of 'race' are portrayed as unimportant in the formation of friendships between individuals. Young people assert that personality, trustworthiness and sharing the same interests and morals are critical to friendship formation. In the following vignettes pertaining to three teenagers attending Fish Hoek Senior High School, we see that family heritage (regardless of 'colour'), religious faith, shared values and long-established friendships are much stronger shapers of identity and of important social relationships than 'race':

> Konrad avoided classifying himself or others in a racial sense and never used any racial categories voluntarily. Even when directly asked if school was mixed, he avoided answering in any detail and said, 'Probably most people are white.' I assumed him to be 'white', but when I visited his home and saw his photographs I realised some family members have 'coloured' physical traits, and he has a surname indicating a possible 'coloured' heritage. He was born in a 'mixed' area of Cape Town and has lived and attended school in Sun Valley since moving there when he was four years old. A photograph of his church youth group shows what he called 'a mixed bunch'. He indicated that his faith and his long-term friends from church are very important to him: 'We help each other, we are quite close…[when you have a problem] you can go to whoever you are comfortable with.' Fish Hoek Middle School also brought him into contact with diversity: 'I only met Xhosa speakers in the last few years. There were also some foreigners, like I had a friend from Zaire…there were some Chinese and some from Belgium, Canada, US, Germany.' (Excerpt from field notes)

> Thayo and Leanne are good friends, and neither of them spoke in racial terms about others or themselves. Both of them identified themselves primarily as Christians: 'It's about a lifestyle and keeping certain values.' They agreed their faith influences who they are friends with, but skin colour or background has no bearing on this. Thayo mentioned the fact that she is Zimbabwean, pointing out she did not grow up with the South African way of categorising people. Both indicated that most of their best friends are from church, although Thayo has a mixed group of friends at school and spent a lot of time with Francis, quoted above, whose father is South African and mother is Tanzanian. (Excerpt from field notes)

Earlier we noted the high levels of mobility and family reorganisation among middle-class children in Fish Hoek. The fact that many pupils at the school were born outside Fish Hoek, had moved several times during their childhood, had experienced varying household compositions and were anticipating moving out of the Valley indicates a high level of diversity and movement in their everyday lives. In other words, many categories that appear fixed by values attached to a middle-class lifestyle – such as the family, home and neighbourhood – are in fact fluid and changeable. In a context in which other important markers of identity are prone to change, it is not surprising that notions of 'race' are also fluid and contingent in their salience to children's everyday lives.

For pupils at Fish Hoek Senior High School, colour or 'race' are not experienced as critical in the formation of friendships or even in constructing personal identities. At the same time, they use 'race' as a label with which to characterise themselves and others. Our data show that these learners use a vocabulary of colour and interact with their peers on the basis of notions of similarity or difference that mimic old ideas of 'race', but are not directly equivalent.

Teenagers commented on the obvious coloured, African and white groups at school, saying 'especially coloureds stick together, and will also stick up for each other no matter what'. They said that these allegiances are problematic and irritating because incidents are made into 'a race issue', even when the context is not understood. For example, when a grade-11 student was reprimanded by a grade-12 student for standing in the tuck shop queue reserved for the higher-grade students, his 'coloured' friends immediately came to join in the argument and accused the grade-12 student of being racist.

Despite the racial labelling used, it transpired that group formation in the playground is more connected to place and community identity than to skin colour or 'race'. Francis (who is African and lives in Fish Hoek) reported: 'When I first came to school, the Masi group expected me to join them…but I just held back to see which people I would relate to.' She subsequently made good friends with a couple of (white) girls who live in her neighbourhood. So it is not a sense of shared 'blackness' that draws a group of friends together, but a shared sense of 'Masiphumelele-ness' – a source of identity that has much more to do with styles of language and social interaction used in a particular neighbourhood than with notions of 'race'.

Conversation with pupils in Fish Hoek revealed an interesting internal contradiction in the way they speak about their personal friends and about the neighbourhoods where these friends live. Unsurprisingly, their descriptions of their friends (who happened to live in Ocean View or Masiphumelele) emphasised the similarities in their interests, values and tastes in music or fashion. However, they clearly felt no connection with, and even some fear or antipathy towards, the areas where their friends live. One of the grade-9 boys commented: 'Our friends from Masi would not invite us [to their homes], and we wouldn't go anyway. We don't want to say this in their face, but we would never come to sleep over.' Although no reasons were given for the impossibility of visiting Masiphumelele, we are reminded of the sensationalist and negative representations of 'other' communities vocalised during map work.

Moreover, the lack of any reference to poverty raises the possibility that middle-class children are reluctant to confront and engage with the huge disparities between their own wealth and resources and those of their friends.

Rather than attempting to engage with their friends' home context, young people tended to dissociate them from their environment and include them in a group of 'us' in the school context. This way they successfully avoided having to confront experiences and notions that did not fit into their ideals pertaining to equality. Such a strategy is useful in the short term for sustaining friendships in a highly racially segregated area. But it curtails friendship's scope to confront and question stereotypes with knowledge that is based on experience. For example, such friendships could enable middle-class children to observe how children and their families manage income poverty, and for poor children may act as a point of access into social networks with greater social and economic capital.

When two teenagers from Fish Hoek were speaking about this issue it soon became evident that they were consciously trying to avoid using racial terminology for political reasons and because it did not fit with their experience. However, they quickly found themselves talking in terms of 'black people' and 'coloureds' or 'coloured people' and hesitantly making comments about 'them'. They confessed they would probably not have spoken so openly had Francis (who is 'African' or 'black') or 'lots of coloured people' been present, as they 'might be hurt or take it the wrong way'.

A similar tension exists between the persistent assertion of the irrelevance of race – the sense that 'we are all the same' or 'everyone is friends at school' – and the labelling of others according to their colour. Like the Durban school students researched by Dolby (2001), pupils in Fish Hoek experience and use racial categorisation in fluid ways based on styles of clothing, speech, body posture, demeanour and social associations. Darren lives in Fish Hoek and would be classified coloured, but actively tries to dissociate himself from the behaviour of a group of 'coloureds' at school (who are mostly from Ocean View and are considered 'common'). He describes the group as follows:

> They walk with a bounce like in American movies, speak loudly, use a mix of lazy English and *kombuis* Afrikaans, are disrespectful towards teachers, and think they are cool, but generally act very immature. [*Kombuis* is Afrikaans for 'kitchen', in this case indicating a simplified, slang form of the language.] (Darren, boy, aged 17, Fish Hoek)

Teenagers recognise that individual behaviour is strongly influenced by the group effect and express some ambivalence around the validity of such classifications, yet they continue to draw on internalised stereotypes in the way they explain 'acting a colour'.

Darren's classmate, Virginia ('white'), laughingly recounted that a few years ago people around her were calling her C.I.T. Amused at the researcher's ignorant expression, other pupils explained that this means 'coloured in training' and was used because she was hanging out with a group of 'coloured' friends at school. Other humorous labels given to those trying to 'act' another colour include 'wannabe white'; 'top deck' (chocolate that has a black and white layer); 'coconut' (black on the outside and white on the inside); and 'half a naartjie' (a variety of orange). (Virginia showed us photographs of her family on the walls of her home and it emerged that she has some coloured heritage, but is seen as white.)

Importantly, while these labels are usually intended as playful insults, young people often actively reject or manipulate them in a way that enables them to assert an alternative identity by 'acting' in the appropriate way and to build friendships across racial boundaries. Yet over time, persistent reminders by peers that they are transgressing certain social codes by subverting their ascribed 'colour' identity often cause young people to abandon friendships with those living in other neighbourhoods.

Interesting in this regard, for example, are the reaction of one of Virginia's best friends at Fish Hoek Senior High School, Justin, to her socialising with 'coloured' friends and her response to this. Justin made regular comments about Virginia's lifestyle, friends and boyfriends, and was a little disapproving of her association with the coloured group and the way she was behaving at the time. She acknowledged: 'I did speak like them [in *kombuis* Afrikaans] when I was with them…it was just natural. People still diss me about it, but I don't take offence to that any more.' She later admitted that she did behave differently herself. More recently, Virginia cut ties with this group after a major argument with her best friend. Having realised that people were talking about her behind her back, she no longer goes to Ocean View. Her decision has attracted the attention of her peers, and she expresses frustration at the associations made between the 'colour' of one's actions and differential status (the significance of such assertions of hierarchy we return to below):

> Now that I have a white boyfriend I get comments from classmates that I have 'gone back to white'. My coloured friends tell me to 'take off my high shoes' and say I am 'acting white' again. By this they mean being all high and mighty…I don't like this at all, because people see white as higher, which really it is not! (Virginia, aged 17, group discussion)

Melissa Steyn (2001: 149), in her study of whiteness in South Africa, reminds us that 'boundaries, to those who have experienced crossing them, become a matter of play rather than an obsession'. Virginia's experiences are interesting with regard to differences among young people in mixed environments in the possibilities they have for overcoming boundaries. Virginia is considered white, and successfully adopted, albeit temporarily, a coloured identity. The objection raised by her coloured friends living in Ocean View to her returning to 'white' suggests that they see themselves as less able to overcome boundaries and play with their identities in the same way. The more rigid sanctions imposed on those attempting to change their identities in Ocean View may be related to the higher levels of racial discrimination experienced in schools in Ocean View compared to Fish Hoek (discussed earlier in the chapter).

Looking closely at Fish Hoek students' ability to play with overtly racial terms, the persistence of certain 'boundaries' becomes evident at the points at which such play is not considered appropriate or legitimate. One of these pertains to the normative code surrounding romantic relationships. Teenagers concurred that, although some white girls have African or coloured boyfriends that they meet outside school, mixed couples are rare and attract attention within the school premises. One (white) teenager cited an example of a white girl dating a black classmate, saying that there was a lot of whispering and 'did you know…?' in the corridors. Her (African) friend added '…and if a black girl would date a white guy…[rolling her eyes]…ooooh!' They quickly added that this had never occurred at their school.

A second limitation to young people's ability to play with and undermine notions of race is found in their relationships with adults. Recognising that the generation above them grew up in a very different political environment, children are careful in their use of racialised language in the company of adults because they predict that their words will be misinterpreted. Through experience, young people have learnt that the older generation has not crossed old boundaries through friendships in the way that they have. As Konrad explains:

> Race really isn't an issue among my group of friends – we are a mixed
> bunch and don't talk about each other in 'that way'. Only when we are
> joking around we use words like 'nigga', to call each other's attention.
> It has nothing to do with a racial issue, it's more like from a movie or
> something. We make jokes like 'why, is it because I am white?' But we
> really don't see it as colour. Our parents probably see it different because
> of apartheid; they might take it the wrong way…it's just for us because we
> are not affected. We are not racist towards each other. But we wouldn't say
> it to just anyone: you have to know who you can joke with.

Students in Fish Hoek reported that race-based language is used in corridor disputes but that there is little, if any, racism between pupils. The only complaints of discrimination related to school rules pertaining to language and the actions of adult teachers:

> The teachers won't allow me and my friends to speak Xhosa; they say
> 'we speak English here'. But then they allow Afrikaans; because they
> can understand. You see they don't understand what we say in Xhosa.
> (Thando, boy, aged 15, resident of Masiphumelele at school in Fish Hoek)

By contrast, overt racism towards pupils and teachers is commonplace in Ocean View Secondary School. Gift, one of the young researchers, recalled that he and his six other isiXhosa-speaking friends at Ocean View Secondary School were forced by older coloured pupils to hand over their lunch money of R2 each day. Although this form of bullying is widespread among coloured boys, Gift perceived it as racist behaviour. During our observation at the school we witnessed isiXhosa-speaking children being reprimanded by teachers for responding in kind to racist comments from local coloured learners. One of the teenagers said that every day he and his African friends are called 'black' in various derogatory ways. Adhikari (2005) argues that a racialised conception of 'colouredness' has grown stronger since the end of apartheid. This, he suggests, has renewed affinities to whiteness and deepened racism towards African people. And although racist behaviour was observed in only the minority in Ocean View, 'white' people are similarly maligned. These practices appear to be part of a wider set of attitudes and behaviours in which putting others down seems to have become a way of coping with bleak prospects (see also Chapters 3 and 6).

Teenagers at school in Fish Hoek are often aware of the persistent tension they confront between an ideology of 'non-difference' across former race groups and the daily experience of racial labelling. Yet their awareness does not seem to translate into an ability to resolve the tension in any other way than divorcing individuals from their context in ways described above. Their reluctance to use a language of race when describing diversity within their peer group, and particularly in relation to friendships, suggests that they consider it unsatisfactory. One reason for their discomfort appears to be a sense that it is not appropriate or acceptable to talk about race in the new South Africa, or even that they are tired of hearing about apartheid and the onus placed on race.

But teenagers in grade 9 pointed out that it is difficult to know how to speak. One of the boys commented: 'If you describe someone as black you are racist! But if he is, what am I supposed to say? Do I say he is really tall and...uhm...?' Francis, who would be considered African or black, asserts a wish to avoid using the word 'black', yet in conversations finds herself referring to 'black people'. Thus it appears that young people lack an alternative vocabulary with which to articulate the affinities and differences they encounter. As we have amply demonstrated, most young people in the Valley have little or no knowledge of the home and community environments of their peers who live in other neighbourhoods. Without the opportunity to observe and analyse their experiences of everyday life in areas outside their own, children and adolescents are unable to construct alternative explanations for the variation in ways of understanding and responding to the world around them. Very seldom, for example, did we hear young people articulate difference on the basis of class, language or cultural practice. The rare exceptions were those who were familiar with another neighbourhood and had made close friendships across neighbourhood boundaries.

For example, 17-year-old Veronique lives in Ocean View and during the two-year period she attended Fish Hoek Middle School made close friends with a girl who lives in Capri, a middle-class and predominantly white area in the Valley. They go to parties together in Capri and Veronique sleeps over at her friend's house. She once took a friend from Ocean View to one of these parties and observed her struggling to fit in. Veronique's reflections about how her friend felt, and why, convey an awareness of the particular manner in which difference is experienced, and what is required to manage or overcome these differences:

> She wasn't very happy...you see she'd never been to a party with just white people before. My white friends behave differently to my coloured friends. My white friends act more childlike, making stupid jokes and laughing at

silly things. My coloured friends wouldn't stand for this sort of thing – they always have a lot to say and act older than what they are. Also, my friend struggles with English as Afrikaans is her first language, so she felt a bit left out. (Veronique, girl, aged 17, Ocean View)

Veronique's comments show that difference is experienced not in terms of 'race' per se, but in terms of language and style of interaction, including forms of speech and humour. Based on her own experience, she does not see these as insurmountable for her friend, but it is clear that considerable time, effort and costs (in terms of feeling marginalised) are required to learn 'new' rules for the way one parties in another neighbourhood. Veronique, in describing this particular incident, demonstrates an awareness of the boundaries created by language difference and particular cultural practices (see also McKinney 2007). Interestingly, she makes no reference to wealth differences as a factor in her or her friend's interaction with wealthier (white) friends.

Middle-class children are certainly aware that they are, in monetary terms at least, wealthier than most children in Ocean View and all those in Masiphumelele. But wealth was never mentioned in discussions of diversity. Reasons for this silence are likely to include some discomfort at historical and contemporary economic privilege, as well as the absence of any direct personal knowledge about what poverty means in terms of its impact on their peers. The fact that they do not spend time in poor neighbourhoods means that they are unable to develop a nuanced understanding of family life and community interaction, including the positive aspects of these that undermine the apparent homogeneity of the term 'poor'. The picture is literally 'black and white' and is described as such by those children who have been unable to build relationships that allow them to move in and out of neighbouring areas.

Studies in other countries have found that the manner in which categories of ethnicity and 'culture' are naturalised in broader society places structural limits on young people's creativity in producing alternative social identities. In a study by Hall (1995) of the manner in which British-born Sikh teenagers negotiate their identities, cultural difference is found to be a social construct that has become naturalised by wider society. In contemporary South African society, the same can be said for racial difference, an invented construct that has become 'real' through persistent unequal treatment by the state, and along with this 'reality' has come to assume a 'natural' status.

Finally, while we have shown that schools offer a fertile ground for the formation of friendships across neighbourhood and 'race' boundaries, they are but one significant sphere of children's social worlds. It is telling that the friendships straddling neighbourhoods that children described as having intimacy and empathy are those that develop in several spheres of their lives. For example, the respective children attend the same school, play in the same sports team and are members of the same church. Such friendships are very difficult to maintain beyond the school grounds (except occasionally through church youth clubs and organisations like OIL) because of costly public transport, reliance on parents to drive them, safety-related fears and other difficulties that children experience in moving between neighbourhoods.

Conclusion

This chapter opened with a question: is this generation of young people living in a more integrated society than that of their parents' childhood? Our analysis has offered an important component of the response through its insights into young people's mobility and their use and understanding of historically entrenched ways of classifying people and the social world. A fuller answer is only possible when these are laid alongside other facets of children's social and cultural lives, and through an exploration of change in the relationship between the actions of the young and the structures of society. This is the work of the book as a whole, and is, therefore, a story that will unfold with each chapter.

Our findings show that the extent to which young people move around, and where they go, are critical factors in their sense of social identity. Striking differences exist between neighbourhoods in the Valley. Differences, for example, in the very limited mobility of Ocean View residents, the frequent geographical movement between kin in distant and nearby poor neighbourhoods by most young people in Masiphumelele and the extensive mobility of many Fish Hoek residents. Long-standing familial associations and current economic restrictions mean that young people largely move in physical and social spheres distinct to their neighbourhood and its history. Across the Valley, few children or adolescents spent any time in the homes, streets and public facilities of other nearby neighbourhoods. And when they did so, it was those from poorer neighbourhoods entering wealthier ones. The young buy into and reinforce negative stereotyping of 'other' neighbourhoods because so few have personal experiences to challenge these. And for those living in Ocean View, who are consistently portrayed least favourably, the social identities ascribed through these processes shape their personal responses to educational and lifestyle challenges.

The context of minimal, one-directional mobility between neighbourhoods demanded careful scrutiny of the nature of social interaction that occurs in shared spaces and institutions. We have shown that the commercial and leisure spaces used by large numbers of children in the Valley afford only very limited social interaction between those from different neighbourhoods. Even in these spaces, young people tend to socialise with their friends, who almost always live in the same neighbourhood. For the vast majority, spending time in shops and on the beach with peers from other neighbourhoods is only symbolic of the potential for crossing these boundaries. Evidence of this potential is found in the fact that the local shopping mall and beach are the chosen meeting places for the few children who have been able to forge friendships across neighbourhoods.

Our data point to the critical role played by schools, churches and development organisations in providing the physical and social space in which young people can interact with their peers from other neighbourhoods on a theoretically equal footing. Friendships begun in these settings have evolved beyond the period in which children shared the space on a regular basis, thereby demonstrating the potential of these institutions to enable the crossing of neighbourhood boundaries.

As yet, there are too few settings and networks of relationships in the Valley for the young – or, for that matter, the older generation – to build familiarity and replace assumptions with knowledge of the physical places and everyday lives of neighbouring communities. Moreover, ethnographic analysis of relationships in the Fish Hoek schools tells us that one aspect of the way young people are managing their personal relationships does not require them to confront their assumptions about a neighbourhood and its residents. When interacting with friends living in different neighbourhoods on an everyday basis, young people recognise similar values, tastes and interests. Yet when speaking about the communities in which their friends live (or even a group of people from that area), they use blanket generalisations and even stereotypes. This disjuncture indicates young people's inability to marry their personal experiences of similarity and connectedness within a peer group of mixed history, language and residence with prevailing discourses that prioritise difference and separateness. Bolstering the bodily knowledge required to do so involves moving within different physical and social spaces to those frequented by their parents' generation. Most young people desire the opportunity to do so, but costs and safety-related restrictions on their mobility pose obstacles, particularly to children, young adolescents and girls.

Tensions also arise in young people's discourses and actions regarding diversity in the school setting. They actively promote notions of equality and try to avoid using racial terms. Yet at the same time they label certain behaviours as being 'black', 'white', 'coloured' or as aspirational to another colour, and actively police these identities using humour and insults. Reflective conversations revealed that young people are aware of these inconsistencies and suggested that they – perhaps like many adults in the Valley – had no alternative vocabulary for expressing lines of difference. We attribute their silence regarding income, resources and sociocultural differences to a lack of opportunity to spend time in each other's homes and neighbourhoods, observing and forming opinions.

In the context of a personal identity and everyday social interaction with peers, 'race' is not the only, or even the strongest, determinant of identity. Friendships are formed and sustained across colour boundaries, especially if young people are able to spend time together in contexts other than school, for example sports teams or church youth groups. Individuals can manipulate their own colour identity by both adopting certain styles of dress, music and language and choosing to socialise with friends from other neighbourhoods. For many, this is a fragile process that requires much effort and resilience owing to transport-related challenges and persistent pressure from peers to conform to the rules associated with their 'true' colour. Interestingly, however, for middle-class children who would ordinarily be labelled 'African' or 'black' or 'coloured', friendships, associations and schooling among the (largely white) local population contribute to their successful rejection of an identity constructed on the basis of colour (or notions of race). This finding suggests that differentiation is substantiated on the basis of place of residence (which, in the Valley, equates to class), rather than colour and 'race'.

In summary, colour is an important dimension in young people's constructs of their own and others' identities, but does not mean the equivalent to 'race' as used in the apartheid era and by the adult generation. The playful use of colour labels does not always imply status difference and, when it does so, does not always reinforce the old hierarchy. That said, acute colour-based discrimination persists in certain settings. Most troubling to young residents of Ocean View, its presence is both a consequence of, and acts to reinforce, this neighbourhood's physical, social and political marginalisation.

The legacy of apartheid planning continues in Cape Town's southern peninsula in the association children make between colour and place of residence, and their set of assumptions about what people do in these places. These assumptions often focus on practices that are bizarre, frightening and redolent of something distinctly 'other' and, therefore, serve to sustain young people's immobility. Although only vocalised as core to their identities by residents of Masiphumelele, 'culture' (meaning sets of traditions, beliefs and values) is regarded as a distinguishing feature of the neighbourhoods in the way young people talk about the social geography of the Valley. In everyday interaction, however, cultural differences are experienced at an entirely different level. One of these pertains to language, both in an inability to communicate and in a choice of language style or accent. The other is a matter of style, namely in the choice of dress, use of humour and forms of socialising in the peer group – the cultural differences that young people encounter as they cross 'colour' boundaries in their friendships.

These experiences, while not described as matters of 'culture', illuminate the basis on which young people have formed a different understanding and experience of integration from that of their parents' generation. Adults working in churches, schools and organisations spoke about 'cultural differences' impeding their efforts to facilitate multi-neighbourhood events. Interestingly, these were often presented as insurmountable, and yet the examples given showed that they were referring to differences in style or habit (such as preferred forms of entertainment) of a similar nature to those encountered by children when they attend parties and events in other neighbourhoods. Yet when young people describe these differences they treat them as interesting, humorous, sometimes challenging, but eminently bridgeable gulfs in the way one socialises within the peer group. Most importantly, they see themselves as able to learn about, work with, manage – and even adopt – different styles. 'Cultural differences' are, therefore, not the immovable barriers to social interaction perceived by many adults, but malleable obstacles that can be worked with if individuals are prepared to put time and effort into the process.

5 The real worlds of public schooling

South African schools have high enrolment rates. Even before the South African Schools Act (No. 84 of 1996) made education compulsory 'until the last school day of the year in which [an adolescent] reaches the age of fifteen years or the ninth grade, whichever occurs first', there was already almost total enrolment among this age group. Indeed, many young people remain in school into their late teens and (until recently) even early 20s. School, therefore, accounts for a huge part of the everyday lives of young South Africans. It is also of considerable consequence for their future. The school is a venue in which young people interact with adults and peers alike. It is a social arena as well as a forum for education. In both respects, schools have been the object of significant policy change over the last two decades. This chapter examines schooling in terms of its formal educational dimensions, whilst Chapter 6 turns to schools as social arenas in post-apartheid South Africa.

Schooling after apartheid: Reform without improvement

Schooling under apartheid was characterised by deep inequalities in the allocation of public resources, the quality of education and educational outcomes. Most children classified as white attended well-resourced schools, with well-trained and motivated teachers, and left school after passing the grade 12 or matriculation ('matric') examination. Children classified as African might not have attended school very much at all. The schools they might have attended were poorly resourced, typically with poorly trained, inadequately qualified teachers who relied on rote-teaching. Many African children dropped out of school at a young age; many of those who persisted learnt little; very few completed the long and arduous journey to grade 12; and even fewer actually passed the matric examination. As recently as 1970, the secondary-school enrolment rate among African children was just 16 per cent, compared to 90 per cent among white children (Pillay 1990: 34). Government spending per African child was about 6 per cent of expenditure per white child (Auerbach & Welsh 1981: 79). Children classified as coloured or Indian had experiences somewhere between those of white and African children.

The consequence was considerable inequality in the skills and qualifications attained by South African children. Because education plays such a pivotal role in so many aspects of life, the unequal distribution of skills and qualifications formed the structure of – and deeply scarred – South African society. This was, of course, part of the purpose of differential education: white South Africans were given the advantages of class that enabled overt racial discrimination in the labour market (through the racial colour bar) to be relaxed with little effect on white privilege (Seekings & Nattrass 2005).

The education system did change from the 1970s. In the final two decades of apartheid, both the enrolment rates and real expenditure per pupil rose rapidly among African children. The number of secondary schools in the sprawling townships of Soweto (outside Johannesburg) rose from 8 to 55 in just 12 years (1972–84). Interracial inequality in terms of spending per pupil declined. Nevertheless, when South Africa became a democracy in 1994, its public (i.e. state) school system was still deeply unequal.

Education had been one of the major concerns of the African National Congress (ANC) for decades. 'The doors of learning shall be open,' it proclaimed in the Freedom Charter of 1955. In its election campaign in 1994, the ANC promised reforms that would enable all South African children to realise their full potential (ANC 1994). The ANC has delivered on almost all of its specific promises (see, on Gauteng, Fleisch 2002). The 17 education departments, which were racially – and mostly also regionally – segregated, were forged into a national system, although one with considerable power devolved to the provincial and district levels. Education became compulsory to grade 9. Public funds were reallocated from formerly white schools (and, to a lesser extent, formerly coloured and Indian schools) to formerly African schools, allowing for reductions in their pupil:teacher ratios and improvements in the physical infrastructure of schools. A new curriculum was introduced in 1997, emphasising skill development rather than rote learning. Considerable investments were made in teacher training.

These changes were dramatic in many respects, but perhaps most so in terms of patterns of public expenditure. The new system of allocating public funds was based on standard formulas: teaching posts were allocated according to enrolment; capital funds according to a formula that discriminated in favour of schools in poor neighbourhoods; pay scales were standardised (Seekings 2001). The result was that the estimated share of public funding spent on African pupils rose from about 58 per cent in 1993 to about 79 per cent just four years later, in 1997, whilst the share spent on white pupils declined in the same period from about 22 per cent to 10 per cent (Van der Berg 2006: 210). South Africa spends more of its national income on education (about 7 per cent) than most other countries, and now spends it in an unusually egalitarian manner.

But inequalities in schooling outcomes persist, and the system fails to enable many, or perhaps even most, children to realise their full potential. Furthermore, many children fail to acquire skills and qualifications despite investing many years of effort, and despite the sacrifices made by their families to keep them in school. This has inevitable consequences for individuals' lives and for society as a whole. Poorly educated children enter a labour market offering few opportunities to unskilled workers, and face potentially long periods of unemployment. Their capacity to enter productively into the informal sector is hampered. They are likely to remain poor. Better-educated children are able to take advantage of the burgeoning opportunities for skilled, white-collar and professional employment. This is especially true of better-educated African children, whose prospects are enhanced by affirmative action policies. These inequalities are also likely to be passed onto the next generation. Poor people are more likely to have children with other similarly poor people and to live in neighbourhoods with inferior schools. In most societies, education correlates with attitudes and values, and the persistence of inferior education undermines tolerance and democracy. Inferior education is one factor locking many poor people into an underclass in post-apartheid South Africa, just as access to privileged education for other children allows them to remain in or enter the prosperous middle classes (Seekings & Nattrass 2005).

The only public measure of the quality of education is the matric examination. The government proudly points to improvements in the pass rate since the end of apartheid. The number of passes per year did rise slowly from the late 1990s, but the dramatic improvement in the pass *rate* was due in large part to the dramatic decline in the number of candidates writing the examination between 1998 and the early 2000s (see Figure 5.1). Moreover, a series of studies cast doubt on whether the quality of a matric pass has remained steady over time. Even though the matric exam has probably become easier over time, and the overall pass rate has risen, the pass rates in key subjects remain very low. Only 5 per cent of the half-million candidates who wrote their matric examination in 2006 passed mathematics at the higher grade. Only one in four of the pupils who *passed* matric passed mathematics at *either* the higher *or* standard grade (Taylor 2007b).

Whatever the actual quality of a matric pass, it is evident that only a small proportion of adolescents even get to write the examination. Only about one-third of each age cohort passes matric, primarily because many young people fail to reach grade 12.

Figure 5.1 *Matric candidates and results (1993–2006)*

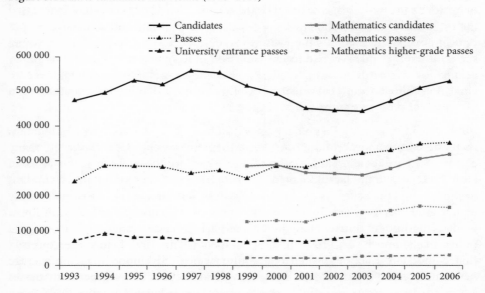

Source: South African Institute of Race Relations (2007)

Figure 5.2 *Grade attainment in the Valley (2001)*

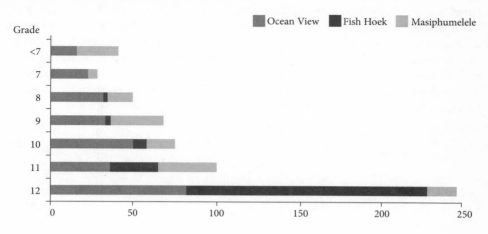

Source: Stats SA (2001)

The Population Census and household surveys indicate that grade attainment – i.e. the highest school grade that people report having completed – has improved over time, but still remains very uneven. Figure 5.2 shows the grade attainment of the approximately 600 young people in the Valley who were aged 19 in 2001, according to that year's census. Of this group, 40 per cent had completed matric, 28 per cent grades 10 or 11 and the remaining 31 per cent grade 9 or less. There are striking differences between the different areas within the Valley. Almost all 19-year-olds in the higher-income areas had passed matric. But large proportions of 19-year-olds in both Ocean View (70 per cent) and Masiphumelele (87 per cent) had not passed matric. Indeed, 39 per cent of 19-year-olds in Ocean View and a massive 53 per cent in Masiphumelele had attained only grade 9 or lower. The numbers of young men and women in Masiphumelele who have not passed matric are swollen by immigration from the rural Eastern Cape, but even taking this into account there are grave inequalities within the Valley. Indeed, the distribution of grade attainment in the different areas of the Valley is a starker, but not atypical, version of the situation in similar areas elsewhere in Cape Town and across South Africa.

Grade attainment, however, is itself an unreliable measure of actual skill acquisition. Many young South Africans sit through years of school without acquiring even basic literacy or numeracy skills. Social promotion (i.e. the promotion of children to higher grades regardless of their skill acquisition) results in children reaching higher grades even when they have not mastered the curriculum taught in lower grades. Intermittent flurries of holding pupils back to repeat grades seems to mitigate rather than remove this problem. This was evident in 1993 before the country's first democratic elections, when one countrywide study found that 'the average African secondary-school leaver, with twelve years' schooling, only narrowly passes a primary-level literacy test, and primary-school leavers fail it miserably' (Moll 1998:

263). Subsequent studies showed similarly alarming results. In 2002, the Cape Area Panel Study (CAPS) conducted a literacy and numeracy evaluation among almost 5 000 young participants. Figure 5.3 shows the combined literacy and numeracy scores for young people who were pupils in 2002, according to the grade in which they were then enrolled. Data are shown only for grades 8, 10 and 12; young people who had dropped out or left school already are omitted. The maximum score was 45. All three lines (corresponding to the three grades) have the shape of an inverted U, with a poor-performing minority, a hump of average performers and a minority of high performers. Adolescents in each grade scored higher than its predecessor, i.e. the grade-10 results are to the right of the grade-8 ones and the grade-12 results are even further to the right. The mean scores rise as students progress through grades. But there is considerable overlap between them. Thus, whilst the poor performers in grade 12 did better than the poor performers in grade 10, who in turn did better than the poor performers in grade 8, it is also true that the top performers in grade 8 scored higher than the worst performers in grade 12.

Cross-national studies show that pupils throughout South Africa perform poorly in comparison to their peers in other countries. In the 2003 round of the Trends in International Mathematics and Science Study (TIMSS), South African grade-8 pupils performed worse in both science and mathematics tests than their counterparts in every other country that participated, including Egypt, Botswana and Ghana. Indeed, the 75th percentile in South Africa achieved about the same score as the 25th percentile in Botswana (Reddy 2006). Other cross-national studies provide a similarly worrying

Figure 5.3 *Test scores by current grade (2002)*

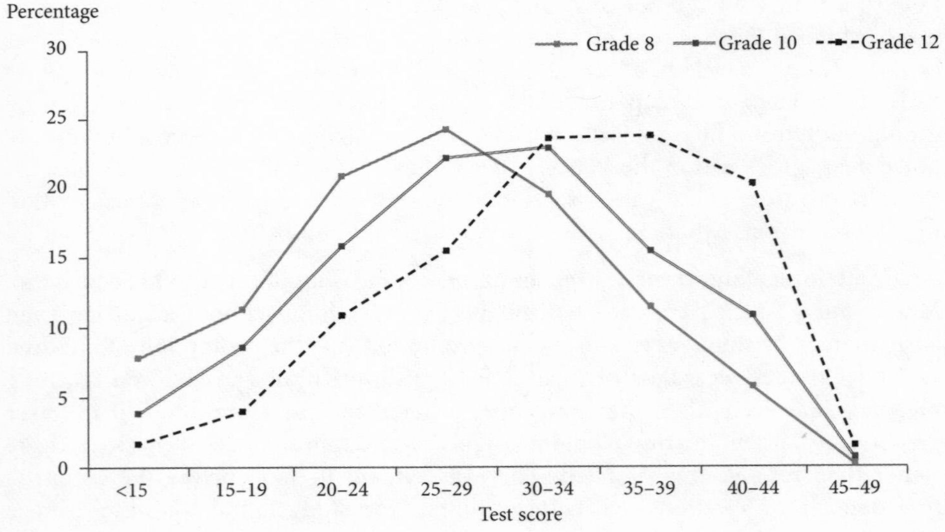

Source: Cape Area Panel Study 2002

and unambiguous message: South Africa performs badly in comparison even with some of its much poorer neighbours. In the 2000 round of surveys conducted by the Southern African Consortium for Monitoring Educational Quality (SACMEQ), South African grade-6 pupils performed worse in reading and mathematics than their counterparts in most of the other 14 countries, including Mozambique, Botswana, Swaziland, Tanzania and elsewhere (Taylor 2007a; Van der Berg 2005).

Not only is the average performance poor, but the distribution of scores in South Africa is also especially unequal. The distribution of test scores in SACMEQ was substantially wider in South Africa than elsewhere, and a much higher proportion of inequality was accounted for by between-school as opposed to within-school differences (Van der Berg 2005). This reality is reflected also in matric exam results. Nationally, two out of three successful candidates in the higher-grade mathematics exam came from just the top-performing 7 per cent of South African high schools, whilst the low-performing 79 per cent of high schools accounted for just 15 per cent of passes in the higher-grade mathematics exam (Taylor, cited in Soudien 2007: 12).

Pupils in the Western Cape perform better than their counterparts in just about every other province, and the provincial government leads the way in testing its pupils. But the Western Cape Education Department's own tests show that even here there are major causes for concern. When the department tested 35 000 grade-6 pupils, only one in six passed the numeracy test and only one-third passed the literacy test at the grade-6 level (Soudien 2007: 10). Moreover, migration into Cape Town means that many young people in Cape Town have been exposed previously to some of the worst schools in the country – in the rural Eastern Cape.

Figure 5.4 *Test scores by neighbourhood income (Cape Town, 2002)*

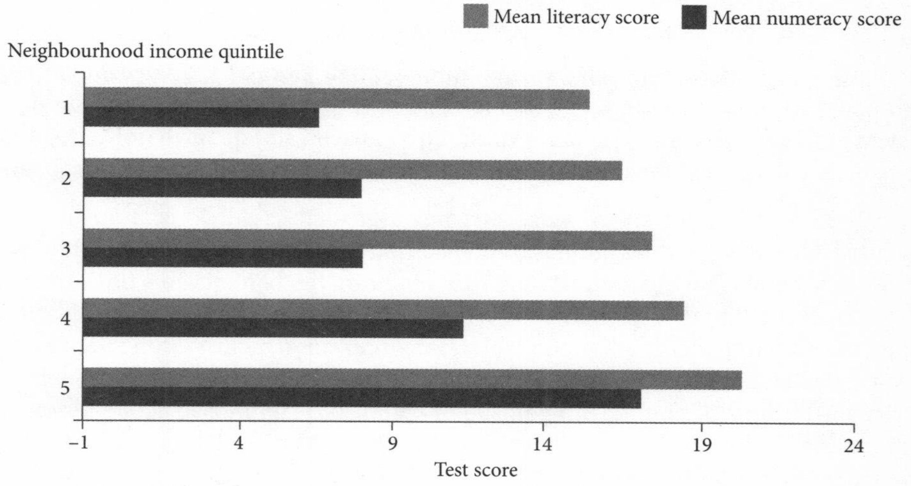

Source: Cape Area Panel Study 2002

Table 5.1 *Distribution of test scores by neighbourhood income quintile (16-year-olds)*

Score	Neighbourhood income quintile					
	1	2	3	4	5	Total
Mean (and standard deviation)	22 (7)	24 (9)	25 (7)	30 (8)	37 (5)	28 (9)
25th percentile	17	20	21	25	35	21
Median	23	25	26	31	38	29
75th percentile	27	30	31	35	42	35

Source: Cape Area Panel Study wave 1 (2002); weighted data
Note: Scores are for numeracy and literacy tests combined, out of a maximum total of 45.

The CAPS data show also that there is a clear correlation between the neighbourhood in which a young person lives and his or her literacy and numeracy scores. Figure 5.4 and Table 5.1 show the distribution of literacy and numeracy scores for 16-year-olds according to the mean household income in the neighbourhood. These use neighbourhood income quintiles, i.e. the neighbourhoods in which young people in the survey lived are divided into five, according to mean household income in the neighbourhood. Quintile 1 constitutes the poorest fifth, or 20 per cent of neighbourhoods, quintile 5 the richest fifth. Figure 5.4 reports the mean literacy and numeracy scores; Table 5.1 shows the distribution. The maximum scores were 22 (literacy), 23 (numeracy) and 45 (combined). At the age of 16, adolescents in rich neighbourhoods perform much better in literacy than adolescents in poor neighbourhoods, and very much better than them in numeracy. Table 5.1 shows that the scores of the 25th percentile, median (i.e. 50th percentile) and 75th percentile pupils rise as neighbourhood incomes rise. The starkness in the difference can be expressed another way: only 1 in 10 16-year-olds from the poorest neighbourhoods (i.e. quintile 1) scored *higher* than 30 out of 45 in the combined tests, whilst only 1 in 10 of their peers in the richest neighbourhoods scored 30 or *lower*.

The difference between innumeracy and numeracy, or between illiteracy and literacy is not trivial – and is certainly consequential. Schollar's research into the problem-solving skills – or, rather, lack of skills – in primary schools in the Eastern Cape provides a rude reminder of the problem. Schollar (2008) conducted numeracy tests among samples of primary-school children in the course of assessing school-improvement programmes. Children used a blank sheet in the answer book to do their 'workings'. Schollar examined these workings in order to try to understand why so many children were getting the answers wrong. He found that many children could not do their times tables, and so reduced simple multiplication exercises to a long series of additions. For example, to calculate 7 × 5, children would write seven marks, repeat this a further four times, and then add up the number of marks. As the numbers involved grew – for example, 11 x 9 – so the chances of error in the addition grew. Children whose numeracy skills are this limited will suffer many handicaps in life.

The problems of poor skill acquisition were evident to us in our research in the Valley. Teachers in Ocean View pointed out that some pupils in the higher grades of primary school and even in high school struggle with reading. We observed grade-6 pupils being unable to read in their first language. A teacher reported that a grade-6 pupil had been unable to read the questions in a class test. In Masiphumelele, those achieving what was expected in the grade-6 primary classroom produced work of a better standard than a large proportion of grade-9 pupils in the high school. Pupils in both neighbourhoods progress into secondary school with impaired reading, writing and numeracy skills. In Ocean View they rarely cope and are likely to be among the first to stop attending class or even drop out of school. In Masiphumelele they struggle, but usually move on through the grades until they reach and fail the matric examination. Reasons for this difference in persistence at school are discussed in Chapter 8, as part of a broader discussion of the ways that educational aspirations and expectations vary between neighbourhoods and change with age.

Resource inequalities in schools

One reason why there continues to be inequality in educational outcomes is that the equalisation of public spending does not mean that all schools have the same *total* resources. Until 2007, all public (or 'government') schools were allowed to charge fees (although there were supposedly strict rules on fee exemptions for low-income parents) and use these funds to appoint additional teachers or improve facilities. The government later introduced a policy prohibiting schools in poorer neighbourhoods from charging fees. Schools in rich neighbourhoods charge higher fees and use this additional funding to continue to have smaller classes, a wider range of subjects on offer and better facilities than schools in poor neighbourhoods. In addition, many enjoy the benefits of the good facilities and human-resource investment accrued under apartheid. For these reasons, and others, they also tend to attract the better teachers.

This is evident in the case of the schools in the Valley. Primary and secondary schools in the Valley reflect much of the highly unequal pattern of public schooling found in the country as a whole. There are 13 public schools in the Valley: three high schools (one in each of Ocean View, Masiphumelele and Fish Hoek); a separate middle school in Fish Hoek; and eight primary schools (three in Fish Hoek, two in Ocean View and one in each of Masiphumelele, Kommetjie and Sun Valley).

The physical structure of the schools reflects both their origins and maintenance. The Fish Hoek schools have large grounds, with pristine sports fields and play areas. The school buildings include reception areas, assembly halls, staffrooms, lockers for pupils, tuck shops, computer centres and facilities for science and art. The Ocean View schools have sports facilities, but they are in a state of disrepair. The Ocean View Secondary School rugby field is overgrown with weeds and grass – somewhere for pupils to go when they bunk class rather than to play sport. Marine Primary in Ocean View has some classrooms in converted containers. Masiphumelele's schools were constructed recently. The primary school was opened in 1993. The high school began life offering just grades 8 and 9 in 2000, sharing the primary school's premises – including emergency classrooms and a staffroom erected on the soccer fields behind the school. It lacked a library, computer room, science laboratories, art rooms, sports grounds and space for administration. In early 2006 – after our fieldwork was completed – Masiphumelele High moved to new and spacious premises on the outskirts of the township. But the sounds of the township still envelop the school in contrast to the quiet environs of the Fish Hoek schools. Masiphumelele High, like Ocean View Secondary, now has the basic necessary facilities, but their educational potential is limited owing to poor maintenance and vandalism. Photos 13–18 show the three high schools in Ocean View, Masiphumelele and Fish Hoek. These pictures, taken by the young researchers, clearly reveal the differences in infrastructure and investment in these schools.

There remain stark differences among the schools in terms of resources because of the variation in school fees, and in their educational outcomes, evident in the matric pass rates for the three high schools. The schools in Fish Hoek are able to supplement the government-funded teaching posts with many posts funded by fees. This has the effects of greatly reducing the pupil:teacher ratio and enabling them to provide a much wider range of subjects. The figures on class size and pupil:teacher ratios overstate some of the differences in practice. In Ocean View Secondary, high rates of truancy reduce de facto class sizes. One grade-8 teacher says: 'There are supposed to be 52 pupils in my class, but I have only ever had a maximum of 36…These kids aren't at home: they come to school, but just don't come to class.'

The lack of teaching posts in the high schools in Masiphumelele and Ocean View means that they cannot offer subjects such as art, drama, information technology, hospitality studies and electrical technology – all subjects that are available in Fish Hoek. In 2004, Ocean View Secondary School could not guarantee being able to offer Xhosa as a first language, which led some African pupils who were commuting from Masiphumelele to Ocean View Secondary School to revert to attending their local high school instead.

Teenagers in Ocean View emphasise the importance of variety in the subjects on offer. In a discussion among grade-11 pupils, one said that 'not everyone can do maths and you shouldn't have to just do the things they want you to do…If they had more subjects, there would be less in a class and then the teacher could give us more attention and we might understand better'. Sixteen-year-old Liam complains that 'school should not be restricted to certain subjects. There should be more subjects because not everyone is good at maths, physics, etcetera'. Constrained resources can undermine teaching directly. Children were making mobiles in a grade-7 art class in Marine Primary when they ran out of the required elastic bands.[1] Sometimes the poorer schools can supplement their meagre resources through charity. Ocean View Secondary School was given a computer room, with internet access and security, by the local Rotary Club. Masiphumelele High relied on 'volunteer' teachers for assistance with some subjects. The volunteers received a small stipend out of the school's fee income and were well placed to apply for fully paid openings when they arose. It had too few textbooks and relied on charity to supplement the resources received from the government. Masiphumelele High reportedly spends much of its fee income on the travel expenses of teachers and on telephones.

The difference in resources is also evident within classrooms. The biology laboratory at Fish Hoek High has colourful posters, stuffed animals and glass specimen jars on the shelves. When the topic of blood pressure came up in discussion in one class we observed, the teacher said that the following day he would bring in a sphygmomanometer. The physical science classroom has molecular models hanging from the ceiling and periodic tables on every wall. Some teachers at schools in Ocean View and Masiphumelele make considerable efforts to create an environment in their classrooms that encourages learning, but, in contrast to Fish Hoek, this is the exception rather than the rule. Three doors were stolen from Masiphumelele High overnight. The next morning, the entire school was instructed to go out and retrieve them – which they did, but at the expense of a morning's study.

The greatly superior resources at Fish Hoek Senior High are no doubt a major part of why it has much better results in the matric examination. Unsurprisingly, some pupils and parents in Ocean View and Masiphumelele regard Fish Hoek Senior High (and Fish Hoek Middle School) as much better schools than Ocean View Secondary and Masiphumelele High. A small minority of children and adolescents from Masiphumelele commute to school in either Ocean View or Fish Hoek, and a small number in Ocean View commute to Fish Hoek. According to the principal of Fish Hoek Senior High, teachers at other schools in the Valley send their children to his school! The preference for schools elsewhere is not universal, however, as we shall see further in Chapter 8. Some pupils at Ocean View Secondary said that 'the level of education' at their school was the same as at Fish Hoek. Given the difference in fees, 'you get a quality education for cheap' at Ocean View Secondary. But 'the big difference is the discipline', which was lacking at Ocean View (Samantha, aged 17; Liam, aged 16).

Many parents and children in Fish Hoek view the Fish Hoek schools with some disdain, because they compare the Fish Hoek schools with better – and typically more expensive – schools elsewhere in Cape Town. The middle school has a poor reputation, being associated with drug abuse and wayward behaviour. Pupils themselves take little pride in their school. 'We do not even have any good sports teams,' complained one. The quality of education is seen to be inferior to the private schools and colleges in the southern suburbs, where the classes are smaller, pupils get more individual attention and there is strict discipline. Reddam College, an expensive private school over the mountains in the southern suburbs, reportedly tried energetically to poach both teachers and pupils from Fish Hoek Senior High and other government schools in the area. The vast difference in fees (Reddam College costs R43 430 a year) as well as the commuting difficulties probably discourage many parents from sending their children over the mountain, but a few do. According to Reddam, 30 out of its 566 pupils lived in the Valley in 2007. Some poorer Fish Hoek families apparently send their children to the government school in Simon's Town, where the fees are lower (R5 200 a year); however, the matric pass rate is also lower (86 per cent in 2006).

Many studies of education in South Africa point to a continuing correlation between race and educational attainment. White pupils continue to perform much better than African pupils, primarily because they continue to attend better schools. Studies therefore point to mechanisms through which formerly privileged schools continue to exclude African pupils (e.g. Soudien 2007). The underlying problem is not exclusion, however, but the persistently low quality of so many schools. When African pupils escape their local neighbourhood schools and attend better schools in other neighbourhoods, their performance seems to improve markedly.[2] We shall examine aspects of school choice – how children and their families choose where to attend school, as well as how schools select pupils to admit – in Chapter 8. The point for this present chapter is that deep inequality persists from one school to the next, and the weaker-performing schools in South Africa perform very much worse than their counterparts in many other African countries.

The process of schooling

The continuation of pockets of privilege does not explain why the huge increase in spending in poor schools has not resulted in greatly improved outcomes. Four reasons seem to be important in explaining the especially low level of skill acquisition despite considerable public investment. Firstly, some schools are managed so poorly that they fail to make use of the resources they have. Salaried teachers are sometimes not teaching, or textbooks accumulate unused in storerooms. Secondly, the quality of teaching is very uneven. In many schools, salaries are paid to teachers who lack the basic competence or motivation to teach properly. Thirdly, it is possible that very high enrolment means that South African schools accommodate children and adolescents from especially disadvantaged family backgrounds. Finally, outcomes might be eroded by a lack of discipline in the school. Both teacher quality and discipline are probably affected by the quality of school management. South African and international research shows that discipline, pupil behaviour more generally and school performance have been found to be highly influenced by exposure to violence in the home and neighbourhood. Mediators in this relationship include substance abuse, depression and anxiety among pupils (Ward et al. 2007).

It is difficult to identify the relative importance of the factors impairing learning in schools. Typically, children from backgrounds that are less conducive to educational success (see Chapter 6) tend to attend the schools that are least likely to equip them with skills. Therefore, there is too close a correlation between family background and school quality. Quantitative studies have begun to tackle this by examining the variation that does occur. The first such research focused on the characteristics of secondary schools and the neighbourhoods in which they were located, and compare these with the results in the matric exam. Crouch and Mabogoane (2001), for example, found that 'schools in very poor areas tend to have matriculation pass scores some 20 (percentage) points lower than schools in rich areas', even controlling for the effects of the different resources that schools received from the state or fee income. The crucial school-level variable, they found, was not class size, but rather the teachers' qualifications. Van der Berg (2005) found that about two-fifths of the difference in matric results between schools with mostly white pupils and mostly African pupils was explained by differences in school fees (which he used as a proxy for neighbourhood income), the pupil:teacher ratio and average teachers' salaries. More than half of the interracial difference remained unexplained even when taking account of these variables, i.e. it reflected factors that Van der Berg was unable to measure. These presumably included the quality of school management, the motivation and competence of teachers and perhaps the motivation of pupils themselves. Unfortunately, such studies lack the data to separate out the effects of teacher competence and motivation, family background, management and school resources. What they can show is that the difference in performance between the better and worse schools in African areas 'cannot be explained by differences in resources and only to a limited extent by differences in socio-economic status' (Van der Berg 2005: 22). The pupil:teacher ratio appears to be of minor importance in distinguishing the better and worse schools in African areas. Competence and motivation – of school managers, teachers and pupils alike – seem to be of considerable importance.

More recent work combines individual- and household-level data from surveys with school- and neighbourhood-level data. Simkins and Paterson (2005) use data from tests in the language of instruction and mathematics, administered to children in a sample of schools in poorer neighbourhoods (including both rural and township schools, but *not* schools in formerly white suburbs). They show that performance in the language test improves with pupil motivation, household wealth, the general quality of the school and whether the language of instruction is used in the pupils' home environment. The mathematics tests were so low that it was hard to detect clearly the determinants of (relative) success.

CAPS allows for analysis of adolescents attending secondary schools in Cape Town. Two findings are striking from the preliminary analysis of these data. First, already by the age of 14 or 15 there are large differences between the numeracy and (to a lesser extent) literacy skills of adolescents. This is true even within grades (as can be seen in Figure 5.3). Second, these differences do not appear to diminish in secondary school. The range of scores in the literacy and numeracy tests for grade-12 pupils is much the same as for grade-8 pupils (see Figure 5.4) and alerts us to the challenge posed to teachers by vastly different capabilities in one classroom. These ranges exist despite the fact that many pupils have been held back or repeated grades in the past. Census data tell us that, at the age of 19, adolescents in Fish Hoek have on average more than one grade advantage over their peers in Ocean View and more than two grades over their peers in Masiphumelele (and this makes no allowance for the fact that many 19-year-olds in Fish Hoek are already enrolled in higher-education institutions, so it underestimates the gap). CAPS data would lead us to expect that, despite this pattern of grade repetition and slow progress in Masiphumelele especially, pupils in any particular grade there would perform well below their (younger) peers in the same grade in Fish Hoek.

Preliminary statistical analysis by Lam, Ardington et al. (2006) suggests that whether an adolescent passes matric or not is explicable primarily in terms of their numeracy skills and educational record three or more years earlier. White adolescents have a much higher probability of passing matric or progressing through grades on schedule. But, when account is taken of initial numeracy scores and grade deficit, then this 'race effect' disappears. The probability of passing matric rises by 16 percentage points for each standard deviation of numeracy score, and falls by 14 percentage points for each grade that the pupil was already behind in 2002. This analysis provides depressing evidence of the long-term consequences of innumeracy at an early age. What makes it especially depressing is the additional fact that about a third of grade-12 pupils in Cape Town did not study mathematics in either grades 10, 11 or 12. Such pupils are disproportionately concentrated in poorer neighbourhoods. These are pupils who have made it to grade 12, but without any advanced mathematics teaching. Even if they pass matric, they will be disadvantaged thereafter.

In short, experiences of disadvantage in primary school and in the early years of secondary school scar many children for life. If they fail to acquire basic numeracy skills, then they will probably perform poorly thereafter. Secondary schooling fails to reduce this already entrenched cognitive deficit.

Studies such as CAPS provide some pointers as to why pupils fail to acquire key skills in too many schools. Secondary-school pupils in poor neighbourhoods are more likely to complain that they do not have enough textbooks and that their classrooms are crowded. They report that there are more pupils in their classes. Pupils in poorer neighbourhoods were less likely to say that their teachers had helped them with their homework, and less likely to have been helped by anyone at home. These bare statistics are corroborated by the few – and dated – qualitative accounts that exist. Ramphele (2002: 87), drawing on research in the early 1990s in the Cape Town township of New Crossroads, writes that 'Verwoerd's ghost continues to haunt the schools of post-apartheid South Africa' in terms of the barriers preventing African adolescents from achieving their aspirations. In New Crossroads, too many teachers lack both competence and confidence, and resort to corporal punishment – since prohibited – to 'encourage' their pupils. The primary school of choice in New Crossroads is a Roman Catholic school, where the teachers are dedicated and motivated, and where discipline relies on positive reinforcement, not punishment. The only high school was 'a caricature of what an educational institution ought to be' (Ramphele 2002: 92): poorly managed, poorly maintained and with demoralised teachers unable to speak good English (i.e. the language of instruction). Parents in the area desperately sought to send their children to secondary schools elsewhere. Pager (1996), in a study based on interviews with schoolteachers in Khayelitsha in the mid-1990s, found that her informants – who were probably a self-selected sample of better, more motivated teachers – were almost unanimous in attributing the problems of township schools to their many incompetent and unmotivated colleagues.

Neither surveys (like CAPS) nor qualitative researchers often collect data from younger children, although it seems to be at younger ages that the deepest disadvantages set in. Schollar (2008) is one of the few researchers to have examined primary schools, as part of his research on primary-school improvement programmes in (especially) the Eastern Cape. Schollar found shockingly low levels of teacher competence in the subjects they were supposed to be teaching. Worse still, very little time was spent teaching in the classroom. Teaching time was reduced because pupils were still being registered for school after term had begun and because schools effectively shut down when sports teams or choirs had important events and more regularly still on monthly pay days, as well as every Friday afternoon. Even when pupils were in class, teachers were often absent. When they were in the classroom, teachers spent considerable time on their cellphones. When they did teach, they generally either wrote notes on the chalkboard or read from a text, with little or no interaction with the pupils. As Schollar wryly comments, it is a miracle that pupils in such schools learn anything at all.

The quality of teaching: Views from Ocean View and Masiphumelele

Ocean View Secondary, Masiphumelele High and the primary schools in the two areas provide good examples of the actual conditions that children experience in classrooms across much of South Africa. The schools include dedicated and good teachers alongside unmotivated and incompetent ones. Under pressure to rush through the curriculum, however, even some of the better teachers find themselves neglecting the needs of weaker pupils, who tend to drop behind. Other teachers do not seem even to make an effort.

Differences between teachers are reflected in the actual physical conditions of classrooms. In Ocean View Secondary, some classrooms are clean, tidy and decorated with posters and children's work. One classroom displayed the undergraduate admission requirements for Stellenbosch University; pictures and names of past Ocean View pupils who had done well in the matric mathematics examination; and a poster exhorting pupils to greater effort ('Only when you push yourself will you achieve your very best'). Other classrooms have graffiti on the walls, and broken windows, doors, chairs and tables. The physical condition of a classroom has an effect on pupils. One grade-10 pupil explained that 'you'll act like the classroom looks'. These differences in classroom conditions cannot be explained in terms of resource constraints alone – or even primarily. In Masiphumelele, unlike Ocean View and Fish Hoek, it is the teachers who move between classrooms, whilst the pupils remain in one room. This means that the teachers have no sense of ownership of any classroom. Most rooms have bare walls.

The most striking differences between schools in the different parts of the Valley are not that they have larger classes or fewer resources, but that the quality of teaching differs enormously. Pupils are quick to point to the failures of *some* of their teachers. Grade-11 pupils in both Ocean View and Masiphumelele complain that some of their teachers cannot speak English properly or spell correctly, so 'how are we supposed to get it right?' Teachers who do not understand fully the material they are teaching are likely to resort to writing notes from the textbook onto the chalkboard and reading through them, rather than engaging pupils with the material. The following was observed in a grade-11 history class in Ocean View:

> Notes on Mussolini coming to power were on the board and the class was copying them down, remaining quiet the whole time. After a while, Miss 'N' began to go over the notes, but was just reading off the board and seemed unsure of her facts. She explained the fact that the Italian king had allowed Mussolini into the government and had not responded to calls from anti-Fascists to dismiss him by saying that he was 'scared of Mussolini'. She was also unable to tell the class which African country Abyssinia was until she looked it up in the textbook. In fact, she generally had to check things in the textbook. She did not explain why Italy had invaded Abyssinia and told the class that it was 'pretty strange' that they 'had come all the way from over there to here'. (Journal notes from classroom observation of a grade-11 history lesson)

In a grade-11 history class in Masiphumelele:

> The words 'Why Bismarck was against the idea of a liberal constitution' were already written on the board before the lesson began – apparently left over from yesterday. Mr 'D' announces that today we will continue with group work and discussion. He gets up to write, but has no chalk. He gives R20 to a male student, who leaves the class. A few minutes later a female student appears with chalk. A student from group E is asked to stand up and read out her answer. She reads verbatim from her notes, making many language errors. Mr 'D' walks around the class, asking for comments and questions. None are forthcoming, so he poses one to the student who read. She replies reading directly from her notes and not answering the question. None of the other pupils are writing and many have their heads down, leaning on bags or with folded arms on desks. He then asks a spokesperson from group A to respond to the question 'Why European countries developed the idea of nationalism?' The female student responding reads from her notes, but does not answer the question. Another student asks why nationalism was not mentioned in her reply. Mr 'D' asks the first student, who looks blank. The second persists with another question: 'What is the meaning of immigration?' Mr 'D' asks a male student at the back of the class, who replies, 'The movement of people from one country to another'. He then asks the whole class: 'What are the factors that contributed to nationalism?' One male student says 'industrialisation'. Mr 'D' looks pleased and moves on to mention the issue of language and the incorporation of German-speaking nations. Another male student asks whether these other countries had their own culture, and if so, how it was incorporated. Most of the rest of the class are not following. (Journal notes from classroom observation of a grade-11 history lesson)

The failure among teachers to explain material was widespread, even when teachers were competent. Few teachers explained how to get the right answers, or why the wrong answers were wrong. By failing to explain work, teachers further undermined the motivation of weaker pupils. We observed a grade-6 class in Ocean View where the teacher said that many children could not read, but failed to help them:

> A girl called her over to point out that the boy sitting next to her and myself was pasting an article into his book that wasn't about a sportsperson (the instruction was find, cut out and paste an article about a sportsperson into their workbooks). [The teacher] came over and pointed to a section in the article and asked [the boy] to read it. He couldn't read it. Pointing to the word *iemand* ['someone' in Afrikaans], she asked him to sound it out. He did this very slowly and did not seem to recognise the word he had just read. She soon gave up on getting him to read the article and asked him if he knew who the people in the picture were. He initially said 'Beckham' [the English soccer captain], but when she kept on asking him, he said he didn't know. It was clear that he had made his selection based on the picture, which he had mistakenly thought was of the soccer star. He had obviously not read the article, as instructed. The teacher then walked away, having not helped him to understand anything more about his article or why his choice was wrong. (Journal notes from grade-6 classroom observation)

Children's lack of skills – or illiteracy, in this case – fuels frustration and apathy among teachers, who feel unable to deal with such huge problems and pass over the opportunity to assist the child. Pupils frequently say that they could not cope because the teachers 'give too much work to understand and move on too quickly' (Patrick, aged 18). A group of grade-11 pupils said similarly that 'some teachers just move on with the syllabus even if you haven't understood the last thing they were teaching'. Veronique (aged 17) said that her 'maths teacher is constantly doing new stuff and doesn't give us enough time to understand'. The weaker pupils particularly get left behind.

Teachers explain that they feel under pressure from the curriculum requirements and move on to new subject material even if the pupils have not grasped a previous section. The emphasis on group assessment in the new post-apartheid curriculum means that the weaknesses of some pupils are hidden. One Ocean View teacher explains how she tries to mitigate this: 'I assign seats to the pupils so that the strong and weak pupils sit next to each other so that the strong ones can help the weak ones. When they do group work though, I have to mix them up because otherwise the strong ones do all the work and the weak ones are able to get a good mark without understanding the work.'

The way in which group work and participatory learning is sometimes implemented seems to undermine the acquisition of skills, such as reading. For example, we observed how teachers would set comprehensions, but then read the comprehension piece and questions out loud to open up discussion and questions. Children could then manage the task without reading and understanding the material for themselves. Participation also sometimes takes the form of repeating answers over and over again. This encourages rote learning rather than understanding. The following journal extract provides an example of this:

> The pupils had been working in pairs on an exercise linking people and animal nouns (such as gypsy and snail) to the nouns for their homes or shelters (such as caravan and shell). Mrs 'Y' asked the pupils to come up and write the answers on the board. She skipped a question twice, but in both cases the pupil called on to write up the answer wrote the answer for the question that *should* have been called out. For example, Mrs Y called out 'hunter' (instead of 'prisoner') but the pupil wrote up 'cell' (instead of 'cabin'). This caused some confusion, but Mrs 'Y' didn't seem to notice that they weren't following the instruction. At first, I was not sure whether this pointed to a lack of comprehension on the part of the pupils, that they weren't actually connecting the home nouns to the animals or people. Later events seemed to support this, however. After all the words were written on the board Mrs 'Y' began reading out an animal/person noun and getting the class to respond with the appropriate home noun. To begin with, she followed the order of the worksheet. When she began mixing up the order the class initially just read out the next word on the list, and continued to struggle, especially with the more obscure nouns. There were also more hands raised for those pairs that had been repeated more often (e.g. gypsy/caravan) in the preceding learning techniques, indicating possible rote learning rather than understanding. (Journal notes from observation in grade-6 English-medium language class, Ocean View)

Individual attention is only given if it is explicitly requested. 'If you need individual attention you can get it, you must just ask and she'll come to you,' says Angelique (aged 12). The teachers 'teach the whole class unless you put up your hand and ask for an explanation or say you don't understand', says Mina (aged 14). Shy or insecure children may not get the help they need because they do not ask. Furthermore, pupils will not request help from a teacher who seems impatient.

> I used to go to the maths teacher for help, but have stopped because he picks on people and it is embarrassing, so now I ask other pupils. Also, I feel I should know the work by now…The accounting teacher will explain if you ask for help, but after he has explained four or so times he expects you to understand and gets impatient. (Nicola, girl, aged 17, Ocean View)

Our observation in classrooms revealed that teachers do not always explain the mistakes that pupils make in assignments or tests. For example, in a grade-11 mathematics lesson, the teacher, who was returning test papers, pointed out a common mistake that had been made on the test and dealt with it by asking what they should have done. Someone gave the correct answer, to which he responded:

'So you know what to do, but you don't do it in the test.' At no point was the work actually explained. Likewise, the accounting teacher also used the technique of getting someone to give the correct answer in response to an incorrect answer, rather than explaining the work.

> The teacher went round the class asking people to read out their answers
> to a homework exercise, getting them to mark their answers as they
> went around. There wasn't that much explanation going on – even when
> people got the answers wrong someone with the right answer was asked
> to read theirs out, with no further explanation given. (Journal notes from
> classroom observation of grade-11 accounting class, Ocean View)

Children also spoke of teachers who spoon-feed them by handing out work and giving them the answers as undermining their understanding of the work. Another common teaching technique that pupils complain about is teaching by getting children to copy information off the chalkboard. This is seen by many pupils as 'boring'.

Teachers are sometimes constrained by a lack of teaching equipment and materials. In the sciences, especially, the absence of equipment means that teachers sometimes have to teach without demonstrations. Teachers also face disruptive behaviour and a lack of motivation among pupils. But it is difficult to tell when teachers are being entirely honest about their pupils' behaviour. When pupils fail to do their homework, some teachers suspend normal teaching to give the pupils time. This is especially true in the run-up to tests, when very little teaching takes place. Some teachers seem too ready to come to class without having prepared any teaching, using the pupils' need to prepare on their own as an excuse. Others use class time to prepare tests, asking pupils to work on their own. The perverse, but unsurprising, consequence was that pupils in both the high school and primary school know that they can often get away with not preparing at home for tests.

More teaching time is lost following tests, as teachers were often observed to be using class time to mark papers and input marks into the records.

> Mrs 'F' was busy marking tests and inputting marks and she told the class
> to use the time to catch up or redo work they had not done well. She
> carried on with her work, but the vast majority of the class did no work
> and were sitting around in groups and talking. (Observation notes from
> grade-8 natural science lesson, Ocean View)

The way in which the unpredictable nature of the school as a whole undermines children's work efforts is revealed by some of the difficulties children face when writing tests. On a number of occasions children complained of having been tested on work they had not covered.

> There had been a problem with the grade-11 biology control test, as
> they had been tested on work that they had not covered. Connor (grade
> 10) had had a similar problem with his business test, as Mr 'Z', who is
> not their teacher, had set it and he had put stuff in that they had not

covered. Apparently, they are usually told what to study, but their teacher had been absent the whole week (he didn't know why – she just hadn't been at school) so they had not been told. Brian also said that the grade-11 accountancy test had been bad because they had been tested on something that they only covered on the day of the test. (Journal notes)

In these cases it was hardly surprising that pupils felt despondent about their school work and that some were reluctant to put in effort in the future. Towards the end of September 2004 the headmaster at the high school, who was also the physics teacher, left after accusations involving the use and sale of drugs (although it seems that no evidence was found to support these allegations). One of the many consequences of this was that they were without a physics teacher for about a month. A week after the new teacher started, a test week was scheduled. On the day of the physics test, pupils were still not sure whether they were going to have a test and the teacher had not told them. In the end, they did not have a test. Again, this kind of uncertainty undermines pupils' willingness to put in effort and prepare.

In Masiphumelele, teachers often spend whole classes reading out aloud from a textbook. If a pupil asks for an explanation, the teacher simply repeats what he or she already said. Classes typically take the form of lectures, with little or no discussion. Teachers and pupils alike are often absent from the room. Even inside the classroom, many pupils are forever playing with their cellphones. Only a minority of pupils do the set homework.

There are teachers who go out of their way to help pupils. Some teachers run extra lessons after school, and there are extra maths lessons on Saturday mornings. But adolescents need to be motivated to take advantage of these opportunities. Unfortunately, the uncertainty in the overall school environment and some teachers' lack of interest demotivate many pupils, who do not take responsibility themselves for their educational progress. At schools in Fish Hoek, children do not need to rely on individual initiative to access the same benefits: the teaching is more even, teachers are more motivated and most pupils live in a culture where it is almost taken for granted that they must invest extra effort. As we shall see in Chapter 8, the educational background of most Fish Hoek parents both reinforces notions of individual responsibility and effort at school and enables them to assist their children with homework when needed.

What makes a good teacher?

Pupils in Ocean View are positive about teachers who make the right effort and are approachable. Both the accountancy and English teachers gave their grade-11 class a lot of homework and expected a lot from them. But the pupils had very different attitudes towards the two teachers. The English teacher is seen as approachable, patiently explains work as much as required, encourages pupils, tries to make lessons relevant to their lives and shows an interest in their lives beyond the classroom. Several pupils told us that they have been to her to speak about personal problems. The accountancy teacher, on the other hand, often fails to explain adequately and is verbally abusive of pupils who try, but struggle with the material. Pupils do not want to be spoon-fed, they want structure in the classroom and do not want to be allowed to get away with not doing work. The English teacher at Ocean View Secondary School stood out. According to Liam (aged 16):

> Mrs N…is very different from the other teachers. She has an amazing personality, she is also an excellent teacher. I hated Shakespeare, but now I love it because she makes it easy to understand and is also someone you can talk to if you have a problem.

Nicola (aged 17), concurs:

> Mrs N is my favourite teacher because she encourages us in lots of different ways. She is straightforward and tells you if you are not going to succeed or make it, because she knows your character after three years. She always tells us to try and do your best and always gives an encouraging note at the end of class. If she sees something uplifting in the newspaper she says that she wants to read it to us.

Although pupils appreciate and respond well to teachers who provide consistent structure in their classroom environments, they also like teachers to be relaxed and informal with them. The popular teachers sometimes stay in their classrooms during breaks and chat informally with pupils.

The characteristics that pupils do not appreciate in their teachers include shouting, not coming to class and not listening to them, respecting them or showing an interest in their problems. Most importantly, they do not like teachers who undermine them academically instead of supporting and encouraging them. Pupils at Ocean View Secondary gave the example of their maths teacher, who instead of helping pupils when they needed it, told them that they should be doing history instead of maths. 'His attitude is that if you don't understand then you shouldn't be there,' said Veronique (aged 17). 'Some teachers will tell you to leave their subject and go and do something else; even when they know that you need this subject for your career, they are not supportive,' said grade-11 pupils in a group discussion. Pupils also dislike favouritism. Weaker pupils especially dislike it when the teacher concentrates on the 'cleverer' pupils and neglects those 'who don't understand'.

In Masiphumelele, pupils also appreciate those teachers who encourage, show respect and help them with problems arising within and outside school. One popular primary-school teacher gave money to a pupil who had been burnt in an accident at home so that the pupil could go to hospital regularly and have her bandages changed. The teacher also encouraged the pupil, telling her she would soon be walking like she did before. Another gave money to a hungry pupil. Practical assistance like this can make the difference between a child attending school or not.

Yet there is another dimension to teacher–pupil relationships observable in Masiphumelele. Most lessons that we observed in both primary and high schools were punctuated by the entrance and exit of pupils running errands for teachers –

delivering a message, photocopying worksheets or bringing a drink. The more competent pupils, who completed class exercises first, were asked by their teacher to mark their peers' books. The readiness with which pupils fulfilled these requests suggests a habitual practice through which teachers reinforce their authority.

But Masiphumelele pupils do not appreciate aspects of this ascribed authoritative status, claiming that most teachers did not think it important to inform pupils about school affairs, let alone consult them. Mr 'S' was one of the most popular teachers at Masiphumelele High, in part because 'he is the only one who talks to the pupils about what is happening at school' (Chloe, grade 11). Concerned with the impact on their education, pupils were immensely frustrated by very regular teacher absence from class. First period is regularly devoid of teaching because teachers arrive late from the staffroom, and more time is lost when there are many announcements to be made. When pupils complained during a student representative council meeting, they were told that it was their responsibility to go to the staffroom and demand that the teachers come to class! Pupils responded, saying, 'We have come here to get an education, and it is the teachers' job to give us that.' But, they say, teachers have brazenly told them that 'the government continues to pay us, whatever we do, so that is the situation'. Unsurprisingly, pupil dissatisfaction and frustration mounted and contributed to a riot in Masiphumelele High that spilled out onto the streets (see Chapter 8).

Like their peers in Ocean View, Masiphumelele pupils are quick to identify a 'good' teacher on the basis of their efforts and competence in the classroom, as well as their interest in and assistance with problems they face at home. Many see the role of a teacher as much in terms of guidance in life as in more formal teaching. Older pupils in particular placed a very high value on teachers' willingness to converse about school matters in a climate of mutual respect. This quality is one that does not sit easily with rigid interpretations of culturally validated authority vested in seniority and professional status, and the corresponding expectation of respectful behaviour from young people. (See Chapter 3 for further discussion on notions of 'respect' that shape intergenerational relationships.) Dissonance in this area fed into a simmering tension between Masiphumelele pupils and teachers and its eruption into violence in the riot referred to above.

There is a more general commitment to education among the principals and teachers at the Fish Hoek Middle and Senior High schools. Take, for example, the case of the history teacher and her grade-11 classes. This teacher clearly had a very good rapport with her pupils, being firm, but fair and understanding, and displaying an interest in them. The pupils themselves saw her as being easily approachable, and indeed often spoke to her about work or other matters after class. Her classroom was very well resourced and decorated, with a carpet on the floor and the tables arranged in two semicircles, instead of the traditional set-up of rows of tables all facing the front. All pupils had copies of the original textbook, which they receive from the school. The class is interactive, as the teacher walks around the class, uses maps on the wall, cartoons and other examples, and the pupils are encouraged to speak and ask questions. The teacher tailors her teaching to the different needs of the two grade-11 classes. She describes one class as 'a slower class, less academic, with [fewer] language skills'. It is 'more noisy and knowing things is not something that they want to show openly'. The other class, she says, includes 'a couple of girls who "pull" the class and they want to do well more openly'.

In each class the teacher guided the pupils through the teaching material, asking someone to read a section and then helping them pick up on the most important points of the text, illustrating and explaining when necessary. She explained to us that teaching pupils reading skills and the ability to summarise the information is an important part of the job. Pupils at times came with questions and remarks, which were taken seriously. They were encouraged to make links with their own experiences and history, and with things they had seen on television or at the cinema (although, as the teacher explained, these are often not accurate historically). Pupils are disciplined and pay attention in class. When the teacher did need to reprimand a pupil, she did not need to shout or threaten.

Other Fish Hoek teachers are similarly diligent in motivating the pupils and ensuring that they understand the material. Exercises are carefully worked through. If a pupil volunteers an incorrect answer, teachers explain why it is wrong. If a pupil does not understand something, the teacher will explain either individually or to the whole class. Teachers and classes go through homework. Teaching is not just about providing the right answer, but helping pupils understand how to get the right answer. Pupils are encouraged to acknowledge mistakes and to ensure that they can correct them. If pupils have not done their homework they risk getting a detention.

This kind of motivation on the teacher's part continued outside of the immediate classroom. In the Fish Hoek schools' staffrooms, teachers would often speak to each other about the best way to teach certain parts of the curriculum, where to find educational materials, how to approach an especially difficult pupil or how to help one who was not performing well. We were present in the staffroom during a discussion about a 16-year-old boy who lives with his sister, does not have parents and has to take care of himself. One teacher, who had been very hard on him before she heard about his home situation, commented that 'no wonder he is so difficult', and felt bad that she had not been more supportive. This interest in the pupils' welfare was perhaps less common among the older, 'old-style' teachers, who used more authoritarian teaching methods and were more distanced from their pupils. And, inevitably, there are some teachers who are fed up with teaching. In general, however, teachers attributed children's behaviour to their home environments, and think that they (the teachers) have opportunities to help pupils overcome their disadvantages. The exception to this is when they are rude and disrespectful, when children do not listen and often talk back. Many teachers see this as a worsening problem and one for which the pupils themselves must take full personal responsibility.

Faced with pupils from what the teachers see as disadvantaged backgrounds, including those whose first language is not English and/or who come from Ocean View or Masiphumelele, teachers say they 'have to teach a bit harder'. If 'they haven't had the advantages that children have had at, say, Fish Hoek Primary', one high-school teacher told us, 'you have to teach hard and help, give them extra help'.

With teachers like these, the new curriculum and its emphasis on group-based problem-solving were implemented without great difficulties and with apparently positive results. One (generally sceptical) teacher said that he was impressed even by the more traditional, older teachers.

> The curriculum has changed, the context of the country has changed and people have had to adapt. I am quite impressed; teachers have got creative and rose to the challenge. People that were incredibly traditional have embraced the democratic challenges. It is interesting watching it and being part of it. OBE [outcomes-based education] is working; the kids are better at working together, working in groups, are more articulate and better at problem solving.

Clearly, a mastery of the subject matter and a general professional commitment to teaching are necessary characteristics of a good teacher. But children and adolescents themselves tend to focus on their personal relationships with their teachers in assessing how good they are. In the Fish Hoek schools, children of all ages refer to teachers as 'supports' in their general lives as well as their schooling careers. 'We do not like teachers who "diss" us,' said grade-6 children. 'Some teachers make fun of us, which makes us feel very bad.' Teachers who listen to pupils and help them individually to do well are valued a lot; strict authoritarian or uncommunicative teachers are not liked. The personal relationship is seen as necessary for good teaching, because the caring teacher takes the time to explain difficult material.

> Bad teachers have no respect, they belittle you, act as if they are better people. They don't want to help you, they are rude, they 'tune' you when you answer back, and get upset. Bad teachers are the ones who only work because it pays, and who don't care. (Composite comments from pupils in Fish Hoek)

Fish Hoek teachers who are 'bad at teaching' are not appreciated and often much disliked. Many times, children mentioned their wish for teachers to support them more by listening, paying more attention to them and taking time for extra classes.

> A good teacher understands us; they are 'straight up'. They don't play games, and help you even after school classes. For example…a teacher who gave out her phone number to call if you needed help. A teacher should be firm, but friendly, someone who listens to our opinions and knows how to keep control. (Composite comments from pupils in Fish Hoek)

Children made a lot of comments on good teachers and how great it is to have a good teacher who explains well, has respect for, and is interested in their pupils. They feel teachers can really make a difference in doing well at school or not. At the same time, teachers feature prominently as a challenge in their lives and are seen as demanding, and children feel that they are under pressure from their teachers to do well.

Grade-9 pupils at Fish Hoek Middle School argued that pupils do not 'fool around' when their teachers show them respect. They added that 'if they want us to act mature, then don't make us feel like children by making us sit on the floor at assembly, for example'. Senior High pupils urged their teachers not to victimise them: 'Make kids feel good and they will work better; detention doesn't solve anything.' Again and again, children indicated that mutual respect is crucial in establishing good relationships between pupils and teachers. When treated with respect, they said, they respect their teachers in turn. Respect is bound up with feeling connected, however. The grade-9 pupils distinguished between younger and older teachers, saying that they connected better with the former.

Pupils across the Valley perceived teachers as crucial to their performance at school, and had a clear sense of what defined a 'good' teacher. Perceptions were broadly similar across the Valley: a good teacher is approachable and caring, about schooling matters and any problems the pupils have in their lives outside of school as well. A good teacher is affirmative and patient, and does not shout at or abuse pupils. A good teacher is well prepared and explains difficult bits in the curriculum. A good teacher is firm, but fair. Of course, what pupils *see* as the qualities of a good teacher may not accord with the actual performance of a teacher in terms of helping their pupils understand their school work or develop other important skills. It is also possible that some pupils, for example pupils who rebel against school and are waiting for the first opportunity to leave, have a rather different assessment. In our observation, however, the teachers who were more popular and commanded more respect from most pupils were precisely those who were more effective educationally.

Unfortunately, many teachers in the Valley, especially in Ocean View and Masiphumelele, failed to perform in the ways that pupils viewed positively. Too many teachers seemed indifferent to their pupils' needs and problems. Too many arrived at class late (or not at all) and ill-prepared; talked *at* rather than *with* their pupils; failed to explain how to get answers right; and either did not bother to maintain order or did so through abuse or force. Differences in the quality of teaching explain much of the gulf between the educational achievement of adolescents in different parts of the Valley. However, pupils are not simply innocent victims of uneven teaching quality. Pupils are also key players themselves in the drama of the classroom, testing teachers – and driving some to desperation.

Peers and discipline

The teacher is not solely responsible for the atmosphere and educational potential in the classroom. Pupils themselves contribute, sometimes constructively, sometimes destructively. Much of the difference among schools in Fish Hoek, Ocean View and Masiphumelele arises from the behaviour of pupils.

Fish Hoek pupils concur that 'good teachers' command respect and rarely need to resort to shouting or punishment to maintain discipline in the classroom. This is why, they say, pupils behave well most of the time. These pupils perhaps underestimate the extent of the problem of bad behaviour faced by their teachers. Pupils might not always listen to teachers, talk in class, fight with one another and even sometimes write graffiti on the tables. By and large, though, the pupils are well behaved. The entire Fish Hoek school system is geared towards inculcating basic discipline and orderly conduct. Pupils at Fish Hoek Senior High School had to sign a code of conduct when they enrolled. The school rules on mutual respect – as well as the penalties for racist, sexist and blasphemous language or behaviour – are readily available, including on the school's website. Uniforms, the school emblem and anthem and events like the yearly Founders' Day all help to instil disciplined order. In assembly and other events, teachers emphasise the importance of keeping up the school's good name (and high pass rates).

In Fish Hoek, school is highly regulated. Although some teachers complain that pupils bunk class, this is probably not common. Pupils must ask the teacher's permission to leave, and if they are late they bring notes explaining why. Attendance registers are taken and homework is checked. Pupils who are performing badly are put onto a system of tracking their attendance and engagement in class. Teachers cover for each other when sick or absent, and classes are rarely left unattended for long periods of time. Teachers are expected to be on the lookout for children who are misbehaving or bunking and reprimand them when necessary. For example, we saw a teacher shout out of the staffroom window during break at children who were in a prohibited part of the school grounds, warning them of detention. Prefects – who are elected – help to maintain order. The deputy principal announces over the intercom which pupils must go to his office and which have detention. One teacher commented that in the beginning she felt like she was in a prison camp, but the pupils are so used to this system they don't even notice.

In general, pupils were happy with the school rules, explaining that otherwise it would be 'total chaos'. Grade-9 pupils even felt that detention – which consists of an hour doing homework after school or on Saturday morning for more severe cases – was not severe enough. Pupils did chafe at the strict restrictions on school uniforms and appearance, and the grade-11 boys were circulating a petition to appeal for more leniency in the rules on the length of their hair. The principal of Fish Hoek Primary, who himself went to school in Fish Hoek, claimed that schooling has changed a lot. 'When I attended school here the rules were very strict, and pupils got a lot of punishment,' he told us. 'Now it is much more relaxed, which I feel is much better. And we do not really have any trouble at school.'

The middle school[3] is the least disciplined of the Fish Hoek schools, and there are regular fights between pupils. Teachers and pupils concur that adolescents at this age are difficult. Teachers described the beginning of adolescence as a time of 'storm and stress', when children have to deal with a lot of 'aggression, hormones and self-awareness'. Adolescent pupils at the middle school said that they and their peers were 'in a certain phase of their lives, and it's about breaking boundaries and rebelling… that's why there's a lot going on'. Teachers and pupils also agreed that it was partly because the grade 9-pupils in the middle school were 'big fish in a small pond', without older pupils to look up to. When pupils moved on to the senior high school, their behaviour changed as they got used to being at the bottom of the hierarchy again. (Only in Fish Hoek was secondary schooling divided between a middle school and a senior high school.)

The physical design of the Fish Hoek schools also facilitates discipline, primarily through assisting surveillance. The schools are all built around enclosed courtyards. Entrance into the schools is controlled. Teachers lock their classrooms when they are not in use. Pupils are not allowed out of school during classes, and the senior high school entrances are locked except during breaks. The result is that it is unusual to find any pupils outside of classrooms during periods.

Incidents do happen, but rarely. About once a month a cellphone gets stolen, but pupils often trustingly leave their bags lying in corridors. Lots of pupils told us about fights at school, but fighting seems to be limited to hitting and kicking and never involves serious injury or the use of knives (or guns). But, to put this into perspective, one girl at the middle school then gave an example of getting hurt by 'balls flying around' during break, and mock or verbal fights are probably much more common than physical ones. As we saw in Chapter 3, Fish Hoek pupils' insecurities concern the world *outside* of school (even though the streets of suburban Fish Hoek are generally safer than those in Ocean View and Masiphumelele).

In schools in Ocean View, the situation is very different. Pupils in Ocean View would agree with their Fish Hoek counterparts that a good teacher commands respect and maintains discipline. Some teachers do indeed run ordered classes. But many teachers in Ocean View either do not or cannot, and a low level of disorder is pervasive. The structure of mutually reinforcing values and practices that underpins discipline in Fish Hoek does not exist in Ocean View.

'Children don't work, [they] "go on", throw paper around, put bubblegum in other children's hair; they actually put someone's hair on fire in English class last year,' said 14-year-old Samantha. Twelve-year-old Angelique added that 'children are always making a noise, running around the class and standing up during lessons'. Patrick (aged 18) said that school stressed him out because 'boys bang on the desks and make a noise when the sir is trying to explain the work'. Fourteen-year-old Mina told us that 'pupils break the windows, write on the walls; they broke the computers and break the handles and locks on the doors. Nothing happens to those that do this because the teacher normally doesn't know who did it'. We observed a grade-8 social-science class:

> Pupils were in and out of her class for the entire period, not asking for permission. Jodie came in very late; another girl got up and went outside to talk to a friend and nothing happened at all – Mrs 'F' didn't even comment. At one point she did tell Jonathan and another boy to '*skryf*' [write]. There was a lot of noise from kids outside the classroom, but nothing was done about it. (Journal notes)

Lessons are disrupted by pupils bunking class, who throw things through open or broken windows, kick doors open or just stand outside classrooms making a noise. Teachers never reacted to those outside the class who disrupted their lessons, meaning that there were no consequences for bunking or for disrupting other lessons. Likewise, teachers seldom attempted to discipline pupils coming late to class (which, pupils say, is often because they are smoking cigarettes in between lessons).

Many teachers struggle to maintain order in their classes. Pupils were observed behaving in ways that were intended to confront and humiliate teachers, using rude language in a way that was seldom, if ever, evident in Fish Hoek and Masiphumelele. We observed Miss 'N's' history class at Ocean View Secondary:

> This class was complete chaos. [The principal] had to be called twice because pupils wouldn't listen to the teacher…Once she called him because two girls had just gotten up and left the room without getting permission. They had gone to get their workbooks. She was angry and frustrated and said they had to ask permission. They in turn became angry that they were getting in trouble for going to get the books that she had asked to see. There was a lot of trouble over homework that hadn't been done. Her punishment was to make pupils squat at the front of the class for 60 seconds, or get a warning in their pupil's file, which then has to be signed by the teacher and pupil. There were 13 pupils who had not done their homework. It took about 15 minutes to determine who had not done their work and to begin the punishment. Some pupils had been squatting at the front of the class since the beginning of the lesson, however, and complained that it wasn't fair that she only started counting the 60 seconds 15 minutes into the class. Some of the boys near me said that 'the miss only caters for certain people, the miss is unfair'. One of the boys said he had explained to Miss 'N' that he couldn't do his homework because his book was not up to date. She said he didn't need the book to be up to date, just the assignment to be done. His response was to sit down at a desk and copy another girl's work, and then took it up to her to sign. She was either too occupied with other pupils to notice this or chose to ignore it. Either way, he was able to get away with doing this. (Journal notes from classroom observation of grade-11 history lesson)

Another method of discipline used by teachers is to make pupils stand on their desks for the duration of the class. Such methods are the subject of ridicule among the pupils. Other, more conventional, methods include making pupils write 'lines' (which teachers themselves admit does not work); detaining children after school to clean classrooms or do extra work; sending them to the office or to another teacher; calling in the principal; making them sign warnings; and even sending them home.

The ineffectiveness of many of these techniques can lead to teachers getting so frustrated that they lose control.

> Teachers shout and say 'stop it!', '*hou jou bek*!' [shut up!] because the
> children make them angry by not behaving. Sometimes they say 'get out'
> and pull you by your top and throw you out. (Mina, girl, aged 14)

Although some of the younger children think that the shouting works, older children
explained that it angers pupils and, therefore, increases bad behaviour.

> They [teachers] shout when no one is listening and they are trying to keep
> the class quiet. Some of them swear. It doesn't work and just makes the
> students angry. (Mandy, girl, aged 17)

Inconsistency on the teachers' part fuels the problem. Pupils push the boundaries
of their behaviour and do not respect teachers because the boundaries they set are
moveable. This in turn increases the difficulty of the situation, which teachers are
ill-equipped to handle.

The fact that teachers resort to apparently bizarre forms of punishment reflects
their frustration and desperation. Corporal punishment is prohibited, and many
teachers simply do not know what to do. Unsurprisingly, corporal punishment is
used occasionally. Pupils at both the primary and high schools reported that teachers
hit them, and we observed a teacher smack a naughty child at the primary school.
Jumat, a 10-year-old, said that he sometimes got a 'hiding' (with a stick) from his
teacher for not doing homework, not listening in class or not doing what he was
told. Sometimes, he felt, this was effective. Clarisa, another 10-year-old, reports that
pupils do not talk 'if the teacher is in the class because they are scared of the teacher
because they don't want to get a hiding'. Even at the high school, 'some teachers get
violent and throw things, like the blackboard duster or they hit students with their
hand', says 18-year-old Patrick.

Unable to control their classes, some teachers get frustrated and demotivated,
which leads to further problems in class. Teachers of grades 8 and 11 at Ocean View
Secondary complained that pupils are rude and try to humiliate them in front of
their classmates, adding that 'there is nothing you can do to improve the situation'.
The secondary school principal told us that a volunteer teacher had been running
a compulsory reading programme, but the teacher could not cope with the pupils'
behaviour and they had to make the programme voluntary. This probably meant
that the pupils who needed assistance most did not get it. The constant threat of
disorder also informs teachers' choices of teaching methods. Many teachers resort
to the 'boring' technique of getting pupils to copy notes off the chalkboard because
pupils tend to be quiet while doing this. Demotivated teachers too easily become
disengaged from teaching. In one grade-8 class, the teacher ignored pupils' requests;
he 'didn't even answer them and just looked worn down, as if he had no energy to
deal with them' (as we noted at the time).

Further undermining pupils' respect for teachers is that children do not always
perceive teachers to be fulfilling their responsibilities in the learning process. This
in turn undermines the effectiveness of discipline. Perhaps the most obvious ways

in which teachers let children down are by not turning up for classes, not being prepared for a class and leaving classes unattended. We witnessed how teachers were sometimes unprepared for later classes and so would leave a class unattended to go and make photocopies or do other preparation. Not only does this leave classes unsupervised, increasing pupil disruption and undermining the ability of the class to get the work done, it also undermines the teacher's attempts to create structure and order in the classroom. For example, a grade-8 class started with the teacher complaining to us about a boy who consistently comes to school without a pen or paper and then comes to the teacher for this stationery. Although he complained about it, he still gave the boy the stationery. He then tried to assert authority by making all the children remove the hats and headscarves that they were wearing, something he had not done in a previous class that we had observed. Almost immediately after this, he left the class on their own for most of the lesson while he went to photocopy notes for his next class. Unsurprisingly, all the headgear was brought out again after his departure.

When teachers leave classes unattended very little learning is accomplished and respect for teachers and rules may be undermined. Sometimes pupils who are bunking class come in and disrupt the others by banging on the desks and making a noise. The consequences of leaving classes unattended can be more serious, as in the following account of a grade-11 class:

> Mahmud had been arguing with one of the 'black guys' over a packet of chips. This is when the teacher was in the class. Patrick had jumped in and was speaking to the black guy, telling him to stop it because they were trying to learn/study. Mahmud told Patrick to stay out of it and Patrick told Mahmud that he would hit him – which he did. They started fighting and the 'sir' came and tried to stop the fight, taking Mahmud to the office…As Mahmud was leaving, he said that he would get Patrick. The teacher was then out the class and Mahmud came back in with a brick… and he hit him on the head and Patrick just fell down and there was lots of blood. (Journal notes from informal conversation with Mandy)

Patrick had to go to hospital for stitches. Aggression, depression and anxiety have all been found among South African children exposed to high levels of community violence (Liddel et al. 1994; Van der Merwe & Dawes 2000).

Even worse than teachers leaving classes unattended during a lesson is when teachers do not come to class at all. Sometimes teachers have legitimate reasons for this, such as being off sick, but this information is often not conveyed to pupils, who end up waiting in vain outside the classroom. Pupils did say that this was not as much of a problem as in the past. According to Nicola (aged 17), 'teachers have really pulled up their socks because, last year, they sometimes used to sit in the staffroom when they were supposed to be teaching a class'. Some teachers, however, still habitually miss class. Pupils say that this reflects the general attitude of some teachers to let them do what they want, and this in turn leads to children not taking the lessons seriously and spending a lot of time just talking. 'I don't like that the teachers sometimes don't pitch up, and the pupils make a noise in class,' said Patrick (aged 18); 'it makes you not want to bother to go to class.'

Schools in Masiphumelele also experience chronic discipline problems. Although these are generally less confrontational towards teachers, they nevertheless disrupt education and pose a threat to pupils' safety. There is a generally high level of noise in classrooms because pupils talk to one another. Pupils reportedly smoke and even have sex on school premises. There is no security, and pupils or non-pupils sometimes bring in knives. The administrator told us that they were considering locking the toilets during class time because pupils bunked class and smoked there, and the administrator worried that there was a real danger of rape (because the toilets were some way away from the main building). Immigrant pupils reported that corporal punishment was used liberally in their former schools in the Eastern Cape, but that it happens literally behind closed doors in Masiphumelele: 'The "school regulation" is two strikes with a stick…When they do this they ask the student to close the door so that other teachers cannot see what they are doing,' says 14-year-old Nomonde. Teachers at Masiphumelele – as in Ocean View – are inconsistent in their treatment of pupils, and this fuels the perception of injustice and then creates dissent.

All of this confirms the findings of Schollar (2008) about the lack of time spent in productive teaching in many schools. The problem is compounded, as Schollar found, by periods in which no teaching takes place. Towards the end of each term in both Ocean View and Masiphumelele, teaching practically comes to a halt, to the point that most of the children we worked with at the high school do not even bother to come into school for the last week to two weeks after exams are completed. The principal of Ocean View Secondary threatened to call parents if their children were not at school, but parents were unlikely to insist that their children attend school when there is no teaching. All of this conveys a less-than-serious attitude to teaching and learning.

In Masiphumelele High School the problem of disruption to teaching time is compounded by the school's demography. Teachers face the difficult challenge of teaching classes of up to 50 pupils, the eldest among them five years older than the youngest. Moreover, up to a quarter of pupils in some of the classes have just arrived from schools in the Eastern Cape where standards are generally much lower.

Even in the face of these challenges some teachers in Masiphumelele and Ocean View remain dedicated and enthusiastic about teaching, set homework and provide structure and a disciplined environment. But the attitudes and behaviour of some of their colleagues make all of their jobs harder. For example, some teachers in Ocean View require notes from parents or doctors when pupils are absent, but their attempts to establish order are undermined by colleagues who are not bothered. Here we witnessed pupils becoming accustomed to pushing the boundaries and getting away with disruptive and disrespectful behaviour. They then began to complain about the teachers who make demands of them, for example by setting homework, thereby undermining their own education.

Teachers in Ocean View felt that they were not supported by the Department of Education. One teacher explained that the department was scared of getting sued by children and parents, so it rarely supported schools that tried to expel and suspend disruptive pupils. Disorder in the classroom was one reason why some teachers, who came across as very committed to their work and teaching, say that they would rather be doing another job.

Pupils say they would like to have more effective discipline and structure at the school. They say that disorder in the classroom undermines their ability to understand their work.

> If teachers don't have control of the class it is a nightmare because then people talk and it is difficult to understand. This is a problem with the new physics teacher. She is trying hard, but it's difficult to understand because the class is disruptive. (Grade-11 group discussion)

They also emphasise that pupils are sometimes disruptive because – to quote Charney (aged 17) – they 'don't understand and are trying to be macho'.

Observation and conversations with pupils and teachers revealed that the reasons for disruptive behaviour in some of the classrooms at the primary and high schools are multiple and stem from the two-way interaction between pupils (including their home environments and their own choices, decisions and behaviour) and the school environment (both in general terms as well as specific teacher behaviour and classroom environments). What is going on in individual classrooms is, therefore, the result of individuals' behaviour, temperaments and personalities within that setting, but these must be seen as being influenced by pupils' and teachers' home and neighbourhood environments (discussed further in Chapter 6) and by the general culture of teaching and learning at the school, its resources (or lack thereof) and decisions and policies implemented at the broader level of the Department of Education.

Conclusion

The standard classroom in a Fish Hoek school and the exceptional classroom elsewhere in the Valley provide pupils with a completely different world to the standard classroom in the Ocean View and Masiphumelele schools. One world is characterised by abundant resources, dedicated teachers and generally disciplined pupils, focused together on school as an institution for learning. The other world is characterised by wasted resources, negligent and demoralised teachers and rebellious adolescents. Public resources to education may have been allocated in a more or less equal fashion since the end of apartheid, but the real worlds of public schooling remain strikingly different across quite short geographical distances. The result is profound inequality in the opportunities for children and adolescents, in part as a perverse result of their own agency as they challenge their teachers.

Resources, teachers and pupils can combine in either a virtuous or a vicious cycle. The presence of a committed and competent teacher, with the requisite resources, encourages pupils to study diligently, complete their homework and behave constructively in class. This in turn encourages teachers to do that little bit more for their pupils. It is much easier to be such a teacher in Fish Hoek, where pupils bring to school values and forms of behaviour that are conducive to educational progress and reinforced in the tightly managed school environment. Faced with teachers who seem not to care, however, pupils will run amok, which further erodes teachers' commitment. In schools where the latter was the norm, certain teachers taught responsively and pupils learnt effectively. The key to the virtuous cycle is not extraordinary measures, but people carrying out their ordinary tasks well. Social psychologists point out that good functioning of ordinary social contexts is critical to resilience in young people (Ward et al. 2007): those whose school system functions well are less prone to anxiety, depression and conduct disorders, which in turn protects the system.

You do not need to spend much time observing classes or talking with pupils in an area like the Valley to appreciate just how different the experience of schooling can be to adolescents. Resources do differ, but it is the quality of teaching that really defines the different worlds of public schooling. Variables such as teachers' qualifications or the pupil:teacher ratio fail to capture all that is entailed in the quality of teaching.

Pupils in most parts of the Valley recognise the importance of teachers explaining how to get the right answers. In Fish Hoek, pupils are perhaps somewhat more appreciative of the actual teaching skills of their teachers. They are also better equipped to take advantage of those skills, in part because they come from homes that are more conducive to educational success. In Ocean View and Masiphumelele, schooling often seems more of an exercise in frustration – or even social control – than in education and skill development. Unexplained teacher absence, over-reliance on textbooks and the habit of setting but not checking homework can contribute to a more general sense of disengagement with learning. Some pupils describe school as boring because 'there is so much sitting around'. And in some classes a large portion of pupils sat through the lesson with their heads buried in arms folded on desks. Too many teachers resort to the safe, but unproductive, methods of writing notes on the chalkboard or reading the texts themselves. What is strikingly rare from the testimonies of adolescents in Ocean View and Masiphumelele – and perhaps even from those in Fish Hoek – is praise for teachers who mark pupils' work, who provide a clear sense of when pupils are and are not performing well, and why. Above we quoted pupils' praise of Mrs 'N' at Ocean View Secondary, but this was almost the only instance of such praise: the silence about teachers' educational commitment in pupils' testimonies is revealing. Tragically, it is not just that many adolescents are not exposed to good teaching, but also that many adolescents as a result have a poor understanding of what educational achievement entails and requires.

Unsurprisingly, perhaps, pupils in Ocean View and Masiphumelele emphasise the encouragement and affirmation that teachers give to their pupils. By encouraging them, and boosting their self-esteem, teachers equip pupils with the confidence to persevere in a world that is plagued with uncertainty, in which it is unclear how to achieve educationally and in which it is even uncertain whether educational success will deliver the employment opportunities to which young people aspire. Given that pupils lose respect for unmotivated teachers and respect those who make the effort to connect with them, and that there seems to be a close link between respect and discipline, it is likely that the teachers who are seen to encourage their pupils tend to be the ones who are more effective as teachers.

Quantitative studies consistently find that the socio-economic characteristics of pupils' families or of the neighbourhood in which the school is located correlate significantly and strongly with educational outcomes, even when controlling for the public resources that are invested in schools. Our observations in classrooms suggest that one important reason for this is that pupils in some lower-income areas – such as Ocean View – are likely to respond to the environment in their local schools in ways that are corrosive of discipline and push teachers, schools and pupils alike into a vicious cycle of inferior schooling. Measures of class, therefore, might pick up some of the differences in the real quality of schooling. However, in other low-income areas – such as Masiphumelele – pupils display extraordinary commitment, at least rhetorically, to education. In the next chapter, we turn to the ways in which the home and neighbourhood environments affect schooling.

6 The social aspects of schooling: Navigating an educational career

> Partying or studying: it's one or the other. (Chloe, girl, aged 17, Masiphumelele)

> My mom never says 'well done' for a test; she says 'what happened to the other marks?' (Veronique, girl, aged 17, Ocean View)

> I was dreading going back in 2004 because of being mocked, because I was the girl who couldn't handle the pressure. (Leanne, girl, aged 17, Fish Hoek)

The uneven quality of schooling is a major factor in the highly unequal outcomes achieved by adolescents at school. But the quality of teaching within the classroom does not explain in full the range of educational outcomes. Even in the better schools, such as those in Fish Hoek, some children fail to thrive, whilst a small minority of adolescents succeed against the odds in schools with generally poor results, such as those in Ocean View and Masiphumelele. Whilst there are indeed differences in innate intelligence and academic potential, some of the variation between pupils in the same school is due to differences in their family backgrounds. Moreover, given that some children attend schools outside of the neighbourhoods where they live, some of the variation within individual schools might reflect neighbourhood influences. Certainly, some of the differences *between* schools are due to differences between the family and neighbourhood backgrounds of their pupils: unequal social backgrounds in general reinforce unequal conditions in schools themselves.

Children and adolescents are to some extent victims of circumstances inside and outside the classroom, but they are not passive victims. In Chapter 5 we saw that conditions *inside* the classroom, and hence the environment for teaching and learning, are shaped by the attitudes and behaviour of the pupils. Children and adolescents also make choices – about which school to attend, how much effort to put into their school work, and whether or not to attend school at all. As we shall show, their decisions are shaped by a widespread, but not universal, expectation that formal education is the route to success and is, therefore, the way to unravel apartheid-era inequalities.

This chapter addresses the social aspects of schooling in contemporary Cape Town. Schooling is a social process in two senses. First, circumstances, relationships and attitudes at home and in the neighbourhood affect children's and adolescents' everyday experiences of school and their educational decision-making. Second, the social interaction that takes place daily at school, particularly among the peer group, and what is meant by school-pupil identity are of central importance to young people with respect to their developing personhood, their sense of well-being and their decisions about formal education.

There is a wealth of comparative literature on the influence of home and neighbourhood on schooling. Devine (2004) details the economic, social and cultural advantages that middle-class parents bestow upon their children in the UK and the USA, thereby reproducing the inequalities of class across generations. Working-class parents generally lack the economic resources of their middle-class counterparts, but some of them are keen and able to try to match their cultural investment – and, Devine argues, actually did so more and more frequently in the second half of the 20th century. Working-class parents can sometimes also mobilise social resources – i.e. connections and networks – to help their children. Strong and effective parental support is generally necessary for children from poor backgrounds to get ahead. But few parents in poor neighbourhoods provide sufficient support to their children for this to happen. Growing up in poor neighbourhoods typically exposes children to a range of influences outside the home that undermine prospects for educational success, whereas growing up in middle-class neighbourhoods often involves exposure to factors that facilitate success (see, for example, Brooks-Gunn et al. 1993; Sampson et al. 2002). Culturally validated attitudes and discourses pertaining to schooling and maturation vary in subtle but important ways across neighbourhoods (Levinson et al. 1996). As classic studies such as Willis (1977) remind us, children and especially adolescents are active agents themselves in generating, or sometimes escaping from, advantage and disadvantage.

In South Africa, as we noted in Chapter 1, most public discourse on and analysis of education emphasises problems within schools, especially with regard to continuing inequalities in school resources (because most middle-class children attend schools that supplement public funds with fees). Public and even academic debate tends to overlook the importance of social factors on the manner in which young people engage with their schooling on an everyday basis and make educational decisions. A few studies have tried to explore the importance of external factors to schools. Anderson et al. (2001) show that mothers' schooling is positively correlated with children's grade attainment, and that children who do not live with either parent are (on average) disadvantaged in terms of grade attainment. But, as they acknowledge with respect to the influence of mothers' education, 'it is not clear what causal mechanisms drive this relationship' (Anderson et al. 2001: 48). Crouch and Mabogoane (2001) try to separate out the effects of neighbourhood poverty from those of school management and resources, using data on matric pass rates by school. They conclude, tentatively, that schools in very poor neighbourhoods have matric pass rates 20 percentage points lower than schools in wealthier areas, even when controlling for the effects of unequal school management and resources.

The purpose of this chapter is to explore the social dynamics of schooling within and across the Valley's neighbourhoods, and to illuminate the changing context of 'education' for young people in contemporary Cape Town. We explore the particular ways in which values, socio-economic influences and personal experience interact to shape the way young people and their families approach schooling, and suggest explanations for the unanticipated differences that emerge both within and among the different neighbourhoods.

Choosing a school

The most basic decision that parents and children make is over which school to attend. In Cape Town geographical school zoning is applied unevenly, and very many children can attend public schools outside of their immediate neighbourhoods. Which school a child ends up attending depends on the parents and children (who might try to select a better school) and on the schools themselves (which can select which children to admit). At the time of research, public schools were charging fees, but the South African Schools Act (No. 84 of 1996) included provision for exemption for low-income parents. The details of this system and the more recent identification of so-called 'no-fee' schools are described below.

Middle-class parents in Fish Hoek, and often their teenage children, choose schools on the basis of perceived educational quality and facilities, as well as the individual child's needs and temperament. Using these criteria, some wealthy parents have opted for more expensive private schools in Cape Town's southern suburbs. Teachers and parents alike tend to keep a close eye on children's academic progress and social interaction at school. When either party is concerned, meetings are arranged to discuss alternative schools for younger pupils or colleges for adolescents. Young people usually participate in these discussions, and schools or colleges are selected on the basis of extensive local knowledge and by visiting the various options.

Similarly, poor parents in Masiphumelele choose what they regard to be the best education available to their children. But the range of options is much more limited. Most move young teenagers from the care of relatives in the Eastern Cape to Masiphumelele so that they can attend a 'better' high school, and prioritise spending on school fees over other household expenses. In some cases, decisions were made to spend limited funds on a 'better' education for one child, which, although appearing to compromise the siblings' education, was consistent with the parents' understanding of schooling priorities at particular developmental stages. For example, Charles decided to send his nine-year-old daughter, Zukiswa, to a Roman Catholic primary school in Kalk Bay that costs five times more than the local primary school and incurs high transport costs. (To put these costs in context, the Kalk Bay school fees are twice those of Ocean View primary schools, but only one-tenth of those of other primary schools in the vicinity of Fish Hoek.) Charles recently took his four-year-old son out of the nearby crèche because he thought it made little educational contribution and he would rather save towards sending him to the Kalk Bay school the following year. When asked about his decisions, Charles spoke of a better standard of teaching in Kalk Bay, as well as a more consistently English teaching environment. He explained his rationale as follows:

> Children of Zukiswa's age need to be in a school where they teach in
> English and where there are pupils from all backgrounds who speak to

each other in English, as well as their home languages. Only then will they become fluent and confident enough to get through high school and get a good job. I see so many teenagers, like our elder son here, who are in the final stages of high school or have just left school, and they cannot speak English. They struggle to find work. (Charles, father of two young children and stepfather of two teenagers, Masiphumelele)

Charles assumes that the local school is not good enough to prepare his children for future employment. Working as a cleaner in a shopping centre in Fish Hoek, Charles's regular wage enables him to commit to paying higher schooling costs. Many other parents in Masiphumelele have similar aspirations, but are unable to afford the alternatives to the local schools. Only a handful of scholarships for places in Fish Hoek and Ocean View schools exist and are distributed on academic merit or donor-defined 'extreme vulnerability' in the household (for example, when a mother is in advanced stages of AIDS). A sizeable proportion of parents struggle to pay local fees; according to the high school administrator, approximately half had not paid the annual fee of R150 by the end of 2004. Young people spoke about asking parents for money to pay fees and being told that they could not raise the full sum. Economic constraints, rather than a lack of commitment to education, appear to underlie non-payment:

In a parents' meeting in December 2004 the principal announced a proposed fee increase from R150 to R200 per year. There was a general intake of breath. However, no one stood up to make a formal complaint. The three parents who did stand up and comment said that they supported the raised fees: 'This is our school and our community and we need to uplift the standards, so we need money to do this.' One made the comment that the alternative is Ocean View Secondary School and that this costs R300 per year plus transport costs. (School administrator, Masiphumelele)

When compared to their counterparts elsewhere in the Valley, parents and pupils in Ocean View exercise little choice regarding schooling: almost all children attend one of the two local primary schools then the local high school. With the exception of Masiphumelele's schools, which are discounted by parents on the basis of language, alternative schools in the Valley are much more expensive (see Chapter 5). Several participants in our study had attended schools in Fish Hoek and subsequently moved to Ocean View, saying that parents were unable to afford the combined cost of much higher fees and transport. That said, the fact that approximately the richest third of households in Ocean View have higher household incomes than approximately the poorest third of households in Fish Hoek (see Chapter 1) suggests that economy is not the only motive for choosing schools within the neighbourhood. Other contributors include perceptions of schools as being an integral part of, and in some ways symbolic of, the neighbourhood and its identity within the Valley.

Poor parents in Ocean View and Masiphumelele, at least within public discourse, position schooling as something that deserves and requires their economic investment. Many struggle to pay the fees even for schools in their own neighbourhood. Yet very few spoke of their decision not to pay or made any reference to the government's commitment to providing free education. Their non-payment was very rarely formalised through exemption applications. By comparison, approximately 15 per cent of pupils at Fish Hoek Primary School – a proportion of whom live in Masiphumelele and Ocean View – applied for fee exemption.

In January 2007, after we had completed our fieldwork, the Western Cape Education Department began implementing the new national 'fee-exemption' policy. Schools in poor neighbourhoods across the country were to be forbidden to charge fees, and would instead receive an additional grant from the government. Categorised in the poorest quintile in terms of household incomes in the neighbourhood, both Masiphumelele Primary and Secondary became 'no-fee' schools. Schools in Ocean View remain fee-paying because they are categorised as falling into quintile 4 in terms of neighbourhood income. In the two primary schools in Ocean View, only about 20 parents apply for fee exemptions, although a larger proportion is probably eligible. These schools report that few parents apply, despite being informed through letters and in meetings, and being offered help with the application forms. They assume that parents are put off by the long forms and the need for proof of unemployment and receipt of social grants. One school staff member in Ocean View described the process as a 'nightmare' in terms of the time required to navigate the bureaucracy for such small numbers of pupils and amounts of money involved (especially as the sliding scale means that some families are eligible only for a reduction, which may translate into having to pay R80 per year instead of R120).

The Western Cape Education Department pays for a body of teachers in all schools based on numbers of pupils and allocates funds for capital and running costs on a sliding scale that favours schools in poor neighbourhoods. But schools in Masiphumelele and Ocean View were quick to remind parents that their fee income enables them to provide certain critical educational resources, and even asked for additional small contributions towards stipends for volunteer teachers. Such requests both rely on, and feed into, widely held understandings that these schools are under-resourced and that their improvement, and with this the overall uplifting of the neighbourhood, is at least partly in the hands of parents. There are strong parallels here with the modus operandi of public schools in Fish Hoek – the difference being that for several decades these schools have been able to charge a wealthier pool of parents much higher fees and buy in additional teachers and resources.

In general, decisions pertaining to selecting a school are taken by the parents and involve little consultation with the children, especially during primary school and the early years of high school. Parents in Masiphumelele mentioned their own undisclosed plans to send teenagers whom they considered to be misbehaving or taking a lazy approach to their studies back to the Eastern Cape to attend a school with stronger discipline. Lack of involvement in the decision or any warning of its implications are particularly problematic for young people when the outcome entails moving both school and home. For example, the teenage immigrants from the Eastern Cape to Masiphumelele mentioned above, whilst comprehending the educational intentions of their parents, sometimes struggled to adjust to a new domestic and peer environment (see Chapter 4). Poor nurture, tension or conflict at home also led to teenagers moving schools, with little or no say of their own in the process. The combined impact of income poverty, mental health and substance abuse in Ocean View contributed to mobility between schools and often between homes. These changes are very challenging at the time, but young people often pointed to the positive effects of a change of residence on their school work:

> When I was 13 I moved to my aunt in Retreat because things were hectic at home in Ocean View. My mother was all over the place mentally, and never at home. My brother was on drugs and I could not handle the pressure. I started high school near my aunt's house and I was really nervous because the place was totally different from Ocean View…Then the next year I had to move back to Ocean View because my mother and my aunt had a big argument. My mother wanted me at home and I didn't want to disrespect her. I was angry I had to leave my aunt and my friends at the new school…As it turned out, I stayed at my aunt's house while studying in Ocean View. Things were much calmer at my aunt's house and I was able to concentrate on my studies. (Brian, boy, aged 18, Ocean View)

Notable in Brian's recollections of moving schools is his fear of a new neighbourhood and his distress at leaving friends and his aunt's home, but the absence of any reference to the relative quality of education. The significance of peer relationships in school aside (see the section below, 'Schools as arenas for negotiating friendship and social identity', for a full discussion of this topic), the two high schools Brian attended have similar attainment profiles and are likely to have provided equivalent learning environments. Those who had first-hand experience of schools in wealthier neighbourhoods in the Valley pointed to the educational shortcomings of Ocean View schools, such as not being able to stay after school to use the computers. Young people without any comparative perspective presented schools in Ocean View and Masiphumelele as offering an equally good education as those in Fish Hoek:

> One good thing is that you get a quality education for cheap. It's the same as Fish Hoek. (Samantha, girl, aged 17, Ocean View)

> The big difference is the discipline. Fish Hoek has it, but Ocean View lacks confidence. But the level of education is the same. (Lenore, girl, aged 16, Ocean View)

Such uninformed assertions that schools in Ocean View are equivalent to those that perform much better make sense in light of young people's understanding that alternative schools are not accessible to them because they are more expensive. Schools in Fish Hoek report offering fee reductions or exemptions to parents who propose moving their children because they cannot afford the fees, which suggests that it is not simply expense that excludes young people from schools that perform better. In 2007, 165 of the 700 pupils at Fish Hoek Primary School were exempt from paying fees, a slight increase over the previous five years attributed to the state policy of providing forms for a subsidy when pupils apply. Approximately half are residents of Masiphumelele and Ocean View, raising the question of why most parents in these areas do not consider Fish Hoek schools if they are available to them economically. Probable explanations include parents' ignorance of the fee-exemption regulations, which derives from the low numbers of pupils attending these schools from their local neighbourhoods, as well as the understanding (reinforced by all schools) that one should be paying fees and a sense of shame or simply being out of place if one cannot do so. What is clear is that a range of such economic, social and personal factors play into decisions to send children to local schools. And parents may respond to their sense of marginalisation and the lack of choice that accompanies these decisions with an increased allegiance to, and optimism about, their local schools. Views of this nature are apparent in young people's rejection of any notions of their own school's inferiority in relation to others in the Valley (see the quotes above). The responses of parents and children to schooling alternatives are further evidence of an awareness of, and reaction to, Ocean View's marginalised position within the broader sociopolitical history and contemporary geography of the Valley and Cape Town as a whole (see also Chapters 3 and 4).

The everyday influence of home and neighbourhood life on children's schooling

The home and neighbourhood in which young people live influence directly and indirectly their daily experiences at school and their abilities to learn in the classroom. Much of the discrepancy in educational achievement in the Valley can be explained by domestic and neighbourhood environments. Home is not only an economic base and nexus of interpersonal relationships that have both positive and negative impacts on children's schooling. It is also an arena in which culturally informed and historically influenced attitudes to schooling are played out, for example in the way family members engage with the everyday demands of schooling. This section explores the mutual interaction between the social worlds of schooling and the home and neighbourhood environment, looking particularly at the possibilities for young people, often with those closest to them, to avoid or overcome constraints to their education.

Periods of extreme income shortage in poor homes in Masiphumelele and Ocean View sometimes result in children going to school without breakfast, and with only a couple of rands in their pockets for a snack or even 'lunch'. Those who snack in the playground to stave off the hunger pangs usually eat cheap, processed chips and sweets that are high in sugar and chemical additives. Research shows clearly that poor nutrition affects children's ability to concentrate, learn and remember at school (Richter et al. 2000), and that processed snack-foods lower concentration and increase irritability (Higgs & Styles 2006). These effects can be exacerbated by anxiety and depression among children exposed to high levels of violence at home or in the neighbourhood (Ward et al. 2007). Dietary constraints on children's ability to engage with their school work help to explain why bright pupils in poor neighbourhoods sometimes describe their school work as difficult and struggle to keep up. These children and their parents are aware that feelings of being left behind reduce motivation in the classroom and regarding homework, but at no point did we hear reference to diet as a possible underlying influence or as one that could be changed.

Further constraints on children's everyday experiences of learning and keeping up at school imposed by material poverty include the demands on children's time and the restrictions of household space. In households in Ocean View and Masiphumelele where parents work long hours in low-paid jobs, children – particularly girls – are commonly responsible for cleaning, fetching younger siblings from crèche and cooking for the family: tasks that cut into the time they need to do homework and socialise with friends (Bray 2003a). Moreover, finding a quiet space to write in very cramped homes poses a challenge. Fourteen-year-old Amanda reported retreating to the yard to sit on the communal toilet to do her homework, and being interrupted by other family members and neighbours who needed to use it.

From young people's perspectives, the impact of material poverty on children's schooling is most acute when combined with a threat to their identity within the peer group and neighbourhood, or with health or social pressures that lead to inadequate nurture or conflict in the home. The life-history narratives of young Masiphumelele residents reveal long periods of school non-attendance, in the Eastern Cape and locally, owing to their families' inability to afford fees, uniforms, books and stationery. Young teenagers said that one of their biggest school-related fears was the stigma of having inadequate uniforms, as this undermined both their status within the peer group and the family reputation:

> You will be teased badly by others in the class. They will say, 'Look, you are so poor that you sleep without food.' It is better to stay at home.
> (Lindiwe, girl, aged 13, Masiphumelele)

Children and adolescents across the Valley spoke of the tremendous strain they felt in relation to their school work during times when their parents were arguing excessively, there was violence in the home, or a conflictual separation was under way. Such situations were often exacerbated by underlying financial strain on parents, or the effects of alcohol or drug use in the family. Nicola, a 17-year-old pupil at Ocean View Secondary School, recalled a period two years previously when she was having frequent verbal fights with her mother, who was unemployed at the time. She began to cut classes with a friend because she was 'close to a nervous breakdown' and had no one to talk to about it.[1] She noticed that the quality of her school work declined sharply and realised that she had to make a conscious effort to reverse this process if she was to remain in school.

The combined effect of life-threatening parental illness and income poverty at home impacts on adolescents' schooling not only by raising anxiety levels and impairing their concentration, but by prompting their reconsideration of both their longer-term schooling and residential arrangements. Seventeen-year-old Noxolo, whose mother and stepfather have AIDS and are on antiretroviral therapy, did not return to high school in Masiphumelele after the long summer holiday. Two months previously, she had decided to contact her father, who lives and works in a town in the Eastern Cape, to ask if he would pay for her to live and attend school in the village where her paternal grandmother lives. He agreed, so she remained at her grandmother's home after the holidays and started at the nearby high school. Six weeks later, Noxolo returned to Masiphumelele, explaining that her grandmother denied her food because she objected to Noxolo's father sending money directly to Noxolo rather than to her. Disappointed that her plan had not worked, she re-enrolled at the local high school, but was struggling to catch up with work that she had missed.

Southern African research consistently points to the manner in which AIDS in the household and community affects children largely by exacerbating existing problems caused by poverty (Booysen et al. 2003; Giese et al. 2003; Steinberg et al. 2003). For example, children's and adolescents' greater involvement in caring for sick adults in the home can lead to erratic school attendance (Giese et al. 2003). When explaining why she had tried to move home and school, Noxolo spoke of her wish to ease the financial, social and emotional burden on her mother and stepfather. Her parents, although often very weak themselves, care for four other children without any regular income. Noxolo then said that she wanted to 'test the relationship with [her] father', a pursuit that is intrinsically important to young people, but becomes more so for those who know that their resident parent-figures are in the advanced stages of AIDS, and want to know whether others who have a parental role are able and willing to offer emotional and financial support. Noxolo's actions, while strategically planned in relation to the possibility of parental death and the absence of anyone to pay her school fees in Masiphumelele, had a negative impact on her academic performance and may undermine her achievement.

The impact of interpersonal tensions and the current or prospective absence of nurture in the home environment can appear to work in the opposite direction, at least in terms of bolstering young people's persistent attendance. In a number of cases, children or adolescents continued to attend school or returned swiftly after a period of absence, but at a serious cost to their educational achievements or personal well-being. Such cases indicate the complex ways in which young people's home lives and school lives are mutually responsive, and illustrate the fallacy of using school attendance as an indicator of current young people's educational engagement or capacity to thrive in their school career.

The tragic and unexpected suicide of a pupil in his penultimate year at Ocean View Secondary School, a boy who attended school regularly and performed reasonably well, prompted one of his teachers to speak to us about what he knew of his home environment. David was living with an aunt in Ocean View who was verbally abusive towards him. His parents, both alcoholics, were living in different homes in Masiphumelele and his younger siblings stayed with his mother. Attempting to fulfil what he saw as his responsibility towards his siblings, he visited his mother's home regularly and when he found her drunk in a shebeen (tavern run from someone's home), would take them back to his aunt's house for a period of time. David's persistent school attendance masked the social and psychological severity of these pressures, and is one reason why no one intervened to prevent him taking his life. And although we shall never know the precise circumstances of his decision, his regular presence at school suggests that it represented a consistent alternative environment to those he was dealing with at home and in his family.

Our findings pertaining to the direct negative effects of material poverty on children's schooling correlate with other South African research (see also the section, 'Who leaves and who stays? Decision-making and the school career'). Less easily observed, but often more salient to children and adolescents, are the indirect effects of past educational and socio-economic inequalities and of contemporary social marginalisation.

Earlier in the chapter we pointed out that parents in Fish Hoek tend to choose schools on the basis of first-hand experience and time spent in the various local and more distant alternatives. A large proportion of these parents are involved in meetings regarding children's attainment as well as extracurricular activities, governance and fund-raising. Such high levels of participation engender both detailed knowledge of their children's experiences at school and a sense of participation in how things are run there. By contrast, parental participation in schools in Ocean View and Masiphumelele is often limited to visiting the school office to pay fees, especially at high school. When Ocean View Secondary called an important budget meeting only 26 parents attended, forcing the school to call another meeting and to put pressure on pupils to ensure that their parents attended. Teachers attributed the declining interest of parents in their teenagers' education to a change in approach as their children get older:

> At the primary-school level parents are quite involved, but when the children come to high school parents are not as interested because they think the children are old enough to look after themselves. (Teacher, Ocean View)

The aunt of two teenagers at Masiphumelele High School commented critically on their mother's inattention to the details of her children's schooling, but explained how ill-equipped and alienated they both felt as a result of their illiteracy:

> She cares about whether they go to school or not, worries about whether or not she can pay the fees, and that's about it. I'm the one who looks at the books. But it's the same for both of us. We don't understand English so well, so we can't read the school work or know how our kids are doing. (30-year-old woman, Masiphumelele)

As we saw in Chapter 1, the education levels of adult residents of Ocean View and Masiphumelele are similarly low. More than half have completed only some primary schooling or up to two years of secondary schooling, as compared to matric or post-matric qualifications obtained by well over half the adults in Fish Hoek. And if we compare matric pass rates in adults aged 40–59, the age group corresponding to the parents of most secondary-school pupils, we find that 77 per cent of this age group in Fish

Hoek had passed matric, whereas in Ocean View and Masiphumelele the proportions were 7 per cent and 5 per cent respectively (according to the 2001 Census).

Illiteracy underlies the disempowerment parents experience regarding their ability to engage with the academic content of their children's schooling. And combined with the brief personal experience of formal schooling (usually in segregated and vastly under-resourced schools), it feeds into unfamiliarity with the contemporary school environment or the possibility of influencing it.

Very few parents in Masiphumelele or Ocean View have even visited schools outside the immediate neighbourhood, including more affordable and accessible alternatives in the Valley. And even parents who, like Charles (quoted earlier), decide to invest in more distant schools do so without particular knowledge of what happens in the classroom. The absence of such knowledge means that parents make financial and emotional investments in schools without full knowledge of what they offer. And more importantly with regard to their children's achievement once enrolled, poor parents are usually in a weak position because either they do not perceive the need to monitor their children's progress and assist them in their school work, or they regard themselves as unable to do so owing to their own minimal education.

Individual children and adolescents who were thriving in schools in these two neighbourhoods were almost invariably those whose parents or other members of the household were closely involved in their daily experiences of schooling. Eleven-year-old Mandisa (whose home circumstances in Masiphumelele are described in detail in Chapter 2) performs very well at the local primary school. Although her parents left a rural high school at the age of about 15, they both ask Mandisa about her homework and try to assist her:

> My parents help me [with my homework] if it is too difficult for me...
> We do it together, and they are there to correct my mistakes if I have
> done it wrong...When they don't know how to help, I ask my older sister.
> (Mandisa, girl, aged 11, Masiphumelele)

In addition to the obvious academic benefits of Mandisa's parents' engagement in her homework, she is bolstered psychologically by the encouragement it provides, as well as the knowledge that the demands of school are understood at home. Longitudinal research in the USA showed that parent support was a strong predictor of children's self-reliance, reduced depression, lower substance abuse and lower misconduct at school, but became less important than school support as children matured into adolescents (O'Donnell et al. 2002).

Surprisingly, perhaps, Cape Area Panel Study (CAPS) data show that there are only small differences from one neighbourhood to the next in the amount of time adolescents in Cape Town claim to spend on their homework. Adolescents in grade 10, for example, in rich white and coloured neighbourhoods report spending an average of 12.5 hours per week doing homework. This is two hours per week more than the time claimed by grade-10 pupils in poor and mid-income coloured neighbourhoods, or very poor African neighbourhoods. Curiously, it is in poor (not very poor) African neighbourhoods that grade-10 pupils report spending the least time on homework – an average of 8.5 hours per week – but even this is only four hours per week less than in the rich neighbourhoods. The differences are less marked among matric pupils.

What does differ, both among different and within individual neighbourhoods, is *who* helps young people with their homework. Figure 6.1 shows that a large proportion (about half) of young people, regardless of their neighbourhood, receive no help with their homework. Evidence presented in the previous chapter suggests that adolescents in largely white areas are more likely to attend schools in which they are well prepared for homework tasks and, therefore, less likely to need help than their peers in other neighbourhoods. Among those adolescents who do receive

Figure 6.1 *Who in the family helps with homework?*

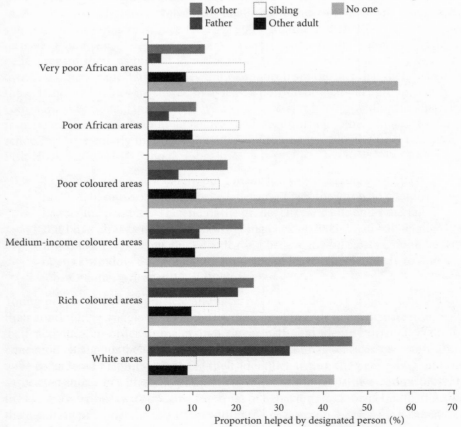

Source: Cape Area Panel Study wave 1 (2002)

help, those in richer – and especially rich white – neighbourhoods are most likely to be helped by parents. In poorer neighbourhoods, and especially in African areas, adolescents are most likely to be helped by older siblings. Part of this difference is due to different rates of parental absence (including death – see Chapter 2). But this pattern seems to be true even among adolescents in such neighbourhoods who live with their parents, and is presumably primarily reflective of the relative educational experience of parents and siblings in the different areas.

Both CAPS and our ethnographic research suggest there is variation *within* neighbourhoods in whether young people are assisted with their homework (and by whom) and in the time spent on homework. The ethnographic data suggest that such variation is shaped to a large extent by the nature and degree of mental engagement in the everyday school-related tasks and by the concern of parents and other close kin or household members. Teenagers also spoke of the difference made to their motivation by the presence of support and encouragement from teachers or friends (we extend our discussion of the peer environment at school later in this chapter).

Charney was one of only two Ocean View grade-12 pupils to pass her matric examination with exemption at the end of 2005. Despite having to clean and cook supper every day, and attend several church and youth meetings each week, Charney spent three to four hours per day on homework, and (very unusually) often did her own revision if no homework was set by her teachers. Her parents rarely assisted her academically, but were willing to do some of her jobs at home so that she could complete her homework. Charney and her mother spoke about her school day every evening, and both her parents were very involved in her decision-making about where and what to study after school.

By contrast, some of Charney's peers spent half an hour or less per day on homework, even though they acknowledged that it is not enough time to get the work done.

> I spend about half an hour per day on homework. It depends if we have been given homework – I won't sit with my books unless I absolutely have to…half an hour is not enough time – normally I don't read the English [set works] and use interval to do maths homework. (Veronique, girl, aged 17, Ocean View)

Veronique attributes her lack of motivation when it comes to school work to her home, school and peer-group environments. She explained that no one since her physics teacher in grade 10 has encouraged her, or told her that she is capable. Many of her friends left school in grade 10 and she spoke of feeling 'abandoned' by them. Most specifically, she found her mother's lack of support and critical attitude regarding schooling upsetting and demotivating:

> My mom never says she is proud of me, or well done for a test. She says 'what happened to the other marks?' (Veronique)

The presence of someone who is interested, willing and able to engage in the daily practicalities of school life has a direct bearing on the personal investment young people make in their school work and, therefore, shapes their attainment. In turn, achieving at school bolsters young people's self-esteem and motivation, which can attract positive input from the home, or at least deter criticism. This relationship holds true for children in all schools across the Valley. However, the presence or absence of the human element of domestic support – though often unrecognised or unfulfilled, for reasons described above – plays an even greater role for pupils in schools in poor neighbourhoods because they often fail to get help from teachers.

Shortfalls in these forms of human-resource provision are problems related to living in a poor household and poor neighbourhood, which children and adolescents are less able to surmount than others, including the limitations of the built environment and population density. Primary-school pupils in Masiphumelele living in cramped and noisy shacks commonly sought and found spaces in the homes of relatives or friends, or in the public library, to do their homework. But their persistence and success in doing so hinged not so much on the space, but on the presence of someone who could guide and assist their work. Better-educated adults in the home are more likely to earn more *and* be able to assist with homework, but this is not always the case (as demonstrated in Mandisa's case above). The interest and empathy shown by adults in very poor homes can provide valuable psychological support for young people in challenging school settings. But the capacity of these settings to sustain sufficient support to maintain good grades is likely to be limited by adult illiteracy and alienation arising from historical poverty and disempowerment. And for children and young adolescents like Mandisa, older siblings or neighbouring friends with a more thorough education often act as a safety net where parents cannot – a role that points to the possible negative consequences on children's educational attainment of sibling separation resulting from adjustments in domestic arrangements (discussed in Chapter 2). This particular safety net weakens in late adolescence because older siblings are less likely to be living at home or to have continued formal education beyond the local school. The emphasis that both Charney and Veronique (quoted above) place on parental interest in, and support of, their school work is partly explained by the fact that Charney's elder brother has moved out, and Veronique has no older siblings and most of her friends have already left school.

Variation in young people's experiences of doing their homework and debating schooling matters at home is but one dimension of a mutually reinforcing interaction between characteristics of the home or neighbourhood and those found within school. The consequence for most young residents of Fish Hoek and a very small fraction of their counterparts in Masiphumelele and Ocean View is a virtuous cycle of investment and achievement. But the dominant experience in poor neighbourhoods is of a vicious cycle in which children, and often their family members and teachers, perceive themselves as disempowered and are, therefore, unable to break it.

What do parents and adolescents expect from education?

The attitudes of family members, particularly parents, as well as those of neighbours, friends and adolescents themselves, towards education represent a further important dimension to the relationship between the home, neighbourhood and school arena, and have a profound influence on educational attainment and well-being more generally. While it was clear that parents across the Valley considered it appropriate that their children attend school and tended to prioritise spending on education above other household expenses, we found important similarities in their attitudes towards education as a preparatory process for adulthood, as well as some subtle, but significant, differences.

Questions asked of parents and adolescents in the CAPS survey offer a particular view of these attitudinal differences. Figure 6.2 shows the responses of parents to the question of what educational stage or qualification they expect their adolescent children to reach. Most parents in all areas say that they expect their children to attain matric and, indeed, post-matric qualifications. The stated expectations of parents in poor and very poor African areas are strikingly similar to those given by residents of wealthy white areas, and only in poor and middle-income coloured neighbourhoods do parents articulate slightly less ambitious goals. Even when children reach their early 20s – and in most cases are evidently falling behind their ambitions – few parents adjust downwards their expectations of their children. This might reflect a perception that educational opportunities are continuing to improve in post-apartheid South Africa.

Adolescents also report very high expectations of their own educational careers and achievements across the wealth and neighbourhood spectrum. Again, much larger

Figure 6.2 *Educational expectations of parents of adolescents aged 14–17, by neighbourhood*

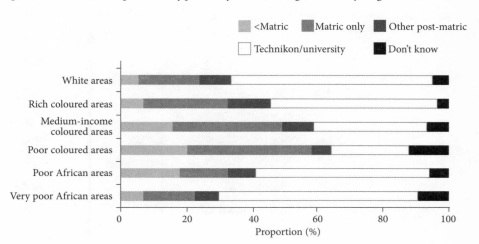

Source: Cape Area Panel Study wave 1 (2002)

217

numbers of adolescents in poor or very poor African neighbourhoods say that they expect to obtain further educational qualifications than do their peers in poor or middle-income coloured areas (see Figure 6.3). Young people's stated expectations become slightly more modest with age (see Figure 6.4). Figure 6.4 needs to be interpreted with caution, however, because adolescents and young people who perform well in school and progress into higher education are more likely to move out of low- and even middle-income neighbourhoods, and perhaps into white neighbourhoods. The majority who achieve less in educational terms and remain at home in poorer neighbourhoods are, therefore, not representative of all young adults born and raised in the area.

Figure 6.3 *Educational expectations of adolescents aged 14–17, by neighbourhood*

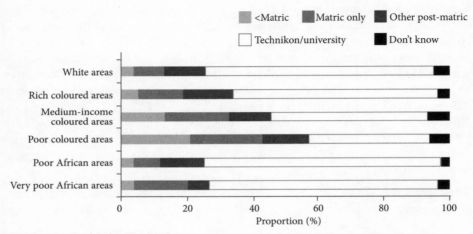

Source: Cape Area Panel Study wave 1 (2002)

Figure 6.4 *Educational expectations of adolescents aged 20–22, by neighbourhood*

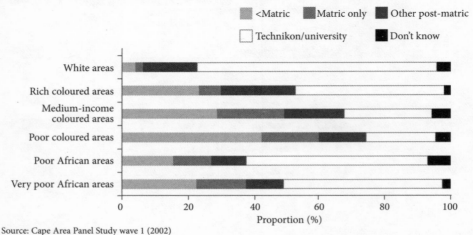

Source: Cape Area Panel Study wave 1 (2002)

Figure 6.5 *Current educational reality of adolescents aged 20–22, by neighbourhood*

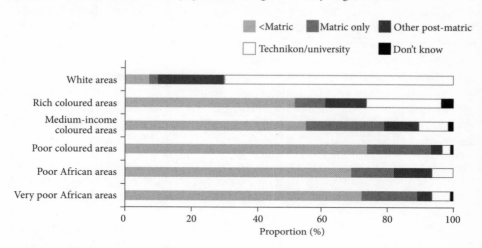

Source: Cape Area Panel Study wave 1 (2002)

Figure 6.5 shows, for young people aged 20–22, either their current level of enrolment (if they are still studying) or the highest level completed (for those who are not). Clearly apparent is the large discrepancy between educational reality and the stated educational expectations of parents and adolescents (as shown in Figures 6.2–6.4). Only in wealthy white areas do the expectations of each generation bear close resemblance to reality. The majority of young adults in low-income neighbourhoods have not even completed their matric, and will not do so, yet they nonetheless continue to say that they expect to attain further education and qualifications.

Looking more closely at the discrepancy between reality and the stated expectations of parents and adolescents, we find it to be especially marked in poor and very poor African areas. The expectations of both generations in poor and middle-income coloured areas are less ambitious than those of their counterparts who are as poor, or poorer, in African areas. These patterns raise questions about what exactly is reflected in the survey responses: have these captured genuine expectations or might at least a portion of responses reflect tenuous aspirations? And for what reasons do all poor young people and their parents express high hopes, yet those in areas where fewest succeed present the most ambitious and unlikely goals? We turn to the ethnographic data for insight into possible sociocultural influences on attitudes to education and to the prospects of the young, which may explain the way both generations respond to survey questions on this topic.

Across the Valley, children in the upper years of primary school stated their ambitions to high-status and high-earning careers, regardless of whether they lived in relatively poor or affluent households. Two boys in Fish Hoek Primary School fantasised about having their own IT company, living in a big house and driving a nice car; one girl had already mapped out her tertiary-education path, with the aim of becoming a successful international lawyer. Their contemporaries in Masiphumelele and Ocean View spoke about becoming doctors, lawyers, football players and singers. At first glance, there seemed little to differentiate the broad and rather grandiose ambitions expressed by this age group in casual conversation about the future. But the opportunity to engage with individuals about their aims, and how precisely they envisaged achieving them, revealed subtle variations within and across neighbourhoods. Furthermore, such opportunities suggested that the expression of ambitious aspirations is reflective of, and responsive to, certain discourses that frame education and the transition to adulthood, and that personal expectations may not cohere with these discourses and, indeed, may be masked by them.

Several children in Fish Hoek knew of the particular steps they would need to take to achieve their goals because they had observed family members and neighbours who had gone the same route. Their peers in Ocean View and Masiphumelele tended to speak in more general terms about 'studying hard so that I can become someone'. When asked more specific questions about achieving their aims, some pupils at Masiphumelele Primary School voiced doubts as to whether their family members would be able to pay for high school then college or university. Others anticipated jealousy from other children or parents should they do well at school and feared that such jealousy could translate into actions that would prevent them achieving their goals, for example theft and witchcraft.

Conversations with adolescents revealed that individuals' perspectives on educational potential and the role of schooling diversify further within and across neighbourhoods with age, as do those of their parents. Journal entries by pupils in grades 11 and 12 at Ocean View Secondary School revealed an awareness of the constraints of their low marks, of the school's decision to enter them for 'standard'-grade matric rather than the 'higher' grade, and of the poor quality of teaching:

> I would like to go to UCT [the University of Cape Town], but it is difficult to get in there. (Davie, boy, aged 17, Ocean View)

> Most universities want a [matric] exemption,[2] but it is hard to get one. (Adele, girl, aged 16, Ocean View)

> We want to finish school and get our matric, but we know this isn't going to be easy because we don't get proper teaching. (Group of grade-11 pupils, Ocean View)

Rarely in Masiphumelele did we hear teenagers express their doubts about the ability to move from school to further education, a concern that was often cited by their peers in Ocean View. Rare too, however, were descriptions of a particular training or qualification, and possible obstacles or contingency plans, should these be necessary. Young people either reasserted the importance of doing well at school as a guarantee to future success, or remained silent on the topic. A skit on the theme of '10 years' time', composed by grade-10 participants in a drama workshop in Masiphumelele, illustrates these future unknowns and assumptions about how aspirations might be realised:

Mother 1: My daughter wants to be a pilot and I don't know what to do.

Mother 2: I know someone who can help you as she is a pilot herself. Let's go and see her.

The mothers walk towards an office, and knock on the door.

Mother 1: Please can you help with some advice? My daughter wants to be a pilot.

Female pilot: What I suggest is that you are very attentive at supporting her with homework, and you help her continue at school so that she can get a matric and carry on with her studies. She needs to be educated beyond school, and to do this must complete school properly first.

Mother 2: What subjects can she chose?

Female pilot: The subjects she may choose include physics and maths, but she must come to me and I will explain it to her. She must not just come home from school and leave her books there, not reading them. To be a pilot you need to learn more and more, and to study hard. Tomorrow evening she can come and see me. Just bring her to me, I'll talk to her and guide her. Here is my name.

The two mothers take the paper and leave, saying thank you.

It comes as no surprise that there are no pilots – male or female – in Masiphumelele. Most parents are domestic workers, gardeners or construction workers. What is more, of the 67 pupils at Masiphumelele High who studied physical science for matric in 2006, only three did so at higher grade (necessary for university entrance) and only 38 per cent of those who sat a science matric passed.

The dialogue in the skit reveals several important contributors to the silence that pervades discussion of career planning among poor adolescents in Masiphumelele. Parents, like adolescents, are often ignorant of exactly what is required to achieve high-status jobs and some of the basic building blocks to achieve these are unavailable to them. Matriculation and, therefore, persistence at school are positioned as critical to success. Personal effort is required on the part of young people to study at home, and to do more than the school requires. Few adults or young people know local residents working in their intended field. But social connections of this nature are vital to gain knowledge of what is required and entailed in any particular career, and may offer the necessary mentoring to reach desired goals.

Across the Valley young people experienced their parents' expectations that they would succeed educationally as pressure to pass their exams. For many in Fish Hoek, the expectation of parents is that they will not only pass, but excel and gain the top marks needed for university entry:

It's my birthday today – got lots of phone calls, and I felt happy that people care. Realised what good friends I actually have. Also realising how stressed I actually am from exam pressure and how important these exams are. I need to get a good mark in order to go to university. I feel depressed. (Diary entry by Justin, boy, aged 18, Fish Hoek)

We want our family to accept us for who we are. We can't get the marks that they want. They mustn't try to fulfil their dreams through us. They try to make themselves feel good by making us get good marks so they can show their kids off...so they feel like good parents. (Grade-11 pupils, Fish Hoek)

Several suicides by middle-class teenagers during the research period were attributed to the psychological pressure exerted by extremely high educational expectations of parents, a link substantiated by the experience of guidance teachers in Fish Hoek schools. Our ethnographic data suggest that white middle-class parents genuinely expect their children to go far educationally and express this in their behaviour towards their children. Middle-class notions of what comprises 'success' are heightened by a perceived narrowing of employment opportunities for white young adults since the transition to democracy. Adolescents in Ocean View and Masiphumelele do not articulate the impact of high (and often unrealistic) expectations in this way. While adolescents in both these neighbourhoods sensed a parental hope that they would achieve educationally, those in Ocean View described mixed messages from parents regarding their expectations of schooling, and those in Masiphumelele tended to see their efforts (and assumed success) at school as their half of a bargain between parent and child. This bargain is framed as a joint enterprise in the context of children having opportunities that the parental generation did not, but does not contain the specific expectations described by young people in Fish Hoek.

Common among teenagers in Ocean View was the observation that parents expect good grades, but do not engage in the everyday practicalities of their schooling, or see themselves as potentially critical supports to the process. One grade-12 pupil recognised this inconsistency and arranged for her mother to meet with two of the teachers of subjects she was struggling with. Some parents have had little education themselves and struggle to interpret reports. Others, say teachers, do not have the maturity to parent pupils in grade 12 because of their early entry into motherhood. We were told that some parents drink, have parties and take drugs with their children without thinking about the consequences for their education. Adolescents in the upper years of high school described their struggle to stay motivated when parents and the neighbourhood in general expressed a pessimistic view about young people's potential. While expecting their children to succeed at school, parents refer to the high matric failure and youth unemployment rates in Ocean View, pointing out that only a handful of young people 'make it' with respect to educational qualifications and a 'good' job. As we saw in Chapter 4, these views are linked to the manner in which people categorised as 'coloured' were positioned between so-called 'whites' and 'Africans' in the hierarchy of privilege legalised during the apartheid era, and to their continuing sense of sociopolitical marginalisation in the new dispensation that is felt to privilege 'Africans'.

Qualitative research in poor residential areas elsewhere in Cape Town with similar demographic and employment profiles as Masiphumelele shows the high value placed on education by mothers and young people (De Lannoy 2005, 2007a, 2007b). Both generations espoused the value of schooling as a route – and often the only route – to material success and social status. Young people in Masiphumelele understand their parents' high expectations in the context of their efforts to meet the costs of their schooling by working long hours and curtailing other expenditure, and in light of the fact that they are one of the first in their families to receive what is perceived as a good education. Investing effort in school work and achieving good results are understood by young people as meeting their half of the bargain. Pelisa's diary entries illustrate this bargain:

> She (mother) told me that she has many plans for me because I am the last born and she will make sure that my dream comes true if I keep doing my school work. (Pelisa, girl, aged 15, Masiphumelele)

Parents in Masiphumelele are often similarly uninvolved in their teenage children's daily schooling challenges as those in Ocean View for reasons that we described earlier in the chapter. Their perspective on teenagers' futures are hopeful, but often unclear as to the actual steps involved, perhaps because they have less direct experience of negotiating the transition from school to further education or work than their counterparts in Ocean View.

Thus far, we have seen that children's experiences of schooling are highly influenced by a range of social, economic, cultural and interpersonal factors operating within the home and neighbourhood. And, although perhaps less recognised in terms of its historical and sociopolitical particularities, the normative environment of expectations and attitudes regarding schooling is found to vary in significant ways that stand to shape profoundly young people's experiences of being a school pupil and of striving to achieve within school. Internationally, links have been made between pupils' expectations for the future and their commitment to school, and to motivation against behaviour that risks compromising their education, such as substance abuse and bad behaviour (Catalano & Hawkins 1996; Hawkins et al. 1992). In order to understand the significance of these influences in the contemporary South African context, we first look at what happens at school in addition to formal learning, and consider how these experiences act alongside influences from the home and neighbourhood to underscore educational decision-making.

Schools as arenas for negotiating friendship and social identity

Our informal conversations about school with children and adolescents throughout the Valley invariably focused on friends and on their feelings regarding their position among their peers. Diary entries report activities and conversations with friends before, during and after the school day, often with elaborate explanations for personal decisions in relation to those of friends or descriptions of the authors' emotional responses to friends:

I walked to school with three of my good friends and told them that I'd been fighting with my brother. I felt good because they listened to me and were worried about me. During class, they told me I should not feel bad, as I was not wrong, but I knew that I was. Then at break time I decided to stay inside, as I had a headache and wanted some time alone. My classmates tried to persuade me to join them outside as usual, but I got my English poem book out and read it. The teacher was very late arriving so my friends and I were planning to pool our money so that we could buy things to share at lunchtime. That cheered me up, as I was very hungry. Then we spoke about a girl who was wearing odd socks. Some were mocking her for being so poor. During lunch break there was a fight between two girls because one was trying to steal the other's boyfriend. (Bongiwe, girl, aged 16, Masiphumelele)

Our observations in the classroom and wider school premises confirm that much of the time and space that ostensibly comprises 'schooling' is occupied by the creation, sustenance or fracturing of relationships with peers (see also Soudien 2007). When teachers are absent or classes are not held, there is more time to pursue these activities and it is unsurprising that they attract more energy and investment from young people than formal learning activities. And we observed that young people were able to participate in, and contribute to, these peer relationships in ways that bolstered their sense of self-efficacy and moulded their social identities in a far more tangible manner than what was possible within the teaching and learning processes available. The significance of friendships, their inclusion within positive experiences at school and contribution to well-being more generally were made apparent when young people spoke of the implications of moving schools:

When…I started high school near my aunt's house I was really nervous because the place was totally different from Ocean View. I met a cool bunch of friends. We got on well because I could share my feelings with them and they with me. We would sing and dance around the school. One of my favourite days at school was a Friday; we would all throw money together and buy pies and chips. We would talk about where we would live and what we will be one day. (Brian, boy, aged 17, pupil in Ocean View)

The excitement, effort and anxiety expressed by grade-12 pupils in relation to their 'matric ball' is a poignant illustration of the significance of school as an arena for forging relationships and developing personal identities. A regular topic of conversation for months before the actual event, the ball is considered by adolescents and their families as the most important event of the school career. And although it is held before final examinations, it is in theory a reward for hard work and an educational rite of passage, similar to a graduation. But the energy and money spent on finding the right outfit, transport and partner convey its wider significance, particularly with respect to a young person's reputation within the neighbourhood and their personal relationships. Brian, quoted above, had selected a design for a suit he wished to wear five months before the ball, and was saving to pay for the tailoring.

Veronique wrote in her diary of her crush on a boy she met who lives in Hout Bay, and her wish to summon the courage to invite him to the matric ball. The event has two stages. The first involves the matric pupils and their partners arriving at the school for a reception with teachers and family members. Each couple attempts to upstage the others by making the grandest entrance; several stretch limousines were hired by pupils in Ocean View and Masiphumelele. After a couple of hours of speeches, awards and photography, parents and teachers watch them leave in their fancy vehicles for the hotel where there is dinner and dancing.

As a focal point in the school career, the matric ball is also an opportunity for family members to position themselves socially, and for parents to exert some control over the choices young people are making. For example, Darren, a 'coloured' grade-11 pupil at Fish Hoek High School, was warned by his father that 'the car taking you to the matric ball will not pass by Ocean View', a statement that conveyed his disapproval (and even prohibition) of Darren taking a girl from Ocean View on a date.

Parents, teachers and sometimes pupils express some ambivalence regarding the centrality of this event to the school career, and particularly the final year. Knowing that it distracts pupils from their studies, schools continually reassess the appropriate timing of the ball in an effort to use it as both an incentive and a wake-up call for pupils. Reflecting back on their experiences, some pupils were aware that the event is used as a convenient scapegoat to mask more fundamental problems affecting their performance:

> Our preliminary exams started the Monday after the Friday matric ball… We did so badly that we had to have a teaching-staff and matric meeting immediately afterwards. But I think that the results had nothing to do with the matric ball being a few days earlier. They were bad because everyone thought studying was a joke – yes, even myself. I thought that reading through your book twice or thrice would help me remember my work. Let me tell you a secret: it does help when you only need to know the first answer to an exam paper with 10 to 15 questions…but it isn't enough when you don't know much about the subject and you have a huge long paper to write. (Ronaldo, boy, aged 17, Ocean View)

The matric ball can be seen as a school-related resource that is equally available to young people across the wealth spectrum. But for the vast majority of pupils in Masiphumelele and a significant proportion in Ocean View who will fail their matric, it neither coincides with nor signifies an educational graduation and qualification. In contexts like these the matric ball seems to offer a culturally legitimised compensation for (and masked alternative to) the rewards of formal schooling. These alternative rewards may lie in the bolstering of social identity among peers, including prospective partners. And because the envisaged formal education course is so fragile, the matric ball is important because it is held within the (highly valued) arena of the school and can encompass both the explicit celebration of the end of a school career and the implicit and often more tangible affirmation of identity and inclusion.

It is not only peer relationships that occupy a significant proportion of time and energy at school. In Masiphumelele we witnessed a very visible consequence of pupil investment in social relationships within the school setting that illuminates the manner in which 'school time' is used to negotiate issues of intergenerational authority and appropriate governance in school. Two weeks into the new school year, pupils walked out of the high school en masse and marched through the streets, protesting against a decision by the acting principal to overrule a teacher who had arranged transport for them to attend a regional sports event (for which many pupils had already paid). The acting principal called the police, who arrived with nine armoured vehicles and large numbers of armed men in bulletproof vests. Helicopters patrolled overhead; some pupils threw stones and police responded with rubber and metal bullets, injuring three residents.[3] The pupils marched for three consecutive days and it was more than two weeks before lessons resumed. Psychological research on resilience would suggest that this event and its ensuing disruption will have had lasting effects on individual pupils, precisely because it interfered so markedly with the normal functioning of one of their core social institutions (Ward et al. 2007).

Reflecting on these events, participants in our study spoke of feeling morally justified in their objections to the acting principal's use of his position, of their allegiance to peers by making a joint stand and of their realisation of the negative consequences on their education:

> The school as a whole has been affected because the teachers have been traumatised. They are scared of the learners, and now the school is taken as a place to hang out, not to learn. (Chloe, girl, aged 17, Masiphumelele)

Pupils' reflections indicate some awareness of how their actions have undermined teachers and eaten into critical schooling time, thereby compromising their educational chances. But they consider changes in the ethic and functioning of the entire school, including the balance of power, that are desired or even necessary in order to address underlying problems, to be beyond their influence as individuals. Collective effort, in the form of a *toyi-toyi* (protest), was, therefore, used to initiate change.

The social aspects of everyday interaction in schools are significant to children, and particularly adolescents, not only in terms of the time and energy they consume, but because they are areas in which they have at least some measure of control. As we saw in the previous chapter, pupils have very little control over major aspects of their academic progress in schools where teachers are regularly out of the classroom, unfamiliar with the subject matter or unavailable for assistance. Young people value schooling for its educational content as well as its potential to provide qualifications for the future. Many expressed the desire to gain knowledge and skills or to learn things about the world that their parents did not know. These desires operate alongside the normative and social influences described above and alert us to the critical role that schooling can – and *should*, from children's perspectives – play in shaping personhood, integrity, dignity and the ability to make sense of one's life. When the balance of effort and reward is shifted away from formal learning, we might expect young people to approach their schooling as one of a number of routes to developing their skills and status, and to choose alternative occupations even when prevailing norms and expectations prioritise formal education. Some do, but, somewhat surprisingly, many more do not.

We turn now to the multiple influences on young people's decisions to stay in school or to leave, and find that choices are often made in response to inadequate support for everyday schooling challenges at home (particularly from parent-figures), as well as to discourses prevalent in the neighbourhood. We also find that, somewhat alarmingly, young people, especially in poor neighbourhoods, are making decisions that are difficult to reverse without thorough knowledge of the alternatives and, therefore, of the implications of their choices.

Who leaves and who stays? Decision-making and the school career

Comparison of the school careers of young people in the Valley throws light on some important differences in when children start school, the consistency of their attendance and when they leave. In Figures 6.6–6.8 we map the educational trajectories from birth to 24 years in each neighbourhood studied (using data from the 2001 Census). We do so because research has shown that early attendance patterns stand to shape attendance later in the school career (Flisher et al. 2010), and that experiences at pre-school and early primary school have a strong influence on achievements in high school and may, therefore, impact upon decisions regarding attendance (Chisholm 2007).

Figure 6.6 *School attendance by age, Ocean View (%)*

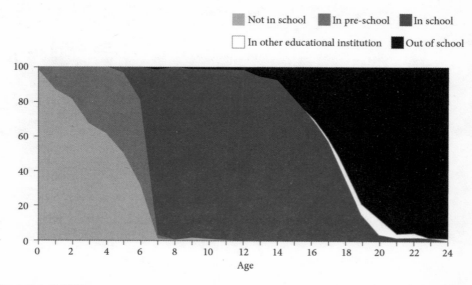

Source: Stats SA (2001)

Figure 6.7 *School attendance by age, Masiphumelele (%)*

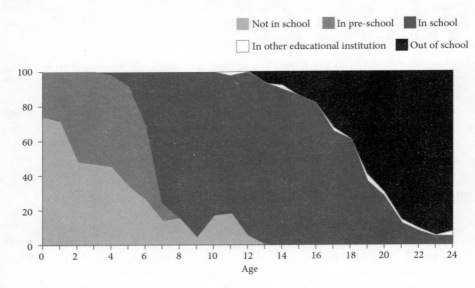

Source: Stats SA (2001)

Figure 6.8 *School attendance by age, Fish Hoek (%)*

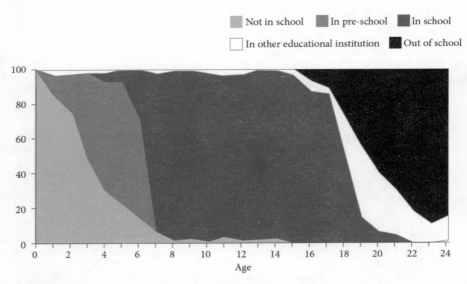

Source: Stats SA (2001)

The majority of children in the Valley begin primary school during the year they turn seven. What happens before and after this point varies considerably between the three neighbourhoods and requires careful interpretation. We see, for example, that more than half of children aged between two and four in Masiphumelele are recorded as attending pre-school – a much higher figure than in Fish Hoek or Ocean View. But children's participation in early education cannot be equated with early educational input and preparedness for school, since most early childhood facilities in Masiphumelele are informal crèches run from people's homes, providing day-care but little or no educational input. On average, in South Africa as a whole, facilities serving African children are of lower quality than those serving the rest of the population (DoE 2001). Not until 2006 did a pre-school open in Masiphumelele that is able to offer care and education (based on a nationally approved curriculum) for children aged two to six.

By contrast, the very large majority of five-year-olds in Fish Hoek attending pre-school will receive some, and usually most, of the grounding needed to thrive during the early years of primary school. Less than half of their peers in Ocean View attend a pre-school, indicating that children tend to start primary school with little familiarity with formal education or basic cognitive skills. Educational research and theory point to the significance of pre-school education for longer-term engagement with, and performance in, school (Chisholm 2007). In this chapter, we recount the problems experienced by pupils and teachers in the upper years of primary school and in secondary school when basic numeracy and literacy are not grasped within the first few years (see also Chapter 5).

Almost all those living in Fish Hoek and Ocean View are enrolled in school between the ages of 7 and 15, i.e. the ages at which children are legally required to attend school. In Masiphumelele, however, a sizeable minority (5–20 per cent) are not enrolled. Some children who have recently arrived from the Eastern Cape do not start school immediately because their families have difficulty affording the fees, uniform and stationery. And we observed some long-term residents missing periods of weeks or even months of schooling owing to illness, sudden drops in household income, a death in the family, their own or their relatives' residential mobility or a combination of such events.

And upon learning more about the home circumstances of poor children who attended school, it was soon evident that a large proportion show tenacity and determination in their efforts to continue attending school. Thirteen-year-old Lindiwe (mentioned earlier), who badly burnt her legs while cooking for her family in Masiphumelele, returned to school in heavy bandages and despite having to attend the hospital in Fish Hoek every other day. Her friend Thandi, who, since the violent death of her stepfather, has lived with her mother and disabled brother in a chaotic and impoverished home, missed school only occasionally when her mother asked her to look after her younger brother. Conversations with young people about their considerable effort to maintain a 'normal' school routine indicated their desire to sustain their studies, be with their friends and avoid drawing attention to the problems they were experiencing at home.

In addition to changing circumstances at home, aspects of the social environment and learning process at school also deterred some children and adolescents from enrolling in school or, if they did enrol, from attending classes. Unfortunately, CAPS did not ask specific questions on reasons for non-attendance, but it did ask about reasons for non-enrolment and why adolescents stopped attending school during a year in which they had initially enrolled. These data suggest that the major reasons for not being enrolled in school are related to employment (see Figure 6.9). The most frequently cited reasons among 15-, 16- and 17-year-olds not enrolled in school were 'I wanted to look for a job' and 'I took a job or was working'. These reasons may reflect poverty – which forces adolescents to work or look for work – or a reluctance to go to school and a preference to get into the real world of work (as is the case with the 'lads' in Willis's [1977] classic study of young Englishmen). A significant minority said that 'school is not important'. About 10 per cent of non-enrolled adolescents cited poverty directly as the reason: 'My family could not afford to send me to school.' Adolescents who stopped attending school during the year in which they were initially enrolled most often gave the reason: 'I could not afford to stay at school.' Small numbers cited looking for or getting a job, being pregnant or falling ill. Small numbers also pointed to problems of crime at school or a lack of interest in school. A Gauteng-based study in three poor and marginalised urban communities found that more than half of children aged between 7 and 15 who were out of school cited 'physical poverty' as the reason they were not in school (Porteus et al. 2000). Flisher et al. (2010) found a strong association among teenagers in Cape Town between belonging to a lower social class (as reflected by number of possessions) and leaving school early. Whether or not other variables such as language and 'race' category were controlled for in this analysis is not clear, raising the question whether income poverty or even social class are sole determining factors.

The difficulties in interpreting these results and the CAPS results shown in Figure 6.9 – especially in distinguishing between cultural and economic reasons behind leaving school and entering into the labour market – indicate the importance of qualitative research.

Teenage girls in Ocean View reported that younger girls are reluctant to attend primary school because they are sexually harassed by male classmates. We found evidence of alleged incidents of this nature in social workers' case files. According to one staff member at Ocean View Secondary School, the reason why just under one-third of pupils enrolled in a certain grade-8 class were consistently absent from class (despite being on the premises) was more related to their poor literacy skills than problems at home or in the peer group:

> The problem is that learners were coming from the primary schools with great reading difficulties and they cannot cope. They do not want to be found out…so they just don't go to class. (Teacher, Ocean View Secondary School)

The starkest differences that we see between neighbourhoods in the Valley are in the age of leaving school (see Figures 6.6–6.8). Only in middle-class Fish Hoek do

Figure 6.9 *Reasons for not being enrolled in school, ages 15–17*

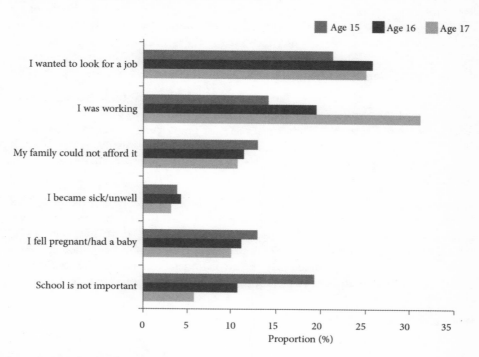

Source: Cape Area Panel Study wave 1 (2002)

the vast majority of children leave at the age of 18 – the age at which most sit their matric examination. The 2001 Census found that 83 per cent of 20- to 24-year-olds in Fish Hoek have matriculated, indicating that exit from school generally coincides with the attainment of matric. In Ocean View there is a dramatic decline in numbers at school from the mid-teens onwards. In Masiphumelele a rather different pattern emerges, with a significant proportion of young adults in their early 20s still at school. These neighbourhood-level variations in when young people end their school career are among the most important features of schooling in the Valley and in Cape Town as a whole, namely the high so-called 'drop-out' rates among 'coloured' teenagers and the remarkable persistence in school by some African young adults (Anderson 2005; Anderson et al. 2001). In 2001, more than 80 per cent of 14- to 16-year-old residents of Masiphumelele were at school, compared to between 60 and 75 per cent of their peers in Ocean View (see Figures 6.6–6.8). This disparity increases with age. Only 15 per cent of 19-year-old Ocean View residents were still at school, compared to 40 per cent of their peers in Masiphumelele. Because matric attainment rates are slightly higher in Ocean View (36 per cent) than in Masiphumelele (28 per cent),[4] and because fewer pupils are 'over age' for their year group, there are fewer 19- and 20-year-olds in a position to consider either staying at school to resit their examination or leaving. In Masiphumelele, persistence in school in the late teens and early 20s is largely due to immigration from the Eastern Cape, which results in large proportions of 'over-age' pupils in the upper classes of high school. These patterns explain some of the differences in school attendance in the late teens and early 20s between these two poor neighbourhoods, but do not account for those occurring in the mid-teens. Nor do they explain why so many adolescents and young adults choose to remain in school in Masiphumelele when the matric pass rate is so very low.

High rates of so-called dropping out worry policy-makers for both educational and social reasons. According to research in mixed communities in the USA, adolescents who leave school early are likely to have fewer employment opportunities, lower incomes, poorer mental and physical health and greater involvement in crime (Beauvais et al. 1996). Quantitative studies in South Africa find similar patterns with respect to employment and income (Anderson et al. 2001).

Several recent surveys in Cape Town have been designed to generate a more detailed picture of school departure than that available from census data. Figure 6.10 presents CAPS data on the rates at which adolescents across Cape Town have left school 'prematurely', by age and kind of neighbourhood. ('Prematurely' is defined as having left school without having passed matric; 'left' is understood as being *currently* out of school and, therefore, does not preclude the possibility of a future return to school.)

Figure 6.10 *Premature departure from school, by age and neighbourhood type*

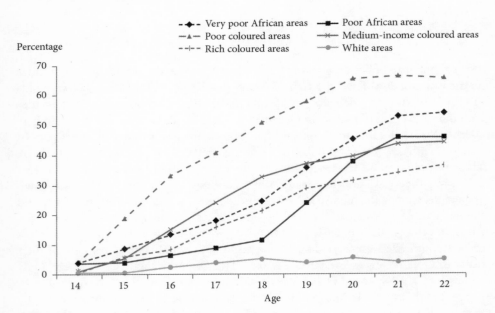

Source: Cape Area Panel Study wave 1 (2002)
Note: The data have been smoothed.

Rates of premature exit from school are highest, at all ages, in poor, predominantly coloured neighbourhoods, and lowest in predominantly white neighbourhoods. Rates of premature exit are higher in poor coloured neighbourhoods than in mid-income coloured neighbourhoods, where rates are in turn higher than in rich coloured neighbourhoods. Similarly, rates are higher in very poor African neighbourhoods than in poor African neighbourhoods. But these rates in African areas surpass those in most coloured areas by the age of 20 or so. In summary, very large numbers of older adolescents living in poor, coloured neighbourhoods leave school without a matric. Similarly large numbers of their peers in poor and very poor African areas do so, although they tend to spend longer at school trying, usually without success, to reach their final year and to pass matric. It is only in white neighbourhoods that there is no significant problem of premature exit from school. These data suggest that young people living in all poor areas tend to experience 'failure' in the formal education arena, but that the point of crisis occurs earlier for those living in coloured areas than in predominantly African areas.

Aimed specifically at identifying aspects of young people's behaviour that influence their departure from school, a team from the University of Cape Town's medical school conducted a panel study in which 1 470 high-school pupils in Cape Town completed a self-report questionnaire three times in the period from 1997, when they were in grade 8, to 2001, when those still at school were in grade 12 (Flisher et al. 2010). Defining 'dropping out' as having left school before the final year of high school (grade 12) or not having gained a matric pass in 2001 or 2002, this study aimed to find out whether dropping out in Cape Town can be predicted by young people's engagement in activities termed 'risk behaviours', such as smoking, alcohol or drug use and sexual activity. The rationale for the investigation was twofold: high recorded rates of tobacco, alcohol and drug consumption among South African adolescents (Flisher et al. 2004), and evidence from high-income countries linking use of these substances to premature departure from school (Aloise-Young et al. 2002; Arellano et al. 1998; Eggert & Herting 1993).

Flisher's enquiry (Flisher et al. 2004) into the possible predictive influences of various 'risk behaviours' revealed no direct causal links between the use of alcohol, drugs, or sexual activity and leaving school early. The only robust association found was with tobacco use earlier in life, but the authors propose this to be an artefact of the two phenomena occurring at different developmental stages and being triggered independently by other social factors, for example social norms, adult behaviour and affirmation within the community (King et al. 2003). Consistent with other longitudinal research into school attrition, this study found that use of alcohol and drugs could not be associated with leaving school when considered independently of family and academic background, school context, academic performance, peer influences and absenteeism (Ellickson et al. 1998; Wichstrøm 1998). As enlightening is their finding that variables relating to school attendance and attainment, home and family environments (including socio-economic status) and residential and care histories were proved to be more consistently associated with – and hence predictive of – dropping out than most of the so-called 'risk behaviours'. They conclude that it is not whether a young person drinks, smokes or has had sex that is going to make a difference, but the nature of their previous and current domestic, schooling and neighbourhood environments.

Important to our discussion is that in most of the sociological and psychological literature, and, indeed, in the popular use of the term 'dropping out', young people's departures from school are viewed as abnormal, caused by poor decisions on their part and resulting in largely negative consequences. In the Valley, as in Cape Town as a whole, only a minority of young people ever actually write the matric examination (and even fewer pass it). The usual experience among young people is, therefore, to 'drop out' of school – to use the prevalent popular and academic discourse – at some point before matriculating.

Surveys indicate the magnitude of such premature exits from formal schooling and point to certain associations between the home environment and educational decision-making. But they are unable to trace the links between economic, interpersonal and sociocultural factors and young people's educational careers, or to provide the subjective interpretations necessary to understand the decisions made by parents and young people themselves about school attendance. We now turn to the ethnographic data for insight into the perspectives of young people regarding their motivations to leave or remain in school, and to the personal consequences of each course of action in particular familial and community contexts.

As we might expect, leaving school before or during one's early teens is experienced differently and has different consequences to the same decision made in late adolescence. For this reason, we present a case study of a 13-year-old primary-school pupil in Masiphumelele who left school temporarily and the responses of those around her. Her experiences are not dissimilar to those of primary-school pupils we worked with in Ocean View who missed long periods of school. We then attend to the experiences and perspectives of adolescents regarding the various factors that influence their decision-making at this stage of life.

> Thirteen-year-old Lihle was described by her teacher at the primary school in Masiphumelele as 'a good pupil who has no problems'. She joined the art club enthusiastically, but after a few weeks was sporadic in her attendance. Her classmates explained that she had not attended school for much of the previous two months. Shortly afterwards, Lihle saw us walking in the street near her home, and ran in the opposite direction. Her teacher, one of the few whom pupils described as attentive and caring with respect to their home lives, told us that she had noticed Lihle's absence and sent two of her friends to her home to make an enquiry and encourage her to return to school. When this visit did not bear fruit, she asked a fellow teacher to do the same, but Lihle did not return.

> A few weeks later, having gained her confidence, we sat with Lihle in the home she shares with her grandmother and great-grandmother – a tiny, dark shack containing two small, single beds, a crate and a stove

with no kerosene. We chatted about her family. Her father had remarried and now lives in Ocean View; her mother died of TB the previous year; and her elder brother drives taxis and visits intermittently. When I asked whether she was happy at school she was silent for a long time, then said that she wanted to continue her schooling, but wished to move from the local school to one in Ocean View, and to move in with her father. The problem, she said, was that her stepmother did not welcome her in their home. And although Lihle made no mention of difficulties at home that prompted her to consider other school options, we learnt from neighbours of her grandmother's recent heavy drinking and of their frequent lack of food. There were also rumours that Lihle had started to drink and smoke cannabis. Her grandmother reported how angry Lihle was when she found out that her teachers suspect her of using drugs. She also said that Lihle was no longer communicating with her. Neither she nor any other member of Lihle's family had been to school to discuss the situation at home or their concerns about Lihle. Somewhat to our surprise, Lihle returned to school a week later without any additional intervention from teachers or ourselves.

Lihle's decision to return to school in Masiphumelele was made under enormous pressure to do so from her family, teachers – and, unwittingly, ourselves. Her own proposed solution to her problems in sustaining attendance at the local school, namely to register at a school in Ocean View, was roundly dismissed as impractical and foolish by her teacher:

> Lihle has been performing well and has had no problems here. The school is near her home and she is learning in her own language; why would she want to go elsewhere? (Teacher, Masiphumelele Primary School)

Returning to school was the best way for Lihle to quell rumours about her family's extreme material deprivation and her use of drugs and alcohol. By conforming to these expectations, Lihle is theoretically in a stronger position to succeed educationally. But her return to school meant that, although the 'problem' (as defined from a schooling point of view) was solved, the fundamental issues affecting both her general well-being and, therefore, her ability to learn at school were not addressed. These ongoing problems are likely to undermine Lihle's chances of thriving at school, meaning that she may well enter high school under-prepared and in a disadvantaged position.

The fact that none of Lihle's family members had ever visited the school or tried to talk to teachers about Lihle's truancy or their home circumstances points to the disempowered position of very poor parent-figures. Furthermore, there is no school social worker in the primary schools in Masiphumelele and Ocean View, and the part-time NGO-funded social worker in Ocean View Secondary School struggles to respond to the large numbers of pupils and parents with complex social issues. In such contexts, the actions of individual teachers play a critical role in identifying and responding to pupils' problems at home. However, Lihle's case study indicates the limitations of such responses when the roots of the problem lie in severe, chronic poverty; the value of school attendance is unquestioned by teachers and the neighbourhood culture; and children's own assessments of a better alternative are rarely taken seriously.

Teachers and pupils in Ocean View made frequent reference to the 'rude' behaviour of pupils and confrontational responses by teachers. And although the relationships were not evident to younger children at the time, older adolescents recalling their early school experiences made links in retrospect between poor-quality relationships in the home and their own destructive behaviour in the classroom. Pupils' efforts to find the emotional connections and responses they lacked at home within the school sphere resulted in confrontation and punishment, which then further undermined their confidence and ability to learn. One young researcher living in Ocean View chose to interview his 22-year-old brother about his school experiences during his mid-teens and his decision to leave early:

> Young researcher: What were the challenges you had to face while you were at school, say from primary school and your few months of high school?
>
> Elder brother: In primary school it was as if the teachers just want to tell you what to do even though you know your school work, as the sir taught you already what you should do. And sometimes the teachers tells you, 'don't your parents teach you manners at home?' Where it comes from is also sometimes where youngsters don't find love at home, now they try to get it at school. But then you still don't get it 'cause every time your parents get contacted then [the teachers] say you did something wrong, whereas you tried to do something good. (Stefan, aged 21, Ocean View)

Lihle's and Stefan's experiences speak of the consequences of past and current material poverty and social marginalisation that interact to undermine the confidence and motivation of young people and the readiness of teachers and parents to offer support. Such consequences very easily result in the vicious cycle of educational underachievement referred to earlier, and an undermining of self-esteem that stands to have implications beyond the educational sphere.

Pertinent to the possibility of young people breaking this cycle is the fact that pupils who miss a few days or weeks of school see this as a temporary strategy rather than a planned precursor to early departure. But results of a recent survey among high-school pupils in Cape Town showed that, as elsewhere in the world, withdrawal from school was often preceded by increased absenteeism (Alexander et al. 2001; Bedi & Marshall 2002; Flisher et al. 2010; Rumberger 1995). Therefore, early departure from school should not be seen as a discrete event, but as part of a process in which a child is responding to a variety of pressures within the home and school, and may – like Lihle – be attempting alternative ways of securing an education rather than rejecting school altogether. Lihle's experiences also bear testimony not only to the impact of grinding poverty on school attendance, but also to young people's tenacity in finding the means of continuing their education. Her intention to move and enrol in another school is a good example. Adults' responses to such efforts often get in the way.

Economic and relationship problems at home also impinge on the schooling experiences of children educated in Fish Hoek, affecting pupil performance and sometimes their attendance. These problems rarely persist unattended because, unlike schools in poorer neighbourhoods, Fish Hoek schools have the financial and dedicated human resources available for responding in a formal manner. The middle school organises free lunches for pupils whose parents cannot afford to provide one. Pupils who struggle to perform academically or behave disruptively are given early-morning tuition or additional sports practice, and regular meetings are held with parents. Guidance teachers have links to professional psychologists and counsellors who are usually affordable to parents.

Conversations with adolescents themselves in the upper years of Ocean View and Masiphumelele high schools reveal further factors that are important in decisions about schooling. Adolescents frequently refer to 'good friends' and 'bad friends'. They spoke of the importance of choosing the former, but avoiding the latter because they will persuade one to do 'bad things', such as bunking school or taking drugs. And, like adults in their neighbourhoods, they made glib and pejorative references to peer pressure when discussing 'dropping out', conveying the impression of a prevailing youth culture that exerts a tremendous pressure to reject school.

> You see, sometimes then you think for yourself 'I don't feel like attending this particular class'. Now it comes to the conclusion you have a friend, you have a lot of friends; they tell you, 'My friend, I don't feel like going to class' and you also consider not to want to go to class and now you go with them, right. I have a cigarette and then we'll go smoke it in the roof or we go and stand against the school fence and speak a lot of nonsense about the teachers – this one has a bald head or this one with glasses and all these things. (Edward, boy, aged 22, Ocean View)

CAPS found that adolescents who stopped studying reported that their friends had not encouraged them to continue studying, and that few of their friends had continued. This was in contrast to those adolescents who had continued studying. In most cases, adolescents who were not encouraged by their friends were also not encouraged by their parents. But some of the adolescents who had stopped studying reported that their parents had wanted them to continue, whilst their friends had not encouraged them. This suggests not only that friends exert some influence on adolescents' decisions, but also that their inputs can be more important even than those of their parents.

Given the opportunity to explain their experiences in more detail, young people said that friends sometimes encourage heavy drinking, drug use, sexual promiscuity and skipping classes, which for various reasons undermine their academic performance and their ability to sustain a school career. Pupils in their final year at Ocean View

Secondary School mentioned classmates who sometimes skipped their own classes to spend time with their girlfriends or boyfriends in other classes. And pupils across the Valley explained that their inabilities to concentrate at school and their tiredness in the classroom resulted from late-night drinking and partying, which may or may not involve casual drug use. Adolescents in Ocean View and Masiphumelele were particularly vocal about the incompatibility between peer-group relationships, including dating, and achieving educational and career goals. Both Lenore (quoted below) and Chloe saw themselves as achieving academically, attending university and having a successful future career:

> I not wish to have a relationship at this point in my life. I feel like if I were to get into a relationship now, it will distract me, and then I would be like off the road of where I want to be. (Lenore, girl, aged 16, Ocean View)

Adolescents across the Valley frequently referred to their personal faith and membership of a religious community in conversations about their responses to the demands of schooling and the possibilities of failure. CAPS found that adolescents who participated in church groups were significantly less likely to drop out of school. Internationally, religious involvement has been found to reduce the likelihood of substance abuse in adolescence (Koenig 2001; Matthew et al. 1998) and behaviour termed 'delinquent' (Pearce et al. 2003). Young people in the Valley with religious beliefs regard these as pivotal in maintaining self-esteem and managing both their own and others' expectations. They draw support from the fact that their beliefs and these associated values are shared by at least a portion of their peer group, family and community. Personal faith often plays a very special role in providing an alternative framework for understanding 'failure' and legitimising other routes to formal schooling, particularly in a high-pressure environment – like the final two years at Fish Hoek Senior High School:

> I got to grade 11, just barely, but I made it. I was dreading going back in 2004, because of being mocked, because I was the girl who couldn't handle the pressure. The end of the grade-11 year came and I did fail. But I had already decided I wasn't going back in 2005, I had had enough! It was like I was being guided to leave. I believe if God closes a door, he opens a window. So I thought I am going to leave school and try to find a job. (Leanne, girl, aged 17, Fish Hoek)

Young people in Masiphumelele and Ocean View made very frequent reference to their continuing struggle to resist the invitations of friends to participate in so-called 'bad' activities, in order to maintain a career path and identity orientated towards education. Religious beliefs and participation in church services or youth groups were considered helpful in defining their identities within the peer group and their associated choice of a lifestyle conducive to the educational pathway. Some presented the choice as one of two opposing extremes of behaviour and social interaction, with the resulting potential for ostracism within the peer group, but for the sustenance of personal integrity. The following excerpt from a young researcher's interview with her female classmate demonstrates their mutual sense of two distinct pathways:

Young researcher: What makes you different from other teens?

Zuziwe: The fact that I don't drink, smoke and be involved in relationships because I am not allowed to. The only thing I do is read the Bible, pray and go to church.

Young researcher: Do you by any chance get negativity from fellow pupils?

Zuziwe: Yes, a lot. They think that if you are saved or if you strongly believe that God is there and you want to worship him, they think you are mad and you don't know what's good about life.

Young researcher: Has there been times when you were just thinking that the negativity around is too much that make you wanna stop?

Zuziwe: Yes, a lot of times when, for example, I make mistakes and people say: 'How can an angel do that?' That makes me feel I wanna stop, but family support keeps me going.

Young researcher: Do you feel you are standing strongly on what you believe?

Zuziwe: I do, 'cause if I wasn't strong on my beliefs and religion I would have given up a long time ago. (Zuziwe, grade-12 pupil, Masiphumelele High School)

Discourse of this nature creates and sustains a moral dichotomy, dividing friends and pursuits within the peer group into two categories, namely 'good' and 'bad'. Such a dichotomy is helpful for adolescents in underperforming schools or who are under tremendous pressure to succeed because it provides a means of managing the anomaly of low attainment despite attendance and effort: poor performance is attributed to wayward behaviour often influenced by friends. And one consequence of this is that it places blame on the peer group and an individual's response to it, and deflects attention away from problems at school, in the home or neighbourhood at large.

Often hidden within a discourse of the negative influences of friends is young people's recognition that friendships can, and often do, bolster children's educational experiences. A large proportion of pupils in the final years of school in Masiphumelele, and a smaller proportion of those in Ocean View, were part of one or more subject-specific 'study groups'. Established by pupils, these groups meet regularly in one member's home or the local library and provide a forum for doing homework and preparing for tests. The advice and encouragement of friends in these semi-formal settings, as well as in everyday classroom interaction, were clearly critical to many children's abilities to keep up with their work and pass internal examinations. But the educational limitations of these groups are evident in the very low matric pass rates. For, even when more knowledgeable friends are prepared to spend time and energy explaining work, they are unlikely to know enough to fill any gaps in classroom teaching. These limitations aside, by providing an arena that combines learning and peer interaction, these groups help teenagers stay motivated even if they do not fully understand the work. One explanation for the persistently high attendance rates in the upper years of Masiphumelele High School is that pupils are bolstered by their peers (as well as their parents and some teachers), but are largely unaware of the limits of their knowledge in relation to what is required to pass their final public examination.

Finally, peer-group interaction is experienced as threatening by adolescents across the Valley because it has the potential to tip an important symbolic balance: leaving school is seen as giving up on the universally validated route to success through education, and is, therefore, indicative of an unwanted change in life path. When asked to brainstorm the challenges they currently face in everyday life, grade-9 pupils in Masiphumelele spoke of 'not achieving my dreams'; 'not being able to succeed in my life'; and 'not becoming someone', and linked these challenges with other fears, such as failing at school or parents being unable to finance their education.

Pupils in the higher grades at Ocean View Secondary School attributed the majority of their friends' early departures from school to drug use or pregnancy. At first glance, these explanations seem to contradict the findings from surveys (such as CAPS and the separate panel study discussed by Flisher et al. [2010]) because young people define these behaviours as independent causes to leaving school prematurely. But a closer look at the interpersonal and sociocultural environments in which responses to young people's engagement in these activities are made reveals that the qualities of relationships and attitudes that exist within the home and neighbourhood influence the ways in which young people view particular activities as either compatible or incompatible with schooling, and their attitudes towards school, their attendance and their achievement.

Teenage pregnancy rates in areas of Cape Town like Masiphumelele are similar to those in areas like Ocean View, but it is more common for young mothers in the former to return to school than for those in the latter areas. Our research in the Valley suggests that the majority of pregnancies are unplanned, but some girls 'choose' pregnancy as a means of making the transition to adulthood (see Chapter 7). The manner in which schools and parents treat pregnant pupils and young mothers received much media attention in early 2007 – a debate sparked by the attempted refusal of one school in Cape Town, and the girl's parents, to allow a pupil back to school after she had a baby and got married, and by a proposed new rule prohibiting pregnant pupils from returning to school for one or two years after giving birth.

Pregnant pupils in both Ocean View and Masiphumelele are the objects of teasing from peers and tacit disapproval from adults. And while some are instructed by parents to leave school in order to seek work and pay for their infants' needs, many have wider options. A number of girls with whom we worked in Masiphumelele took several months off school over the period of the baby's birth, then returned to the same class and continued to express high expectations of their educational career:

> Interviewer: How did teachers and your fellow students respond to
> your pregnancy?

Nosango: Students created jokes on me, saying, 'How can a child of a saved person get pregnant?' I just ignored them. The teachers said nothing, as if nothing happened.

Interviewer: What are your hopes/dreams for your future?

Nosango: I want my son to get more education, for him to be educated although I'm not sure what I want him to be in the future. I want him to look after me because now I'm looking after and taking care of him. For myself, I want to be a medical doctor. My subjects are physics, maths and biology and I am very good at them.

Interviewer: What do you think is necessary to enable you to achieve your dreams?

Nosango: To work hard at school so that I can get very good results at grade 12 and that's the way to university to study medicine, to be a medical practitioner.

Interviewer: Do you have any concerns about your own or your child's future?

Nosango: No, I am not worried about my future nor about my child's because I know he will get what he wants and be what he wants to be in the future. (Nosango, aged 16, Masiphumelele)

Young mothers who managed to return to school without repeating a grade described the practical and emotional support provided by partners, friends, family and teachers. In Nosango's case, her mother looked after her infant during school hours; her boyfriend contributed to the cost of baby clothes and infant formula; certain teachers and fellow pupils ensured that homework tasks were taken to and from her home; and her friends explained the school work when necessary. Such examples of practical support are critical in their own right and give young mothers a sense that others are standing by them in the face of social norms that regard pregnancy during school years as 'a mistake'. Thus pregnancy and early parenting are in the medium term often incorporated into, and even normalised by, existing domestic and peer relationships (see Chapter 7). When this is the case, the schooling of adolescent girls is not necessarily compromised.

Conversely, pregnant teenagers or young mothers tend to leave school when a combination of local attitudes and economic constraints means that family members, friends and boyfriends are unwilling or unable to offer them such support. Adolescent girls in Ocean View said that a fairly common reaction from parents was to deny their responsibilities with regard to a 'choice' made by a young person and leave them to cope with the consequences: 'She is grown up now so she must look after herself and her baby,' or 'She's made her bed, so now she must lie on it'. When such parental attitudes are combined with a general neighbourhood discourse that positions adolescents as likely to fail at school and in the employment arena, there is little incentive for girls who conceive to stay in school.

While the concern is usually directed at the impact of childbirth on girls' education, our data suggest that young parenthood has a significant, and often greater, impact on schooling among adolescent boys and young men. Young fathers in Masiphumelele, and sometimes in Ocean View, are expected not only to pay 'damages' for making their girlfriends pregnant, but to make regular financial contributions to the baby's upkeep. The typical charge for 'damages' in Masiphumelele is approximately R5 000 (equivalent to about 50 days' work for someone in casual, unskilled employment). We do not have access to precise figures, but it is clear that while many young fathers distance themselves and evade these duties (see Chapter 7), a sizeable proportion leave school and seek full-time work in order to fulfil them.

Adolescents' decisions are influenced by their peers in other ways too. Throughout this volume, we have shown that one of the reasons friendships operate so powerfully in young people's lives both within and beyond school is because friends are notionally equal in terms of age status. Therefore, when the strictures of the education system differentiate peers (for example by passing some and failing others), young people are confronted with uncomfortable changes in identity within their circles of friends. The experience or even the prospect of these changes deters adolescents from continuing at school:

> A lot of people do not come back to school after failing. Friends will laugh
> at you if you do, and you'd have to see your friends being ahead of you.
> (Pupils aged 16–18 in grade 10, Ocean View Secondary School)

Young people who fall behind at school are not only confronted with the indignity of failure and the need to repeat the year, but are separated from their peer group with whom they have formed close attachments. In addition to the consequences of alienation within the peer group, our data show that decisions about whether to continue in or leave school are influenced by changes in roles and activities that accompany maturation and the transition to adulthood, and that these are demarcated in a number of ways.

In Masiphumelele, formal initiation into manhood usually occurs between the age of 16 and 20. Many boys are taken to the 'bush' (usually their paternal ancestral home in the Eastern Cape) to be circumcised in the school holidays during their penultimate or final year. Recent initiates spoke of the incongruities of returning to Cape Town to continue studying in a class comprising mostly 'boys' (who may or may not be younger than they are). A large proportion of high-school pupils in Masiphumelele face this tension because frequent grade repetition during their earlier school years has meant that many are still at school in their early or even mid-20s.[5]

Work becomes a priority for boys and girls across the Valley when they reach late adolescence, a shift that they explain in terms of the need for spending power and a wish to become independent from their parents. Having a disposable income is linked to ensuring inclusion in the peer group by purchasing fashionable clothes or technology, and to personal integrity associated with entering adulthood. In Masiphumelele and Ocean View young people are often also required to fulfil family responsibilities (such as those of young fathers described above). Boys feel the pressure most keenly to earn money, in part because of the pervasive and powerful gender norms that position them as providers to women and children.

Many older teenagers in Masiphumelele and Ocean View try to find work that they can do whilst continuing at school. Very few succeed. In 2005, only 6 per cent of adolescents in Cape Town reported combining study and work, and very few of these were either poor or African. Figure 6.11 shows the study and work status of adolescents by age in rich neighbourhoods (including both white and coloured ones), poor coloured neighbourhoods and poor African neighbourhoods. In poor African neighbourhoods almost everyone is studying and almost no one is working or has worked recently (defined here as in the past 12 months). In poor coloured areas fewer adolescents are studying, and a higher proportion of those who are not studying are working – although unemployment is high among the non-pupils. It is only in rich neighbourhoods that adolescents study and work. Among the older adolescents (i.e. aged 18 and 19), approximately equal numbers are studying and not working, studying and working (including those who have worked recently), and not studying. These data indicate the extreme scarcity of employment opportunities for poor – and especially poor African – youths.

Most young people who leave school to find work, or felt they had no alternative but to do so, struggle to get a job. Unemployment rates among 20- to 24-year-

Figure 6.11 *Study and work status, by age and neighbourhood type*

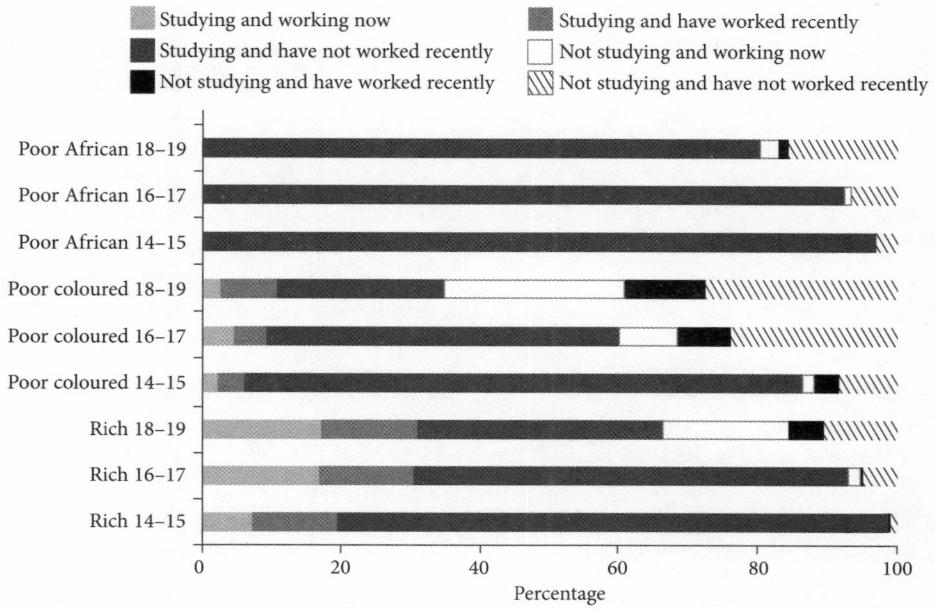

Source: Cape Area Panel Study wave 1 (2002)

olds in 2001 were as high as 31 per cent among women in Ocean View; 37 per cent among men there; 68 per cent among men and a massive 73 per cent among women, in Masiphumelele (as we saw in Chapter 1). In other words, for every young woman in Masiphumelele with a job, there were three other young women who were unemployed.[6] Employers prefer adults with similar qualifications but more experience than young people. Of those who did find employment, it was mostly casual or irregular work – including especially menial work in the service sector – that they considered helpful in fulfilling an immediate need to earn money, but inadequate in relation to their aspirations for a high-status job in the future.

The difficulties of finding work experienced by young men in Ocean View and Masiphumelele can have an indirect effect on the decisions of girls regarding their schooling:

> [Young women] are badly influenced by the boys…you want to go to school maybe, you stay there [at your boyfriend's house] overnight then when you want to go to school in the morning, then he doesn't want you to go to school because…he doesn't understand. Because he doesn't himself go to school. So he doesn't understand that. (Zanele, girl, grade 12, Masiphumelele High School)

The dismal employment prospects described above underlie the decisions of some young people seeking social status and an income to engage in other activities that they observe as a feasible alternative in their neighbourhoods, such as gang membership and crime. Our ethnographic study generated very little data on these activities owing to our use of schools as an entry point, the age group with which we worked and because gangsterism is widely believed by local residents to be less rife in the Valley than other areas of Cape Town, such as the Cape Flats. But because gang membership is a choice made by a proportion of young people, mostly adolescent boys, in Ocean View and Masiphumelele, we include a case study generated in a qualitative study conducted in the same period in Khayelitsha, a settlement on the Cape Flats that, although much larger, is demographically similar and intimately connected to Masiphumelele.[7] The decisions taken by this young man and his family reflect the particular influences of the home and neighbourhood discussed earlier in the chapter, and show the manner in which these experiences articulate with discourses that value education in shaping decision-making in the transition to adulthood.

Nineteen-year-old Nezile spoke of his sporadic school attendance throughout his teens and, at the time of being interviewed, he had been out of school for a few months. He recalled becoming involved in theft from the age of 13, his quick addiction to drugs, joining gangs and his early fascination with weapons. Looking back, he recognises that he established his own gang primarily in order to achieve social status and power within his neighbourhood and among his peers:

> The thing is that we wanted to get known…like when we enter in a place where they (another gang) are known, everyone would just fear, they are

scared. We wanted it to be like that with my gang…We wanted to be the most feared…

Gang membership offers young men social status from the moment they join (Bility 1999; Kinnes 2000). And several years later, while Nezile asserts that he is trying to leave gang life and 'bad' criminal activity behind, he still enjoys exerting his position of power among younger friends:

> …they gonna do it and I'm not gonna stop them. I like it when they do it also…like, let's say right, mhh…let's say you are walking down the street, I come and rob you. My friends are still here: they don't know about robbing, they don't know that stuff. I rob you. I'm gonna tell them to do it and force them to do it, seeing at the same time that it is wrong, but I want them to do it.

Nezile experienced gang life as exciting and rewarding in terms of his position within the peer group and sense of self-efficacy. In contrast, he found school 'a boring place' where teachers were often absent, easily irritated, very slow or always upset, in other words an environment where he felt under-stimulated and disempowered. He reported being unable to focus or to understand questions, and as a result usually failed tests. He considers that he 'only passed properly until grade 4', implying that he felt close to failure throughout his high-school years. At home, his mother and stepmother would call him 'stupid', further undermining his sense of his own ability and his motivation:

> And then, if someone always calls you stupid, why would you still make an effort?

The central role of gangs in the identities and everyday lives of young men, and by association some women, in large sections of Cape Town has been amply documented (Pinnock 1982a, 1982b; Steinberg 2005). Such gangs exert a powerful influence on social interaction in many neighbourhoods that is often either beyond the reach of, or incorporates, local police. Perhaps sensing the grip that gang life had on her son, Nezile's mother tried to help him by enrolling him at a boarding school outside Cape Town. Although grateful of his mother's considerable efforts to make education and a career available to him, Nezile reports that he could not settle there. He was expelled after a few months and his mother enrolled him at a different boarding school in Pretoria. There he was again expelled, having experienced the same problems: persistent bad behaviour even when he was made a prefect or given other responsibilities, and feeling 'stressed out' by the fact that he was so far away from his mother and could not check if she was managing financially. Returning to Cape Town, Nezile re-enrolled at the local high school, but left later that year. He was working as a waiter at the time of being interviewed, a job that he described as 'fine' because it meant that he was not sitting at home doing nothing. However, a few weeks later he walked out of this job.

Nezile is one of many poor adolescents for whom time at school has been profoundly dissatisfactory and time spent in illicit or normatively 'antisocial' activities has offered at least some aspects of the social and personal development he sought at the cusp of adulthood. At several points in Nezile's narrative he apparently rejects an educational career for himself ('there is nothing in education for me'), but he remains equivocal about the potential benefits of the schooling he could have had. When recalling his feelings of regret each time he was expelled, Nezile appears to remind himself of the reasons he courted expulsion: 'At the same time, this person does not like school.' Despite these personal realisations, he never directly challenges the notion that schooling is the best, and indeed only, route to a good job and to success in life more broadly. Why then does he maintain a belief that education can enable young people to fulfil these aspirations when he has had such negative experiences?

The answer to this question appears to lie, at least in part, in the problems inherent in the alternatives to schooling. Lack of employment opportunities removes the possibility of combining school and work, and of finding a job that provides income and social status. And gang life is quite literally life-threatening: Nezile has witnessed the deaths of several friends, deliberate or accidental, as a result of gang-related activities. And in the light of the mortality statistics for young men living in Cape Town's poorer neighbourhoods, he has reason to wonder about his own chances of survival:

> You can't know what tomorrow is gonna bring, so I prepare myself for everything...I just wish I can make it to 2010 maybe because I know one of these days something is gonna happen...

In light of the real costs of involvement in criminal and gang-related activities, quite apart from the social costs of being considered morally 'bad', Nezile does not consider a career in these activities to be a feasible alternative to that of schooling. It is almost as if, in the vacuum of opportunities left by massive unemployment, he has to believe in at least one route to success for himself and all his peers in a similar position. He holds onto the possibility of following this route and achieving its promised outcome even though he knows it to be unrealistic given his age and schooling history:

> I feel bad [about dropping out of school] 'cause somebody on TV, you see, you see like, you see people on the TV, and I saw this advert yesterday, this guy who has a briefcase and a suit and he was driving. So I'm like, if I finished my standards and everything, would I have been that person immediately or would I have to struggle to be that person? You see?...So I thought maybe next year I will try again, try to be that person on TV.

In the excerpt above, Nezile openly wonders how long it would take to achieve a position in an office having completed school, and, indeed, whether the process between would have been smooth or not. The fact that such questions are glaringly absent from the narratives of school pupils in Masiphumelele and Ocean View is perhaps explained by the fact that they had not made a decision to leave, and that because they saw themselves on the path that leads from schooling to work and success, it was not helpful to question the efficacy of this route. The absence of voiced doubts does not mean that these adolescents assume that their progress along this path will be unproblematic. We saw earlier that members of the art club in Masiphumelele worried that their parents would not be able to afford the costs of further education or that their success would be undermined by jealous neighbours or peers.

What the silence does suggest is that a large portion of poor adolescents in school have a very minimal understanding of the educational, training and recruitment processes beyond their everyday experience of school and the casual labour market. We compared grade-12 pupils' exposure to information on higher education and careers across the Valley: local universities and technikons displayed stands in Fish Hoek Senior High school; a visit to the University of the Western Cape was organised by Ocean View Secondary School; and Masiphumelele High School asked pupils to pay R30 for a trip to the University of Cape Town, then cancelled the trip because too few had contributed to pay for the transport. In this context, it is highly likely that poor adolescents who currently attend school privately question whether they will achieve their goals, but cannot afford to verbalise their doubts because they have invested so heavily in schooling and regard themselves as following the 'right' path.

Striking in young people's narratives across the wealth and cultural spectra is the absence of an anti-schooling ideology or subculture, such as was found among teenage boys from poor families in England (Willis 1977). Unlike in 1970s England, we hear little of the opportunity costs of education, namely the supposed 'freedom', earnings and expenditure associated with work. In the light of high rates of unemployment, it is understandable that Capetonian adolescents equate leaving school without a matric pass with continuing poverty, and that education is seen as something that *should* make a difference. Even adolescents living with HIV-positive mothers or whose mothers have died from AIDS-related sickness, describe education as the route to success, an opinion that is understood as revealing the high value placed on education even when life expectancy becomes more uncertain (De Lannoy 2008). What is perhaps more surprising is the lack of rebellion – at least at the level of public discourse – against the culture of mainstream education, and the persistent veneration of education as *the* proper (or only) solution when everyday experiences show it to be a highly problematic process with dubious rewards.

The completion of schooling, including at least the notion of passing matric, is one of several transitions into adulthood that young people envisage and experience in a period spanning their mid-teens to early 20s. Some of these transitions are considered by wider society as consistent and compatible with schooling (such as initiation), but experienced by young people as problematic. Others are considered incompatible (like pregnancy and early parenthood), but can, with certain provisions, be incorporated into an educational career. In all cases, however, the fact that these transitions are occurring in parallel to the culmination of schooling means that young people are likely to confront a number of points where difficult decisions need to be made.

Teenagers in the final three years of high school in both Ocean View and Masiphumelele are aware that a very large proportion of their friends have left school, with or without a matric pass, and have not found work. Yet only in Ocean

View did young people express a pessimistic view of the potential of education, and of their associated intention to follow their peers in leaving school early:

> When you look around in Ocean View there are people with matric that are sitting around at home without jobs, so it doesn't seem to make much difference. (Bianca, girl in grade 10 at Ocean View Secondary School)

In the light of even higher unemployment rates among young people in Masiphumelele, we must ask why adolescents in this community do not point to the futility of education as do their peers in Ocean View. Our data point to two distinct but related influences on young people's perceptions of their opportunities in contemporary Cape Town. The first relates to the social and political identities of young people as members of communities that were, and in many respects still are, afforded different opportunities. The second pertains particularly to African adolescents, and springs from a response to living in ongoing structural poverty where there are no viable alternatives through which to realise, or speak about realising, the aspirations one holds as a member of a generation with greater opportunities than those of one's forbears.

During conversation with Brian, an 18-year-old pupil in Ocean View, we spoke about his attempts to secure training or work for when he matriculated. He explained that there were some jobs he could have applied for, but they were looking for 'black' candidates. He, like many young people in Ocean View, identified himself as 'coloured' so wrongly assumed that these jobs would not be available to him. One of his classmates said that there are people in Ocean View who believe that affirmative action policies are taking jobs away from them, and that 'black people are getting everything and that they [coloured people] are not getting much'. This view was reiterated by one teenager and linked with his self-perception as being marginalised and inadequate:

> I must say, we did a great job as far as the ten years of democracy is concerned but I really think that apartheid is going in reverse, especially with this black economic empowerment thing going as far as you must get a job according to your skin colour…I don't want to be looked at as a coloured that's not white enough to be black enough, so I can't get the job. So I think that we sort of, feel very degraded by that, making me as a person feel that I'm not good enough for this country. (Ivan, boy, aged 16, Ocean View)

A large proportion of young people we worked with in Fish Hoek spoke of their intentions to travel and work overseas after they had completed school. Many saw this as an opportunity for broadening their experience beyond the Valley or for connecting with relatives or friends. But some also referred to their perception of themselves as being the 'wrong colour' for the current and future employment market.

Young people in Masiphumelele were largely silent on the topic of identity and employment prospects. (Our study, however, did not focus on work-seeking behaviour in late adolescence – a topic that deserves further investigation in light of the findings presented in this volume.) Their stated intentions to enrol in a higher-education institution, or to seek work in the retail outlets and restaurants in the Valley, convey a perception that these jobs are available to them and that by completing their schooling they can achieve these goals. Their absence of knowledge of further education, plus the minimal evidence of increasing employment prospects in their neighbourhood, perhaps explain why young people made little reference to an era of opportunity through affirmative action.

A further, less obvious influence on adolescent experiences of schooling, their sense of what school can offer them and, therefore, their decisions to stay or leave is the extent to which the neighbourhood permeates the school. Schools in Masiphumelele and Ocean View were observed to be porous: both adults and children moved on and off the premises fairly freely. Outsiders, often described by children as 'gangsters', came into school and persistent 'bunking' by pupils was largely ignored by teachers. Only in 2006 were the gates in Ocean View Secondary School locked and community police brought in to round up those 'bunking' class and expel outsiders from the premises. And in the same year, Masiphumelele High School installed gates and fences and employed a security guard for similar reasons. By comparison, schools in Fish Hoek tend to be enclosed and any movement in or out closely monitored. Long-established in the Valley and now educating pupils from beyond the immediate neighbourhood, these schools have identities that are linked to, but distinct from, the Fish Hoek community. The identities of relatively new schools in Masiphumelele and Ocean view are to a much greater extent bound up with those of the surrounding community. In these settings, it is more difficult for young people to maintain a sense of belonging to an institution that offers something different to what exists in the broader neighbourhood.

Very rarely did adolescents in Masiphumelele attribute the high failure rates to the quality of their schooling. Some explained it as arising from the fact that the high school is young and has only run the matric exam for two years, and that teachers and pupils are still getting used to the system. But many made no reference to the failure of the system, possibly because, despite its weaknesses, it is still experienced as offering a better-quality education than that which they experienced in schools in the Eastern Cape.

Conclusion

Earlier in the chapter we raised the questions of why such a high value is placed on education by poor children and adolescents, particularly those living in Masiphumelele. We also asked why, in the face of low pass rates, so many poor African adolescents across Cape Town remain in school, whereas a large proportion of their slightly less poor coloured counterparts leave from the age of 15 and upwards.

Across the social and demographic spectrum of post-apartheid Cape Town, being a school pupil is associated with doing what is 'good' and 'right'. The value placed on education – particularly in neighbourhoods populated by adults who were themselves denied quality education – affords a positive social status for the individual child and his or her family. It gives young people a sense – albeit often an illusion – of investing energy in ways that will improve their own future and that of their family. And, in terms of young people's daily experiences, schooling in all neighbourhoods is largely about the formation, development and remodelling of friendships and, often, dating relationships. While these commonalities provide pupils with a sense of a shared identity and life path, they mask large inequalities in educational provision, support from the home and neighbourhood and perceptions of future opportunities.

Pupils in Fish Hoek schools struggle with the pressure not only to pass, but to excel in their school work. Most regret, and some fail to cope with, their perception that the marks they gain at school define their value to their parents. In schools in poor neighbourhoods, such as Ocean View and Masiphumelele, peer-group dynamics assume a greater importance in young people's experience of school because they have at least some measure of control over these, which they do not have over important aspects of their formal learning and academic progress. The active assistance and interest of family members is critical to young people's abilities to perform well and to stay motivated in schools where performance is generally poor. However, very low parental education levels mean that it is exceptional for secondary-school pupils in these latter neighbourhoods to have parents with the schooling to assist them with their own homework, or even perhaps to understand the demands of secondary schooling and the opportunities that follow. Pass rates are low and the persistently high attendance rates in the upper years of Masiphumelele High School therefore surprising. A key contributor is the support from peers, as well as from parents and some teachers, as a result of a strong social consensus. Adults and children alike believe that this is a generation with vastly increased opportunities for social and economic status through education. They are largely unaware though of the limits of their knowledge regarding what is required to pass their final public examination. In Ocean View, by comparison, parental disengagement from school is often accompanied by pessimistic attitudes towards young people's future potential. Doubting their abilities to pass exams and observant of high unemployment among those who have, a large portion of adolescents opt to leave school early.

There are subtle, but significant, differences in the value attached to education between neighbourhoods, and the knowledge underpinning these values, which helps explain survey responses about educational expectations. In Fish Hoek and Masiphumelele, education is seen as *the* route to success, whereas in Ocean View it is seen as *a* route to success for the small minority. The unquestioned value of education in Fish Hoek is supported by the fact that the vast majority of pupils move through school at the expected pace, pass their matric and enter further education or other forms of training. In Masiphumelele, however, its value persists in the context of unfamiliarity on the part of parents and children regarding the mismatch between what is happening in classrooms and what is required to pass matric and move into further education and high-status employment. Here, adolescents see their contemporaries and adult relatives struggle to find even menial or casual work, but at the same time maintain their own aspirations to high-status jobs. They are able to do so because they consider the casual, manual employment sphere of their parents to be totally separate to that of white-collar professions, and they observe the occasional local resident get into university or acquire a well-paid job, but know little about what is required to obtain such positions. For, despite the redirection of resources since 1994, few African adolescents in Cape Town have access to formal information on higher education or careers, or to the knowledge that is passed through personal networks.

In Ocean View, where formal education is widely regarded as a possible route to success, the aspirations of adolescents were more conservative and tempered by anticipated obstacles to further education and seeking employment. They observe young adults who have matriculated but have not found work, and have more direct and indirect knowledge of the local labour market than their counterparts in Masiphumelele because their families have participated in it for several generations (see also Beutel & Anderson 2008). Furthermore, some young people regard themselves as being in a weak position to enter further education and high-status employment because they understand affirmative action policies as favouring black African people.

A further contributor to the discourse that venerates education is material poverty. In contexts where economic resources are scarce and unpredictable, young people who have genuinely positive attitudes towards education face various pressures alongside that of educational success, which undermine their ability to achieve at school. The impact of domestic demands, illness, income fragility and the social manifestations of poverty and disempowerment, such as alcoholism and drug use among parents, have been documented above. Poverty also contributes to the tensions adolescents experience in their social identities. Poor adolescents state how difficult it is to be a successful pupil and simultaneously considered trendy and attractive within the peer group. High status in the peer group requires wearing and owning costly items. And given that poor parents can rarely afford these and do not always wish to provide them, young people need to earn either through work, dating relationships or crime. For most, these pursuits are incompatible with schooling on practical and social grounds (see also Chapter 8).

One way in which young people can manage these incompatibilities is to think and talk in terms of a moral dichotomy between the 'good' career through school and into high-status work, and a 'bad' career entailing educational failure. Discourse of this nature has considerable currency across the Valley, but is a particularly powerful way of organising and explaining the world in Masiphumelele. And it can only be fuelled by the absence of viable and sustainable alternatives for adolescents, such as local apprenticeship or employment, which makes it simply too dreadful to contemplate the notion that education may not produce success. Through these mechanisms, young people are unknowingly strengthening a culturally validated discourse that venerates education and acts as a robust veneer over other ideas and realities that pertain to school experience.

We worked with several adolescent pupils in Ocean View and Masiphumelele who at once espouse the view that education will lead them into successful careers and privately question whether they will achieve their goals. However, they could not afford to verbalise their doubts because they have invested personal effort and family resources so heavily in their schooling that they consequently regard themselves – and are seen by their families and friends – as following the 'right' path. But in maintaining this silence, young people preclude the possibility of receiving advice or support that could help them with their school work and bolster their self-esteem. The decision by one highly competent grade-12 pupil at Masiphumelele High School arose out of this dilemma and resulted in her failing her matric.

Chloe had performed well throughout her career in Masiphumelele High School and made an effort to study at home and in the library. At the beginning of her grade-12 year, she told us that she expected to pass her matric examination and had plans to enrol in college. To our surprise, she failed, but received a 'supplementary exam' (a chance to resit mathematics and accounting). Several months later, it emerged in conversation that Chloe had elected not to attend the maths exam, knowing that it would jeopardise her chances of passing. She said that she did not believe she would be able to understand and complete the questions so thought it best not to try. She spoke to no one about her decision and later said that 'pretending I was on the right track was driving me crazy'. Chloe was later told by a teacher that her marks in other subjects were high enough to have enabled her to pass if she had attended the maths exam.

Evident in Chloe's experiences is the fact that in contexts where education is highly venerated, there is considerable symbolic, social and emotional value in adolescents maintaining a discourse that divides the world between those who are 'on the right track' and those who are not. The reality is much more nebulous. Young people move quickly and sometimes even unconsciously from the former to the latter, and some vice versa (for example, some young mothers), although this is much more difficult without a high level of support from family, teachers and friends. In poor neighbourhoods with poorly functioning schools where young people are faced with 'failure' (either midway through or at the end of their school career), one reason why young people persistently uphold the value of formal education as a route to success is that it represents a 'definite', and therefore allows them to retain a sense of integrity associated with predictability, in what are, in reality, highly unpredictable circumstances.

Young people's active participation in such discourse serves important short-term purposes, including fulfilling obligations to family and bolstering self-esteem, which, in turn, serve to strengthen their chances of overcoming obstacles at school. In the long term, however, its perpetuation is disempowering of the young because it mutes other discourses within and between generations that acknowledge the dissonance between ideals and realities. The bald reality of poor employment prospects and difficulties entering further education are left unexamined, and young people make no serious demands on the state or contemporary civil society to change this scenario.

7 Freedom, 'fitting in' and foreign territories: The world of friends, dating and sex

> When I was younger…back *then*, it was just like: *me*. You know? *My* feelings and *my* mind and *my* stuff…But now, you're thinking of everyone around you…it's just, like, snowballed into this huge big picture of, like, *everybody* that I know: my family, my school, my friends, boyfriends, where am I going to work one day, what money will I get in…You know, *all these things*…You have to *learn* how to manage your feelings and stuff. Or else it just gets *unmanageable*…(Leanne, girl, aged 17, Fish Hoek, group discussion)

One of the most demanding and often traumatic changes for adolescents in every part of the Valley is their entry into the world of dating and sexual relationships. What marks young South Africans out from others traversing this 'normal' terrain of adolescence is a history of legitimised power relationships between groups categorised by 'race', the effects of which, articulated with culturally inscribed gender roles and age-based hierarchies, produce additional challenges to adolescents. In this chapter we examine the post-apartheid world of the peer group, its increasing importance and influence with age, the normative environment in which young people make decisions and their interaction with adults on the topic of sex. Histories of segregation between neighbourhoods are likely to have resulted in differences between neighbourhoods in the way that boys and girls experience relationships and sex. But what is the nature of these differences and of the less explored similarities? In what ways are adolescent friendships and sexual relationships affected by the increasingly pervasive consumer culture and global imagery of status present in the media? And, echoing Mandela's (1995) vision quoted at the beginning of Chapter 1 of this book, does contemporary society create and nurture informal or formal institutions that are 'eloquent with care, respect and love', necessary to redress past wrongs and prepare the youth for a future involving healthy intimate relationships?

One of the most serious challenges to South African youth is that of HIV and AIDS. The presence of AIDS further intensifies issues of knowledge, power and self-care[1] that pervade relationships between young people, and those between generations. The pandemic has prompted considerable research on adolescent sex, but most early studies were primarily quantitative, telling us more about *what* young people are doing than *why*, and neglecting the 'societal, normative and cultural contexts' (MacPhail & Campbell 2001: 1614; see also Campbell 2003; Kelly & Ntlabati 2002; Parker 1995). The result is a proliferation of explanations of youth sexual behaviour that were denuded of social meaning and divorced from the specificities of historical, socio-economic and cultural contexts. Only recently has research turned to adolescents' *own* understandings and experience of their behaviour within given contexts (Burns 2002).

Recent South African research has started to examine the social processes and pressures associated with young people's sexual practices (Alexander & Uys 2002). Both boys and girls experience their sexual socialisation in contradictory terms. Henderson (1999) discusses the contradictory pressures on girls living in New Crossroads, as their families emphasise their girlhood and encourage them to preserve their virginity, whilst boys at school and in the neighbourhood demand sex. Salo (2004) notes the importance to mothers in Manenberg that their daughters remain chaste (and be 'good daughters'), but this can trap their daughters in a position of continuing dependency. For their part, boys are expected to conform to a rigid definition of masculinity. In the absence of jobs, many men turn to violence to demonstrate masculinity (Barker & Ricardo 2005; Henderson 2006; Shefer & Potgieter 2006). Qualitative research shows that violence against women is widespread in young people's heterosexual relationships (Varga & Makubalo 1996; Wood & Jewkes 1997; Wood et al. 1998). This is not without costs to some young men whose emotional vulnerability, doubts and insecurities are at odds with the predominant, macho image of sexual bravado, experience and power (Barker & Ricardo 2005; Holland et al. 1994). And out of this dissonance can emerge defensive strategies on the part of men, which reproduce and reinforce male dominance (Barker & Ricardo 2005; Holland et al. 1994).

Boys' voices and experiences are still largely silenced within the prevailing research agenda, and boys tend to be represented uncritically as 'problems' (Pattman & Chege 2003), with girls cast as 'victims' of male sexuality. A promising shift in focus is evident in recent research on how young men and women resist pressure to conform to gendered expectations. For example, one study of young people in the African mining township of Khutsong, south-west of Johannesburg, found that a minority of young men heatedly defended the rights of women in sexual relationships and challenged the idea of coercive sex, while a minority of female participants spoke of successfully fending off coercive sexual advances from males or expressed admiration towards those who took up active strategies of resistance (MacPhail & Campbell 2001).

'Problems' such as sexual violence and teenage pregnancy are often attributed to 'tradition' and 'culture'. Such explanations are often crude, sometimes verging on racist (Macleod & Durrheim 2002), and serve to excuse problematic male behaviour and power (Shefer & Potgieter 2006). Delius and Glaser (2002) argue that violence is untraditional in that it reflects a profound historical shift in male peer pressure from managing and restraining adolescent sexuality to a celebration of the commodification and control of women. Furthermore, given the overlap between race category and class, sexual violence might as readily reflect socio-economic as cultural factors (Eaton et al. 2003). Indeed, one ethnographic study in a poor township in the Eastern Cape suggested that the lack of economic and recreational opportunities available to young men and women led to sexual relations being used as a means for gaining respect and social status (Wood & Jewkes 2001). Material factors are also integral to the phenomenon of 'transactional' sex, with young women exchanging sex for material support (Adams & Marshall 1998; and – for a study across 'race' groups –

Kaufman & Stavrou 2004). In South Africa, transactional sex generally entails conspicuous consumption rather than subsistence needs (LeClerc-Madlala 2002, 2003). In this context, 'women typically see multiple boyfriends as a means of gaining control over their lives, rather than acts of desperation…although the two of course are linked' (Hunter 2002: 112). Hunter's point deserves attention: young women may seek sexual exchanges of the kind that expose them to violence, and although their motivation is very rarely physical survival, there are significant consequences for their social identity and sense of self-efficacy (see also Chapters 4 and 8).

In this chapter we heed the calls to examine young men and women living in all kinds of neighbourhoods, to engage with the positive as well as the negative aspects of sexual relationships and to resist stereotypes (Alexander & Uys 2002; Lesch & Kruger 2004; MacPhail & Campbell 2001).

We refer to relationships between boys and girls as 'dating'. We do not mean by this the *activity* of going on a date (as in American academic and popular discourse), but rather the *relationships* between boys and girls. Few young people in the Valley spoke about going on formal or structured 'dates' with their boyfriends or girlfriends, and interaction between boys and girls who are paired off often takes place in the context of group-based socialising with peers. We employ this imported concept because, across the Valley, there is no single term used by boys or girls to describe their relationships with the opposite sex. We refrain from using the term 'sexual relationship' to describe such relationships, as not all young people who have boyfriends or girlfriends are sexually involved. We are also hesitant to refer to 'romantic' or 'intimate' relationships because, as shall be seen, relationships with the opposite sex can be motivated and characterised by factors other than 'romance' or 'intimacy'.

Relationships in adolescence

The importance of relationships beyond the family in adolescence is well recognised within academic literature. Achieving independence, marked by an increasing social distance between adults and youth and the establishment of sexual relationships, is often seen as a marker of 'normal' adolescence (Marshall et al. 1999). Much literature surrounding relationships in adolescence has focused on the changing salience of relationships within family and relationships with friends (Giordano 2003). Studies of peer relationships are common within the domain of developmental psychology, which characterises these relationships as an integral part of social development in adolescence. Social development in adolescence is characterised by an increasing interest and involvement in the peer group, motivated by an intense desire to 'belong' (Thom et al. 1998). Increasing interaction with the peer group provides interpersonal contact beyond family relationships, playing an important role in adolescents' psychosocial development, contributing to their emotional needs and serving as an important source of information and opportunity for socialisation. Studies document changes in the peer-group structure that occur during adolescence, including cliques, crowds, friendships and the development of 'romantic' relationships (Thom et al. 1998). These ideas have generally been developed within the domain of developmental psychology, which often ignores the role that contextual processes play in shaping the contours of such relationships. Researchers have warned against making universalistic assumptions about relationships in adolescence at the expense of engaging with social specificities that shape adolescents' relationships in a variety of ways (Marshall et al. 1999). Internationally, sociological work has provided a broader lens through which to view these relationships in adolescence and draws attention to the manner in which adolescents' social addresses and locations (gender, race and social class) influence many aspects of these relationships, including their intimacy and influence (Giordano 2003). As we saw in Chapter 4, historical patterns of racial segregation in South Africa are still a powerful mediator in shaping young people's friendships, patterns of integration and socialising.

Across the Valley, younger teenagers tend to have friends of both sexes. 'Best friends' are generally of the same sex; friendship groups or cliques at school are largely segregated by gender. Few of these younger teenagers have boyfriends or girlfriends. They rarely mention 'dating' relationships, and when they do, they do not refer to them as if they were of primary importance in their current lives. For example, in art club sessions, boyfriends and girlfriends were rarely (if ever) mentioned in discussions and drawing sessions about intimate relationships, support and challenges. While dating relationships are evident during late childhood, these do not yet involve the level of intimacy or depth experienced in familial relationships and friendships.

At the same time, conversational banter and teasing during art sessions with young people aged 11 to 13 from all parts of the Valley showed their growing interest in this topic, and in the opposite sex, as well as a greater self-consciousness about appearance. Towards the end of the fieldwork, many of the girls in the Ocean View art club had started to have boyfriends. We observed this group tease those with boyfriends, but always with an underlying sense of envy. The dynamics between the girls demonstrated the ambiguity at this stage of their lives as they develop a new interest in boys. Girls would try to embarrass each other by telling about SMS messages others had sent to or received from boys; however, embarrassment was also mixed with pride in the attention they were receiving from boys. 'Who loves who' was often a topic of much interest and teasing in our group sessions with this age group. Darren at Fish Hoek Primary School introduced a 'names and numbers test' that results in a percentage indicating how much someone 'loves' another person. This was a cause of much teasing and laughter – and a secretive business: when it was Annie's turn to do this test for some boys she liked, she would then cross out the names furiously. Darren managed to steal her paper and started calling out the names, which resulted in a screaming and running session in the corridor.

Pre-existing friendship networks are important in shaping the manner in which young people pair off. Among young people in their early teens, we observed that same-gender cliques are sometimes attached to cliques of young people of the opposite gender, and that these cliques merge over time. It is within this context that young people start forming attachments with members of the opposite sex. For example, Samantha, Mina and their friends in Ocean View – all in their early teens – gave themselves 'gang' names, like 'The Young Little Bastards' and 'The Fiesta Girls'. (The term 'gang' refers to a group of friends in this context, *not* a group of 'criminals'.) These gangs were attached to similar gangs of boys, and individual girls and boys would form dating relationships within these boundaries. The girls' gang would take on additional names to mark their connection to the boys' gang. For example, Mina referred to her gang as both the 'Fiesta Girls' and the 'Naughty by Nature' girls because a number of them were dating boys from the 'Naughty by Nature' gang. Friendships are also affected by dating relationships: young people often spoke about fights at school between former friends over boyfriends and girlfriends.

Among younger and older teenagers, both boys and girls get caught up in the idea of 'love'. They start to experience new and confusing feelings for the opposite sex, often accompanied by experiences of rejection. For grade-11 young people in Fish Hoek, the topics of boyfriends, girlfriends, break-ups, heartaches and relationship problems came up regularly in their timelines of memories of growing up, and in diagrams of current supports and challenges. 'Relationships' and 'love' mostly appeared as 'challenges'; few people mentioned their boyfriends or girlfriends as sources of support. As teenagers' interest in dating and sex increases, they also report that school gets harder and the pressure to do well and think about the future increases substantially. They indicated that balancing social lives and studying for school was their main struggle. Turbulent feelings and events related to relationships (both of a romantic nature as well as relationships with family and friends) were put forth as major issues they had to deal with.

In a discussion about memories about growing up, grade-9 boys in Fish Hoek agreed that, from about the age of 13, sex becomes a major interest for them. They recognise this interest to be a combination of physical changes and a desire for a 'cool' social image. Boys and girls described increasing social pressure to date and have sex during high school, and felt that this was an important part of 'fitting in' and 'being cool'. Although young people often expressed the view that dating and sex are 'the norm' and that 'everyone is doing it', among the older teenagers with whom we worked closely, girls and boys alike, there were considerable variations in their experience of dating and sexual relationships. In fact, a significant proportion were not dating and had not had sex.

Figures 7.1 and 7.2 show the proportions of adolescent girls and boys in Cape Town who report that they have had sex, by age, using Cape Area Panel Study (CAPS) data. (These figures also show the proportions of respondents who report having been pregnant or having made a girl pregnant, which we discuss further below.) The differences between girls and boys are small. About one in five 16-year-olds and about half of 18-year-olds reported having had sex. At the age of 22, four out of five people have had sex. These data suggest that it is unusual for a teenager to be sexually active until the ages of 17, 18 and 19, i.e. at about the age at which students complete their schooling, unless (as is often the case in poorer neighbourhoods) they have repeated grades and fallen behind.

Figure 7.1 *Sexual activity and pregnancy among girls, Cape Town*

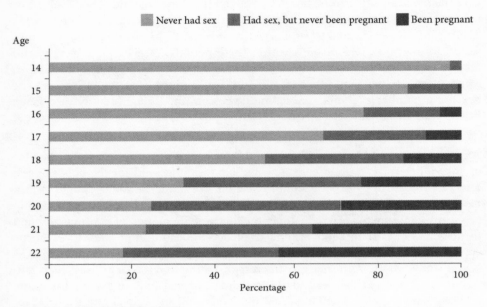

Source: Cape Area Panel Study wave 1 (2002)

Figure 7.2 *Sexual activity and impregnation among boys, Cape Town*

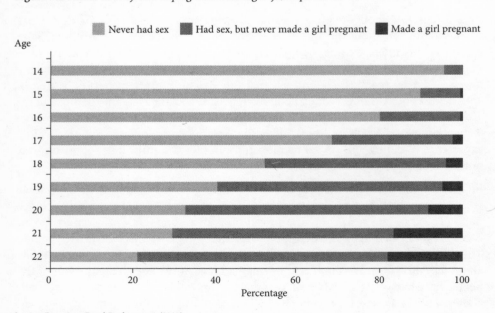

Source: Cape Area Panel Study wave 1 (2002)

Figures 7.3 and 7.4 show the differences for selected ages (15, 17 and 19 years) in different neighbourhoods in Cape Town. There are striking differences between neighbourhoods in Cape Town, as in South Africa as a whole. Both girls and boys in African neighbourhoods report having sex at younger ages than do girls and boys in poor coloured neighbourhoods. The latter, in turn, have sex at a younger age than boys and girls in non-poor coloured neighbourhoods, who in turn have sex at a younger age than boys and girls in white neighbourhoods. The poorer the neighbourhood, the younger the age of first sex. Average income in the neighbourhood, however, does not in itself explain why the average age of first sex differs. To understand the causal mechanism we must examine the character of social relationships and norms in these neighbourhoods.

Figure 7.3 *Sexual activity and pregnancy among girls, by type of neighbourhood and age, Cape Town*

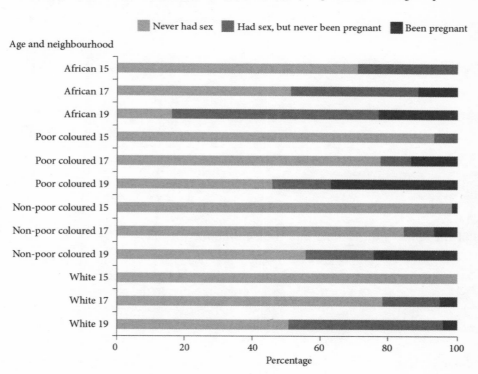

Source: Cape Area Panel Study wave 1 (2002)

Figure 7.4 *Sexual activity and impregnation among boys, by type of neighbourhood and age, Cape Town*

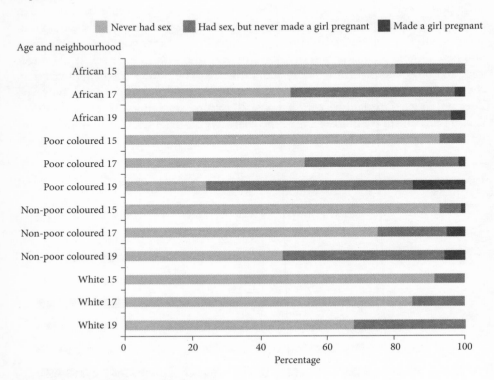

Source: Cape Area Panel Study wave 1 (2002)

Parent–child interactions and their influence on sex

> …secrecy in human society is often an integral aspect of, and…a major mechanism for, maintaining existing relations of power and patterns of respect. So is an increasing social distance between the generations as children 'grow up'. An aspect of this may be the 'silences' over sex and reproduction between generations…typical of many societies across the globe. (Preston-Whyte 2003: 90)

The manner in which adults speak to their young about dating and sex, as well as the silences that they keep, are central to the meaning and value that young people attach to dating and sex, and their practices in these areas.

Adult discourse surrounding dating and sex: Repressive talk, repressive practices

> …My mommy hasn't really spoken to me about periods, puberty, boyfriends, sex, STIs and stuff like that. *I* had to find the stuff out for myself! Do you think that's right? I don't think that's right!…I ask my

> friends…Because my mommy doesn't [tell me], I don't know *why* or
> *what* or *when* or *how*…I can't go to my mommy and say, 'I got this crush
> on some *outjie* [guy] and I'm really upset about it, because he doesn't
> feel the same way.' We don't have that type of relationship. I don't know
> if she's *scared* to speak to me or *what*, but she doesn't talk to me about
> anything…(Veronique, girl, aged 17, Ocean View, informal conversation
> with researcher)

Most adults – including parents, teachers and pastors – keep a pervasive silence surrounding dating and sex. Young people told us that when adults do talk to them about dating and sex, such discussions tend to be framed in negative terms, and communication is one-way, consisting of adult advice and directives to avoid dating and to abstain from sex. Adults are said to emphasise the negative consequences of sex, referring frequently to disease and pregnancy and advocating abstinence. They speak of dating and sex as 'inappropriate' and as distractions from what young people 'should' be doing – i.e. school work, chores at home or activities organised by schools or churches. There is also a strong religious or moral component to adult messages surrounding dating and sex: sex before marriage is 'bad' or a 'sin'; having boyfriends or girlfriends is a temptation that may lead to 'sinful' behaviour.

Repressive adult talk is accompanied by repressive practices, especially for girls. Girls from across the Valley described the advent of their teenage years as a time in which parent-figures became increasingly 'strict', regulating and monitoring their activities closely. Parents seem to fear that their children might be 'badly influenced' by friends and get caught up in 'chasing boys'. In a discussion with grade-12 girls in Masiphumelele, the group maintained that whenever they move beyond the confines of the home, particularly at night, parents 'assume' that they are 'chasing boys' and 'having sex'. Adult monitoring and regulation of girls because of dating and sex appear to be part of a more general adult monitoring of girls' activities and relationships that do not take place under spheres of adult supervision. This monitoring appears to serve the purpose of keeping girls 'safe' from the negative influence of friends and boys, and keeping them 'good' – keeping them from engaging in socially deviant or morally inappropriate activities, and making sure that their energies are invested in age-appropriate activities and pursuits, such as school work, housework and religion.

Girls recognise the gendered double standards surrounding parental regulation. While their own sexuality is closely monitored and is spoken about in negative, repressive terms, boys' sexuality tends to be 'ignored', and their social movements are far less subject to adult regulation. Grade-12 girls in Masiphumelele complained that their younger brothers are allowed to go out until late at night without being questioned. If they were to do this, their parents would cry, 'You'll get pregnant! You'll get AIDS!' One consequence of the scarce monitoring or expressions of concern by parents towards boys' sexuality is that boys – perhaps even more so than girls – are kept in the dark about 'the facts of sex'.

Silence, secrecy and maintaining intergenerational boundaries

Henderson suspects that the silences between African children and adults in New Crossroads concerning sex do not so much denote 'emptiness' as 'mark lines of power and may become the symbolic means whereby respect is demonstrated by young girls and boys towards their parents. Lack of verbal expression concerning sexuality circumscribes the boundaries between generations' (1999: 136–137). Preston-Whyte argues, in a similar vein, that silence and secrecy play an important role as intergenerational 'boundary keepers' (2003: 91). She argues that the silence and secrecy that adults enforce surrounding dating and sex serve to construct and maintain two parallel worlds where dating and sex are concerned: 'that of adults, who know everything' and 'that of children, who, parents presume, do not' (Preston-Whyte 2003: 90). Our material suggests that adults as well as young people are complicit in upholding this presumption.

Many young people describe parents or parent-figures as resistant, uncomfortable and even fearful in discussing dating and sex with them, but also talk of their own uncertainty in broaching these issues with their parents. There seem to be no conventions or scripts available to guide intergenerational communication on such matters. As one girl expressed it: 'I don't know if *we're* the ones that are supposed to be open with them, or they are the ones that are supposed to be' (Nobuntu, aged 18, Masiphumelele). Girls often avoided such discussions with parent-figures because they thought that they would not 'understand' their feelings and experiences. This generation gap was experienced in particularly forceful terms by girls in Masiphumelele, whose mother-figures are often their grandmothers (see Chapter 2).

Both adults and young people appear to feel a great need to preserve a sense of moral integrity in their interactions with one another. According to some young people, parents quietly accept that their sons and daughters will have girlfriends and boyfriends (and may be having sex), and turn a blind eye to these relationships and practices as long as they are kept separate from the parent–child relationship and, for girls, as long as they do not fall pregnant.

For girls more so than for boys, there appears to be greater restriction upon open displays of interest in dating and sexual matters, and of sexual knowledge and experience in their interactions with adults – and parent-figures in particular. This resonates with traditional norms surrounding appropriate expressions of femininity, where femininity is associated with sexual naivety and chastity (Weiss et al. 1996, 2000). In the Valley, adults seem reluctant to permit girls to bring their boyfriends home or to incorporate them into their family lives. Girls must carry out these relationships in spaces beyond the home, or within the homes of their boyfriends. Girls can only bring their boyfriends home when their parents are out, and they say that they would be severely reprimanded if they were caught. Girls have to hide their dating and sexual practices. They told us they feared that should they talk about or bring their dating into view of their parents, this would break down trust and cause parental disappointment. Thayo (aged 19, Fish Hoek) told us that many girls 'don't *allow* their moms to see them as they really are'. Leanne (aged 17, Fish Hoek), talking about her 'first kiss', said in a group discussion that she felt unable to confide in her mother about this experience, as it would shatter her mother's illusion that her 'daughter is so pure':

> ...there's like two faces of me...I want to keep like that whole image of angel in front of my mom, but then I know in myself that I'm not an angel...And I just kind of wish that she would know that, but in a way I don't want her to know...I think she wouldn't trust me then. So...I just prefer her just to think I'm an angel...

Through their own practice of silence and secrecy, young people thus sustain 'the presumption of innocence' surrounding sexuality that parent-figures hold in relation to their young, and daughters in particular. This enables adolescents to preserve an appearance – and even an internal sense – of moral integrity in their interactions, but the cost is to further bolster walls of silence and misinformation between generations and to block potential support from adults to whom they feel closest.

Adults across the Valley appear to be more in acceptance of boys having girlfriends and bringing them home. Findings from developing countries, including South Africa, suggest that boys are socialised more positively into their sexuality than girls (Weiss et al. 1996, 2000). This does not mean that boys integrate their dating relationships into their relationships with the family to a greater degree than girls. We found that when boys bring their girlfriends home, they typically see their girlfriends in their private rooms. Once boys in Masiphumelele reach their late teens, a room with a separate entrance (*iintanga*) is often built onto the main shack or house in order to give them a level of freedom that is considered appropriate to their age and gender. Parents generally stay out of these rooms and only if their son asks for advice does the father and, occasionally, the mother, enter. *Iintanga* are usually built after a boy has been initiated into manhood. But because some boys are initiated at a later age (owing to costs, schooling and recent state advice to delay the initiation until 21), many uninitiated boys in their late teens in Masiphumelele live in *iintanga*.

The absence of communication between adults and adolescents serves to maintain existing relations of power and patterns of authority and respect between the generations. But it also leaves young people to explore and learn about their sexuality within 'a world that is essentially closed to their parents and older generations... Adolescents are shutting their parents and the older generations firmly out of their increasingly public, but age- and generation-limited world' (Preston-Whyte 2003: 91). The increasing social distance between young people and adults, enforced through denial and silence on the part of adults, and secrecy and the upkeep of a 'hidden world' by the young, marks one of several fault lines in young people's social relationships.

Rebellion, peer pressure and anxieties

Many young people told us that adults' negative comments, centred on 'the consequences' of sex, leave them feeling that there is 'something more' that is being kept hidden from them. For Charney (girl, aged 17, Ocean View), 'it's not exactly the *real stuff*, like, the personal details, how you feel, and stuff like that...all things that youngsters expect, think it's like'. Adult secrecy and boundary-keeping is experienced with a sense of frustration by young people, but also with a sense of anticipated excitement about achieving entry into this foreign and forbidden territory. According to Preston-Whyte (2003: 91): 'Things hidden, things not normally spoken about, carry the irritation of exclusion but also the excitement of achieving entry...All these elements...combine...in the secrecy surrounding rituals centring around sex or rites of passage, be they into adulthood or secret societies.' Young people often spoke about dating and sex as part of a package of forbidden activity, which sometimes seemed 'dangerous' or socially deviant, but sometimes also – or even because of this – immensely exciting and attractive. This package of activity included 'hanging out with friends', staying up and being out late at night, 'partying', drinking alcohol, smoking cigarettes and experimenting with drugs. These were often spoken about in opposition to what was seen as a package of 'adult-prescribed' pursuits, which included participating and doing well in class; doing homework and chores; and getting involved in activities organised by schools or churches. Here, we find a close alignment between the manner in which adults and young people respectively talk about teenage dating, sex and social pursuits: both generations speak about these practices with reference to a stark moral dichotomy surrounding what young people 'should' and 'should not' be doing (see also Chapter 6). While the talk of young people reflects that of adults, young people construct their values surrounding these pursuits in opposition to the adult-defined value system.

Adolescents viewed the pursuit of the 'deviant package' of activities as an important part of 'being a teenager' – which, as Chloe (aged 17, Masiphumelele) described, is bound up with 'being free, having fun, and doing whatever I want to do', complaining that parent-figures do not recognise this. Grade-12 girls in Fish Hoek agreed that the teenage years are a time in which 'you take back your life from your parents'; grade-9 boys in Fish Hoek described this period as a time of experimentation and rebellion. These ideas resonate with theories found in developmental psychology literature, which construct independence and autonomy as 'universal goals' of adolescent development (Thom et al. 1998). In the Valley, teenagers and adults often saw these pursuits as a way in which young people react against negative elements in their families (such as parental conflict and neglect) and neighbourhoods (such as poverty, violence and limited opportunities); make a symbolic escape from their immediate situations; and attain a rare sense of control over their lives.

The attraction of 'deviant' pursuits lies in the rejection of adult authority, the sense of entry into the world of adults (and concomitant escape from the position of a dependent child) and the sense of independence, power and authority that comes with these. Many of these pursuits have legally defined age restrictions: sex, smoking and drinking represent a symbolic entry into foreign, adult territory. Grade-9 boys in Fish Hoek told us that the challenge among boys is to have sex before the legal age of 16, and that successful completion of this challenge earns one the respect and admiration of other boys. (Few boys complete this challenge!) In this sense, dating, and sex in particular, are seen as a rite of passage – one that grants one quasi-adult status within the peer group. In a discussion with grade-12 girls about why young people have sex, they said that this is because they want to be seen as 'brave', 'stand out' and 'show off' to other girls and boys: 'It shows people that they *know pain* and that they've *been through it.*' Young people who have experience in the world of dating and sex often broadcast their experiences publicly, among peers:

> I think that a lot of girls and guys think that if you want to be popular
> you must lose your virginity or something, I think because they think it's
> cool to sleep around with people…Some people, even though they don't
> want to, just to be popular will sleep with somebody. And they'll tell
> their friends, and almost everybody they know who they come across,
> they tell…(Denise, girl, aged 18, Fish Hoek, interview)

As Denise's comment suggests, dating and sex, as a rite of passage to being 'popular' and 'cool', are also associated with much pressure. We found that, although dating and sex are valued by young people, they also inform intragenerational boundary-keeping over information, and processes of inclusion and exclusion.

Lacking knowledge about what is perceived as the 'real stuff' of dating and sex, young people rely on their peers for information. Much of the conversation between young people of the same sex, in all parts of the Valley, revolved around dating and sex. Older teenage girls explained that close friendships are important because within them they can confide their experiences, feelings and concerns surrounding dating and sex; ask questions; and find identification and affirmation. The price of information and support, however, is often encouragement or pressure to experiment. In many cases, we found, young people who have no experience in the world of dating and sex are excluded from conversation on this subject by those who do, and information on these matters is often only given on condition that one has experiences of one's own to 'share' or exchange. In this respect, although dating and sex are subjects of much discussion among young people, we found that boundary-keeping, secrecy and exclusion operate between young people in much the same way as between generations. Young people who have dating and sexual experience become 'gatekeepers' of this knowledge in the same way as adults.

Girls did not see boys as an alternative source of information surrounding sex, as they felt that initiating such discussions would make them the subjects of crude jokes and sexual remarks, and would be taken by boys as a sexual advance. Boys, it might be surmised, have difficulty in engaging with girls on these issues in alternative ways because of pressure to keep up an image of manly bravado. Boundaries are thus also maintained between boys and girls (see also Henderson 1999; Preston-Whyte 2003).

Other studies have observed that, in Africa and worldwide, young men are expected to be knowledgeable about sex and, consequently, boys fear admitting ignorance on these matters (Rivers & Aggleton 1998). This may fuel the difficulty that boys experience in obtaining information on sex-related matters from friends. Too often, young people, and especially boys, enter into the world of dating and sex ignorant and emotionally unready. The need to display sexual bravado and prowess sits uneasily with emotional vulnerabilities, doubts, uncertainties and insecurities (Barker & Ricardo 2005; Holland et al. 1994).

Young people who do not date or have sex may feel anxiety or experience exclusion when in the company of more experienced friends. Charney, reflecting on an experience at a youth camp, told us that 'all the girls were bonding' by talking about the boyfriends they had had, and that when it came to her turn to confide, she 'had nothing to tell'. She had been forced to admit to the other girls that she had 'never had a boyfriend' and that she did not 'even know how to flirt with a guy'. This admission was met with laughter from the other girls, and had left Charney feeling 'excluded' from the group bonding process. This kind of experience inclines young people to 'grab the chance' to pair off when a boy or girl expresses interest in them 'just to fit in', rather than because they are particularly attracted to the person. In this respect, early attraction is, to a large extent, bound up in the socially attractive aspects of having boyfriends and girlfriends. Young people who have not had sex have not undergone this 'rite of passage' and are denied entry into, and membership of, the 'elite' social group. They may experience feelings of inferiority:

> You actually feel less than them because they say 'no, you are still a kid', and they are adults. And you actually want to be on the same level as they are. Because, if they are going somewhere, they like, 'no, we're not going with *kids*; we're older than you'...even if they're younger than you by age, since they're not virgins they're older than you. Now you're this *kid*, you mustn't go with them; you mustn't go walk around with them at school or something, because you're this *kid*. They don't want to talk of such things with the *kid*...(Chloe, group discussion)

Sex represents a rite of passage into perceived adulthood. This is one reason why so much 'boy-talk' involves sex, including boasting about sexual conquests, and why boys often have fun making sexual jokes and crude remarks. Through (claimed) sex, boys show themselves to be 'manly'. Those who have no sexual experience feel inferior and childish. According to one girl:

> Guys, they're very insecure about being a virgin; they just want to find a chick and lose their virginity and everything. Because it's a *big man* thing that you have to sleep with someone; you have to *feel* like a man; you have to *be* like a man; you have to smell like one...They don't want to mention the fact that they're virgins...because that will brand them a loser: it's one of the unwritten social rules, that if you're a virgin, then you're a loser. (Kim, aged 17, Fish Hoek, interview)

Young people who do not date, and those who have not had sex, often saw themselves as in the minority, or as the 'odd one out' among friends. The perception that young people who do not date and who have not had sex are in the minority, and the feelings of social isolation that accompany this, seems to reflect more the prevalence of exclusionary discourses (and silences) than any behavioural reality. Because of the social stigma attached to being single or a virgin, such young people tend to keep quiet; it is those who date and have had sex who tend to broadcast these experiences publicly. Kim told us that some of her closest friends tease her in public about the fact that she is a 'virgin', despite the fact that they themselves are sexually abstinent and do not have boyfriends and, during more intimate conversations, maintain that they are 'proud to be virgins'. Kim felt that they teased her publicly to cover over the fact that they too are sexually abstinent – and insecure about this. Many of the young people with whom we worked closely confided during individual interviews and individual diary work that they were not dating, and many told us that they were sexually abstinent, but during group discussions they often covered over this fact – possibly unaware that any of the other participants in the discussion were in the same position! Silencing and secrecy deny abstinent young people the possibility of identification with peers, which in turn might alleviate some of the pressure on young people to conform by dating and having sex, 'even though they don't want to'.

While girls and boys alike experience pressure from the peer group to engage in dating and sex, we found that there are gendered double standards at play within the youth population. While it is acceptable – and even expected and applauded – for boys to have many girlfriends (even at one point in time), girls who do the same are judged negatively by boys and other girls. Girls may see these double standards as unfair, but they themselves are complicit in perpetuating them. Kim told us that a (sexually 'promiscuous') girl in her class, Tessa, had called her a 'nun', because Kim is a virgin. Kim retorted that Tessa may think she is above her because she has sexual experience, but 'personally, I just think it's a way of telling people that you're a slut. I mean, sleeping around with so many guys obviously will brand you a ho [whore]'. She felt that Tessa only called her a 'nun' because she was perversely 'jealous of the fact' that Kim had *not* slept with anyone, whereas she 'gave up that innocence long ago'. In this respect, girls feel competing pressures surrounding their sexuality: they are both pressurised to display their experience in the world of dating and sex, if they are to be accepted and feel valued among their peers, yet can face rejection and stigmatisation – from girls, boys and adults – if they display this too overtly. It appears to be a fine line for girls to navigate, and easy to fall either way. It is also important to note that these gendered double standards do not translate simply into experiences of sexual freedom for boys: this 'freedom' is accompanied by powerful social expectations and pressure to prove oneself as a 'man' through macho displays of sexual prowess – or to risk being seen as 'unmanly'. These gendered double standards, and the expectations and pressures that surround them, strongly shape the dynamics of young people's dating relationships, which will be discussed later.

Style and status

Young people may retreat into a somewhat 'closed world' in the face of adult and even peer pressures, but the meaning and value that they attach to dating and sex are not constructed in a vacuum. Beyond the surrounding influence of relationships with adults is a broader and, in some respects, more powerful world of popular culture. Explicit and enticing references to and images of sex proliferate on radio and television, in popular magazines, and are splashed across advertising billboards. Young South Africans appear to look to, embrace and take ownership of this 'world of sex' in the interest of both status acquisition and of asserting autonomy and freedom in relation to the 'world of adults'. 'The world of sex is now the world of the young – of the teenage generation for whom it has become a symbol of success, of their independence from the older generation and the secrets that once gave the latter control over the youth, and of the world' (Preston-Whyte 2003: 90).

How young people present themselves and are seen within this public world becomes more and more important to them. Young people across the Valley agreed that the teenage years are a time when is becomes important to 'look good'. As Chloe told us, 'for all young people, outside image is very, *very* important'. 'Looking good' is bound up with conspicuous consumption and global style: designer clothes, nightclubs, expensive beverages and the latest cellphone. Dating and sex appear to be an important part of 'looking right' for young people, and this means not only asserting freedom from adult authority, but also transcending the social boundaries of the neighbourhoods in which they live in order to display their connection with and recognition within the wider world.

Establishing this connection seems to be particularly important for young people living in Masiphumelele and Ocean View because it entails a symbolic escape from feelings of social and economic marginalisation. Posel (2004) observes that, amid the post-apartheid demobilisation of political movements, sex has become 'the' sphere in which new-found freedoms are asserted and celebrated. She argues that, for 'black' youth (the author probably means what we term 'African'), asserting a sexualised freedom is a statement of the rupture between apartheid and post-apartheid generations, as much as a symptom of erosion of parental authority. In this sense, asserting and openly displaying a bold sexuality is a key way for black youths to construct their identities in the 'new' South Africa. Economic disempowerment and the absence in many areas of recreational facilities probably contribute further to the importance of sex as a source of respect and status (Barker & Ricardo 2005; Wood & Jewkes 2001). As Posel notes, 'sex is consumed, at the same time as consumption is sexualised', making for an 'overt sexualisation of style, status and power' (2004: 56; see also LeClerc-Madlala 2004).

According to Charney from Ocean View, a partner (with whom one is assumed to be having sex) can become a fashion accessory:

> If the guy has this very fine girl and she's sexy…and he's having sex with
> her, he gets status…And girls also get status from their boyfriends if
> they have a hunk or something…So it's basically their *egos*…To them, a
> boyfriend is just like an *accessory*. Like, you know, you buy yourself a *bag*
> or a *bangle* or something, something to make you look good or nice or

pretty or something. Like, just another accessory that brings them across as being cool, confident or sexy or something – because of the amount of boyfriends, or the type of boyfriends that they've had.

For young people, being sexy or attractive, catching the attention of the opposite sex, and displaying success in the world of dating and sex are symbols of personal success. Girls and boys spoke about daing and sex as an important way for young people to compete with members of the same sex for popularity. Boys in Fish Hoek and Ocean View agreed that having a girlfriend is 'cool', and that a boy who dates the most beautiful girls at school automatically becomes popular. Girls across the Valley agreed that having a boyfriend, particularly one who is good-looking, is an 'accessory' that displays success. Across the Valley, young people agreed that ideas about what is considered sexy are drawn from popular culture and the media in particular, and that young people take their cues from popular movie stars, models and musicians. For both girls and boys, this appears to turn to a large extent upon fashion, style and accessorising. Wearing expensive designer clothes, owning globally desired brand-name products (e.g. Nike, Levi, Diesel) or having the latest cellphone models are an important part of cultivating 'sex appeal', and competing with same-sex peers for the attention of the opposite sex – and, in turn, the status that is conferred by this attention.

> …In some cases, just walking down the street, you'll see a group of girls wearing just certain brands, like Diesel or Nike, or something. I think there is competition between girls about the way they dress. And they think that what guys go for is the brand and that. (Denise, interview)

Young people appear to seek out internationally desirable brand-name clothes and accessories in the interest of embodying some of their exclusivity and desirability. In turn, members of the opposite sex who embody this lifestyle are sought out as boyfriends or girlfriends, as conferrers of style and status. For girls, we also found that boyfriends are not only 'objects' of consumption, but also vehicles for consumption: across the wealth and racial spectra of the Valley, it was considered normative and expected that boys will 'provide' for their girlfriends. Boys who are in a financial position to provide their girlfriends with consumer products and pay for entertainment that aids the display of a consumer lifestyle are sought after as boyfriends. Boyfriends are important for girls, both as conferrers of social status (through their own display of style), and through the provision of goods and a lifestyle that confer this status.

Being seen out and about, displaying style through consumer items, using style as a means of displaying success in the world of dating and sex and using dating and sex as a means of acquiring consumer items are all ways that young people present themselves to the world as individual 'successes'. However, while dating, sex and style have a similar value to young people across the Valley, we found that economic disparities strongly shape young people's experiences and pressures, and feed into gendered processes, pressures and dynamics of power within young people's dating experiences.

While fashionable, brand-name products and displaying a lifestyle of conspicuous consumption are important aspects of how young people construct their social and sexual identities, they also feed into processes of exclusion and boundary-keeping among the youth. Young people feel excluded, both from the 'popular' cliques and from the competitive world of dating, when they are unable to afford these products: 'Sometimes you just feel, oh! maybe if I had that Levi jeans, he'd like me…then I'd get a boyfriend,' says Charney. Young people who cannot afford these products sometimes feel undesirable to the opposite sex and undesirable among their peers. This places particular pressure upon young people who live in less affluent neighbourhoods and share the aspirations of a consumer lifestyle with their wealthier peers in Fish Hoek, but have fewer means to achieve it. Their aspirations may, indeed, be more pronounced precisely because of the absence of alternative ways of displaying personal success.

Class structures the relationships between boys and girls. For girls and boys living in the more affluent neighbourhood of Fish Hoek, parents often provide not only the day-to-day necessities, but also sought-after consumer commodities and brands. In the context of material exchanges within dating relationships, these girls do not rely on their boyfriends to provide them with consumer commodities or pay for their entertainment. Insofar as boys are expected to provide, most have the means to do so. For girls in Masiphumelele and Ocean View, however, boyfriends are sometimes the only route through which they are able to access a lifestyle of conspicuous consumption.

> Most of the time, girls want money from a relationship…They say, 'I can't go out with someone who's still at school, because he's not going to provide for me: when I need the jeans, who's gonna buy a jeans for me? So I have to have someone who's working'…I think there's a problem because [girls] don't have money in their families, so when you want something from your parents, they're going to tell you [they] don't have the money…So they think it's a good idea to have someone who's going to support you from outside. (Zanele, girl, aged 17, Masiphumelele, interview)

Because of this, gendered expectations surrounding material provision in dating relationships operate with particular force within the less affluent neighbourhoods. Some young people living in these areas told us that girls want 'nothing to do' with boys who do not have money to their name, and feel that such boys are 'not worth going out with'. They pointed to the fact that girls unashamedly 'use boys' in this respect. LeClerc-Madlala (2002, 2003) and Hunter (2002) argue, on the basis of research in KwaZulu-Natal, that the way in which young women 'exploit' their sexual relationships to meet 'new' consumer needs should be seen as a means whereby young women consciously and deliberately assert agency in relationships that have been traditionally a site of female disempowerment. Grade-12 girls in Masiphumelele and Ocean View report that other girls often seek out older, sometimes married, men – or 'sugar daddies' – because they are better able to provide material benefits. If younger men cannot compete, they may end up feeling emasculated (Barker & Ricardo 2005).

Young people and adults worry that girls are even attracted to 'gangsters' because of their perceived wealth, status and power. Research in Johannesburg found that the hegemonic understanding of masculinity is embodied in the notion of the *ingagara*, namely someone who is well respected and considered macho. This is associated with having many girlfriends, an expensive car and fashionable clothes, and wielding power over women, who are seen as possessions. At the opposite extreme is the *isithipa* (sissy), who does not have many girlfriends, does not wear fashionable clothes, is not involved in crime and wants to achieve educationally. Boys are, therefore, under pressure to acquire immediate wealth and success – if necessary, through deviance and criminality – and are discouraged from pursuing education (Selikow et al. 2002; see also Chapter 6).

While there are added pressures on boys to be providers for their girlfriends in less affluent communities, these boys also attach greater value to being a provider than their peers in more affluent neighbourhoods. We found that, for boys, being able to provide for a girlfriend is an important strategy for achieving and displaying status and manliness. Grade-12 girls in Masiphumelele described these exchanges as a way in which boys 'pay their girlfriends to look nice' – so that when these boys introduce their girlfriends to their friends visiting from other areas, they can do so with pride. These girls noted that a boy who has a girlfriend who 'does not look nice' or 'wear nice clothes' will 'pretend' that he does not have a girlfriend, or 'point out another girl' who is better dressed. This suggests the importance that young men attach to girlfriends as vehicles for displaying their material and social success. In the poorer parts of the Valley, displaying sexual achievement and claiming ownership of beautiful women is one of the few routes through which young men can display manliness and personal success.

Boys' claims to ownership over their girlfriends through the provision of material goods extends to the assertion of control and power, particularly when it comes to sex. Girls may exercise agency in negotiations over material provision, but the price is that they provide their men with sex whenever the men want it. Girls in Ocean View and Masiphumelele told us that gifts or money are almost always given by boyfriends with an unspoken expectation of – or entitlement to – sex. Girls who receive things from their boyfriends are indebted and unable to deny sex to their providers.

> …if he says that he wants to sleep with you, you won't be able to say 'no, I can't', because you will think about the things that he bought you, the things that he's given to you. It would be like, ok, let me do it. (Nobuntu, girl, aged 18, Masiphumelele, interview)

This suggests that not only do boys have a sense of 'owning' their girlfriends, but girls internalise this and come to see themselves as 'owned', and at the (sexual) service of their boyfriends. Furthermore, girls can come to internalise the idea that they 'need' a man to support them financially. Girls in Masiphumelele and Ocean View told us that (other) girls give up their education and career ambitions in the expectation that they will find husbands to provide for them. As girls in Ocean View themselves observed, adult women in their neighbourhood who end up financially dependent are disempowered. According to Talia (aged 18, Ocean View): 'Men feel that they have the *right* to control the lady, because she is at home: "I bring in the money, so I will control." I think that it's the money." Ocean View girls also understood that this often contributed to violence, which boys learnt from their fathers:

> In most cases, the guy, if he sees his mother being beaten by his father, then he will become like his father; he will end up abusing his wife. (Nicola, girl, aged 17, Ocean View, group discussion)

Abused girls, like women, might not be able to escape because of their material dependence:

> It could be that they are so dependent on the person – I mean, if you are a girl in high school and you have a boyfriend who's working, obviously he's gonna buy me things, and…gifts…and, you think to yourself, you're not gonna get that anywhere else, so you might as well just stay and get this. Because you're getting something. (Charney, group discussion)

(Mis)trust and infidelity

> There is this thing at school that people say: no one loves anyone; it's just a big game! It's a love game…It's more like we're just playing; it's a game. Because people play with other people's feelings; that's the way it is…Especially guys; yoh, they'll play with girls' feelings…they don't feel ashamed to have four or five girlfriends. (Chloe, group discussion)

> It's hard to find a guy you can *really* trust…you can't really trust boys. I have been hurt so many times. So, it's not like so easy to trust a guy, even if he is honest or anything. It's not that easy. You've been there, done it; it's like it's going to repeat itself again. (Nobuntu, interview)

Adolescent boys and girls engage in dating and sex amid pressure and competition, exacerbated by the disadvantages of class and (for women) gender. In this environment, dating relationships and existing friendships become tenuous and often transient.

Girls look for, but rarely find, trust, fidelity and commitment in their dating relationships. The general view (often a product of experience) was that boys are likely to cheat or 'use' girls and, consequently, girls have to be wary of this. Girls across the Valley often spoke about the difficulty of finding love and intimacy in dating relationships. They often saw boys as a 'barrier' to building relationships on these terms – and felt that sex is part of the problem. Girls tended to hold the view that, while they 'want love' and commitment from their dating relationships, boys 'only want sex'. They agreed that boys tend to 'use' girls for sex, and then tend to 'dump' them once they have got this. These girls said that boys think sex is a 'joke' and a way of 'having fun' – which often leaves girls feeling hurt, rejected and used. They also said that boys cheat on girlfriends who refuse to have sex with them, and that boys are 'not satisfied' by one girlfriend. As a consequence, girls felt that dating relationships tend to be transient and lacking in trust, intimacy and commitment.

Although girls saw boys' sexual 'needs' as an obstacle to building committed dating relationships, it appears that they are complicit in sustaining this scenario. Across the Valley, girls do not feel that boys can be held responsible for their actions when it comes to dating and sex. Girls assign themselves and one another the responsibility and blame for their boyfriends' transgressions. Lara (aged 17, Fish Hoek) spoke of a friend's relationship:

> She doesn't trust him at all…She thinks that he is seeing someone else… She gets really angry when he even *looks* at another girl. [I tell her] give him a bit of freedom; don't spend *all* your time with him, because if you spend all your time together you will get irritated with each other. I tell her not to be clingy and not to expect so much of him: he is only male.

The phrase that girls should not 'expect too much' of their boyfriends came up repeatedly in conversations with girls from across the Valley. Girls' expectations and acceptance of male infidelity dovetail with dominant gender norms across the whole Valley. Mandisa (aged 19, Masiphumelele) told us that she is aware that her boyfriend is cheating on her, but that she is 'just taking it' because she 'does not want to upset the relationship'. She justified the situation by telling us that her boyfriend is 'still young and at that stage of life of wanting to have many girlfriends…They can have all those things now when they are young, but when they are older they can be asked more of'.

By failing to confront unfaithful boyfriends, girls help sustain this culture of male infidelity (and their own unhappiness). Girls avoid confronting boyfriends because they do not want to jeopardise the relationship, which, in turn, is due to the social desirability of having and keeping a boyfriend and the accompanying material support. The status quo is maintained, giving boys little incentive to question their approach to relationships or modify their behaviour.

Girls also tend to blame other girls for trying to break up their relationships rather than their unfaithful boyfriends. They expect that other girls cannot be trusted to respect their relationships and will try to steal their boyfriends – and frequently succeed. Girls are seen as conniving and untrustworthy, boys as blameless. Both younger and older teenage girls across the Valley said there are often fights *between* girls *over* boys. If a girl finds out that her boyfriend is involved with another girl, she goes to 'get her', and if she succeeds, will also try to 'win' back the errant boyfriend. Occasionally, girls will band together to confront unfaithful boyfriends. Thayo told of a situation where three girls 'worked out that the guy they were seeing was the same one, then they all ganged up and went to get him!' Girls will sometimes keep tabs on their friends' boyfriends and inform their friends if their boyfriends are cheating. (This can sometimes backfire if the friend suspects that the informant is trying to break up the relationship.) In Masiphumelele, if a girl challenges an unfaithful boyfriend or tries to leave the relationship, he is likely to beat her. Girls in other neighbourhoods did not mention this kind of sanction.

Infidelity is not the domain of boys only. Some girls also have multiple boyfriends, or pursue boys when they are already in relationships. It was suggested to us that girls were challenging dominant gender norms by actively taking up multiple partners at one time, to 'get back' at boys:

> Guys…they play with girls' feelings…they don't feel ashamed to have four or five girlfriends…so I think girls are realising that, because, now, even girls are playing with guys' feelings. (Chloe, group discussion)

Leanne said she thinks 'more power to you, girl; that is how guys behave, so why not the girls too?' But such an open challenge to dominant gender norms appears to be limited to *talk* (of 'girl power') rather than actual practice. Indeed, in reality, as one of the girls told us, getting back at boys 'does not really work'. In Masiphumelele, there is a real threat of violence. Girls there told us that if a boy finds out his girlfriend has cheated on him he is likely to beat her. This appears to be both a means whereby boys punish their girlfriends and reclaim 'ownership' over them, so that they will be unlikely to 'stray' again. Other South African studies have documented such violent punishment of young women for alleged infidelity (Eaton et al. 2003). More generally, girls risk their reputation. Boys in Fish Hoek described this gendered reality in words that would apply to every part of the Valley:

> It's cool for a guy to be a 'player' and have many girlfriends, and 'players' talk a lot about girls and recommend girls to each other, but girls who have more than one boyfriend are called sluts. (Boys' consensus in a grade-9 discussion, Fish Hoek)

Older teenagers agreed that it was considered 'fine' for boys to be seeing more than one girl at a time – even 'good', as he'll be considered a 'real man' by his male friends. Girls, on the other hand, are looked down on, and seen as 'hoes' (whores) if they do this.

These gendered norms not only place constraints upon girls, but also pressures on boys to conform to dominant notions of what it means to be a 'real man'. Mandy (aged 17, Ocean View) explained that, when her boyfriend cheated on her, he attributed his behaviour to the fact that the girl in question had propositioned him and, as a 'man', he could not turn her down. He explained that he 'had' to accept her offer or the other boys would have laughed at him and thought that he was a *moffie* (homosexual). In South Africa, generally:

> …manhood appears to be rigidly associated with heterosexuality and the ability to be sexual with multiple women. Thus, those who do not conform or are not successful in this realm may be punished or stigmatised. Alternative sexualities, either homosexual or those resistant to traditional macho masculinity, are still not well tolerated in South African communities. (Shefer & Potgieter 2006: 117; see also Barker & Ricardo 2005)

In many settings, if a boy does not have sex with a girl, his reputation suffers among his peers (MacPhail & Campbell 2001). Having multiple partners helps to demonstrate masculinity, especially in poorer areas (Barker & Ricardo 2005; Morrell

2006; Silberschmidt 2001). Insofar as sex is more about a display of competence and achievement than an act of intimacy (Barker & Ricardo 2005), girls become mere sexual objects or conquests. Like many girls with whom we spoke, Mandy said she was left feeling as if her boyfriend had just been trying to get her into bed: he had 'just taken what he wanted' – sex – 'and left'.

Boys are also implicated in trying to break up each other's relationships. Conflict between boys appeared to stem from cheating and infidelity, and boys are often involved in physical altercations with other boys who are trying to 'get' their girlfriends. Boys seem to gain status if they are involved in and win such a fight, and girls are more attracted to these boys. However, if a boy starts a fight and then loses, his credibility (among boys) and attractiveness (to girls) diminishes. Among boys and girls alike, infidelity is bound up with social standing and reputation, not with trust and intimacy. Anger (directed against competitors) distracts both girls and boys from communication and building trust within relationships. Anxiety, jealousy and suspicion become pervasive, making teenagers controlling and demanding with their partners and further undermining relationships.

Young people felt that the difficulty that girls and boys have in building committed, intimate relationships is also a product of the fact that young people have few role models of relational intimacy and commitment available to them.

> I know that some girls sleep around…I think they don't actually care…
> because most parents are divorced here, or their dad or their mom is
> having an affair with so and so, and they've had an affair with so and so.
> (Thayo, interview)

Young people mentioned the high rates of divorce and extramarital affairs among adults. Furthermore, dating and sex are commonly represented within the media – particularly within the daily soap operas that many girls watch faithfully – as inevitably tumultuous and non-committal, and are even valorised this way. Young people said that children growing up watching these shows and seeing the adult relationships around them are socialised into a world in which dating and sex are displayed as casual and transient and, as a result, take up a similar approach to dating and sex when they get older.

In rare instances, some boys and girls with whom we worked closely were involved in long-term, committed dating relationships, which appeared to be founded upon trust. We identified a pattern of characteristics common to such relationships. Foremost, what appears to set such relationships aside from the normative character of dating relationships among young people is the nature of communication between boyfriend and girlfriend. These young people often have conversations with their partners that centre on their relationships. These involve voicing their fears, worries and concerns about the relationship; discussions about potential threats to the relationship with their partners; and communicating what they want from their relationship and for the future.

For example, Patrick (aged 18, Ocean View), who had been going out with his girlfriend for about a year at the time of the fieldwork, said that he and his girlfriend had both raised fears about infidelity and concerns about the attention that the other gets from other boys and girls. He also told us that during the early stages of the relationship, other boys used to 'go after' his girlfriend and try to break them up. Over time this had stopped happening, as people realised that there was 'no chance' of breaking up the relationship. Young people who build long-term, committed relationships can earn quiet respect from friends. Building trust was sometimes a tenuous process, and there were instances in some of these relationships where a boy had betrayed his partner, or vice versa. However, instances of infidelity only characterised the early stages of relationship-building. Through open dialogue, these issues were resolved, and sometimes young people felt that the process of working through such problems had actually strengthened the relationship. In this way, young people can build relationships that are fulfilling and characterised by sharing, support and commitment.

An interesting commonality among young people who spoke of building trusting and intimate relationships was that they were often practising sexual abstinence or had delayed sexual relations until after establishing trust and intimacy. This strategy may serve to avoid some of the gendered power dynamics that accompany sex, and thereby make room for building relationships under mutually negotiated terms. In other respects, what appears to be key to the enduring nature of these relationships is that when having problems with a girlfriend or boyfriend, these young people address the issue with their partners, rather than looking outwards for support or blaming others for the problems, which, as we have seen, is more commonly the case. However, relationships that match young people's ideals are rare, and often seem to be vulnerable to attack from peers motivated by jealousy. Young people who stay in committed relationships are sometimes seen as 'boring' by friends, who encourage them to move on. Sustaining intimate and trusting relationships is a difficult process that is highly demanding of personal resources.

Pregnancy and parenthood

In Cape Town as a whole, one in four 19-year-old girls has been or is pregnant (see Figure 7.1). Pregnancy is less common, but not unknown, among younger teenagers. Teenage pregnancy is very unusual in white middle-class neighbourhoods. It is most common not in the poorest African neighbourhoods, but in poor coloured neighbourhoods, where more than one in three 19-year-old girls has been or is pregnant (see Figure 7.3). Indeed, teenage girls in poor coloured neighbourhoods who have had sex are more likely to have been pregnant than not. Figures 7.2 and 7.4 show that only a tiny proportion of boys aged less than 20 reported having made a girl pregnant.

The striking differences shown in Figures 7.1 and 7.3 for Cape Town as a whole are not reflected in what girls in Fish Hoek and Ocean View say. In both neighbourhoods, girls say that teenage pregnancy is rife. Grade-12 girls in Fish Hoek referred to an 'epidemic' of teenage pregnancy. Their Ocean View peers maintained (with irony) that pregnancy was 'in fashion': 'In the past, it was different, but now, in our community, it's an everyday occurrence.' But discussions with adults (and other young people) in Fish Hoek suggested that early pregnancy is not common locally, whereas similar conversations in Ocean View confirm that it is all too common there.

Questions of prevalence aside, it is clear that when girls do fall pregnant, it can be a traumatic experience, and it certainly has a great impact both on their own and others' lives. Such experience, coupled with the way teenage pregnancy is represented as a social rupture in family and community life and attracts excessive gossip and speculation, may contribute to the idea that teenage pregnancy is a 'big issue' (even when it is not an 'everyday occurrence') across the Valley.

Why girls 'fall pregnant'

> Most of them want to be grown-ups before their time. Because they
> don't want to be told what to do, and they don't want to do this, and
> they don't want to do that. And when you're pregnant or have a child,
> it's like, you're *older* than what you really are…Because you think you've
> got a child, you're not a child any more…They want to do things that
> adults do, and not be like all childish, and go to school, and be good.
> (Veronique, girl, aged 17, Ocean View, group discussion)

Young African men and women, particularly those living in traditional-minded rural areas, may seek to conceive in order to demonstrate virility or fertility and thus manhood or womanhood (Preston-Whyte & Zondi 1991; Varga & Makubalo 1996). Recent studies suggest that education is prioritised over early childbearing in urban contexts (Kaufman et al. 2000; LeClerc-Madlala 2002; MacPhail & Campbell 2001). Data from CAPS and other surveys (e.g. Pettifor et al. 2004) suggest that most girls who have been pregnant had not wanted to be. In 2002, CAPS asked young women across Cape Town whether they expected to have a child in the next three years. Even among 19-year-old girls, only 1 in 10 said that they expected to do so (see Figure 7.5). When we re-interviewed exactly the same girls three years later, in 2005, we found that many more girls had been pregnant than had expected to be. Pregnancy is not unusual for girls in their late teens, but it is a largely unanticipated experience.

None of the girls in the Valley with whom we worked closely said that they wanted to fall pregnant any time soon. But, contrary to what is suggested by survey data, they suggest that *other* girls who do fall pregnant often do so intentionally, as a way of asserting power. As the quotation from Veronique at the beginning of this section suggests, falling pregnant is sometimes seen as a strategy whereby girls rebel against or undermine the authority of parents, and attempt to take up a new position of perceived seniority and independence within the home. Salo (2004), in her study of Manenberg, a neighbourhood not unlike Ocean View, describes how poor, young coloured women who cannot afford a *skoon troue* (clean marriage) choose to have at

Figure 7.5 *Young women's expected and actual ages of maternity (2002–2005)*

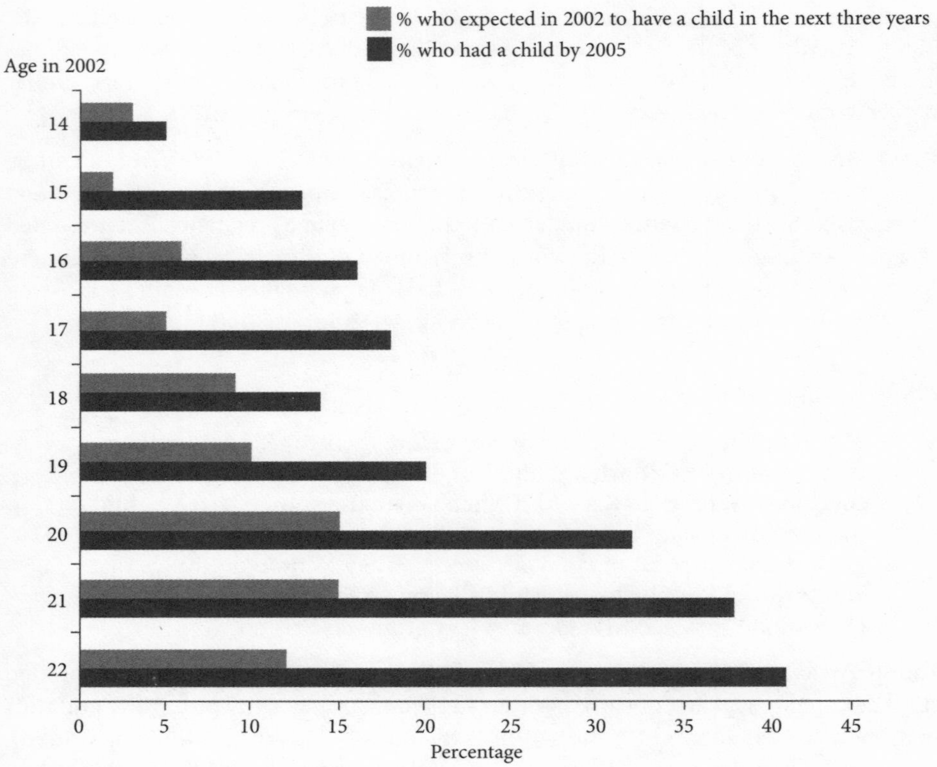

Source: Cape Area Panel Study wave 1 (2002) and wave 3 (2005)
Note: These data exclude girls who were or had been pregnant at the time of the initial 2002 survey.

least one child before marriage as a way of obtaining a more senior status than that of a dependent child: 'A young pregnant woman is perceived to have usurped the mother's power illegally to confer seniority upon herself, as she and her partner have initiated their own passage into a new phase of life' (Salo 2004: 163). The idea that falling pregnant is something girls do 'to' their mothers resonates with material we gathered from girls who do *not* want to fall pregnant:

> We, as young girls, we don't live our lives the way we want to. We just live our lives to impress our parents. That's all. To be what our parents want us to be. So, when you get pregnant, you think 'so what is my mother going to think?' (Nobuntu, interview)

> Everything I do, I want to satisfy my mother; I like to impress my mother. When I do have sex, I try all the time to use condoms. Because I don't want to become pregnant…When a girl falls pregnant, they say you've disappointed your mother. (Nozazi, aged 19, Masiphumelele, interview)

This material suggests that girls often see their choices, particularly surrounding sex and reproduction, as 'not theirs to make', because of overriding social pressures. Girls take steps to avoid pregnancy if they want to maintain their relationships with their parents as well as (or rather than) for their own reasons.

Some girls also suggest that pregnancy can be part of a deliberate attempt to get attention from parent-figures – as in 'maybe my mommy will take notice of me now that I'm pregnant'. Alternatively, falling pregnant might be a rebellious reaction. Older girls in Ocean View discussed how a girl might fall pregnant 'out of spitefulness', to 'get back at parents' (for a divorce, perhaps) or even to bring social disgrace upon parents. These dynamics accord with Salo's (2004) discussion of how an unchaste daughter in Manenberg detracts from the respectability of her mother. Adults in Ocean View, however, argue that not all pregnant girls come from 'troubled homes', as the arguments above would suggest. They say that many girls who have fallen pregnant come from stable and supportive families.

Pregnancy was also seen as a means by which girls attempt to take control and exert agency within their heterosexual relationships. As noted, girls commonly experience betrayal, and sometimes abuse, within their relationships with boys. In a discussion with grade-12 girls in Ocean View, the group maintained that girls try to fall pregnant in an attempt to 'hold onto a boyfriend' who 'has a wandering eye'; get 'revenge' on a boyfriend who has dumped them (by saddling them with the burden of a child); or believe that this will stop an abusive boyfriend from 'beating' her. However, the group was critical of girls who thought that, should they fall pregnant, their boyfriends would 'change' for the better. It would be better, they said, if the girl 'just lost the loser and just got on with her life'. This assertion does not, however, take into account that girls often feel trapped within abusive relationships, or feel unable to leave boyfriends upon whom they are materially dependent.

While the idea that girls want to fall pregnant was a common one, it is also evident that girls fall pregnant unintentionally, often because they do not use or are unable to get access to contraceptives. Contraceptive use is made difficult for many girls by their parents' efforts to 'manage' (or deny) their daughters' sexuality. Some girls told us that when parents are 'too strict' with their daughters and do not allow them to 'see boys', girls often hurriedly take the opportunity to have sex when parents are out, or cut school to meet their boyfriends. The unplanned nature of such sexual encounters means that girls often do not have condoms with them. In this respect, as other South African studies (e.g. MacPhail & Campbell 2001) suggest, parental supervision can have a negative effect on contraceptive use, especially when it is coupled with a lack of communication about sex. Girls throughout the Valley said that it was common for parents to forbid their daughters from using birth control, such as the oral pill or the injection, because this would 'encourage' their daughters to have sex. This appeared to be the case even when parents knew their daughters were sexually active. Parental denial of their daughters' sexuality appears to be powerful enough to override the evidence in front of them – and their reluctance to acknowledge their daughters' sexuality can contribute to their falling pregnant.

Finally, discussions with older teenage girls from across the Valley suggested that it is difficult for girls to acquire contraceptives from the local clinic because of the social stigma attached to being seen there. They told us that girls who are seen going into the clinic become the subject of speculation and gossip. Ironically, girls avoid getting contraceptives from the clinic for fear of being presumed pregnant, but may then fall pregnant as a result. Girls can also get a hostile reaction from clinic staff if they go there for contraceptives (Eaton et al. 2003). Grade-12 girls in Ocean View pointed out that the local library displayed posters encouraging girls to go to the clinic for contraceptives, but when girls go there they are made to feel uncomfortable and unwelcome, and that clinic staff themselves may initiate gossip and rumour.

What happens when a girl falls pregnant?

Young people tended to associate teenage pregnancy with negative outcomes. Girls across the Valley rarely saw abortion as an option, ascribing this view to moral and religious considerations, and social stigma. In a discussion with grade-12 girls in Ocean View, the group said that girls only resort to abortion in the face of physical threats by boyfriends who do not want the child. One girl had reportedly gone to the local clinic for an abortion, only to retreat in fear having been told by the doctor that she would be 'haunted by the sound of the suction and the baby's cries for the rest of her life'.

Across the Valley, young people said that pregnant teenage girls suffer a loss in social standing, and experience difficulties within their interpersonal relationships. They become the subject of gossip and are seen as bringing shame upon themselves and their families. People are content to gossip about pregnant teenagers, but not to provide support. Pregnant teenagers are also seen as 'easy' by boys and men. Pregnant girls may receive support, advice and acceptance from other girls, particularly from friends who have also had babies (further discussed in relation to schooling in Chapter 6). But on the whole, it seems that most pregnant girls feel rejected by their peers, resulting in experiences of social isolation. Across the Valley, girls pointed to the fickle nature of friendships when it comes to pregnancy: 'They may be the people who encourage you to open your legs – and when you fall pregnant, then they're the people that actually turn their backs on you' (Veronique).

The reaction of parents to teenage daughters who fall pregnant was also seen to have a devastating impact on the lives of these young women. Young people recounted dramatic tales of girls who had fallen pregnant and, on their parents' discovery, had been rejected and thrown out of the home. Alternatively, and more commonly, young people felt that parents often redirect care and attention towards the baby, and away from their daughter:

> The parents will look after the child and *not you*…They won't look after you any more, because they have to look after your child. So you're no longer their child, right? (Nobuntu, interview)

While girls may wish to fall pregnant as a means of becoming a 'grown-up before they really are', the change in age status that accompanies pregnancy and childbearing can take an unexpectedly burdensome form, and is often not welcomed by teenage girls. Nosango explained why she did not enjoy being a mother:

> When the baby is crying my mother shouts at me, saying it is all my fault and I have to face it [her parenthood], that I must not let the child cry because he is disturbing them. When she is shouting I just quit the house and stay at nearby neighbours, leaving the baby crying with my mother and I come back when she is cool…I'll never have a baby again because it is painful to give birth, and I don't have rights as I used to in my home…My mother doesn't buy clothes for me; she only buys them for my sisters and brothers, especially Baballwa. She is my mother's favourite. (Nosango, aged 17, Masiphumelele, interview)

According to girls in both Ocean View and Masiphumelele, emotional care and material resources are both redirected to the new baby. Girls see this as a means for parents to punish daughters, for example by buying her nappies while her siblings are bought new clothes. As Nosango suggests, spending decisions were also seen as a signal to the teenage daughter that she can no longer hold the position of 'child', and hence a 'dependant'. In some cases, parents instruct daughters who fall pregnant to leave school and find work to support the child. Pregnant girls and teenage mothers are quickly burdened with new, adult responsibilities, may be forced to stay at home (when not working) and are often unable to participate in the activities that teenagers around them are typically enjoying. Adjusting to the new responsibilities accompanying parenthood and the ensuing shift in status in the family and among friends are often described as the most challenging aspects of early motherhood.

However, while these new responsibilities are often spoken about by girls as ones that are enforced on pregnant teenagers by parents, and as 'punishment', this appears to be an important part of a process in which patterns of parent–child authority and respect are reinstated, ruptures in the parent–child relationship repaired and girls socialised into a responsible and respectable adulthood. Salo (2004) notes that when teenage girls in Manenberg fall pregnant, this is initially experienced as a 'social crisis' within the household and community. However, social harmony can be restored and girls can 'recuperate their standing in the community as they distinguish themselves as more mature and responsible than their childless peers… by exhibiting their growing repertoire of parenting skills and as they assist the older women in policing and protecting the economic and social respectability of their households' (Salo 2004: 312). Her findings echo material we gathered in our own observations of and discussions with girls who had fallen pregnant. While parents often react initially with shock, anger and disappointment, they do not reject their pregnant teenage daughters, as is the dominant belief, but with time come to accept and even welcome the idea of a grandchild. Furthermore, relationships with parent-figures can reach a new level of closeness that seems to result from them sharing the pregnancy journey and preparation for the baby's arrival.

> As time passed by…the support I got from my family really helped me. My granny really helped me, and we are starting to build a really nice,

good and honest relationship. We talk a lot and share whatever we are feeling and she comforts me a lot. (Extract from Chloe's life story, aged 17, Masiphumelele)

Deconstructing a one-sided account: Where do boys fit in?

The old saying of 'boys will be boys' is still very much alive – where it would be socially acceptable if a boy spirals out of control or gets someone pregnant – 'oh, he's sowing his wild oats' – and that kind of thing. And he doesn't have to really take full responsibility. (Interview, school social worker, Ocean View)

As is evident from this extract, there is silence surrounding the role that boys play in impregnating girls, why boys may wish to conceive a child and the effect that conceiving children and fatherhood has upon the lives of teenage boys. Figures 7.2 and 7.4 show that, by the age of 19, very few boys report having made a girl pregnant. Girls themselves typically report that the boyfriends who made them pregnant were older than them. Even when young men do admit to being fathers, they have limited contact with their children. CAPS found that, in Cape Town as a whole, only 7 per cent of fathers under the age of 20 said that their children lived with them. The equivalent figure for mothers was 87 per cent. Children born of young parents almost always live with their mothers and their mothers' kin.

Young people in the Valley consider that fatherhood makes much less difference to a boy's everyday life than pregnancy or motherhood to a girl's. 'The girl can't go out any more, and other guys won't go near her, because she is pregnant, but the guy can carry on as normal' (male youth leader, youth meeting, Ocean View). This sentiment was supported by Chloe, who fell pregnant during the study. Referring to the father of her child, she complained that:

His life is the same, whereas mine has changed for good…he just carries on as normal, still goes to parties and stuff, whereas I have to stay home and feel sorry for myself…It's not that I blame him for the pregnancy, as we were both in it together, but it's that he carries on with life, going to parties, doing what he wants as if nothing has happened, whereas my life has completely changed. It doesn't seem fair. (Extract from Chloe's life story)

Girls and boys alike say that few teenage fathers take responsibility for their children. Nor do boys who impregnate girls appear to suffer the same negative social consequences in terms of gossip. 'Irresponsible' girls are blamed for falling pregnant, and even for bringing 'fatherless' children into the world. A social worker in Ocean View told us how pregnancies are 'written off' by the parents of a teenage father: 'They wouldn't bat an eyelid…wouldn't even acknowledge the child.' In the meantime, she said, their sons will have their 'next two or three victims'. In some cases, fathers may be inhibited by poverty. Morrell notes that fathers who are 'unable to meet what they consider to be a father's responsibility to provide for their family are more likely to deny or flee the fatherhood role' (2006: 20; see also Desmond &

Desmond 2006; Ramphele & Richter 2006; Wilson 2006). But even in the face of limited means, some boys do in fact take on the role of provider. The social worker in Ocean View told us that, in a few cases, the parents of the teenage father will take responsibility for child maintenance, and even compel the teenage father to take on a casual job to contribute. In defence of their peers, some grade-11 boys in Ocean View pointed out that it is often difficult for boys to face up to their responsibilities regarding pregnancy, as they are afraid of the reaction from the girl's parents. Boys are also slow to turn to school social workers and clinics, perhaps because they are considered 'women's spaces' and in conflict with a 'macho' identity. They, like girls, need, but often do not receive, the support of their parents in this.

Furthermore, in the experiences of some girls who fall pregnant, teenage fathers can be committed and involved partners and fathers, on both a practical and emotional level. This was evident in the case of Nosango, who had given birth five months before the interview. She told us that the baby's father buys food and clothes for the baby every month, both willingly and out of a sense of duty. According to Nosango, he enjoys being a father and his family has 'accepted' the pregnancy, often asking her to visit with the baby. Salo argues that, when a young man acknowledges responsibility for a pregnancy by visiting the home of the girl, and apologising for bringing shame on the girl and the household, this is an important step in enabling the young mother to 'prevail as a new adult woman...while their household's and their mother's moral reputations are restored' (2004: 167). This restores the 'natural order' of the household and, for the young man, at the same time serves the purpose of showing him as honourable. In this manner, fatherhood becomes reconciled with gendered expectations that men should claim their right to sex, which is 'considered an aspect of men's personhood and agency' (Salo 2004).

HIV and AIDS

> It's something I don't really, like, focus a lot on, AIDS and HIV, because I don't think I'm really worried about it myself so much. You know?...I don't think it's, like, such a big issue, because I think the media has sort of like, in a sense, shoved it down everyone's throats: so, like, all the teenagers now are AIDS-aware...I mean it's so insane, because they teach it to you at school every single year. And like, it's so much that it becomes: oh, well! It's just AIDS; you know, nobody cares, you know? And then they show you these pathetic videos on it...They might show you some skeleton of a person – but it's nothing to someone. Or they give you the statistics: we don't care about the statistics. (Thayo, aged 19, Fish Hoek)

The post-apartheid generation of young South Africans faces a challenge not encountered by any previous generation at their age: AIDS. Demographic models of the pandemic in South Africa suggest that about 5.4 million people (out of a total population of about 48 million) were HIV-positive in mid-2006, and about 600 000 were sick with AIDS (Dorrington et al. 2006). Prevalence rates are lower in the Western Cape than elsewhere in South Africa. Modelling suggests that 7 per cent of 15- to 24-year-old women in the Western Cape were HIV-positive in 2006, as were 1.3 per cent of young men. Whilst there are HIV-positive people in every 'racial' group in South Africa, prevalence rates are much higher among African people, including in Cape Town. Until the public health system began providing antiretroviral drugs, the inevitable consequence of the pandemic was rapidly declining life expectancy. The public provision of AIDS treatment has changed this somewhat, especially in Cape Town, which pioneered and continues to lead the roll-out of treatment. Nonetheless, the lives of many young people in the Valley will surely be transformed by their experience of AIDS, either directly through infection themselves or indirectly through sickness or death among kin, neighbours and friends.

The HIV/AIDS pandemic has prompted massive educational campaigns about risk and protection aimed especially at young people. Across the Valley, however, we observed a pervasive silence surrounding HIV/AIDS. When asked directly, young people seemed to be knowledgeable about HIV and preventing infection, reflecting general exposure to public campaigns. But few young people identified HIV/AIDS as a personal concern. Concerns about pregnancy were more important than concerns about HIV in informing decisions about sex and contraception, and, in any case, 'unsafe sex' was widespread among sexually active boys and girls. While young people can 'talk the talk' when it comes to HIV, there appears to be a large 'gap' between knowledge and awareness, on the one hand, and perceived vulnerability and practice, on the other, in the Valley as elsewhere in South Africa (Eaton et al. 2003).

Close discussions with older teenage girls revealed some of the factors explaining this paradox. At the core of these lies the invisibility of the virus. In all neighbourhoods of the Valley, young people are continually targeted with HIV educational messages – in the home, at school and by the media – but they rarely see what they describe in their own words as the 'true impact of what AIDS is'. Few young people said that they had had personal contact with someone who was infected with the virus, or who had died of AIDS-related causes. CAPS found low levels of respondents who had personal knowledge of people who were HIV-positive or sick with AIDS. Although many people known to respondents have died, the immediate cause of death is often diseases such as pneumonia or tuberculosis, which were already widespread (although not as widespread) before AIDS, and so deaths need not be presented or understood in terms of AIDS. Young people in the Valley told us that stigma results in HIV-positive people keeping their positive status secret. In Masiphumelele, social workers informed us that it is common practice to keep people who are sick with AIDS at home, 'hidden', or for such people to be moved to the Eastern Cape, often to die there. Given this, it may be understandable that young people have difficulty internalising the risk of HIV/AIDS, in the face of little tangible evidence of its existence and 'real' consequences.

This may feed into the following scenario, which came up in a discussion with grade-12 girls in Masiphumelele. The group said that many young people believe that 'it's a myth that HIV exists', and even that parents invented this myth to 'scare' their children 'away' from sex, 'because the parents don't want their children to get pregnant and to have sex'. The girls said that parents sometimes use the threat of HIV/AIDS in an attempt to control and restrict the movements of their young. For example, one of the participants said that when girls have 'done something wrong', such as going out too late at night, their parents tell them: 'You'll get AIDS!' This could further compound girls' suspicions that HIV/AIDS is part of a parental scare tactic and a means of controlling them.

The issue of visibility arose again in a discussion with grade-12 girls in Ocean View, who told us that young people tend to evaluate their partners' health status on the basis of how he or she 'looks' – and, particularly, on the basis of the appearance of wealth:

> If they see you looking nice, you dressing well, they think, oh, he's dressing well, he's looking well; why would he have HIV? They're just looking from the outside. (Talia, girl, aged 18, Ocean View)

They said that if someone comes from a 'poor family' and looks 'dirty', then 'people tend to think, OK, you look like someone who has HIV – because he's a *dirty* one'. The manner in which young people evaluate a potential boyfriend or girlfriend – attaching value to his or her clothes and displays of wealth – appears to influence the manner in which they evaluate his or her health status. The idea that wealth is a determinant of health suggests how, particularly in the less affluent areas of Ocean View and Masiphumelele, both social and physical integrity are deeply bound up in one's presentation as a materially successful person.

The final scenario we explore suggests, in turn, that young people tend to place a higher value on their social integrity than their physical health and well-being. As noted before, while girls exhibited concern about falling pregnant, and took up practices to prevent this, they displayed contrastingly little concern about HIV. In a discussion with grade-12 girls in Masiphumelele, the group agreed that if a girl has had unprotected sex, she would be scared that she might fall pregnant – and may go to the clinic for the 'morning-after pill' – but that she would 'not even *think* about HIV'. When asked why this was the case, the following responses were prompted:

> HIV is not a big issue. Because if you have HIV/AIDS, some people won't even notice you have the disease. If you are pregnant, people will see that you're pregnant. (Precious, girl, aged 18, Masiphumelele)

> The thing is, if you get pregnant, then everyone will see that you are pregnant. But when you are infected [with HIV], it will take a while for people to see. Because if you're HIV-positive, no one can recognise until you're in the later stages; you going to die. So I think that's the problem, you don't want people to know. (Chloe, girl, aged 17, Masiphumelele)

These responses point towards the high priority that young people attach to social reputation and standing – to the point that social well-being is valued above physical well-being. The social repercussions of unprotected sex are of greater concern to girls than are its implications for physical health. The more immediate threat to social integrity that pregnancy poses appears to outweigh the more long-term threat of HIV/AIDS to physical integrity. Both 'bodily conditions' are seen as posing threats – not in themselves, but because of the potential negative social reaction that each condition may provoke. The 'problem' is about *hiding* from others one's sexual 'transgression' – 'you don't want people to know' – rather than the physical implications of this 'transgression'. Young people appear to employ a frame of logic that concerns itself with what people will think when weighing up the health and reproductive risks associated with sex. The importance that young people attach to 'outside image', 'keeping up appearances' and social reputation – particularly in the context of limited other means to display success – appears to play a troubling role when it comes to young people's sexual health-related concerns.

Image, choices and self-care

> [Some people will] change their whole self to become popular, and that's basically what you are: you lose your self-identity…You like *lose yourself* in this *whole messy cycle* of popularity…That's what happens: it's like a rock star. (Leanne, aged 17, Fish Hoek, group discussion)

For young people, one's external image is a key vehicle for displaying social success. Markers of such success include being seen out and about; socialising in sought-after places; pursuing a lifestyle of entertainment; owning fashionable clothes and accessories; being surrounded by friends who are dressed and accessorised in a similarly fashionable manner; and being seen at the hip of trendy boyfriends or girlfriends. However, the world of social success is also a highly competitive one, which makes both friendships and dating relationships tenuous, and popularity hard to maintain. It is not surprising then that the young people with whom we worked tended to see this world in ambivalent terms: while it is enticing and exciting, it is also highly pressured, and easy to get caught up in at the expense of other goals and priorities.

Additionally, this world is (somewhat deliberately on the part of young people) one that is separate from the influences of the adult generation. For most, entering this world requires rejecting what young people present as 'adult' ideas of what they 'should' be doing: participating in class, doing school work, staying at home doing chores and religious pursuits. Those who engage in such pursuits are often seen as 'boring' and 'not cool'. Young people appear, in this respect, to be caught in a very stark moral dichotomy wherein 'fitting in' and 'being cool' means rejecting pursuits and relationships in which, in many cases, they are deeply invested, but failure to reject these comes at the expense of 'fitting in' and 'being cool'.

Young people also drew attention to the fact that 'being cool' is more of an 'attitude to keep up', and that relationships with adults, religion and schooling are also important for many, especially if one wants to 'get somewhere in life'. However, it is difficult for young people to 'keep up the attitude' while doing something different in practice. For most young people, keeping up a cool attitude requires, in practice, taking up the whole package of 'cool' pursuits – and succumbing to pressure in one arena makes one more susceptible to pressure to succumb in other arenas. Likewise, those who are determined to 'get somewhere in life' feel that they have to keep themselves on the straight and narrow and resist conformity to all that is considered 'cool' (see also Soudien 2007).

Discussions with older teenage girls across the Valley revealed the sentiment that young people often go 'off track' when they succumb to peer pressure to 'hang out with friends', 'party' and 'have fun'. This pathway of 'deviance', while providing immediate social integration and status among peers, is seen as a 'dead end'. Many young people spoke about 'fitting in' and 'being cool' as part of a 'cycle of deviance' in which young people get caught up – and in the process end up 'losing themselves' in the 'messy cycle of popularity'. Being cool and fitting in were often spoken about as coming at the expense of 'being (and bettering) oneself' in other respects.

Young people saw the pursuit of popularity as costing them educational attainment in particular. They often said that having fun in class rather than focusing on school work was seen as cool, while those who participated in class were seen as boring. While dating is seen as cool, it is also associated with negative consequences for educational advancement. Young people spoke of being distracted from their class work when they had girlfriends or boyfriends in class, and also felt that 'being in love', and the exciting but confusing emotions that accompany this experience, can be a distraction from school work. Charney (girl, aged 17, Ocean View) said that when dating relationships end, young people think that 'all their dreams are useless' and 'feel there is no purpose, and turn to sex and drugs'. This should be seen as a particularly likely outcome because of the transient nature of relationships, underpinned by competition over boyfriends and girlfriends, and the rifts in friendships that accompany this. This emotional turmoil should also be understood as embedded in a context of complex social problems and limited opportunities for young people to achieve and display success. It makes holding onto dreams difficult, and hurt and disappointment can easily lead to choices that may have a negative impact on the type of future young people can achieve.

Older teenage girls, particularly those living in the less affluent neighbourhoods of Ocean View and Masiphumelele, felt that dating has particularly negative implications for girls. Lenore (aged 16, Ocean View) observed that many girls saw boyfriends and husbands as an alternative route to material success – to that of education and pursuing a career – and tend to give up ambitions for individual achievement once they have found a committed partner and see marriage impending. She said that because girls have so much invested in these relationships, they tend to put their partners first and 'neglect themselves' and, in the process, lose sight of their goals and dreams. She felt that this leads to many women being in unfulfilling marriages where they are 'trapped', often in abusive circumstances. Girls in Masiphumelele agreed that young women are 'badly influenced by their boyfriends'. They said that many boys were 'doing nothing' with their lives, and encouraged their girlfriends to leave their homework and go out late at night partying.

In this respect, young people's talk reflects that dating and sex, as part of a package of pursuits that provide the immediate means to fitting in and being cool, ultimately lead to a dead end. On the other hand, not conforming to peer pressure and instead choosing the socially accepted or straight-and-narrow route of education and often religion is seen as a somewhat lonely road. In this respect, young people see the choices available to them as limited and restricting, and always accompanied by loss or sacrifice in some form. Picking and choosing between available pursuits is not seen as an option.

The conformers: Deviance and dead ends

> All my friends were having sex. That was the main thing that was pulling me to do that. They were stressing me – talking about sex and all of that. And they were like, 'Chloe, we like girls who have sex'…Peer pressure is the most *powerful* thing. You want to fit in. So if people like people who are not virgins, it's better for you to *not* be a virgin so you can fit in…So, what the hell, I must just do it and get it over with and be the same with them. (Chloe, interview)

> When you lose your virginity, it's more like you've opened the gate to – now I'm not a virgin – so I can sleep around with anyone that I want. But when you were still a virgin, you were like, no, I'm scared to do this; I shouldn't do it; it's wrong…But now, once you're not, it's like, 'What the hell! I did it, so let me continue.' (Chloe, interview)

Chloe's life-story, which we constructed with her over many months and which extended beyond the official end of the fieldwork, illustrates the dilemmas young people face, and the limited nature of the choices available to them. Her story tells of her competing desire to make a success of her life, by completing her education successfully and pursuing a career, on the one hand, and fitting in and being cool on the other. Her story is illustrative of how young people 'live' the discourse of 'deviance and dead ends'.

She told us during the early stages of the fieldwork that she had made a 'promise' to herself to postpone having sex until she had finished school, as she did not wish to compromise her education by falling pregnant and limiting her possibilities of pursuing a career. By her own admission, however, Chloe reneged on this promise at the age of 16 when, under great pressure from friends, she had sex. She spoke about her feelings afterwards in ambivalent terms. She told us that, having had sex, she gained the acceptance and respect of her friends, and was no longer 'laughed at in school' and seen as a 'child' by her sexually experienced friends. On the other hand, however, she had also felt 'dirty' and 'angry' with herself, as she had broken her promise to herself to postpone having sex until she had completed her schooling: 'I told myself that I want to lose my virginity when I finish school. But it just happened. It happened because of friends.' She explained that, after a girl 'loses' her virginity, it becomes difficult to return to a sexually abstinent lifestyle, and easy to fall into a pattern of 'sleeping around'. It seems that once young people have broken out of the moral constraints surrounding sex, it becomes easier to remain outside of these and take up a 'what-the-hell' attitude. Additionally, succumbing to peer pressure in one respect appears to make young people more prone to succumbing to peer pressure to engage in other 'deviant' activities, and get distracted from other priorities, such as education. In her life-story, written after her grade-12 year, Chloe wrote:

> I had a fabulous matric year: I enjoyed my year and had the time of my life on my matric ball. Also what happened is that I partied too much and forgot about my books. At the end of the day I got burned coz I didn't pass my matric; I got a supplementary[2]…It's not that I blame friends…but I have to say that friends were the major reason, as we were encouraging each other to party. A few people said I'm not going to party this weekend, I'm going to study, but they seemed not cool…It's not possible to do both partying and studying – it's one or the other.

Although Chloe had the opportunity to do a supplementary exam and to pass her matric year, she fell pregnant shortly after her matric year, which has led her to postpone taking these examinations. As Chloe's account suggests, young people appear to be positioned within a very stark, morally imbued dichotomy: in this context, once one has subscribed (or 'given in') to one 'package' of pursuits, one's behaviour becomes almost wholly influenced by what is expected in this package. Also, once one has 'succumbed' to pressures to engage in the 'unwise' package of activities, such as 'partying' and sex, it appears to be very difficult for young people to discontinue their involvement in that set of pursuits, or redirect themselves along an alternative path. As Chloe's story suggests, young people appear to become 'trapped' in a cycle characterised by negative practices from which it is very difficult to disengage.

Part of this scenario appears to rest on the fact that young people make their choices within a very narrow frame of reference. Older teenage girls across the Valley agreed that many young people look to their peers – in the absence of adult role models or advisors – as a frame of reference to decide whether what they are doing is 'right' or 'wrong'. Many expressed the view that even when young people are aware that the choices they are making are detrimental to themselves in some way, they seek comfort and reassurance in the fact that, as Chloe put it, 'everybody else is doing it' so 'it must be alright' – 'even though they know that it is wrong'. Young people are, therefore, conscious of the limits to what friends can provide, but nonetheless find comfort in conformity.

The non-conformers: The straight-and-narrow, but lonely, road

Across the Valley, young people who chose not to date and have sex often made this choice as part of a broader strategy of decision-making that involved non-conformity to peer-group values surrounding 'partying' and 'having fun'. Investment in religion and education, and a desire to meet parental expectations of 'making something of themselves' in life were the main reasons that young people gave for resisting peer pressure. Both boys and girls who were not dating or having sex often said that these practices went against their religious values, and would compromise their 'morals'. Zuziwe (aged 17, Masiphumelele), who described herself as a 'saved' Christian, told us that because of her religious beliefs, 'I don't and am not allowed to drink, smoke and be involved in relationships. The only thing I do is read the Bible, pray and go to church.'

Even more salient than religious values appeared to be the value that many of these young people attached to their education. These young people had chosen not to date because they saw dating as a distraction from school work. For grade-12 girls in Ocean View, the choice to avoid having a relationship was, in part, linked to concerns relating to their productive and reproductive futures, centring specifically upon achieving career goals and financial independence as adults, and 'making a better life' for their children. These aspirations need to be understood as deeply related to the social and material contexts in which these girls are living, where unemployment and poverty are common; opportunities for realising career aspirations – particularly for young women – are limited; and gender-based inequality and disempowerment is often a function of women being financially dependent upon their male partners. The goals of building a career and independence are very high aims in this context.

Young people who chose this package of pursuits often spoke about themselves as 'different' from other young people:

> What I like about myself is that I am unlike other children. I have no boyfriend and I don't do dating. Also I work hard at school so that I can go far with my studies. I respect adults. I listen to adults and take advice from those who encourage me, for example, my pastor. (Lindiwe, girl, aged 13, Masiphumelele, interview)

Although, as Lindiwe's words suggest, this difference is not always perceived in negative terms, we found that for the majority of these young people, being 'different' is also experienced as being 'the odd one out' in a more negative sense. Young people who choose not to conform with peers are often resented by their peers. They spoke of being the subject of 'silly jokes', and said they were seen as 'boring' by their conforming friends. Young people who resist peer pressure and follow the more 'straight-and-narrow' path of school work and, in some cases, religious faith, often feel that they have chosen a somewhat 'lonely road' of individual values and success – a road that does not intersect with pathways to social acceptance and status among peers.

We found that, particularly in the poorer areas of Masiphumelele and Ocean View, young people who attempt to break out of negative social cycles of poverty by focusing on education feel 'pressed down' by others who have resigned themselves to the fact that such success is unachievable.

> They don't get the support most of the time from their parents and from their friends, because if someone says, 'oh, I'm going to be this'...then

they're like, 'oh, but you's too stupid!'…They just press the person down, and concentrate on the negative instead of encouraging the person. (Lenore, group discussion)

As Lenore and Charney, grade-12 girls living in Ocean View, told us, people would rather try and 'bring you down' than see you as a positive role model to aspire to, and would feel threatened by other people's success. Envy and tactics of 'spoiling' that accompany this make it very difficult for young people to sustain a journey up the ladder to success (see also Chapter 5). It is clear that young people who do not conform to peer-group norms – which appear to be reflective of community norms more generally – are a threat to those who do. The difficulty that young people have in disengaging from a cycle of negative practices, discussed before, may fuel the resentment that they level towards non-conformers. Talia, a 'non-conformer', confided that sometimes problems at home and the pressures of school work and from peers were overwhelming and made her feel she should 'just give up and be like the others…smoke a cigarette, get drunk, have sex, drop out of school'.

We found that young people have particular difficulty in remaining on the 'straight-and-narrow' pathway into adulthood because they are surrounded by few young people or adults whom they see as role models for this direction. Many young people reject this pathway, often concealing their 'deviant' activities for fear of judgement by peers. And, as we have seen, few adults in the community are role models or examples. For these reasons, the 'straight-and-narrow' pathway is, to a large extent, an imagined one, rather than one that has been tangibly mapped out by others before them. This imagined and intangible pathway is, by nature, easy to lose sight of in the face of a competing reality. Choosing or falling back on the alternative pathway – one that provides immediate rewards of social value and self-validation – is, therefore, an attractive, and perhaps the only realistic, option.

Making inroads and negotiating the crossroads: The road less travelled

My boyfriend, he's good to me; he's taught me a lot of things that I didn't know…He taught me about love; how to love a person. If you love a person, you don't love them with money, or stuff: you love them in your heart. You have to have feelings for someone you love…In the future, what things you want to do; like, he asked me those things. And he also explained, if you want to be someone in the future, you have to do that and that and that. (Precious, interview)

We found a small group of young people who appeared to be able to negotiate the 'moral dichotomy' in more flexible terms. We call these young people the 'negotiators'. These young people were building committed dating relationships while keeping sight of other goals and priorities – in particular, focusing on school work, thinking about their future career prospects and about building families one day. These young people were both forward-looking and focused on the present relationships and pursuits that would help them to achieve their future goals. They also showed a more discerning approach to how they select their friends and dating partners, and choose those who share similar aspirations and provide motivation and support. Contrary to the sentiment upheld by many girls that boyfriends are a 'bad influence' on girls' educational attainment and success, these girls seek out boyfriends who similarly invest in their education. What distinguishes these girls and boys is the manner in which they communicate with their partners, and avoid too much pressure from friends. These young people spoke extensively with their partners about what they want from their relationships and in the future, and often experience their dating relationships as sites of sharing, support and inspiration. Their narratives illustrate the abilities of the young to act in an empowered and decisive manner and to prioritise looking after themselves through the conduct of their relationships, even when the pressures against doing so are immense.

Conclusion

Negotiating decisions, feelings and experiences involving dating and sex is a complex and new territory for adolescents. In post-apartheid Cape Town, 'playing the love game', as one person put it, entails learning and playing by rules of relationships that are new to adolescents, but have historical roots, in the face of both old and new sets of pressures and desires.

Few girls or boys are able to speak openly with parents or other adults about dating and sex, in part because of adults' unwillingness, and in part because they themselves keep parts of their lives secret in the interest of preserving adults' trust and respect. Institutions purporting to offer health and social services to adolescents often fail to connect with and respond to their concerns. In the absence of adult input, young people turn to peers for information and support. But peer advice comes with pressure to experiment. Across the Valley, dating and sex are bound up in a rebellion against adult authority, asserting control and autonomy and cultivating style and status. For young people who perceive many areas of their lives to be out of their control, dating and sex can represent an arena in which they can harness some sense of control and power.

For all young people, decision-making about dating and sex is largely linked to concerns surrounding self-representation and social reputation. For boys who have few material resources and poor prospects, masculinity can become dependent on heterosexual success with girls, and even on violence and coercion. Girls in poor communities whose consumer aspirations do not fit with parental means of provision can become dependent on boyfriends, which can lead to submission in the face of sexual demands and acceptance of sexual coercion and violence. Fear of exclusion from the peer group or of losing access to social and material success can disempower girls in relation to their providers. Girls may also avoid using contraceptives out of concern to preserve an image of chastity. Boys, fearful of admitting ignorance, can also find themselves unprepared for intimate and sexual relationships.

Young people negotiate dating and sex within a stark moral dichotomy that contrasts a package of responsible activities with a package of dangerous ones. The former, the morally approved pathway, is almost impossible to sustain. There is little or no moral legitimacy attached to a pathway that encompasses a mix of 'good' and 'bad' activities. The starkness of the choice disempowers young people.

Most of the factors and processes discussed in this chapter are common across the spectrum of cultures and wealth in the Valley. In all parts of the Valley, girls face socialisation practices, norms, expectations, pressures, power dynamics and inequalities that are strongly gendered – although many of these are exacerbated by poverty. Many of the *silences* in discourses are also common throughout the Valley.

8 The quiet violence of contemporary segregation in Cape Town

Thus far, this book has drawn on what young people themselves do and say to analyse the intricacies of the lives of ordinary children and adolescents in the various domains where they spend time and build relationships. In this chapter, we look closely at the ways individual young people growing up in contemporary Cape Town are able to maximise their chances of thriving, and how the responses of individuals and institutions serve to bolster or undermine these processes for the young. Young people certainly face circumstances that would ordinarily be considered adverse: pervasive violence; very high unemployment; poor schools; families and communities that struggle to retain coherence; and cultural change. In such a context, what power do they have to safeguard their own well-being, or even – as Mandela (2000) put it in the words quoted at the beginning of Chapter 1 – to 'heal not only themselves but their societies as well'? And, central to these questions, how do children and adolescents themselves view their own capabilities in relation to the challenges of their everyday worlds?

Enquiry into children's agency internationally has gained momentum since the work of European sociologists in the early 1990s, termed the 'new sociology of childhood'. Their core contention was that scholarly focus on the socialisation of children had failed to capture the manner in which children shape their physical and social environments. Used liberally and often without definition, the term 'agency' has become problematic insofar as it is simply shorthand for the general recognition that the young have some kind of power to influence their own and others' worlds, even when these worlds present considerable obstacles to their well-being. It tells us nothing about the source, nature and effectiveness of this power, or how it is managed by either the young or adults close to them.

This distinction is especially important in South Africa, where many young people forcefully asserted their 'agency' during the township revolts of the mid-1980s. Many commentators worried that this evident political agency was not matched by a similar capacity to engage with social and economic issues, including some that were perhaps consequential to young people's political activism. In describing young people as a 'lost generation', the media implied that their active participation in, or at least exposure to, political conflict, together with interrupted schooling and disrupted family life, had undermined young people's knowledge of and capacity to build healthy social relationships and navigate a positive individual life course (Seekings 1995). Even Nelson Mandela and other ANC leaders warned of the dangers posed by apparently unsatisfied and alienated young people (Seekings 1996). Scholars criticised the 'lost generation' thesis on two grounds: first, by extrapolation, it applied to an entire generation the experiences of what was probably a small minority of young people; second, it underestimated the resilience of young people even in the face of adverse circumstances. Large-scale research in the early 1990s concluded that there was 'no such "youth crisis" but a range of intractable problems in which young people find themselves' (Van Zyl Slabbert et al. 1994: 26). A national survey showed that most went to church, played sports and were positive and ambitious about life (CASE 1993). But very little attention had been paid to how young people themselves interpreted the sociopolitical environment, and hence their capacity to respond constructively, as well as destructively, in the social arenas of everyday life as much as in the visible political realm.

Anthropologists working in poor African neighbourhoods began to address children's participation and influence in their social arenas during the late 1990s. Henderson (1999) concluded that in the face of severe, chronic poverty and disempowerment, African children in New Crossroads show initiative and dexterity in using the available social, cultural, discursive and imaginative resources to make sense of highly problematic familial and neighbourhood relationships, and to reduce the pain caused by them. But, she attests, because their strategies are inadequate to the task of solving or preventing the reoccurrence of these problems, children incurred high short-term and long-term costs to their well-being in their efforts to cope. Other anthropologists working in the same neighbourhood have also linked the restrictions on young people's efforts to find care, support and guidance to the inabilities of adults close to them (including parents, wider kin, neighbours and teachers) to fulfil their obligations. These inabilities are traced to the culpability of the apartheid state in undermining the family as an institution within the African population (Reynolds 1995) and the enduring influence of patriarchy (Ramphele 2002). More than a decade later, the post-apartheid state claims to be redressing the injustices of the past, although our chapters document continuing evidence of patriarchy in familial, neighbourhood and peer relationships across Cape Town's cultural and wealth spectra. How then have the possibilities for self-determination and nurture in their broadest sense changed for this generation of children?

Psychologists have long recognised that self-efficacy and high self-esteem, alongside social competence, good cognitive skills and intellectual functioning (particularly problem-solving abilities) are key indicators of 'child adjustment', i.e. the ability of children to cope with, and even thrive in, adverse environments (Black & Krishnakumar 1995; Garmezy 1996; Masten & Coatsworth 1998; Quinn 1995; Rutter 1985; Werner 2000; Werner & Smith 1989). The thrust of more recent enquiry has been to explore and explain resilience, or the child's ability to adapt to and develop within environments that pose significant challenges (Luthar et al. 2000; Masten 2001; Masten & Coatsworth 1998; Ward et al. 2007). Resilience is achieved through the mutual interaction of intrapersonal factors (including perceptions of self and behavioural choice) and protective factors in the wider environments of family, neighbourhood, peer group and school. Like agency, this concept foregrounds the attributes, perceptions and actions of young people as critical in their responses to their environments. But it is perhaps more helpful in recognising the two-way and context-specific nature of this process. Where the challenges lie, particularly in a South African setting, is in attending to the part that very localised histories, culturally nuanced norms and socio-economic realities play alongside shared aspects of the sociopolitical landscape. Interdisciplinary, comparative research is of enormous value in probing these questions. Our efforts to do so build on the foundations laid by earlier scholars and extend the analysis beyond poor African neighbourhoods to encompass the demographic spectrum of contemporary Cape Town.

This chapter begins by exploring adolescents' own assessments of how much control they consider themselves to have in their lives, as reflected in their responses to questions posed in the Cape Area Panel Study (CAPS). We then reflect on these responses in light of ethnographic data pertaining to how children position 'self' and their sense of autonomy in relation to their participation in social relationships. Our data suggest that adolescents' responses to survey questions about self-efficacy are guided by culturally validated discourses in which choice is placed in the hands of the young and described in moral terms, and may, therefore, be a poor reflection of how young people think about their ability to look after their own interests and influence the world around them. The bulk of the chapter pays close attention to the ways in which children and adolescents achieve control of self within and through their everyday relationships at home, among their peers and in the neighbourhood. We look at why some of their choices may protect or empower young people in the short term, but – in their own opinion – are problematic in the long term, and what sustains these processes. Finally, we consider the implications of our study for furthering understanding on the transition to adulthood, and provide some suggestions for more research.

Adolescents' responses to questions about personal control

Young CAPS participants were asked to rate the degree of control they consider themselves to have over their own lives. Analysis of their responses produces a somewhat unexpected picture. Figure 8.1 shows the responses by type of neighbourhood in Cape Town for adolescents aged 17–20 in 2005. Young people from poor and very poor African neighbourhoods are more likely to say that they have total control over their lives than young people from coloured or white neighbourhoods. Young people from wealthy neighbourhoods, either predominantly white or coloured, are least likely to say they have total control over their lives. How far young people feel they are able to shape their everyday lives seems to vary *inversely* with the degree of historical privilege and advantage. Multivariate regression analysis suggests that there are no significant differences between white and coloured young people on the basis of race alone, but that class matters. However, there are big differences between white and coloured young people, on the one hand, and African young people, on the other. Few of the former report that they have control over all aspects of their lives, whereas more of the latter report being 'totally in control'. These differences are statistically significant even when we control for class.

Figure 8.1 *Control over life, by neighbourhood (17–20-year-olds, Cape Town)*

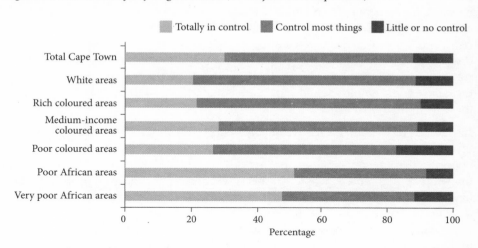

Source: Cape Area Panel Study wave 3 (2005)

Notes: These figures are net of a very small number of 'don't knows'. 'Neighbourhood' refers to 'neighbourhood of origin', i.e. it is the neighbourhood where the participants lived at the time of the first CAPS interviews in 2002; they may have left those neighbourhoods since then.

How then should we interpret these findings? Most immediately striking is that the vast majority of young people across Cape Town describe themselves as in control of most things, or everything, in their lives. Other studies have found similarly high levels of optimism and self-assurance among young people nationally, even amid negative experiences in their homes and neighbourhoods (Finchilescu & Dawes 1998; Leoschut & Burton 2006). These mark a shift away from the high levels of depression reported in the decade before the transition to democracy (Soudien 2007).

At first glance, these South African data appear to fly in the face of most psychological research internationally that finds a low locus of control in very poor people, and a high one in wealthy people (Lachman & Weaver 1998). It is unusual to find the poorest and historically most disenfranchised section of the population reporting higher levels of control over their lives than their wealthier counterparts. The discrepancy might owe something to the precise wording of the questions. Lachman and Weaver (1998), for example, report on studies that probe responses to statements such as 'I can do just about anything I really set my mind to'; 'When I really want to do something, I usually find a way to succeed at it'; and 'Whether or not I am able to get what I want is in my own hands'. The wording in CAPS, however, is somewhat more general, and might tap into sentiments of optimism about the future more than self-control. The wording was also somewhat ambiguous with respect to time, and might have been understood as referring either to current everyday lives or life paths in the future. This question was, however, followed by one asking, 'What opportunities do people like you face in the future?' The pattern of responses shown in Figure 8.1 was only partially replicated: young people from poor coloured neighbourhoods assessed their opportunities most pessimistically, whereas there were insignificant differences between young people from African, white or rich coloured neighbourhoods, who almost all assessed their opportunities to be 'good'. The fact that poor African and rich white (or coloured) adolescents considered that they had similar opportunities does suggest, however, that the optimistic responses among poor African people are robust. Even though poor African adolescents face pretty grim prospects in reality, most have grand ambitions and expectations and think that their chances of realising these lie in their own hands.

Insofar as 'race' matters, it presumably reflects in part the prevalent discourses of affirmative action and black economic empowerment, which suggest that opportunities are opening up for African people and (arguably) closing down for white and coloured people – especially poorer coloured people. Adolescents living in poor coloured areas are the least hopeful about the future of people like themselves, but range most widely in their responses regarding control in their lives. A greater proportion report having little or no control in their lives, but slightly more residents of poor coloured areas say they are in total control than do residents of wealthier coloured or white areas. Assertions of control in everyday life cannot only pertain to perceived social identity and its implications for achieving future goals. It is likely that adolescent CAPS participants' responses to the first question about control in their lives also reflect a varying sense of decision-making power within everyday domestic, peer and neighbourhood interaction. The fact that white and coloured adolescents from richer neighbourhoods recognise that they face good opportunities, yet far fewer assert total control over their lives, presumably reflects a sense of restriction to their control in ordinary and everyday matters (such as who they live with, whether and where they go to school and where they socialise) rather than collective 'racial' disempowerment.

We are left, however, with the paradox of great optimism and strong perceived self-control among young men and women in poor African neighbourhoods. As we saw in Chapters 6 and 7, this general optimism is also reflected in expectations that adolescents would achieve educational success and would not fall pregnant until much later in life. Sometimes these expectations are realised, but it is much more often the case that they are dashed. Survey data provide us with little understanding of precisely how and why so many young people in poor neighbourhoods are so optimistic and positive for so long, and what happens when they run up against the brutal reality. We don't know whether 'control over one's life' – as measured in questions in surveys such as CAPS – matters to young people, and if it does, in what ways.

Understanding personal efficacy

Emerging from the qualitative data is a keen sense among young people of the importance of some level of self-determination to their well-being more generally, and of the various barriers to developing and exercising it which, while varying in form, are encountered across the class, cultural and geographical spectra. Children and adolescents across the Valley agreed that being able to make decisions and instigate change mattered to their well-being, but the broader discourse in which possibilities for doing so were framed differed between neighbourhoods and reflected the particular constraints to their achieving the level and nature of self-determination they desired.

Young children and teenagers in Masiphumelele frequently referred to their own choices and actions as instrumental in protecting themselves and ensuring their continued well-being. Nine-year-old participants in a focus group spoke of their own responsibilities to eat healthy food, keep themselves clean and resist the temptation to steal from supermarkets. Such assertions could be interpreted as young children repeating the rules set by adults in the home, but their consistent presence in the discourse of younger and older teenagers suggests a cognisance of self-determination that has developed within an environment where material resources are often very scarce – as are social and emotional ones. Pupils aged between 15 and 19 at Masiphumelele High School were asked to map and write about the challenges they face and the means by which they saw fit to address these. Responses to the latter emphasised improving personal attitudes and decision-making above appeals for resources or assistance, and included: 'Think before you do things; make good choices; love yourself and care about what you do; share everything you have; communicate with others and work together as a team; focus on your future; be happy all the time; forget about stress.' What we see in this discourse is a repertoire of self-efficacy as both present and pivotal in managing everyday life. The extent to which young people and their peers respond to challenges in this manner is not clear: at what point does the ideal fail to hold the reality, and, in reaching that point, does it undermine the discourse?

While foregrounding personal actions in solving problems, young residents of Masiphumelele said that the major constraint to their making better decisions for themselves was lack of knowledge. In the writing exercise described above, pupils wrote that the means to meet challenges included '[having] more knowledge about life; [knowing] how to handle challenges and deal with enemies; [knowing] what is wrong and what is right; [learning] about how to cope on my own and how to take control of self'. And where these teenagers identified a need for assistance and support from family members, schools or services more broadly in meeting challenges, we were struck by the fact that they placed more store on acquiring knowledge and expertise through their relationships with these figures or institutions than on their provision of greater material resources in the home and school, or better neighbourhood infrastructure.

In a similar mapping exercise, teenagers in Ocean View were asked to show their sources of support, challenges and suggested responses to challenges (see Map 9). They also drew attention to the importance of control over self, both one's attitudes and actions, as critical to well-being, but unlike their peers in Masiphumelele, concluded that very few young people position themselves as highly influential over their current and future lives. For most, the barriers to doing so in this neighbourhood appear to be too great to sustain even the notion that a young person can have complete command of their own life path. One of these barriers, say teenagers, is that local child-rearing practices do not teach young people to be accountable to themselves:

> What people really need to do is stop looking for someone else to
> blame and take ownership of themselves, to face up to what they've
> been doing wrong and stop blaming someone else for their mistakes…
> If you not good at a subject you going to say it's the teacher's fault,
> but you not doing anything exactly to improve yourself so that you
> can improve. I mean it's so easy to blame someone else instead of
> blaming yourself because then you don't have that guilt. (Charney,
> girl, age 17, Ocean View)

Across the Valley we witnessed various culturally informed practices relating to raising children and to notions of personhood more generally that effectively limit young people's abilities to exercise power in their own lives. Often describing feelings of despair, despondency and frustration in relation to problems they were currently facing, middle-class adolescents in Fish Hoek were also grappling with how to achieve their desired level of self-determination. They linked their confidence in this arena to the quality of their everyday interpersonal relationships, pointing specifically to how their own relatives and teachers responded to the general expectation that adults should be the ones making decisions for their children until they reached their 18th birthday. Within this normative framework, some parents largely excluded their children from decisions until they reached 'adulthood' then left them to their own devices, whereas others encouraged their children to think and act more independently as they grew older (even if they often overruled their decisions). Those young people who enjoyed open and consultative relationships with parent-figures expressed their appreciation of both parental support and guidance, as well as their ability to give them a certain amount of independence. Some spoke of being encouraged by parents 'to make my own mistakes'.

Why, we might ask, if cognisance of self is in such short supply, did such large proportions of adolescents report in a survey questionnaire that they were in control of all or most things in their lives? And why do black Africans assert greater confidence in this regard than their coloured or white peers, who are much more likely to achieve their personal goals? In the previous section we noted that collective 'racial' empowerment (or otherwise) appears to influence adolescent responses to survey questions about control in their lives, but it does not explain all the variation. We suggested that culturally validated discourses about the young and their future prospects may also shape the way young people responded to these questions. The reader will recall the powerful and pervasive nature of discourses linking formal education to personal success, wealth and social status described in Chapters 6 and 7. In this light, it is likely that when posed a question about control over one's life as part of a survey, many young people responded in line with the worldview that gives power to individuals who follow the ascribed route. Only in conversations that try to make sense of everyday experience, which was often equated to failure when judged in relation to such worldviews, do young people speak about other realities, including their incomplete knowledge, disillusionment and feelings of disempowerment.

One plausible hypothesis is that such large proportions of adolescents assert high levels of self-determination in their survey responses because they subscribe to the discourse of achievement through personal adherence to education and career development, and either may not have had cause to challenge it through personal experience or choose to avoid contemplating other possible outcomes. Our conclusion raises questions about how young people regard the actions of self, the nature and degree of power they attribute to themselves and the sources or catalysts of this power. Our conclusion also points to an opportunity for further research in this vein, namely to explore any correlation between individual-level variables in the CAPS data and the responses shown in Figure 8.1.

Perspectives on what shapes control over self

Even in their pre-teen years, young people are aware that aspects of individual personality, particularly temperament, shape their responses to difficult circumstances. They speak about friends who are easy-going and sociable, eager to develop friendships and unperturbed by being teased for being different, even when circumstances at home are judged to be unstable and worrying. Some recognised that their own character traits differed in certain ways from their peers and could explain, at least partly, their feelings of discontent and powerlessness. In an art club exercise designed to facilitate the expression of a problem young people are currently struggling with and how it makes them feel, 12-year-old Neliswa of Masiphumelele drew a fierce giant. She explained her drawing as follows: 'My problem is like this big giant. I feel it in my head, I am unhappy, rude, angry and I shout at everyone in my family and at my friends. It happens when someone does something that I don't like, and I say to him or her that I don't like it and they do it again.' While recognising that she is being provoked by other people's actions, Neliswa depicts the problem as an internal battle and regards her own temperament as partly responsible for why she seldom feels satisfied and in control of self. But in many respects, Neliswa is in a stronger position than many of her peers in her neighbourhood: she is one of only two art club members living in a brick house; her mother has a salaried nursing job; she speaks of love and support from family and friends; and she often comes top of her class. But in spite of (or perhaps because of) her comparatively secure and promising socio-economic position and success at school, Neliswa says that she feels 'small and horrible' at school, seems consistently frustrated about who she is and what life offers and was aware that because she stands out in this regard she has to maintain a front. Under her self-portrait – in which the absence of a smile and addition of a T-shirt with 'Bad Girl' across the chest make an arresting combination – Neliswa wrote: 'In this picture I feel happy, but not too happy. People think that I am not happy, but I am happy. I am thinking about the things I have to do at home.'

Temperament is not considered by the young as the only or most important influence on their sense of internal integrity and control over self. Rather, they emphasised a number of other personal attributes that are developed in their relationships with others. These include nurturing a belief in oneself that emerges in the interpersonal exchange that occurs within high-quality intimate relationships, and particularly those in the domestic and familial spheres. Relationships of this nature are also recognised by the young as the arenas where they learn the skills needed to empathise and communicate with others. And, when combined with confidence in one's own integrity, social and communication skills are seen as critical in being able to negotiate with friends who persuade them to act in ways that they would otherwise choose not to, while at the same time reducing the possibility of being excluded from the peer group. These lines of cause and effect are also reported by psychologists, who find that children with good social and communication skills are more resilient because they are more able to engage other people and access social support (Werner 2000).

A second important stimulus to belief in self among young people throughout the Valley is personal faith in God and the moral guidance offered by adults and peers with a similar faith both within and outside religious institutions. Few South African surveys probe people's strength of, and commitment to, religious (or other moral) beliefs. Surveys typically ask only 'what is your religion?' and (sometimes) 'how often do you attend services?' CAPS asked only the first question. Given that only 1 in 10 adolescents in Cape Town answered 'none', it provides little indication of the relevance of religion in the lives of young people.[1] As long ago as 1993, as part of an enquiry into just how 'lost' the younger generation was, one survey found that half of young women and one-third of young men reported attending church frequently (Everatt & Orkin 1993: 8). A more recent survey of high-school pupils in Gauteng found that 88 per cent said that religion was either important or very important in their lives (Emmett 2004).[2] Literary accounts of contemporary adolescence are also generally silent about these issues. One psychological study by Mary Schwab-Stone found that personal involvement in religion (such as private prayer and scripture reading) reduced delinquency, but the effects were not only seen among children who attended church, mosque or temple (O'Donnell et al. 2002). Our ethnographic research further accentuates the importance of this generally neglected dimension of young people's lives, and points to the significance of young people's personal investment in and ownership of their religion in influencing their actions:

> The world we live in today allows youngsters to do and experience a lot
> of things like drugs, alcohol, to be pressed down by peer pressure and
> teaching our youngsters of safe sex and not of abstinence. You will forever
> have a choice and always it will conclude to you making the right choice.
> God made us with a choice so that we can make up our own mind and
> that means that only you can make the right choice and in all my time
> that I was faced with peer pressure I always remembered teaching of what
> was right and what was wrong. If there hasn't been someone who taught

you these principles then seek someone today still because it helps a lot.
(Ronaldo, boy, aged 17, Ocean View, life story account)

The onus on self-determination becomes more powerful in the context of a morally imbued discourse in which life paths are considered 'right' or 'wrong'. Such a discourse is often supported by a wider religious worldview and morality. Most young residents in the Valley describe themselves as Christians, but there are also Muslims (particularly in Ocean View), and the wide variety of belief systems encompassed within the term 'Christian' include conservative evangelicalism to faiths that incorporate the reverence of ancestors. There is a strong religious ethos in all three neighbourhoods and the beliefs and activities of the young make a significant contribution. A large proportion of children and adolescents report reading the Bible or other religious texts and attending church services or events regularly – even daily. Their response to personal religious involvement and the general ethos within the community varied over time within an individual life course and according to context. At times, young teenagers from all three neighbourhoods spoke about feeling intimidated and confused about their 'wrongs'. In an anonymous essay-writing project set by the religious-studies teacher, most grade-9 Fish Hoek pupils expressed confusion and guilt about going to parties, drinking and using drugs, as well as about their relationships with friends and family. Writing about what they perceived as their wrongdoings, these pupils conveyed a negative self-image and internal confusion about their own capabilities to deal with situations in their lives:

> I used to go to church, but then sum stuff happened and I got involved with the wrong people and things. I felt very guilty…I feel very guilty because God has done so much for me but I have done nothing in return.

> I deleted all the bad 'satanic' music from my computer, like 'Slipknot', but I am so scared I am listening to the wrong music.

> If God does exist then why does he make people's lives 'hell'. My friend has many bad family problems and all she does is pray for help, but does she get it? NO!

The fact that these essays were written in a religious-studies class may have enhanced young people's attention to a highly moralistic interpretation of their own behaviour. Yet the sense of a religious foundation to moral polarity of this nature was not unusual among children and adolescents throughout the Valley. For many, religious belief and membership of a religious community enabled young people to assert decision-making power in relation to their choice of friends and decisions to avoid drugs or sexual activity. Their sense of personal legitimacy and self-efficacy in relation to such a stance is partly derived from personal faith and partly from the legitimacy gained from the sharing of, and respect for, religious belief among local adults and peers. We often heard young people in the Valley describe their religious belief as involving a highly restrictive behavioural framework. Describing having to avoid drink, cigarettes, sex and even dating relationships while pointing to siblings or friends who were unable to sustain these commitments, teenagers were tacitly acknowledging that the bar is set extremely, if not impossibly, high.

Balancing relationships with peers requires continual effort and skill refinement. For reasons that we return to below, it is described by the young as one of the most difficult tasks of late childhood and adolescence. Small wonder, therefore, that young people place so much emphasis on the qualities of their everyday relationships with adults that strengthen their internal resources and social ties. As we saw in Chapter 2, the presence or absence of joint activities, open communication, reciprocity and mutual respect – and the vulnerability of these qualities in the face of the pressures on adults to manage poverty, separation and cultural conformity – has enormous bearing on children's experiences of nurture and care in the home. Critical to such provision are the emotional, social and mental resources available to children in making decisions that are coherent with their cognisance of self and have a positive influence on their broader social relationships.

Making a decision to strive for a particular goal, and in doing so to live by certain codes, is another important means by which young people consider they can achieve greater control over self and the world around them. This strategy, which is described particularly frequently by poor adolescents in Ocean View and Masiphumelele, seems to be more effective because it is less contingent on the quality of relationships with other people. It is about an individual decision to be someone who has chosen a path that is considered 'good' now and promises reward in the future:

> I decided to change my personality. I'm someone who everyone can just push me and I'll do nothing about it. I want to start standing up for myself more. I also used to be quite a party girl and now I want to concentrate more on my studies and school work and also to stop going out with all these guys. (Mandy, girl, aged 18, Ocean View)

> We decided not to drink [at the party] as it's not nice to see a woman drunk. I came up with the idea as I know how much people drink. But they looked happy when I said it, and we decided together. My brother was listening and laughing. Perhaps the friends thought they could hide from me, and I wouldn't see that they were drunk. I went home about 8.30, there was dancing and music, but I decided to go home as I didn't want to see them drunk as I don't like alcohol…The next day, they came here to tell me all about it, and I told them I didn't want to hear and I'm not interested. (Bongiwe, girl, 17 years, Masiphumelele)

The manner in which young people describe their conscious choices and goals suggests that they obtain a level of personal strength and sense of control over self that, by implication, will enable them to stand up to external pressures. But what was only very rarely articulated is the fact that in asserting a decision to strive for certain career goals and lifestyles consistent with these, young people are unwittingly capitulating to a worldview that divides the pursuits of the young – schooling, leisure activities, consumption habits and even certain relationships –

into 'good' and 'bad'. Like the highly restrictive behavioural codes that are described by teenagers as integral to their religious beliefs, these discourses fail to enable young people to manage everyday realities in a manner that is internally coherent. And the polarisation of young people's behaviour reinforces two of the most powerful and insidious myths that inform the transition from childhood to adulthood. The first, mentioned above, is the promise that current allegiance to certain behaviour and institutions, particularly school, will result in health, happiness and success in the future. The second is that the choices and actions of an individual at any particular moment and in any one sphere define that person's moral integrity, regardless of the obstacles and barriers imposed by social structures and institutions beyond the control of the individual. Setting goals and reinforcing their legitimacy using a discourse of morality in environments like Masiphumelele and Ocean View can be understood as a logical and sensible way of responding to very low rates of educational and other forms of personal achievement or social status. For those who follow the 'good' route, such strategies have the effect of bolstering a sense of self-efficacy and self-esteem: two of the interpersonal qualities recognised by psychologists as protective of well-being, which we mentioned above. But, as we saw in Chapter 6 (with respect to pursuing formal education), attempts to control self by living the myths work only until something happens to knock young people off track. In this sense, goal setting is helpful as a long-term strategy for only the very few poor adolescents who manage to sustain a lifestyle that is consistent with their goal and achieve 'success', as judged by parents, the wider neighbourhood and the educational system. For the large remainder who do not, it is a strategy that enables them to achieve a sense of control over their lives in the short term. But this sense of coherence and of self as determinants of positive outcomes is undermined over time because the feelings of having failed oneself and one's family add additional weight to this failure, and can bring subsequent disillusionment in young people's personal capacities.

Looking back on his teenage years and his involvement in heavy drinking and gangsterism, Keith, a 22-year-old resident of Ocean View, describes his persistent attempts to live according to his goals despite experience that rendered them less and less realistic.

> At this point when I came to high school I started focusing on one thing, that was to become a lawyer. Then I didn't go for it, but I wasn't also focused – then I thought, 'Hey, I can still do that at another time, I can just push that aside and enjoy myself a little bit.' Without knowing, I kept on enjoying myself, enjoying myself until it came on a later stage, standard 7, when I failed the one year. Then I thought it's not the end of the world and I went back. The next year I passed so it went on until I came in matric but then my dream was totally gone. All the stuff that I'd done, all the stuff that I'd seen and experienced, I can say that actually stopped me from achieving what I set for myself in standard 6 and primary school. (Keith, male, aged 22, 'Tri' interview)

Keith articulates his failure to achieve his goals in terms of his own behaviour ('all that stuff I'd done') and makes no mention of the failures of the institutions that purport to nurture young people: the family, school, community and, not least, the state.

Young people throughout the Valley live within – and participate in creating – a moral world in which ideals that have religious, social and cultural legitimacy are used to bolster self-determination and guide personal decision-making. These ideals are not in themselves undermined by particular features of the immediate neighbourhood, or the broader cultural and sociopolitical environment. Indeed, their rootedness in long-standing inequalities and norms means that such codes have symbolic and instrumental value to young people. But the question remains as to how effective these codes are in enabling the young to muster the personal and social resources needed to meet the challenges encountered at home, among peers, at school and in the neighbourhood. The next four sections pull together conclusions drawn in earlier chapters that illuminate the responses of individuals and institutions to young people's efforts to enhance their own well-being. We find that post-apartheid Cape Town is characterised by persistent and often scarcely visible segregation of various kinds that encumbers and even foils the efforts of children and adults alike to achieve the quality of relationships they desire and in turn their goals relating to education, skills, interpersonal networks and social identity.

Intergenerational reciprocity and nurture in the home

Despite the ravages on family life wrought by apartheid, children and adolescents from Cape Town's different class and cultural spectra currently portray the parental role as one centred on material and emotional provision, even when their parents have not always lived with them or nurtured them on a daily basis (see Chapter 2). Children say that their parents, and particularly mothers, should meet diverse needs – and should do so indefinitely. In assigning such a role, young people both uphold and oblige parents in their duty to care. And although never explicitly intended, the result of their affirmation of the parental role can be seen to be protective of their own nurture. It is a strategy that is consistent with the awareness articulated by many children that poverty can limit their parents' ability to assemble a simple evening meal or meet school expenses.

The fact that the majority of parents in Masiphumelele and Ocean View manage to feed, clothe and nurture their children on low incomes is testimony to their human tenacity and resourcefulness. But there are very high costs to parents' mental health and their capacity to care that arise from the persistent scarcity of resources and related anxiety, particularly when there is illness or substance abuse in the home. The implications for children are not always highly problematic precisely because they too shape the nature of care. As we have demonstrated in this book, relationships in the home are intimate and caring in both directions: children influence and support parents – and, by extension, the nurturing hub of the home – in several other ways than affirming their role as providers. The scope of their influence is found to be related to the extent to which children's cognisance and capacities are recognised and articulated. For example, children living in Masiphumelele and Ocean View clean, cook and run errands for the household, both because they are expected to do so and because they wish to do so. They gain satisfaction from their contribution and status and respect in the home. And, importantly, even young children nurture their adult carers, particularly when they are sick, for example by reminding them to take medicines and monitoring their emotional state. Although so-called 'tradition' in these two communities serves to segregate childhood and adulthood in ways that prevent recognition of the younger generation's reciprocal participation in care relationships, the diffuse and inclusive manner in which domestic activities and care are practised more generally allows young people the opportunity to take command of their actions and nurture others in ways they see fit. By contrast, middle-class children in nearby Fish Hoek rarely have cause to worry about whether their daily needs will be met, but often describe an absence of emotional engagement, effective communication or nurture in the home. As elsewhere in the Valley, the limitations placed on young people's abilities to influence their domestic environments arise from the interactive combination of culturally informed worldviews and socio-economic realities. Young Fish Hoek residents are often restricted in their efforts to engender or contribute to higher-quality relationships by the fact that there is sufficient financial and residential security to support the culturally validated segregation between adults who work, provide and decide, and children who learn, receive and comply. In a context that allows no room for reciprocal nurturing relationships between generations, children have little opportunity to demonstrate their expertise or gain a measure of respect from adults that results from making positive contributions to family relationships. Therefore, the notion that adults should make decisions for children without even consultation persists unchallenged. Teenagers in Fish Hoek often describe capitulating to these decisions and feeling disempowered as a result:

> I hate school with a passion, always. I would be a lot happier going to a college, but my family says: 'No, go to school, stay in school, get a matric.' I can get a matric in college, but they don't seem to understand. Fine. I will get a matric, even though I have to be miserable. I have been talking about this since grade 10, but they make the decision for me. I got fed up and said, 'OK, fine, do it your way.' But I am not happy and am not doing as well as I could be; I am not really enjoying what I am doing. (Lara, girl, aged 18, Fish Hoek)

Similar examples of non-negotiable decision-making by parents were also found in Masiphumelele. Children and young teenagers are frequently moved from grandparental homes in the rural Eastern Cape to attend what they deem better schools in Cape Town, and adolescents who are considered unruly or easily distracted from their studies are sent to stay with extended family in the Eastern Cape because schools there are thought to exert greater discipline. Yet at the same time, the bargains struck between poor children and their parents regarding their respective commitment to, and investment in, education indicate a certain level of influence by young people within the domestic and care nexus, and a means by which they can help sustain the role of parent-provider even when the economic means of doing so are very fragile. In reality, of course, both a mother's promise of continuous financial support and a child's of educational achievement are more reflective of good intention than reality: poor women whose marketable skills are limited to domestic assistance and childcare cannot guarantee a sustained income, let alone the sums necessary to finance further education. Similarly, children's efforts in their local school rarely translate into educational success. The discourse and ideal are ones that assign power to both adult and child, but the highly restrictive and disempowering nature of many classrooms and of the job market renders this an empty power. The articulation of these commitments does, however, serve a different purpose, namely to strengthen relationships and enhance young people's conviction in self and is, therefore, important for the reasons described earlier in the chapter. Moreover, rational negotiation of contributions towards a positive future outcome is consistent with, and can be articulated in terms of, notions of respect that exist between generations. Children who consent to parental guidance and desires are fulfilling their duty to respect their seniors. Often understood as ubiquitously serving to place an unbridgeable gap between the generations, we found that notions of 'respect' (*ukuhlonipha* in isiXhosa) served as a common principle from which young people were able to both build and articulate relationships of *reciprocal* respect with parents and other adults. The cultural rubric guiding social relationships in Fish Hoek and Ocean View does not include the explicit articulation of respect as integral to the bond between the young and their seniors. Unlike their counterparts in Masiphumelele, young people in these two communities do not have such a reference point and struggled to engender reciprocal relationships of care and trust with parents.

Adolescents and parents in Ocean View also draw on the discourse of success through education to strengthen their respective commitments to each other, but its effect is diluted by the presence of other discourses. These include the denigration of the capacity and potential of the young by the older generation. Everyday conversations reiterate the widespread view that only the exceptionally talented few will succeed, while the majority of young people will end up jobless and poor. Adults in Ocean View recognise the negative effect of such discourse on young people's motivation, the absence of so-called role models (who are important because they offer an alternative to the predicted pattern) and speak about being trapped in a cycle of negativity (Jardien & Collett 2006). Only a small portion of adolescents, often – but not exclusively – those with a history of high-quality intimate relationships in the home, good communication and social skills and a robust, but flexible, temperament are able to sustain the personal coherence and integrity to carve a path through these barriers. Perpetuated through local discourse and processes of socialisation, general predictions of failure severely curtail young people's sense of self-efficacy. Often misleadingly attributed to so-called 'coloured culture', the view that only the minority will achieve must be understood as emerging from a historical and contemporary sociopolitical identity characterised by a particular form of discrimination and marginality (described in Chapters 2, 5 and 6).

Seeking particular types of support from individuals within the neighbourhood or kin network as a means of supplementing care within the home and the ready adoption of parent-figures are two other ways in which poor children use their own mobility and more general domestic fluidity to ensure self-care. Young residents of Masiphumelele and Ocean View move between homes during the day, and commonly move into a relative's or neighbour's home to avoid resource constraints or conflicts. Such a strategy entails a child entrusting his or her body and emotions to the adults who make up this wider network of care, a strategy that is found to be largely protective, but that can result in abuse, injury or death. For these networks of care include men whose roles as providers in the home and community have been undermined by continuing unemployment, the psychological implications of which are not yet fully understood, but are associated with alcoholism, drug use, violence and abuse. A common response to the horror of conflict or abuse within intimate relationships is silence on the part of children of all ages. Non-disclosure is sensible in that it enables the young to retain some degree of personal control over the situation; it also enables them to sustain social relationships and hence familial integrity. In the longer term, silence may allow time for problems to be tackled and resolved. Far more likely is that neglect or abuse continues undetected because young people's decisions to remain silent arise not out of their relational ideals, but out of entrenched age and gender hierarchies that segregate children and adults and women and men, and devalue the testimony of young people – especially girls.

Consideration of the manner in which children and adolescents act to influence their intimate and caring relationships at home raises questions of how adults in these spheres respond to the cognisance and actions of the young. Parents for the most part, and particularly mothers, are encouraged by their children's actions to continue working and earning to sustain their children's nurture and education. The determined pursuit of the material, social and emotional resources needed to raise children by poor South Africans is given scant recognition in the popular media (Meintjes & Bray 2005) and remains rather buried in academic writing on the family (Ramphele 2002; Reynolds 1993, 1995). Some lip service is paid to the fortitude of mothers and grandmothers, particularly those caring for children orphaned by the AIDS pandemic, but the true extent of their provision and that of men is consistently under-acknowledged (for a recent exception, see Richter & Smith 2006). Poor parents, like their middle-class counterparts, are expected to protect and provide, but live in the knowledge that they cannot always fulfil their responsibilities. In many of Cape Town's neighbourhoods, parents cannot guarantee protection from the violence of hunger any more than from the violence of a drunken and disillusioned neighbour. The magnitude and implications of the disempowerment of those who have duties to care for children are rarely recognised or debated in the public arena, even when their presence is obvious. In mid-2007, the abductions and murders of four children in Cape Town in separate incidents received front-page news coverage on consecutive days. One article included a life-size photograph of a dead child's mother, head in hands, crying in anguish because she had been unable to protect her child from a killer in her own neighbourhood.[3] None drew attention to the particular demands on parents and characteristics of the social and built environment that link these tragedies to poverty in its broadest sense.

Mothers are validated in their caring role by strongly gendered divisions of responsibility that operate across wealth and cultural contexts. This position of privilege means that the maternal care role carries particular weight: children who lived apart from their biological mothers and who perceived them to have in some way chosen not to fulfil their maternal role were somewhat critical and even resentful of their mothers – feelings that seem to stem from a sense that they have been denied a vital ingredient of nurture in its fullest sense. Fathers, on the other hand, are given little or no public credit for their contribution to child rearing, and their absence from the home is not viewed as remarkable. The differing expectations of mothers and fathers arise from continuing expressions of patriarchy that position men as outside the domestic and nurturing realm despite ethnographic evidence of their participation in it. Fathers are depicted as negligent or, at best, a source of money that could and should be tapped. It is in the context of this powerful myth that children strive to sustain connections with fathers who live in other households or some distance away. Although difficult to quantify, we have evidence of fathers responding with generosity and affection to their children's efforts, some providing both material and emotional care for a period of childhood and others enabling older teenagers to change homes and/or schools should they wish to. That said, a large proportion of young people struggled with their father's decision to stay out of touch or do little more than provide occasional funds. And consistent with young people's greater weighting of care towards women (and mothers in particular) is their, at least partial, recognition of the context in which fathers choose to keep their distance. Adolescents and even younger children could see that obstacles to fathers doing otherwise include the assigning of gendered roles that easily exclude men from the care-giving nexus, their obligations to other families and – in poor communities at least – their very limited earning capacity.

Geography, mobility and claiming community

Laying claim on 'community' is a dimension of both individual and social identity that is as important in childhood and adolescence as it is in adulthood. Often it is assumed that only adults make decisions about how neighbourhoods are organised and used by their residents. The significance of place and social space to the young and their efficacy in these spheres are often underestimated. The extent to which children growing up in post-apartheid Cape Town can exert control over their own use of physical space and shape the character of this space varies considerably. High levels of independent mobility enjoyed by older children and adolescents in Masiphumelele and Ocean View allow them some choice in the individuals with whom they cultivate social relationships and a degree of power in the pace at which these relationships develop and the kinds of resources they choose to derive from them. Young people there consent to the mobility restrictions that adults place on very young children and girls because they understand their greater susceptibility to danger. That said, from an early age they are entrusted with responsibilities over younger siblings for large parts of the day while adults work. In a built environment where there are open sewers, narrow streets that double up as cricket pitches and pathways and play spaces hidden from view, monitoring children's safety is practically impossible. Accidents, abductions and even murders occur, and the implications of such neighbourhood-level violence for adolescents charged with the care of young children remain unknown.

Neighbourhood-level violence of a different nature dominates the concerns of children in Ocean View, and to a lesser extent in Masiphumelele, because it directly undermines personal integrity and is something they see themselves as being unable to curb or address effectively. Adolescents persistently identify rumour and gossip as social practices that characterise and, in some ways, define Ocean View. Some of their peers in Masiphumelele anticipate the possibility of being undermined in their career pursuits by jealous neighbours through the medium of witchcraft. As we showed in Chapter 5, some young people respond to denigrating rumours by attempting to refute their truth – a battle that is hard to fight. Others feel so utterly disempowered that they respond by capitulating and behaving in ways that the rumour mill expects. The fear of being the subject of gossip and its consequences to personal integrity and control of self alert us to the darker side of children's experiences of living in close-knit neighbourhoods. And while being targets of antipathy in the neighbourhood is certainly seen as a possibility by young residents in Masiphumelele, their peers in Ocean View considered it inevitable because they witness its prevalence in their own and their parents' generation. Teachers, police and social workers who reside and work in Ocean View concurred, linking extensive gossip to the 'cycle of negativity' (referred to above) that has emerged from a history of forced removals and continuing poverty and social marginalisation. In their eyes, many residents continue to feel excluded from local political structures, employment opportunities, voluntary-sector development activities and the state's poverty-reduction strategies (as demonstrated in a violent street protest to delays in housing provision[4]). The stereotypical and pejorative attitudes of those living elsewhere in the Valley (and often made explicit in the local press) are testimony to the persistent social violence that underscores perceived marginalisation among residents of Ocean View. In this context, adults doubt their own and their children's ability to benefit from society, and respond to the possibility of other people doing so – in some cases even their own children – by denigrating their efforts and spreading negative rumours.

Young residents of Fish Hoek perceive Masiphumelele as a very different neighbourhood to their own because it has what they describe as 'community spirit'. For middle-class children who are largely at home or ferried to and from sporting or leisure activities by parents, the ability to move about and interact with neighbours freely is simultaneously foreign, risky and attractive. Despite their stated wishes to have greater control over their social lives, children in Fish Hoek usually consent to adults structuring their time and mobility. They enjoy the range of sports and leisure pursuits on offer, and acquire skills, status and a social network through their participation. But they also perceive themselves to be at risk of crime and rarely challenge adults on this matter. Regardless of its actual prevalence, crime is a social reality for these young people because it dominates local newspapers and is a frequent topic of conversation within families, neighbourhoods and schools. Children in Fish Hoek know that personal assault and theft occur regularly in their locality as they do in other middle-class suburbs in Cape Town. What they are less aware of is that their own risk of being seriously assaulted or caught up in adult violence is far less than that facing their peers in poor neighbourhoods like Masiphumelele and Ocean View.

The spatial organisation of residential communities in Cape Town has a continuing bearing on young people's familiarity with neighbourhoods beyond those they reside in, as well as on their attribution of a common community identity in juxtaposition to that of other communities. This is particularly true of Ocean View, where a sense of geographical isolation further reinforces its residents' perceived social marginalisation linked to the shaping of community identities through recent history described above. Young residents of Ocean View say that they would like greater involvement in activities across the Valley and even in the city, but few travel. Adults and children alike perceive distances to be great and travel expensive. As a result, the majority find it difficult to generate a sense of community that stretches beyond their own neighbourhood.

The physical mobility of children and adolescents around the Valley is almost always from poorer neighbourhoods into wealthier ones. Children and adolescents from Masiphumelele and Ocean View travel into Fish Hoek to shop, use recreational facilities, go to school and occasionally to work. Few young people ever travel in the opposite directions. Young people, like adults, tend to stick to the familiar. In this regard, very poor children living in Masiphumelele stand to be more geographically knowledgeable than their often wealthier peers living elsewhere, purely because they have spent time in other neighbourhoods and gleaned knowledge from this. Young residents of Fish Hoek, by comparison, have rarely been to Ocean View or even know where it is, and few of those who have entered Masiphumelele have stepped out of a car. As pointed out earlier, these children's mobility is largely determined by parental design and a middle-class lifestyle that tends to value organised sports and leisure pursuits more than cultivating friendships in other neighbourhoods. Young people, therefore, have little latitude to alter habitual adult decisions and family patterns, particularly when safety is used to justify patterns of mobility and sociality. Earlier we noted the impact of physical and socio-historical isolation on young Ocean View residents' cognisance of self in relation to community membership. It is also important to observe that these young people are further disempowered by the fact that they are the least visited by those living elsewhere and, therefore, the least known about and the most easily stereotyped. The flow of human, financial and social resources from white middle-class communities to poor black African townships represents efforts of the general public to redress the inequalities of apartheid through targeted charity efforts. But without political influence, children and adolescents can do little to alter long-standing patterns of work and volunteering in ways that would increase movement in and out of all neighbourhoods (and most pertinently Ocean View) and thereby engender the kind of knowledge needed to build understanding and undermine stereotyping among Valley residents.

Targeting resources to Masiphumelele, while (at least until very recently) largely ignoring the needs of Ocean View residents is one way in which institutions are unwittingly reinforcing difference on the basis of 'race'. Children in the multiracial environments of Fish Hoek schools draw on a language of race, albeit through playful adaptations of terminology, but at the same time desire to abandon these terms because they are inappropriate to their personal experiences of friendship formation. They often fail to find appropriate vocabulary to describe their experiences because they have rarely spent time in other neighbourhoods and seem to have little familiarity with the concept of class difference. Teenagers' descriptions of differences that they encounter in terms of style, humour and use of slang indicate a search for an alternative vocabulary with which to make sense of their social worlds. But persistent economic and social inequalities are absent from their discourse. Vast differences in wealth that are so startlingly obvious to any outside observer do not, it appears, form part of discussions at home or in the classroom. By default and through a lack of knowledge among the young, they too participate in supporting the myth that 'race' (as expressed by neighbourhood, language and culture) is the source of difference rather than a marker of difference largely attributable to persistent social and economic inequalities.

We encountered a general, popular belief that in the context of a long period of apartheid-dominated governance in South Africa – perhaps reinforced by the continuing spatial and economic segregation of contemporary Cape Town – change and, more specifically, racial integration, will occur through the actions of the young. Indeed, there is some evidence that there are many spaces where the new multiracial middle class is integrated racially to an extent that was almost unimaginable under apartheid (Nkuna 2006; and see also Chapter 6). But in the context of the barriers described above, this notion is experienced by a large proportion of this generation's youth as little more than another myth over which they have few negotiating powers:

> The camps that OIL [Ownership, Invest, Live] organise are great. We
> get to stay in a dorm with teenagers from all around the Valley. I wasn't
> so sure about it the first time I went, and I didn't speak to anyone for a
> couple of days. Then I just got chatting with this white girl and we became
> friends. We see each other a lot now. But the camps only happen a couple
> of times a year…there should be more things like this where we do stuff
> together. (Anele, girl, aged 16, Masiphumelele)

Our research suggests that young people would spend more time with those who live in different neighbourhoods if they could do so easily. Churches, schools and youth-oriented NGOs provide some of the very scarce physical and social space to enable this in the Valley. But control remains largely in the hands of adult facilitators (because dominant, culturally validated understandings of childhood, competence and adult responsibility mean that they have not considered an alternative to this). For the most part, children or adolescents are unable to influence the design or geographical reach of the various educational institutions, leisure opportunities or sports teams that have been established for the youth.

Schooling and control

Earlier in this volume, we showed how the nature and quality of relationships within the classroom and school vary within and among neighbourhoods (see Chapter 5). Relationships between teacher and student, and among students, have a profound influence on young people's abilities to learn, and a range of cultural and structural factors impede the young in shaping these relationships to their advantage. Corporal punishment – although officially banned and, according to children in Masiphumelele and Ocean View, used less frequently in recent years – was reputedly occurring behind closed doors and is an extreme manifestation of adult authority within the school realm. The reluctance of many teachers (in all schools, but particularly those in Ocean View and Masiphumelele) to inform pupils of management decisions or to engage them in debate about better alternatives in school practice is further evidence of a power divide between teachers and pupils, and one that in Masiphumelele is legitimised by broader notions of respect for one's seniors, mentioned earlier. Pupils in Masiphumelele express frustration when such attitudes render them unable to use even formal channels (such as the representative council of learners) to influence their learning environment.

We found striking variations within, but especially *among*, neighbourhoods in the abilities of children and adolescents to engender support from teachers and schools for their academic progress and their management of domestic problems impinging on their performance. In Fish Hoek, teachers are available to individual students seeking academic assistance, partly because the space is arranged in such a way that teachers have their own classroom where they can be found after hours or in breaks. Guidance teachers and, very recently, a dedicated social worker, provide a formal channel through which students can seek support. Their links with professional social and psychological services and the ability of most parents to pay for these largely private services mean that students in Fish Hoek are aware of, and can draw support from, adults at school. In Ocean View and Masiphumelele, where human and institutional resources are less available (for reasons described in Chapters 3 and 6), some children make successful use of interpersonal relationships to derive social or financial support, but individual academic support is much less available. Students in these two neighbourhoods could name only a handful of teachers on whom they could rely for this, pointing to a serious limitation in their ability to take effective action about their own academic progress. While fellow students in informal study groups and adults or older siblings at home provided valuable support and encouragement, they rarely had the specific knowledge needed to fill major gaps in understanding. The inability of local social networks to plug these gaps is partly attributable to low levels of education and white-collar employment among adults in poor communities like Ocean View and Masiphumelele. But the fact that the gap persists despite widespread knowledge of the apartheid legacy of gross educational inequalities points to the continuing failure of the state in its educational provision.

Again, variations were observed both among neighbourhoods and within individual schools in the extent to which students acted, and were responded to, as individuals. Schools are vastly different both socially and educationally. And teachers approach their roles and relationships in the classroom in very different ways. One grade-6 class in Masiphumelele was characterised by lively individual responses when questions were posed to the whole class. In another grade-6 class, pupils' facial expressions conveyed interest and personal opinion, but none spoke or raised their hand unless the whole class did so. Reasons for such conformity are difficult to isolate, but its practice speaks of major limitations to young people's self-efficacy in learning and communicating their comprehension, or, indeed, their incomprehension. In Ocean View, relationships between teachers and students are often confrontational, both within the classroom and on the school premises more generally. Student truancy and disruptive behaviour can be interpreted as an expression of power by the young. However, the fact that teachers and students alike express frustration that confrontation like this poses a major barrier to learning, partly because of the greater individual and collective stress that it causes, indicates that young people do not have access to other ways of influencing their learning environment. Again, reasons for the prevalence of confrontational behaviour are not easily identifiable and appear to stem from a combination of structural and cultural factors. An even starker example of pupils' attempts to resist the manner in which teachers' authority is employed and alter the forms of school governance can be seen in the street demonstration that was mounted by pupils of Masiphumelele High School, referred to in Chapter 6. By not only considering the option of mass public protest to be available, but also by actually pursuing this route, these pupils employed similar strategies to youth activists in the apartheid era. Their choice is understandable given that street marches are locally familiar and meaningful, and that there is a strong likelihood that they have limited knowledge of, and access to, other ways of expressing discontent. But the heavy-handed police response and local press coverage was also alarmingly familiar. The photograph of armed police in riot gear attempting to block the path of large numbers of children, splashed across the front cover of the *Cape Times*, could easily have been taken in the 1980s. Implicit in such an image and its accompanying text was the message that young people can still perpetrate collective violence and that the authorities continue to respond with a certain level of violence and a demonstration of their capacity to act with greater force. These pupils effectively communicated their objection to what they perceived as inappropriate use of school authority, but they seem to have achieved little in the long term except to demonstrate peer solidarity in confronting such inappropriate authority. The Department of Education made some temporary changes to staff positions, but the dominant style of leadership, teaching and communication in the school remained the same.

Dating, sex and status in the peer group

The arenas of friendship and dating are experienced as at once exciting, sustaining, demanding and worrying by teenagers throughout the Valley. Adults have relatively little control in these arenas and they are a primary means by which the young negotiate status and learn and practise new forms of intimacy. Regardless of wealth or cultural background, being seen with others who wear designer labels, or having a girlfriend or boyfriend who dresses well and has the latest cellphone brings a sense of personal inclusion and well-being, as well as denoting both social and material success. But the ability to display a lifestyle of conspicuous consumption is all the more important to teenagers living in poor neighbourhoods, where not only the means of earning are scarce, but so too are those by which they can achieve and demonstrate success and maturity in other areas. In cases where parents and elder siblings earn too little to dispense the money needed for the latest fashion items, and there are few sports, leisure and educational institutions that can provide consistent skill development, then a teenager's image within the peer group holds greater sway for them, and often leads to decisions that are not consistent with their personal aims for their physical or emotional well-being and provision for the future.

Teenagers experience close relationships within the peer group that sustain and give pleasure through the simple act of sharing of ordinary activities. School is a fertile ground for developing and negotiating these relationships, particularly when the learning environment lacks stimulation or personal challenge. At the same time, however, friendships and dating relationships are demanding because they require continuous care and management, and can create conflict or exclusion. Young people reflecting on some of the decisions they made regarding their friendships demonstrate a sophisticated balance between personal considerations for their own well-being and attempts to guide or assist their friends:

> People define you because of your friends – that's the way…I had two really good friends, but they started doing drugs in middle school and I stood back. They changed completely: because I stepped back they didn't want to be friends with me any more. First, I tried to help and said don't do that, but they just went down. It was just the type of people they were. They like the idea of fitting in; they had to satisfy the need to look good in front of others; I don't have that. Middle school, that's when the crowd thing starts. But if you don't go to those parties you don't know about it [drugs]. I decided to step out and concentrate on school work. (Justin, boy, aged 18, Fish Hoek)

Like his peers across the Valley, Justin points to the responsibility of the individual in making 'good choices', in other words, those that will bolster and protect personal well-being, as well as conform to society's expectations. Even for middle-class children, achieving this balance is found to be difficult and dependent on personal qualities and capacities, the latter often attributed by teenagers to positive relationships within the home and familial sphere (described earlier in this chapter).

When adolescents start, in their words, to 'play the love game' and form dating relationships, friendships are further complicated by competition and jealousy, but at the same time are needed even more for the advice and stability they provide. Dating relationships are precarious and easily ruptured by suspicions of infidelity. By increasing their investment in and reliance upon close friendships, young people maintain a sense of personal integrity and control through periods of change, and in the face of pressure to conform and feelings of personal vulnerability. Throughout the Valley, the advice and support of friends is especially valuable to teenagers because adults in the family tend to avoid the topic of intimate and sexual relationships, or merely lay down rigid rules for girls designed to prevent pregnancy or illness. Parental reticence in matters of sex and intimacy is propped up by culturally validated notions of the type and level of knowledge that children should be party to. Although these notions vary slightly in their expression in the different neighbourhoods in the Valley, they seem to have an equally undermining impact on young people's ability to care for their physical and emotional selves.

Throughout the Valley, adolescent boys are given greater latitude by adults to make their own decisions, but are consequently provided with even less information in conversations at home. Very few seek support from professional services, meaning that boys rely even more heavily on their friends for information and make decisions based on what they observe and are told in the peer group. Both boys and girls find that friends do not know enough to enable them to make what they consider to be good decisions regarding dating relationships. Moreover, friends use their relative knowledge to exclude and, therefore, put pressure on their peers. They are willing to share information only if the recipient is engaged in the same sexual activity and will share their personal experience. Therefore, teenagers make largely unguided and pressured decisions about their physical and emotional well-being in a context where social status, inclusion within the peer group, and access to knowledge about sex and intimacy are contingent upon at least some level of experimentation. It is perhaps this vacuum of knowledge that prompts young people to draw heavily on a discourse of morality as they strive for personal protection, care and integrity in their intimate relationships. By describing their social and relational worlds in terms of a choice to pursue activities that are 'good', for example schooling, obedience to parent-figures and church attendance, or those including truancy and sexual relationships, considered 'bad', teenagers assign themselves certain decision-making powers. The reiteration of this dichotomy seems to help young people persevere in their school work and efforts to build trusting relationships with their partners despite the odds against them and in the absence of any better compass. But it is ultimately disempowering because it presents a person's actions in terms of two absolute pathways – and the morally approved one is almost impossible to sustain. Moreover, it does not give any moral legitimacy to an alternative route that might involve a young person's participation in activities that are considered both 'good' and 'bad'. In reality, of course, most adolescents do just that. They persist in attending school and fulfilling teachers' expectations; they attend and enjoy churches of their own choosing; they respect parental rules, but break them occasionally; they cultivate friendships and begin dating; and they see advantages in sexual abstinence, but capitulate to pressure from within the partnership and the wider peer group. Thus when a teenager makes a decision to have sex or fails at school, it is considered indicative of moving off the 'good' pathway and onto the 'bad' one. And some adolescents report that they tend to reduce their efforts towards self-care having made one so-called 'mistake', because they regard themselves as already labelled a failure and cannot see how to navigate a pathway that incorporates this decision into their personal cognisance, or engenders the adult recognition and support they need to do so.

Using this discourse to explain the consequences of personal decisions is another example of young people's unwitting capitulation to the myth that the individual chooses either right or wrong actions, and that his or her moral worth is determined by these decisions. In dispensing rules or avoiding discussion of intimacy and sex, adults at home, in schools, in clinics and the social services are reinforcing this worldview because they assume that their strategy will guide, or more accurately, control, adolescents' decision-making. In doing so, they are also suppressing discussion of how teenagers' personal efforts towards self-care and inclusion within the peer group intersect with the possibility that they may contract a sexually transmitted illness, such as HIV, or become parents before they intended to. These practices reinforce the divide between theoretical knowledge (espoused by adults) and experiential knowledge (about which adults keep silent), and block communication between generations. It is in this context that teenagers in Ocean View, Fish Hoek and Masiphumelele are largely silent about AIDS as a possible challenge in their own lives, despite its rising prevalence in all areas and very high risks in Masiphumelele.

High rates of pregnancy and rising HIV prevalence in the young must be understood as arising from a multifaceted vulnerability that involves a lack of access to knowledge that would assist girls and boys in making decisions about their own self-care. Girls who live in poor households make decisions under an additional set of pressures related to the intersection between material poverty and strongly gendered power relationships. Across the wealth and cultural spectra of the Valley, boys are seen as material providers and girls as recipients (whose consent to sexual intercourse can be expected in return). But without access to personal income, the stakes are much higher for poor girls should they challenge this relationship. For many poor girls, the only means of acquiring the material goods that bring status within the peer group is to enter into a relationship with an older man in which there is a tacit understanding that dating and sex are available in exchange for gifts. To object to, or place conditions on, sexual activity (such as demanding condom use) risks forfeiting the personal reassurance of being included in the peer group and the opportunity to demonstrate social and material success. These economic limitations also increase girls' vulnerability to verbal and physical violence from a boyfriend, particularly in communities where masculinity is explicitly linked to sexual prowess.

In summary, young people's efforts to care for themselves and make positive choices are often highly successful in the short term owing to the skills and tenacity of both generations. But many are constrained in acting to safeguard their longer-term well-being by the limited capacities of adults and institutions to provide the necessary knowledge, emotional support, consistent quality of relationship, finance or access to everyday social networks. A portion of what has undermined social institutions and intimate relationships can be directly attributable to the continuing legacy of apartheid, for example the underemployment of those not categorised 'white'; the spatial segregation of neighbourhoods; and persistent inequity in the provision and quality of schools and recreational facilities. Other social forces that have had an equally, or arguably greater, undermining effect are strongly gendered role divisions and lines of authority, as well as norms defining childhood, adulthood and the appropriate forms of communication between generations. There are differences between neighbourhoods in the way these norms are articulated and negotiated. More striking is the consistent manner in which they restrict the possibilities for children and adults to achieve nurturing relationships and longer-term goals, especially when combined with material poverty.

Transitions to adulthood: Directions for further research

Amartya Sen's definition of a successful transition to adulthood prioritises young people's capabilities 'to enhance the substantive choices they have' (quoted in Lloyd 2005: 24). This notion is useful firstly in foregrounding young people's self-efficacy in a context of various kinds of limitations as described thus far in the chapter. Secondly, it allows for individual and cultural variability in the value of different markers in the transition, and, therefore, opens discussion of the implication of differences in timing and sequence of changes that mark entry to adulthood. Close analysis of this period of life is beyond the scope of this book. The purpose of this section is to draw on the information we have recorded through our ongoing relationships with a small group of older adolescents in order to suggest directions for further research.

As we would expect, none of these adolescents, irrespective of their neighbourhoods, moved smoothly from childhood to adulthood, whether or not this change of status is defined subjectively or according to a preselected set of indicators, such as those used by Biddecom and Bakilana (2003) and described in Chapter 1. Their narratives are helpful in identifying markers of adulthood most pertinent to young people and in drawing attention to various and unexpected routes towards achieving these changes in status.

When asked what they perceive to be a marker of becoming an adult, young residents in the Valley emphasised financial independence and the ability to choose how to spend their own money as an important step towards adulthood, but one that was insufficient in itself, as well as potentially reversible. We note that employment per se was not regarded by young people as evidence of a shift into adulthood, indicating a cautious use of the objective indicator 'working'. A cursory look at the nature of work illuminates this logic. Jobs are often short term, low paid and considered to have immediate utility in easing financial burdens, as opposed to being the kind of work young people aspire to in the longer term. The reader will recall the CAPS findings quoted in Chapter 1, showing the much greater proportion of 22-year-old Capetonians who have ever worked than those who are currently employed.

The second, more decisive, indicator of adulthood identified by young people was the move out of their childhood homes. In middle-class Fish Hoek this move often happens around the age of 18 and coincides with the beginning of further education, work experience or overseas travel, which necessitate moving to a new geographical location. The timing of these moves is generally consistent with norms that circumscribe the end of childhood dependence and (total) adult responsibility. By contrast, many residents of Masiphumelele and Ocean View in their late teens and early 20s with part-time or full-time jobs – and often with children of their own – continue to live at home. They commonly devote most of their income to personal expenditure but contribute substantially to the running of the household. They see themselves as having adult responsibilities but neither regard themselves or are regarded by others as having attained adult status. Markers of this transition tend to happen later and at the point when young people have worked for some time, formed long-lasting partnerships and even had children. Two examples serve to illustrate these processes:

> Sixteen months into his full-time job in a supermarket deli and on the point of moving out of his aunt's home and into a flat with his partner, 19-year-old Brian was anticipating his first experience of taking a gift of groceries to the head of his family (his grandmother) at the beginning of Ramadan. Known as *fideah*, this practice is expected of all single Muslim men and Brian's participation therein marks an irreversible change of status.

> Chloe became a mother when she was 18 and living in her childhood home, a shack in Masiphumelele. During her pregnancy, she declined her child's father's suggestion that the three of them set up home in a rented flat in Fish Hoek, primarily because she anticipated wanting and needing the close emotional support of her family. She and her baby have relied on consistent (if, at times, meagre) financial support from her grandmother's household. Her ex-boyfriend, a member of the navy, has contributed very little. Five months after giving birth, Chloe found work as a cashier at the cinema and was quickly promoted to supervisor. She has steadily become a more regular and significant contributor to the household budget. And although her grandmother approved of her plans to marry and establish her own home, Chloe is under pressure to remain at home for as long as possible. She understands that her grandmother has strong

emotional bonds with her and her baby, and she knows that her financial contributions have become central to the domestic budget. Six months after her boyfriend proposed, Chloe called the marriage off and discovered that she was pregnant for the second time. Three years later, she is still living with her grandmother, mother, siblings and two daughters.

Both Chloe and Brian regard moving out of their childhood home as symbolic of a new status because it denotes that they no longer need the everyday care of their grandmother and aunt (both of whom are mother-figures), and marks a shift in their relationship with these women. Neither was confident to make this move even when they had sufficient money to meet their everyday expenses and had long-term and apparently committed partners. Chloe's experiences suggest that the economic roles of young adults in very poor households may influence other transitions to adulthood associated with social status and emotional attachments. More could be learnt about this relationship by looking at the spending patterns of young adults in relation to the nature of their jobs, the sums they earn and their subjective understanding of status within the home and peer group.

Chloe and Brian's narratives also illuminate the variety of routes through which young people achieve steps in the journey towards adulthood and question common assumptions of what may be necessary or optimal preparation for these changes. Chloe left school without a matric and did not find work until 10 months later, during which time she had a baby. She is the only one to have been recruited by the cinema who does not have a matric. Her boss told her that they made an exception because she came across as capable, energetic and eager to learn. Her narrative demonstrates that events or sequences of change that are considered 'pre-mature', or that are unplanned, can be adjusted to at an emotional level by young people and those closest to them, and hence incorporated into their sense of progression into adulthood. Although her pregnancy entailed elements of a change of status from child (who could expect to be provided for and enjoy freedom of mobility) to adult (with domestic responsibilities and restrictions on behaviour), Chloe remained reliant on her grandmother's household economically and emotionally, and did not see herself as being in a strong position to gain independence in light of her matric failure. In other words, becoming a mother was not regarded by Chloe or those around her as an assumption of all the roles and responsibilities of adulthood. But her success as a mother bolstered her self-esteem and confidence: the very factors that enabled her to get a job that should technically have been unavailable to her. With hindsight, we can see that Chloe's experience of mothering and her identity as a mother assisted her in finding salaried work with promotional opportunities.

Brian, by contrast, matriculated with clear, stated ambitions to be a chef, but found himself unable to make telephone calls or initiate processes to achieve his chosen career goals. Only through his aunt's church networks and assistance did he gain a place on a training programme. He completed his one-year course, was offered a permanent contract by the retailer with which he had a training placement and started to spend nights in his partner's flat. He has followed a more conventional route through education and further training into adulthood. But he is anxious, has little appetite and is often unwell. He states that he is glad to have a 'good' job and a loving partner, but is frustrated because he sees no practical means of moving into social work (where he feels his talents lie) and positions himself as powerless: 'I worry that I may be on a "downwards spiral" and I can't change it.' His sense of being unable to enhance the choices he has available to him lies in stark contrast to Chloe's sense of self-efficacy in her home, at work and in her intimate relationships. Yet it is Brian who made choices to prioritise his school work, passed his matric and enrolled in further training. And it is Chloe who failed her matric, has had no further formal training and became a mother.

What we learn from these narratives is that jumping through the culturally idealised hoops of matric, training and employment undoubtedly has social value for adolescents and may also have instrumental and economic value. On the other hand, they do not guarantee work, financial security and career opportunities. Paradoxically, perhaps, it may be the less visible interpersonal and internal shifts in a young person's relationships and sense of self that enhance the choices available to them. Individual temperament is likely to play a role here, but so too might young people's perceptions of their abilities to apply their personal skills and competences developed within one arena (for example, their local school or neighbourhood) in other less familiar arenas. Research could usefully ask how the social identities of young people and the role of local neighbourhood histories in shaping these identities feed into such perceptions, and in turn influence self-efficacy in the contexts of work and relationships.

These observations cast a different light on the routes through adolescence and into adulthood that Biddecom and Bakilana (2003: 15) describe as 'characterised by more disorder than order in terms of the variety of combinations and chronological sequences of important social and family formation traditions'. What Chloe's and Brian's narratives suggest is that approaching the study of transitions to adulthood from the point of view of the young reveals logic and coherence to the decisions of each generation. They also point to differences in the way young people (as well as their elders) define and prioritise markers of adult status, and the appropriate timing of their achievement, when compared to the steps of transition laid out in demographic studies. Moreover, both these variables are constantly shifting over time and over social or cultural 'space', including neighbourhood, class or 'race' groups. Their study requires clear reference to the interface between historical ideals and realities, as well as to those emerging in the contemporary landscape.

9 Conclusion

Childhood and adolescence are periods in which new opportunities are constantly opening as young people become more mobile and extend their horizons beyond familiar settings. At the same time, opportunities remain constrained for young people – and adults – by their positions in society. Young people's experiences of growing up in contemporary South Africa are characterised above all by the coincidence of the widening range of opportunities that arise from age alone and the changing opportunities and constraints in society as a whole as apartheid is dismantled. More than a decade into the new political dispensation, young Capetonians aspire to possibilities denied to their parents. They participate in creating a society that is in some respects conducive to the achievement of their dreams, yet remains unequal, difficult and often dangerous at the same time.

Much has changed in the legal and sociopolitical landscape since the demise of apartheid. Official racial classification no longer restricts people in where, or with whom, they can live, play or attend school. There are equal rights to state services for all; there is a public discourse of diversity and equality. Young people at school in Fish Hoek or Ocean View and those attending certain churches have networks of friends crossing a race and class spectrum that could only have been imagined 20 years ago. And all young Valley residents aspire to progress far in the education system, find well-paid work and achieve material and social success. At the same time, there are persistent, large inequalities in earnings and in the quality of schooling and healthcare available to people despite broadly equal public funding for these facilities. Neighbourhood demographics have changed little in the past decade: few families have moved into or out of areas other than those designated to their race groups during apartheid.

In order to make sense of young people's experiences of growing up in post-apartheid Cape Town one needs to take seriously both the changes that have occurred in less than one generation and the differences that remain. Studies that emphasise only one of these cannot elucidate why dreams retain their appeal, and hence why contradiction and ambivalence remain at the core of the experience of growing up in places like the Valley.

Put very simply, neighbourhood (still) matters. The particular suburb or township in which children or adolescents live shapes profoundly almost every aspect of their everyday lives and their future opportunities. Its effects reproduce many of the effects of the racial hierarchy imposed by apartheid, including a restricted range of family dynamics, income levels, social networks and notions of race. At the same time, as we have demonstrated in this book, there are increasing similarities in young people's lives across neighbourhoods. Tellingly, few of these converging experiences are recognised as such by the young.

For young people today, the physical and social characteristics of the neighbourhood spaces created during, or as a result of, apartheid have a profound impact on mobility, personal safety, social identity, choices in peer relationships, certain dimensions of family life, educational and economic opportunities and, ultimately, personhood. Although Capetonian children and adolescents live in a more integrated society than their parents at their age, almost all of them inhabit *local* spaces that remain highly segregated. Most young people learn, play, socialise – and the lucky ones even earn and spend – within neighbourhoods that are almost entirely racially homogeneous (in apartheid classificatory terms) and distinct in crucial respects. Being from Fish Hoek or Masiphumelele is now a more significant social locator among the young than race group per se. But since material differences between neighbourhoods tend to correlate with their racial composition or profile, race retains some social and cultural importance, although less emphatically than in the past. Some children and adolescents use racial terminology unquestioningly, whereas others wrestle with the terms and seek another language to describe their own and others' identities. The result is an expression of belonging to a neighbourhood community that is riven with ambivalences: a combination of pride, frustration, hope and fatalism. Schools within each neighbourhood generate these apparently contradictory responses. They are supposedly more equal than in the past in that they currently receive broadly equal state funding. However, their former and present ability, or otherwise, to gain income from fees and other kinds of support from the local neighbourhood means that they provide profoundly different learning experiences.

From neighbourhood to neighbourhood, young people increasingly share experiences of family life. Throughout the Valley, access to an income that is regular and sufficient to meet daily expenses enables parents to live and work in the same neighbourhood and reduces pressure on marital relationships. The positive implications of this association can be increasingly seen in historically very low-income neighbourhoods, where some adults are now commanding higher, stable incomes. The negative implications are becoming apparent in separation or divorce, underpinned by financial strain, in areas like Fish Hoek, where incomes have in the past been high. Strikingly similar aspirations were expressed by young people in all neighbourhoods regarding the qualities of intimate relationships sought with kin and other people. Although the idiom for reciprocity, trust and open communication varies across neighbourhood cultures, children and adolescents stand in broad agreement on the kinds of intragenerational and intergenerational relationships that create nurture and those that compromise their own and others' well-being.

Set against these convergences are some persistent familial and domestic patterns within each particular neighbourhood, and some that vary between each. These include the people with whom children share a home until adulthood; their scope to contribute care, support and advice to family members of all generations; and the ways in which parental absence or other potential compromises to care are managed by adults. Young people living in historically privileged neighbourhoods are still much more likely to live with both parents throughout their childhoods, but struggle to influence or enhance relationships at home. They are also increasingly likely to experience one parent's departure and must contend with a set of neighbourhood ideals that problematises non-nuclear families more explicitly than in historically disadvantaged areas. Children and adolescents in poorer neighbourhoods work very hard to sustain and enhance connections with absent parents, often achieving coherence through heavy investment in one or two intimate relationships – often with a mother-figure. Doing so, however, does not necessarily protect young people from incurring damage to their emotional well-being, such as that resulting from absent or abusive parents or exploitative relationships within larger networks of kin and neighbours, which they have little power to avoid or overcome. The limits of young people's agency within the familial and home setting are evident here.

Across the board, young people are keenly aware that the neighbourhood they live in poses particular, and often increasing, threats to their safety, and that it differs in fundamental respects to other neighbourhoods just a few kilometres away. But neither they nor their parents 'see' the entire spectrum of neighbourhood-level influences clearly. From childhood to late adolescence, young Capetonians position their families as central to their social worlds and to their physical and emotional well-being. Mothers, fathers and grandparents remain the primary role models. Their presence and emotional engagement is actively sought in the home and they are the main focus of young people's efforts to nurture reciprocal relationships that balance duty and entitlement. Young people consistently place family and, specifically, parent-figures, in the role of protectors in much the same way as social psychologists position family as the filter or buffer zone between neighbourhood influences and effects on individual children. Our findings question the suggestion that we are seeing an increasing 'detachment from elders' (Soudien 2007: 6) in this generation of South African children. There is plentiful evidence of the expected social distance between teenagers and their elders, who struggle to communicate over matters of socialising and sex. However, adolescents in all neighbourhoods remain firmly emotionally and socially attached to their parent-figures, looking to them in a crisis and strengthening their loyalties and trust in these adults, even when they are barely coping. Mothers especially are vested with superhuman powers as providers and considered a moral compass for young people in their decision-making.

Remarkably, many parents and families live up to young people's expectations by providing sufficient care and fulfilling basic material needs even in settings of extreme poverty, illness, hunger and violence. In this respect, little has changed since apartheid times. But the reason we conclude that neighbourhood differences still exert a significant influence over young people's well-being is that parents who see more and more reason to protect their children from physical and social dangers in the neighbourhood are less and less able to do so. More women in particular are working long hours and cannot be at home to monitor and protect. And as expectations of the young have risen in the wake of democracy, so have the stakes for families in facilitating their 'success'. Parents, particularly mothers, talk about their income as being critical to bolstering their children's chances by enabling them to pay for things such as youth camps, transport to a better school or fashionable clothing.

Some of the neighbourhood-based dangers identified by young people – such as denigrating discourse, the use of alcohol or drugs, and violence in intimate relationships – emerged when this generation of adults attempted to cope with state-engendered oppression during their own youth (often by undermining the moral authority of their parents). These problems have since become entrenched, habitual forms of behaviour in domestic and community interaction. Most pervasive in neighbourhoods created for coloured people, they are also evident in those largely populated by African people and to a lesser extent those formerly zoned white. The demise of apartheid intensified some threats and added others: drugs move more freely between neighbourhoods, as do the criminal gangs pushing their sale. The corollary of media freedom is the pressure that has been brought into homes across the entire income range to wear designer labels and own the latest technology. HIV rates have risen sharply over the last 15 years, posing a new threat to sexually active adolescents. Economic and cultural characteristics of neighbourhoods combine to increase young people's risks of infection and early parenthood. Adults who earn very little struggle to provide food and other basic needs, which compromises their half of the intergenerational 'bargain' and undermines their attempts to influence young people's behaviour. And very rarely are they able to advise and protect their children through open, intimate communication because this runs counter to the way in which respect has traditionally been upheld between generations. Both these phenomena are strongest in African neighbourhoods, where the adolescent journey into the world of dating and sexual relationships is characterised by missing information (on the part of parents and children alike) and misinformation, as young people fail to get access to individuals or services that can give them an accurate picture of the implications of their actions. Such information gaps, persistent gender imbalances and the rising power of material goods in defining social identity – especially in contexts where schooling largely fails adolescents – help to explain higher AIDS rates in these settings.

Class exerts an increasingly strong influence on other dimensions of family life. While income inequality across the demographic spectrum is increasing in Cape Town, as it is throughout South Africa, some households in wealthier neighbourhoods have experienced declining incomes and some in poorer neighbourhoods have experienced rising earnings. Such shifts, when accompanied by decisions by adults – often women – to work for an income away from home, create conditions under which children's experiences of 'family' are converging across neighbourhoods. In a post-apartheid context of high, and even increasing, mobility among adults and children across all neighbourhoods (especially in households that earn least), the conditions for family stability most salient to children are flexibility in normative ideas about what constitutes a 'family' as well as in gender roles in the home. Also important is the ability of parent-figures to maintain their emotional availability (and thus mental health) when under pressure to earn and nurture simultaneously. Their success in this regard will depend on access to support, both informal and formal, for adults and children alike. Here, neighbourhood economics, once again, is critical: historically wealthier areas have a range of professional services geared to prevent or respond to social and psychological difficulties. Some of these are provided by the state or civil society and are freely and readily accessible to children, adolescents and parents (including guidance teachers and church youth workers); others are private, but affordable to most families. In low-income areas, services are scant, overburdened and often poorly co-ordinated. Mental-health issues are largely neglected.

Race remains a social marker in that it is used unconsciously by young Capetonians. Importantly, however, it is not a vocabulary that is sought or desired by young people and functions as a default option in a context where alternative ways of thinking about or articulating difference are unavailable. Being from Ocean View or from Fish Hoek, for example, exists alongside a broader identity as a Capetonian or South African, as well as a sense of belonging to, and pride in, a cultural identity associated with particular ethnic histories and language. Race-based labels, although still deeply acknowledged and engrained, are often asserted by the young only secondarily to belonging to the country or city. For some, refusing to admit a racial identity is a political statement in support of democracy, and is most evident among 'white' young people, who tend to refer to themselves as South Africans. In describing themselves confidently and even proudly as 'black', young people from impoverished neighbourhoods, such as Masiphumelele, convey their legitimacy and even superior social standing in the new era – at the same time as they identify themselves as Xhosa, South African and perhaps even Capetonian. The diminished significance of race as a social marker is linked to the possibility of upward mobility and adherence to middle-class ideals: those with the greatest opportunity to avoid race-based labelling by others and to create an alternative social identity are those children and adolescents whose families have moved into formerly 'white' areas and attend schools, sports clubs and churches there.

Young people's multiple (and often neighbourhood-related) expressions of social identity are consistent with the importance they place on the minimal, piecemeal and spatially defined opportunities available for interaction with residents of other neighbourhoods. The significance of shared spaces, such as the shopping mall, churches and youth camps, lies in the networks of friendships that can be cultivated there – not possible in their parents' youth – and in their symbolism of young people's desires to cross old boundaries. Obstructing this process are parental fears – many of which are also voiced by their children – for young people's safety when they are in other neighbourhoods, and assumptions that they will pick up 'bad' behaviour there. Structuring children's and adolescents' activities (and hence their social interaction) with the intention of building their skills is part and parcel of the middle-class lifestyle fiercely adhered to in 'white' areas – and increasingly aspired to in poorer neighbourhoods. Few parents encourage their children to spend time 'hanging out' with their peers in spaces outside the local neighbourhood, even if it is precisely this kind of agenda-less interaction that is valued by young people, and has the potential to build lasting relationships between individuals and their families of the kind able to undermine stereotypes.

The persistent separate development of children and adolescents is more challenging in the first decade of the 21st century precisely because it is caused not by easily identified state enforcements, but by a set of social realities and learnt perceptions, some of which are glaringly obvious and others difficult to spot and understand. Poverty prevents most families in the Valley from owning plots, building houses and paying for higher education, thereby separating them from middle-class ideals and realities. Although language is an obvious potential divider, contemporary urban youths are increasingly conversant in English. Their challenge lies in their inexperience in managing differences in styles of humour, dress and conviviality that they observe between race groups in ways that allow friendships to develop. A history of isolation has led to an internal orientation and reliance on the small set of services existing within the neighbourhood. These can be reinforced by prevailing adult perceptions that so-called 'cultural' differences between groups given race labels will impede social interaction, the precise nature of which is never clarified. There is a difference between generations in that children experience integration as achievable in ways unfamiliar to their parents. At the same time, they slow the process by pressuring each other to conform to behavioural codes linked to race – for example, to act as a 'true' coloured or to 'stop trying to be someone they are not'. These are perhaps understandable responses to their venturing into uncharted territory.

The post-apartheid environment is one characterised by an opening of possibilities for all young people to achieve educational, social and material success. In practice, this operates more as an idea than a reality, as young people encounter boundaries and tensions in their relationships with adults and peers that are consistently disempowering. By and large, they experience their neighbourhoods as fearful, judgemental and unforthcoming in terms of advice and services in response to their health and social needs. It is here that we identify a quiet violence that limits young people in achieving the quality of relationships and personal goals they aspire to. For example, the supposed freedom to make choices about schooling and dating is in reality tightly circumscribed by what is acceptable and possible within a particular neighbourhood. Choosing an educational pathway gives a young person a socially valued goal and personal aim. But the path through compromised schooling is full of pitfalls. Then parents and other adult family members may not have the finances or know-how to guide young people beyond school and into training and their desired careers. Schools and other community facilities in poor neighbourhoods are also likely to lack such knowledge and fail in their support role. For these reasons, the few children and adolescents who have had opportunities to cultivate social networks beyond the neighbourhood value these contacts for their instrumental and symbolic content, often drawing on them to plot a route out of school and into further education or work.

There is little solidarity among the young. Political rhetoric is of equality and 'room for all' in a diverse nation. Those still most disadvantaged are kept going by the promises of success, status and wealth through education and their officially advantaged political position. And because some achieve, there is no consistently legitimised grievance against the state. Young people achieve a lot through their 'head work' (Soudien 2007: 1) in the realm of personal goal setting, identity creation and strategies to cope with uneven, unpredictable resources – both material and emotional – from their parents and at home. But they rarely actively challenge the institutions or systems that fail to deliver services of the quality or regularity needed to ensure their healthy development. Critical here are knowledge gaps that can seriously undermine the effectiveness of 'head work' in late adolescence, such as a lack of awareness among parents and their children of precisely what is required to succeed in schooling, enter further education and attain certain white-collar jobs. The absence of concepts and terminologies with which to debate difference and inequalities in post-apartheid South Africa across all neighbourhoods is another example.

Ethnographic analyses of childhood have been described in the past as limited in their contributions to anthropology or to social science more broadly by the absence of cross-cultural comparison or theory building (LeVine 2007). In this book, we have sought to respond to these shortcomings through a multidisciplinary and comparative approach to data collection and analysis. In-depth comparisons within and among three neighbourhoods, including the discursive interaction of young researchers from different backgrounds, have enabled us to identify gaps in young people's knowledge that are fundamentally disempowering to them as individuals, and reveal larger social issues in contemporary South Africa. One of these is the sketchy or non-existent awareness of educational processes and requirements for employment, described above. The presence and implications of strongly gendered roles are another feature of the social environment about which young people are unaware of their own ignorance. Although these operate in a generally direct fashion according to neighbourhood in determining young people's health and well-being, the fact that gender prescriptions are manifest across all sectors of society is a feature of South African society around which little momentum for change can occur, precisely because young people are not aware that they face similar gendered dynamics in the home and in dating relationships. A third finding to have emerged through careful listening to what children and adolescents say about their everyday lives and experiences is that the nature of neighbourhood sociality has a greater impact, both positive and negative, on their self-esteem, personal integrity, ambition and overall well-being than the quality of physical infrastructure and the presence of services. These nuances were made evident through careful attention to children's multi-vocality within age, gender, class and cultural groups – a feature of analysis that has been lacking in child-focused research internationally in recent decades (James 2007).

These findings have both theoretical and practical significance. We are sorely in need of conceptual tools with which to understand the nature and implications of young people's highly uneven knowledge about the world in which they live, and possible ways to fill knowledge gaps and precipitate social change that arises with increased social integration. At a practical level, there are direct consequences of these findings to service design and delivery. For example, the types of social interaction within a young person's neighbourhood will either cohere with or conflict with the style of interaction within the institutions designed to provide services to children or adolescents. The results can be an accurate, attentive response appropriate to the individual young person's familial and neighbourhood sphere. These usually arise from a local, informal interpretation of the scope of the service, the responsibilities of adults therein and the degree of decision-making afforded to children. Rare examples of such coherence discussed in the book include the Art Vibrations club for adolescents in Ocean View, the temporary fostering of children by soup-kitchen cooks in Masiphumelele and the roles played by guidance teachers and youth workers in Fish Hoek. The more common scenario is a complete mismatch between institutions working to a set of predefined 'needs' and services and the ways young people understand everyday challenges and desire to tackle them. Schools, clinics and youth-focused organisations consequently fail to engage children and adolescents in ways they intend, meaning that critical compromises to well-being and gaps in information and life skills persist into young adulthood.

The combination of persistent material or economic differences and the social and cultural legacies of apartheid have resulted in the subsequent reproduction of deep differences between, and even divisions in, social worlds across the Valley. As we have shown, some of these differences are real and some are assumed or imagined, precisely because similarities between social worlds are not recognised. Young people are powerful agents of change, both in their efforts to source and nurture relationships of intimacy and support they recognise to be crucial to their well-being, and in their demands for greater socio-economic opportunity and connectivity to social spheres beyond their immediate neighbourhoods and historical identities. At the same time, they engage in conversations and actions that reproduce perceived differences and actual inequalities across the Valley. How, we must ask, might the legacy of division and difference be transcended? Over the long term, there is clearly the need for change in material circumstances at the household and neighbourhood levels. In the foreseeable future, however, greater contact between young people of different classes and race-group backgrounds would facilitate more interaction, understanding and scope for mutual support. Institutions have a key role to play in actively promoting such interaction by adopting a broad-based approach to community participation and service provision. So too do we ordinary citizens by seizing opportunities to befriend, mentor and encourage young people whose backgrounds differ from our own.

Notes

Chapter 1

1. See http://web.wits.ac.za/Academic/Health/Research/BirthTo20/.

2. See www.caps.uct.ac.za.

Chapter 2

1. An accurate picture of the various means through which parent-figures discipline young people, particularly adolescents, is not easily gained through observation because the presence of a visitor, particularly a researcher, alters behaviour. Group drama exercises proved a useful forum through which young people could express the character of intimate personal relationships, presumably because the role-playing process is ostensibly unlinked from their own, personal experiences.

2. The threats to well-being posed by the physical and social aspects of young people's local environments are described in detail in Chapter 3, as are the ways in which certain actions are represented as morally 'good' or 'bad' as a means of managing a high-risk environment.

3. Historically, gifts to children in isiXhosa-speaking communities were given at Christmas, but not at birthdays. Norms appear to be changing in Masiphumelele and this generation of mothers and children report that small gifts (such as a T-shirt or a chocolate bar) and sharing cakes and fizzy drinks is common, and there is now an expectation that parents provide these at birthdays.

4. OIL (standing for 'Ownership, Invest, Live') is an NGO supporting peer education among high-school pupils across the Valley.

5. Studies conducted in diverse cultural contexts identify a link between strong norms of filial piety and children's vulnerability to sexual abuse (on Puerto Rico, see Comas-Díaz 1995; on China, see Tang 2002, cited in Townsend & Dawes 2004).

Chapter 3

1. Very unusually, just before our research, a student 'from another school' had stabbed a 14-year-old girl just outside the gates of Fish Hoek Middle School. Although extensively covered in the local papers, the incident did not seem to cause much anxiety amongst pupils at the school or other young people in the neighbourhood.

2. Greef, Inspector R, personal communication, 2007.

3. Smetherham J-A, *Cape Times*, 4 April 2005.

Chapter 4

1. Few teenagers (or adults) in Fish Hoek cycle to and from their neighbourhood, and those who do make the trip for the purpose of fitness rather than transport. It is common for men living in Masiphumelele to cycle to work and a small number of young people belong to a Masiphumelele cycle club.

2. See, for example, 'Children selling sex to buy tik', *Cape Times*, 4 April 2005; 'Street talk – time to shout out loud about tik before it wrecks new generation', *Cape Argus*, 25 May 2005; and 'Premier goes walkabout to launch anti-tik drive', *Cape Times*, 29 June 2005.

3. Umkhonto we Sizwe (Spear of the Nation) was the active military wing of the African National Congress between 1961 and 1990.

Chapter 5

1. It should be noted that it is often difficult to distinguish between the absolute constraint of scarce resources and the consequences of budgetary choices made by school managers. Schools might choose to spend less on things like stationery and more on other items.

2. Van der Berg (2005) shows that African pupils attending racially mixed schools perform much better than African pupils at all-African schools, but this might be because they are middle class and might not even live in poor neighbourhoods.

3. Fish Hoek Middle School and Senior High School merged in 2009 to become Fish Hoek High School.

Chapter 6

1. The poor provision of school social workers and counsellors in all three neighbourhoods, but particularly Ocean View and Masiphumelele, is discussed in the section headed 'Who leaves and who stays? Decision-making and the school career'.

2. An exemption is given when the composite mark for a pupil's subject-specific examinations is high enough to allow for university application.

3. This event, reminiscent in form of protests during the late apartheid era, was extensively covered by the media. See, for example, 'SAPS investigating: Live ammo used against school children', *Weekend Argus*, 12 March 2005.

4. These attainment rates are for 20- to 24-year-olds in each neighbourhood, using data from the 2001 Census.

5. CAPS did not ask about participation in initiation rites, and we can find no other survey that has done so. This makes it difficult to be precise as to the prevalence and age of participation.

6. Data from the 2001 population census. Note that the unemployment rate is calculated exclusive of people who are studying or are otherwise not in the labour force.

7. This small qualitative study on educational discourse and decision-making was conducted in 2006 by our colleague, Ariane de Lannoy (2008). It is with her permission that we include Nezile's narrative.

Chapter 7

1. Psychologists sometimes use the term 'self-care' to refer to daily routines such as washing, brushing teeth, getting dressed, etc. We use it to refer to young people's efforts to protect and bolster their own well-being in the broadest sense.

2. Pupils who achieve a certain matric grade, but fail certain subjects, are allowed to rewrite examinations for subjects they have failed.

Chapter 8

1. CAPS also asked if young people were members of a 'religious group'; one-third replied 'yes'. There is no relationship between responses to this question and perceived self-control, even controlling for race and class.

2. Of the 1 890 pupils that participated in this survey, 68 per cent were African; 19 per cent were white; 6 per cent were coloured; and 6 per cent were Indian. Ninety per cent of these participants were in urban schools.

3. Little Sonja was murdered, *Cape Times*, 3 July 2007.

4. Rubber bullets fly, 12 held as housing demo turns ugly, *Cape Argus*, 31 May 2005.

The authors

Rachel Bray is an independent researcher and former research fellow at the Centre for Social Science Research (CSSR) and the Department of Social Anthropology at the University of Cape Town (UCT). She has a PhD from the University of Durham and is co-editor of *Monitoring Child Well-being: A South African Rights-based Approach*. Imke Gooskens and Sue Moses graduated from UCT in 2006 with master's degrees in social anthropology and development studies respectively. Sue currently works at the Children's Institute at UCT. Imke has begun research for a doctorate at UCT. Lauren Kahn completed a master's degree in psychology at UCT in 2008 and is currently working as a researcher at the Young Foundation in London. Imke, Sue and Lauren have all held scholarships and junior research positions at the CSSR. Jeremy Seekings is Professor of Political Studies and Sociology at UCT and director of one of the units within the CSSR. He has a PhD from Oxford University, and has held visiting appointments at Oxford, Yale and Princeton Universities. His books include *The UDF: A History of the United Democratic Front in South Africa* and *Class, Race and Inequality in South Africa* (co-authored with Nicoli Nattrass).

References

Adams H & Marshall A (1998) Off target messages: Poverty, risk and sexual rights. *Agenda* 39: 87–92

Adhikari M (2005) *Not white enough, not black enough: Racial identity in the South African coloured community.* Athens: Ohio University Press

Alexander KL, Entwisle DR & Kabbani NS (2001) The dropout process in life course perspective: Early risk factors at home and school. *Teachers College Record* 103: 760–822

Alexander P & Uys T (2002) AIDS and sociology: Current South African research. *Society in Transition* 33(3): 295–311

Aloise-Young PA, Cruikshank C & Chavez EL (2002) Cigarette smoking and perceived health in school dropouts: A comparison of Mexican American and non-Hispanic white adolescents. *Journal of Pediatric Psychology* 6: 497–507

Altbeker A (2007) *A country at war with itself.* Cape Town: Jonathan Ball Publishers

ANC (African National Congress) (1994) *The Reconstruction and Development Programme.* Johannesburg: ANC

Anderson KG (2005) Relatedness and investment in children in South Africa. *Human Nature* 16(1): 1–31

Anderson KG, Case A & Lam D (2001) Causes and consequences of schooling outcomes in South Africa: Evidence from survey data. *Social Dynamics* 27(1): 37–59

Arellano CM, Chavez EL & Deffenbacher JL (1998) Alcohol use and academic status among Mexican American and white non-Hispanic adolescents. *Adolescence* 33: 751–760

Ashforth A (2005) *Witchcraft, violence and democracy in South Africa.* Chicago: University of Chicago Press

Auerbach F & Welsh D (1981) Education. In S van der Horst & J Reid (Eds) *Race discrimination in South Africa: A review.* Cape Town: David Philip

Barbarin O & Richter L (2001) *Mandela's children: Growing up in post-apartheid South Africa.* London: Routledge

Barker G & Ricardo C (2005) *Young men and the construction of masculinity in sub-Saharan Africa: Implications for HIV/AIDS, conflict and violence.* Social Development Unit, Conflict Prevention and Reconstruction Papers No. 26. Washington, DC: World Bank

Beauvais F, Chavez EL, Oetting ER, Deffenbacher JL & Cornell GR (1996) Drug use, violence, and victimization among white American, Mexican American, and American Indian dropouts, students with academic problems and students in good academic standing. *Journal of Counseling Psychology* 43: 292–299

Bedi AS & Marshall JH (2002) Primary school attendance in Honduras. *Journal of Development Economics* 69: 129–154

Behr M (1995) *The smell of apples.* London: Abacus

Beutel AM & Anderson KG (2008) Race and the educational expectations of parents and children: The case of South Africa. *The Sociology Quarterly* 49: 335–361

Biddecom A & Bakilana A (2003) *Transitions into sex, parenthood and unions among adolescents and young adults in South Africa.* Cape Town: University of Cape Town

Bility KM (1999) School violence and adolescent mental health in South Africa: Implications for school health programs. *Sociological Practice: A Journal of Clinical and Applied Research* 1(4): 285–303

Black M & Krishnakumar A (1995) Children in low-income urban settings: Interventions to promote mental health and well-being. *American Psychologist* 53(6): 635–646

Booysen F le R, Bachman M, Matebesi Z & Meyer J (2003) The socio-economic impact of HIV/AIDS on households in South Africa: A pilot study in Welkom and Qwaqwa, Free State province. Interim report. University of the Free State and the Centre for Health Systems Research and Development

Borneman J (1992) *Belonging to the two Berlins: Kin, state, nation.* New York: Cambridge University Press

Boyden J & Ennew J (1997) *Children in focus: A manual for participatory research with children.* Stockholm: Radda Barnen

Boyden J & Holden P (1991) *Children of the cities.* London: Zed Books

Brandt R, Dawes A, Bray R, Mthembu-Salter L, Tomlinson M & Swartz L (2005) *An exploratory study of the impact of primary caregiver HIV infection on caregiving and child developmental outcome in the era of HAART: Piloting the methodology.* Report for the Organisation for Social Science Research in Eastern and Southern Africa (OSSREA)

Bray R (2003a) Predicting the social consequences of orphanhood in South Africa. *African Journal of AIDS Research* 2(1): 39–55

Bray R (2003b) Who does the housework? An examination of South African children's working roles. *Social Dynamics* 29(2): 95–131

Bray R (2009) How does AIDS illness affect women's residential decisions? Findings from an ethnographic study in a Cape Town township. *African Journal of AIDS Research* 8(2): 167–179

Bray R & Brandt R (2006) How do childcare and childcare relationships operate in the context of unemployment and HIV/AIDS? In P Graham (Ed.) *Inheriting poverty: The link between children's well-being and unemployment in South Africa.* Cape Town: Institute for Democracy in South Africa

Bray R & Brandt R (2007) Childcare and poverty in South Africa: An ethnographic challenge to conventional interpretations. *Journal of Children and Poverty* 13(1): 1–19

Bray R & Gooskens I (2006) Ethics and the everyday: Reconsidering approaches to research involving children and young people. *Anthropology Southern Africa* 29(1): 44–55

Broadbridge H (2002) Negotiating post-apartheid boundaries and identities: An anthropological study of the creation of a Cape Town suburb. PhD thesis, Stellenbosch University

Bronfenbrenner U (1979) *The ecology of human development.* Cambridge, MA: Harvard University Press

Bronfenbrenner U (1986) Ecology of the family as a context for human development: Research perspectives. *Developmental Psychology* 22: 723–742

Brooks-Gunn J, Duncan G, Kato Klebanov P & Sealand N (1993) Do neighbourhoods influence child and adolescent development? *American Journal of Sociology* 99(2): 353–395

Budlender D & Bosch D (2002) *South African child domestic workers: A national report*. Report submitted to the International Labour Organisation (ILO) International Programme for the Elimination of Child Labour (IPEC), Geneva (May)

Burman S & Reynolds P (Eds) (1986) *Growing up in a divided society: The contexts of childhood in South Africa*. Johannesburg: Ravan Press

Burns C (2002) A commentary on the colloquium, Instituting Gender Equality in Schools: Working in an HIV/AIDS environment. *Agenda* 53: 6–10

Calder M (1999) *Assessing risk in adult males who sexually abuse children*. Dorset: Russell House Publishing

Campbell C (2003) *Letting them die: How HIV/AIDS prevention programmes often fail*. Cape Town: Double Storey

CASE (Community Agency for Social Enquiry) (1993) *Growing up tough: A national survey of South African youth*. Johannesburg: CASE

Catalano RF & Hawkins JD (1996) The social development model: A theory of anti-social behaviour. In JD Hawkins (Ed.) *Delinquency and crime: Current theories*. New York: Cambridge University Press

Chisholm L (2007) Monitoring children's rights to education. In A Dawes, R Bray & A van der Merwe (Eds) *Monitoring child well-being: A South African rights-based approach*. Cape Town: HSRC Press

Christensen P & James A (1999) *Research with children: Perspectives and practices*. London: Falmer Press

Christopher AJ (2001) Urban segregation in post-apartheid South Africa. *Urban Studies* 38(3): 449–466

Christopher AJ (2005) Further progress in the desegregation of South African towns and cities 1996–2001. *Development Southern Africa* 22(2): 267–276

Coetzee JM (1998) *Boyhood: A memoir*. London: Vintage

Comas-Díaz L (1995) Puerto Ricans and sexual child abuse. In L Aronson Fontes (Ed.) *Sexual abuse in nine north American cultures: Treatment and prevention*. Thousand Oaks: Sage Publications

Cooper A (2009) 'Let us eat airtime': The relationship between violence and youth identity in a low-income neighbourhood in Cape Town. CSSR Working Paper No. 263, Centre for Social Science Research, University of Cape Town

Courtenay B (1989) *The power of one*. London: Heinemann

Crouch L & Mabogoane T (2001) No magic bullets, just tracer bullets: The role of learning resources, social advantage and education management in improving the performance of South African schools. *Social Dynamics* 27(1): 60–78

Dawes A & Biersteker L (2009) Improving the quality of ECD interventions through results-based monitoring and evaluation. The Sobambisana Early Childhood Development Initiative Paper presented at the Pan-African Early Childhood Development Conference, Johannesburg (20–23 July)

Dawes A, Borel-Saladin J & Parker Z (2004) Measuring and monitoring. In L Richter, A Dawes & C Higson-Smith (Eds) *Sexual abuse of children in South Africa*. Cape Town: HSRC Press

Dawes A, Bray R & van der Merwe A (2007) *Monitoring child well-being: A South African rights-based approach*. Cape Town: HSRC Press

Dawes A, Bray R, Kvalsvig J, Kafaar Z, Rama S & Richter L (2004) *Going global with indicators of child well-being: Indicators of South African children's psychosocial development in the early childhood period*. Phase-three report for UNICEF South Africa. Cape Town: Human Sciences Research Council, Child, Youth and Family Development

Dawes A, De Sas Kropiwnicki Z, Kafaar Z & Richter L (2006) Partner violence. In U Pillay, B Roberts & S Rule (Eds) *South African social attitudes: Changing times, diverse voices*. Cape Town: HSRC Press

Dawes A & Donald D (Eds) (1994) *Childhood and adversity: Psychological perspectives from South African research*. Cape Town: David Philip

Dawes A, Long W, Alexander L & Ward C (2006) *A situation analysis of children affected by maltreatment and violence in the Western Cape*. Report for the Directorate Research and Population Development, Department of Social Services and Poverty Alleviation, Provincial Government of the Western Cape, delivered by the Human Sciences Research Council

Dawson M (2003) Identity and context: Friendship and friction in a South African high school. MA dissertation, Rand Afrikaans University

De Lannoy A (2005) 'There is no other way out': *Educational decision-making in an era of AIDS: How do HIV-positive mothers value education?* CSSR Working Paper No. 137, Centre for Social Science Research, University of Cape Town

De Lannoy A (2007a) *The stuff that dreams are made of…Narratives on educational decision-making among young adults in Cape Town*. CSSR Working Paper No. 190, Centre for Social Science Research, University of Cape Town

De Lannoy A (2007b) *Educational decision-making in an era of AIDS: Exploring the narratives of affected young adults in the Cape Flats*. CSSR Working Paper No. 191, Centre for Social Science Research, University of Cape Town

De Lannoy A (2008) Educational decision-making in an era of AIDS. PhD thesis, University of Cape Town

Delius P & Glaser C (2002) Sexual socialisation in South Africa: A historical perspective. *African Studies* 61(1): 27–54

Desmond C & Desmond C (2006) HIV/AIDS and the crisis of care for children. In L Richter & R Morrell (Eds) *Baba: Men and fatherhood in South Africa*. Cape Town: HSRC Press

Devine F (2004) *Class practices: How parents help their children get good jobs*. Cambridge: Cambridge University Press

Dlamini SN (2005) *Youth and identity politics in South Africa, 1990–94*. Toronto: University of Toronto Press

Dockett S & Perry B (2007) Trusting children's accounts in research. *Journal of Early Childhood Research* (5)1: 47–63

DoE (Department of Education, South Africa) (2001) *Nationwide audit of ECD provisioning in South Africa*. Pretoria: DoE

Dolby N (2001) *Constructing race: Youth, identity and popular culture in South Africa*. Albany: State University of New York Press

Donald D, Dawes A & Louw J (Eds) (2000) *Addressing childhood adversity*. Cape Town: David Philip

Dorrington RE, Johnson LF, Bradshaw D & Daniel T (2006) *The demographic impact of HIV/ AIDS in South Africa: National and provincial indicators for 2006*. Cape Town: Centre for Actuarial Research, South African Medical Research Council and Actuarial Council of South Africa

Eaton L, Flisher AJ & Aarø LE (2003) Unsafe sexual behaviour in South African youth. *Social Science & Medicine* 56: 149–165

Eggert LL & Herting JR (1993) Drug involvement among potential dropouts and 'typical' youth. *Journal of Drug Education* 23: 31–55

Ellickson P, Bui K, Bell R & McGuigan KA (1998) Does early drug use increase the risk of dropping out of high school? *Journal of Drug Issues* 28: 357–380

Emmett AB (2004) Youth civic engagement in a period of transition in South Africa. Pretoria: Human Sciences Research Council

Emmett T, Richter L, Makiwane M, Du Toit R, Brookes H et al. (2003) *The status of youth report 2003*. Pretoria: Human Sciences Research Council

Everatt D & Orkin M (1993) *Growing up tough: A national survey of South African youth*. Braamfontein: Community Agency for Social Enquiry

Finchilescu G & Dawes A (1998) Catapulted into democracy. South African adolescents' socio-political orientations following rapid social change. *Journal of Social Issues* 54(3): 563–583

Finchilescu G & Tredoux C (2007) Intergroup contact, social context and racial ecology in South Africa. Prepared for U Wagner, L Tropp, G Finchilescu & C Tredoux (Eds) *Improving intergroup relations: Building on the legacy of Thomas F Pettigrew*. SPSSI Series on Social Issues and Interventions. Malden: Blackwell Publishing ·

Fleisch B (2002) *Managing educational change: The state and school reform in South Africa*. Johannesburg: Heinemann

Flisher AJ, Evans J, Muller M & Lombard C (2004) Test-retest reliability of self-reported adolescent risk behaviour. *Journal of Adolescence* 27: 207–212

Flisher AJ, Townsend L, Chikobvu P, Lombard C & King G (2010) Substance use and psychosocial predictors of high-school dropout in Cape Town, South Africa. *Journal of Research on Adolescence* 20: 237–255

Garmezy N (1996) Reflection and commentary on risk, resilience and development. In RJ Haggerty, LR Sherrod, N Garmezy & M Rutter (Eds) *Stress, risk and resilience in children and adolescents: Processes, mechanisms, and interventions*. Cambridge: Cambridge University Press

Giddens A (1984) *The constitution of society: Outline of the theory of structuration*. Cambridge: Polity Press

Giese S, Meintjes H, Croke R & Chamberlain R (2003) *Health and social services to address the needs of orphans and other vulnerable children in the context of HIV/AIDS in South Africa: Research report and recommendations*. Report submitted to HIV/AIDS directorate, National Department of Health (January). Cape Town: Children's Institute, University of Cape Town

Giordano PC (2003) Relationships in adolescence. *Annual Review of Sociology* 29: 257–281

Gooskens I (2006) Boundaries and crossing points: Children, geography and identity in the Fish Hoek Valley. *Social Dynamics* 32(1): 135–168

Greig A & Taylor J (1999) *Doing research with children*. London: Sage Publications

Guma M & Henda N (2004) The socio-cultural context of child abuse: A betrayal of trust. In L Richter, A Dawes & C Higson-Smith (Eds) *Sexual abuse of children in South Africa*. Cape Town: HSRC Press

Hall K (1995) There's a time to act English and a time to act Indian: The politics of identity among British Sikh teenagers. In S Stephens (Ed.) *Children and the politics of culture*. Princeton: Princeton University Press

Hawkins JD, Catalano RF & Miller JY (1992) Risk and protective factors for alcohol and other drug problems in adolescence and early adulthood: Implications for substance abuse prevention. *Psychological Bulletin* 112: 64–105

Hecht T (1998) *At home in the street: Street children of northeast Brazil*. Cambridge: Cambridge University Press

Henderson P (1999) Living with fragility: Children in New Crossroads. PhD thesis, University of Cape Town

Henderson P (2006) South African AIDS orphans: Examining assumptions around vulnerability from the perspective of rural children and youth. *Childhood* 12(3): 303–327

Heyns M (2008) *The children's day*. Cape Town: Jonathan Ball Publishers

Higgs J & Styles K (2006) Principles and practical aspects of healthful school vending. *Nutrition Bulletin* 31(3): 225–232

Holland J, Ramazanoglu C, Scott S & Thomson R (1994) Achieving masculine sexuality: Young men's strategies for managing vulnerability. In L Doyal, J Naidoo & T Wilton (Eds) *AIDS: Setting a feminist agenda*. London: Taylor & Francis

Hunter M (2002) The materiality of everyday sex: Thinking beyond 'prostitution'. *African Studies* 61(1): 99–120

Hunter M (2006) Fathers without *amandla*: Zulu-speaking men and fatherhood. In L Richter & R Morrell (Eds) *Baba: Men and fatherhood in South Africa*. Cape Town: HSRC Press

Huston AC (2002) Reforms in child development. In *Children and welfare reform: The future of children* 12(1): 59–77. Available at http://www.futureofchildren.org

Jacobs R (2003) The Manuel family. In *Group portraits: Nine family histories*, compiled by Paul Faber. Cape Town: Kwela

James A (2007) Giving voice to children's voices: Practices and problems, pitfalls and potentials. *American Anthropologist* 109(2): 261–272

James A & Prout A (Eds) (1997) *Constructing and reconstructing childhood: Contemporary issues in the sociological study of childhood*. London: Falmer Press

Jardien R & Collett K (2006) Case study report on Marine Primary School. Building school communities as nodes of care and support to promote the well-being of children and youth. Children's Institute, University of Cape Town

Jenkins R (1996) *Social identity*. London: Routledge

Jenks C (1996) *Childhood*. London: Routledge

Jewkes R, Levin J & Penn-Kenana I (2002) Risk factors for domestic violence: Findings from a South African cross-sectional study. *Social Science and Medicine* 55: 1603–1617

Johnson V & Ivan-Smith E (1998) Background to the issues. In V Johnson, E Ivan-Smith, G Gordon, P Pridmore & P Scott (Eds) *Stepping forward: Children and young people's participation in the development process*. London: Intermediate Technology Publications

Jones S (1993) *Assaulting childhood: Children's experiences of migrancy and hostel life in South Africa*. Johannesburg: Wits University Press

Kahn L (2006) Narratives of sexual abstinence: A qualitative study of female adolescents in a Cape Town community. *Social Dynamics* 32(1): 75–101

Kahn L (2008) Sexual subjects: A feminist post-structuralist analysis of female adolescent sexual subjectivity and agency. MA dissertation, University of Cape Town

Kaufman CE, De Wet T & Stadler J (2000) *Adolescent pregnancy and parenthood in South Africa*. Policy Research Division Working Papers No. 136. New York: Population Council

Kaufman CE & Stavrou SE (2004) 'Bus fare please': The economics of sex and gifts among young people in urban South Africa. *Culture, Health and Sexuality* 6(5): 377–391

Kelly K & Ntlabati P (2002) Early adolescent sex in South Africa: HIV and intervention challenges. *Social Dynamics* 28(1): 42–63

King G, Flisher AJ, Mallett R, Graham J, Lombard C et al. (2003) Smoking in Cape Town: Community influences on adolescent tobacco use. *Preventive Medicine* 36: 114–123

Kinnes L (1995) Reclaiming the Cape Flats. *Crime and Conflict* 2: 5–8

Kinnes L (2000) Gang warfare in the Western Cape: Background. In monograph No. 48 *From urban street gangs to criminal empires: The changing face of gangs in the Western Cape* (June). Accessed 7 July 2009, http://www.iss.co.za/Pubs/Monographs/No48/Gangwarfare.html

Koenig HG (2001) Religion and medicine III: Developing a theoretical model. *The International Journal of Psychiatry and Medicine* 31: 199–216

Lachman M & Weaver SL (1998) The sense of control as a moderator of social class differences in health and well-being. *Journal of Personality and Social Psychology* 74: 763–773

Lam D, Ardington C & Leibbrandt M (2006) Progress through school in urban South Africa: Evidence from panel data. Paper presented at DPRU/TIPS Conference on Accelerated and Shared Growth in South Africa, Johannesburg (October)

Lam D, Seekings J & Sparks M (2006) *The Cape Area Panel Study (CAPS): Overview and technical documentation for waves 1–3*. Cape Town: Centre for Social Science Research (CSSR), University of Cape Town

Leatt A (2007) Support for children: Social services and social security. In MA Kibel, A Westwood & H Saloojeeh (Eds) *Child health for all: A manual for southern Africa* (4th edition). Cape Town: Oxford University Press Southern Africa

LeClerc-Madlala S (2002) Youth, HIV/AIDS and the importance of sexual culture and context. *Social Dynamics* 28(1): 20–41

LeClerc-Madlala S (2003) Transactional sex and the pursuit of modernity. *Social Dynamics* 29: 1–29

LeClerc-Madlala S (2004) *Transactional sex and the pursuit of modernity*. CSSR Working Paper No. 68, Centre for Social Science Research, University of Cape Town

Lee R (2002) Locating 'home': Strategies of settlement, identity-formation and social change among African women in Cape Town, 1948–2000. PhD thesis, University of Oxford

Leibbrandt M, Woolard I & Woolard C (2009) A long-run perspective on contemporary poverty and inequality dynamics. In J Aron, B Kahn & G Kingdon (Eds) *South African economic policy under democracy*. Oxford: Oxford University Press

Leoschut L & Burton P (2006) *How rich the rewards? Results of the 2005 National Youth Victimisation Study*. Monographic Series No. 1. Cape Town: Centre for Justice and Crime Prevention

Lesch E & Kruger L (2004) Reflections on the sexual agency of young women in a low-income rural South African community. *South African Journal of Psychology* 34(3): 464–486

Leventhal T & Brooks-Gunn J (2000) The neighbourhoods they live in: The effects of neighbourhood residence on child and adolescent outcomes. *Psychological Bulletin* 126: 309–337

Leventhal T & Brooks-Gunn J (2003) Indicators of children's well-being in a community context. In RP Weissberg & HJ Walberg (Eds) *Long-term trends in the well-being of children and youth: Issues in children's and families' lives*. Washington, DC: Child Welfare League of America

LeVine R (2007) Ethnographic studies of childhood: A historical overview. *American Anthropologist* 109(2): 247–260

Levine S (1999) Bittersweet harvest: Children, work and the global march against child labour in the post-apartheid state. *Critique of Anthropology* 19(2): 139–155

Levine S (2002) In the shadow of the vine: Child labour in the Western Cape. Seminar presented at the Centre for African Studies, University of Cape Town (February)

Levinson B, Foley D & Holland D (1996) *The cultural production of the educated person: Critical ethnographies of schooling and local practice*. Albany: State University of New York Press

Liddel C, Kvalsvig J, Quotyana P & Shabalala A (1994) Community violence and youth: South African children's involvement in aggression. *International Journal of Behavioural Development* 17: 613–628

Lloyd C (Ed.) (2005) *Growing up global: The changing transitions to adulthood in developing countries*. Washington, DC: The National Academies Press

Lloyd C, Behrman JR, Stromquist NP & Cohen B (Eds) (2005) *The changing transitions to adulthood in developing countries: Selected studies*. Washington, DC: The National Academies Press

Luthar SS, Cicchetti D & Becker B (2000) The construct of resilience: A critical evaluation and guidelines for future work. *Child Development* 71(3): 543–562

Macleod C & Durrheim K (2002) Racializing teenage pregnancy: 'Culture' and 'tradition' in the South African scientific literature. *Ethnic and Racial Studies* 25(5): 778–801

MacPhail C & Campbell C (2001) 'I think condoms are good but, aai, I hate those things': Condom use amongst adolescents and young people in a South African township. *Social Science and Medicine* 52: 1613–1627

Magwaza A (1997) Sexual abuse: A sociocultural developmental perspective. In C de la Rey, N Duncan & T Scheffer (Eds) *Contemporary issues in human development: A South African focus.* Johannesburg: International Thomson Publishing

Mandela N (1995) Speech at the launch of the Nelson Mandela Children's Fund, Pretoria (8 May). Accessed 12 February 2008, http://www.anc.org.za/ancdocs/history/mandela/1995/sp950508.html

Mandela N (2000) Speech at the Annual Children's Celebration, Pilanesburg. Accessed 12 February 2008, http://www.nmcf.co.za/Reports_Speeches.htm

Mann G (2003) *Family matters: The care and protection of children affected by HIV/AIDS in Malawi.* Stockholm: Save the Children Sweden

Marks M (2001) *Young warriors: Youth politics, identity and violence in South Africa.* Johannesburg: Wits University Press

Marshall H, Stenner P & Lee H (1999) Young people's accounts of personal relationships in a multi-cultural East London environment: Questions of community, diversity and inequality. *Journal of Community and Applied Social Psychology* 9: 155–171

Masten AS (2001) Ordinary magic: Resilience processes in development. *American Psychologist* 56(3): 227–238

Masten AS & Coatsworth JD (1998) The development of competence in favorable and unfavorable environments: Lessons from research on successful children. *American Psychologist* 53(2): 205–220

Matlwa K (2007) *Coconut.* Johannesburg: Jacana Media

Matthew DA, McCullough ME, Larson DB, Koenig HG, Swyers JP & Milano MG (1998) Religious commitment and health status: A review of the research and implications for family medicine. *Archives of Family Medicine* 7: 118–124

Matthews H & Limb M (1999) Defining an agenda for the geography of children: Review and prospect. *Progress in Human Geography* 23(1): 61–90

McKinney C (2007) 'If I speak English, does it make me less black anyway?' 'Race' and English in South African desegregated schools. *English Academy Review* 24(2): 6–24

Meintjes H & Bray R (2005) 'But where are our moral heroes?' An analysis of South African press reporting on children affected by HIV/AIDS. *African Journal of AIDS Research* 4(3): 147–159

Meintjes H & Hall K (2008) Demography of South Africa's children. In S Pendlebury, L Lake & C Smith C (Eds) *South African child gauge 2008/2009.* Children's Institute, University of Cape Town, http://www.ci.org.za/depts/ci/pubs

Meintjes H, Moses S, Berry L & Mapane R (2007) *Home truths: The phenomenon of residential care for children in a time of AIDS.* Children's Institute, University of Cape Town and the Centre for the Study of AIDS, University of Pretoria

Meursing A, Vos T, Cutino O, Moyo M, Mpofu S et al. (1995) Child sexual abuse in Matabeleland, Zimbabwe. *Journal of Social Science and Medicine* 41(12): 1693–1704

Moll PG (1998) Primary schooling, cognitive skills and wages in South Africa. *Economica* 65: 263–284

Morgan J (2007) *Hero book anthology: A collection of hero stories from southern Africa*, http://www.children-psychosocial-wellbeing.org/download-center.html

Morrell R (2006) Fathers, fatherhood and masculinity in South Africa. In L Richter & R Morrell (Eds) *Baba: Men and fatherhood in South Africa*. Cape Town: HSRC Press

Moses S (2005) How do space and place matter? The role of neighbourhood-level factors on the everyday lives of children and young people living in a Cape Town community established under apartheid. MA thesis, University of Cape Town

Moses S (2006) The impact of neighbourhood-level factors on children's everyday lives, well-being and identity: A qualitative study of children living in Ocean View, Cape Town. *Social Dynamics* 32(1): 102–134

Newfield D & Maungedzo R (2005) *Thebuwa: Poems from Ndofaya Lamula Jubilee High School, Soweto*. WITS Multiliteracies Research Project. Central Printing, University of the Witwatersrand

Niehaus IA (1994) Disharmonious spouses and harmonious siblings: Conceptualising household formation among urban residents in Qwaqwa. *Journal of African Studies* 53(1): 115–135

Nieuwenhuys O (1994) *Children's lifeworlds: Gender, welfare and labour in the developing world*. London: Routledge

Nkuna L (2006) 'Fitting-in' to a 'classy place': The zone and youth identity. In P Alexander, M Dawson & M Ichharam (Eds) *Globalisation and new identities: A view from the middle*. Johannesburg: Jacana Media

Ntsebeza L (1993) Youth in urban African townships, 1945–1992: A case study of the East London townships. MA dissertation, University of Natal, Durban

O'Donnell DA, Schwab-Stone M & Muyeed AZ (2002) Multi-dimensional resilience in urban children exposed to community violence. *Child Development* 73: 1265–1282

Pager D (1996) The culture of learning in Khayelitsha secondary schools: Teachers' perspectives. M.Soc.Sci thesis, University of Cape Town

Paranzee P & Smythe D (2003) *Domestic violence and development: Looking at the farming context*. University of Cape Town: Institute of Criminology

Parker RG (1995) The social and cultural construction of sexual risk, or how to have (sex) research in an epidemic. In H Brummelhuis & G Herdt (Eds) *Culture and sexual risk: Anthropological perspectives on AIDS*. Australia: Gordon and Breach

Parkes J (2007) Tensions and troubles in young people's talk about safety and danger in a violent neighbourhood. *Journal of Youth Studies* 10(1): 117–137

Pattman R & Chege F (2003) 'Dear diary, I saw an angel, she looked like heaven on earth': Sex talk and sex education. *African Journal of AIDS Research* 2(2): 103–112

Pearce MJ, Jones SM, Schwab-Stone M & Ruchkin V (2003) The protective effects of religiousness and parent involvement on the development of conduct problems among youth exposed to violence. *Child Development* 74: 1682–1686

Pettifor AE, Rees HV, Steffenson A, Hlongwa-Madikizela L, MacPhail C et al. (2004) *HIV and sexual behaviour among young South Africans: A national survey of 15–24-years-olds*. Johannesburg: Reproductive Health Research Unit, University of the Witwatersrand

Pillay P (1990) The development and underdevelopment of education in South Africa. In W Nassan & J Samuel (Eds) *Education: From poverty to liberty*. Cape Town: David Philip

Pinnock D (1982a) *The brotherhoods: Street gangs and state control in Cape Town*. Cape Town: David Philip

Pinnock D (1982b) Towards an understanding of the structure, function and cause of gang formation in Cape Town. MA thesis, University of Cape Town

Porteus K, Clacherty G, Mdiya L, Pelo J, Matsai K et al. (2000) 'Out of school' children in South Africa: An analysis of causes in a group of marginalized, urban 7- to 15-year-olds. *Support for Learning* 15(1): 8–12

Posel D (2004) 'Getting the nation talking about sex': Reflections on the discursive constitution of sexuality in South Africa since 1994. *Agenda* 62: 53–63

Preston-Whyte E (2003) Contexts of vulnerability: Sex, secrecy and HIV/AIDS. *African Journal of AIDS Research* 2(2): 89–94

Preston-Whyte E & Zondi M (1991) Adolescent sexuality and its implications for teenage pregnancy and AIDS. *Continuing Medical Education* 9: 1389–1394

Quinn J (1995) Positive effects of participation in youth organizations. In M Rutter (Ed.) *Psychosocial disturbances in young people: Challenges for prevention*. Cambridge: Cambridge University Press

Qvortrup J, Bardy M, Sgritta G & Wintersberger H (Eds) (1994) *Childhood matters: Social theory, practice and politics*. Aldershot: Avebury

Ramphele M (1993) *A bed called home: Life in the migrant labour hostels of Cape Town*. Cape Town: David Philip

Ramphele M (2002) *Steering by the stars: Being young in South Africa*. Cape Town: Tafelberg

Ramphele M & Richter L (2006) Migrancy, family dissolution and fatherhood. In L Richter & R Morrell (Eds) *Baba: Men and fatherhood in South Africa*. Cape Town: HSRC Press

Rauch J (2005) *Crime prevention and morality: The campaign for moral regeneration in South Africa*. Pretoria: Institute for Security Studies

Reddy V (2006) *Mathematics and science achievement at South African schools in TIMSS 2003*. Pretoria: HSRC Press

Reynolds P (1989) *Childhood in Crossroads: Cognition and society in South Africa*. Cape Town: David Philip

Reynolds P (1993) *Paring down the family: The child's point of view*. Children and Families in Distress Working Paper No. 5. Research Programme on Marriage and Family Life, Human Sciences Research Council, Pretoria

Reynolds P (1995) *The ground of all making: State violence, the family and political activists*. Pretoria: Human Sciences Research Council

Reynolds P (2000) The ground of all making: State violence, the family and political activists. In V Das, A Kleinman, M Ramphele & P Reynolds (Eds) *Violence and subjectivity*. Berkeley: University of California Press

Richter L, Griesel D & Rose C (2000) The psychological impact of a school feeding project. In D Donald, A Dawes & J Louw (Eds) *Addressing childhood adversity*. Cape Town: David Philip

Richter L & Higson-Smith C (2004) The many kinds of sexual abuse of young children. In L Richter, A Dawes & C Higson-Smith (Eds) *Sexual abuse of children in South Africa*. Cape Town: HSRC Press

Richter L & Morrell R (Eds) (2006) *Baba: Men and fatherhood in South Africa*. Cape Town: HSRC Press

Richter L & Smith W (2006) Children's views of fathers. In L Richter & R Morrell (Eds) *Baba: Men and fatherhood in South Africa*. Cape Town: HSRC Press

Rivers K & Aggleton P (1998) *Gender and the HIV epidemic: Men and the HIV epidemic*. New York: UNDP HIV and Development Programme

Ross F (1995) *Houses without doors: Diffusing domesticity in Die Bos*. Co-operative Research Programme on Marriage and Family Life. Pretoria: Human Sciences Research Council

Ross F (1996) Diffusing domesticity: Domestic fluidity in Die Bos. *Social Dynamics* 22(1): 55–71

Ross F (2009) *Raw life, new hope: Decency, home and housing in a post-apartheid community*. Cape Town: Juta

Rumberger RW (1995) Dropping out of middle school: A multilevel analysis of students and schools. *American Educational Research Journal* 32: 583–625

Russell M (1995) *Parenthood among black migrant workers in the Western Cape: Migrant labour and the nature of domestic groups*. Co-operative Research Programme on Marriage and Family Life. Pretoria: Human Sciences Research Council

Russell M (2003) Are urban black families nuclear? A comparative study of black and white family norms. *Social Dynamics* 29(2): 153–176

Rutter M (1985) Resilience in the face of adversity: Protective factors and resistance to psychiatric disorder. *British Journal of Psychiatry* 147: 598–611

Salo E (2004) Respectable mothers, tough men and good daughters: Producing persons in Manenberg Township, South Africa. PhD thesis, Emory University

Sampson RJ, Morenoff JD & Gannon-Rowley T (2002) Assessing neighbourhood effects: Social processes and new directions in research. *Annual Review of Sociology* 28: 433–478

Scharf W (1990) The resurgence of urban street gangs and community responses in Cape Town during the late eighties. In D Hansson & D van Zyl Smit (Eds) *Towards justice: Crime and state control in South Africa*. Cape Town: Oxford University Press

Schenk K & Williamson J (2005) *Ethical approaches to gathering information from children and adolescents in international settings: Guidelines and resources*. Washington, DC: Horizons, Population Council, IMPACT, Family Health International

Schollar E (2008) The Primary Mathematics Research Project, 2004–2007. Unpublished report for the Shuttleworth and Zenex Foundations

Seekings J (1993) *Heroes or villains? Youth politics in the 1980s*. Johannesburg: Ravan Press

Seekings J (1995) Media representations of 'youth' and the South African transition, 1989–1994. *South African Sociological Review* 7(2): 25–42

Seekings J (1996) The 'lost generation': South Africa's 'youth problem' in the early 1990s. *Transformation* 29: 103–125

Seekings J (2001) Making an informed investment: Improving the value of public expenditure in primary and secondary schooling in South Africa. Report for the Parliament of South Africa

Seekings J (2006) Beyond heroes and villains: The rediscovery of the ordinary in the study of childhood and adolescence. *Social Dynamics* 32(1) (Special issue: Childhood and Adolescence in southern and eastern Africa): 1–20

Seekings J (2008) The continuing salience of race: Discrimination and diversity in South Africa. *Journal of Contemporary African Studies* 26(1): 1–26

Seekings J (2010) Poverty and inequality in South Africa, 1994–2007. In I Shapiro & K Tebeau (Eds) *After apartheid: The second decade of democracy*. Charlottesville: University of Virginia Press

Seekings J & Nattrass N (2005) *Class, race and inequality in South Africa*. New Haven: Yale University Press

Selikow T, Zulu B & Cedras E (2002) The ingagara, the regte and the cherry: HIV/AIDS and youth culture in contemporary urban townships. *Agenda* 53: 22–32

Shefer T & Potgieter C (2006) Sexualities. In T Shefer, F Boonzaier & P Kiguwa (Eds) *The gender of psychology*. Cape Town: UCT Press

Shelmerdine S (2005) *Relationships between adolescents and adults: The significance of narrative and context*. CSSR Working Paper No. 119, Centre for Social Science Research, University of Cape Town

Silberschmidt M (2001) Disempowerment of men in rural and urban East Africa: Implications for male identity, sexuality and sexual behaviour. *World Development* 29(4): 657–671

Simkins C & Paterson A (2005) *Learner performance in South Africa: Social and economic determinants of success in language and mathematics*. Cape Town: HSRC Press

Soudien C (2001) Certainty and ambiguity in youth identities in South Africa: Discourses in transition. *Discourse: Studies in the Cultural Politics of Education* 22(3): 311–326

Soudien C (2004) Constituting the class: An analysis of the process of integration in South African schools. In L Chisholm (Ed.) *Changing class: Education and social change in post-apartheid South Africa*. Cape Town: HSRC Press

Soudien C (2007) *Youth identity in contemporary South Africa: Race, culture and schooling*. Cape Town: New Africa Books

South African Institute of Race Relations (SAIRR) (2007) *South Africa Survey 2006/07*. Johannesburg: SAIRR

Spiegel A (1996) Introduction: Domestic fluidity in South Africa. *Social Dynamics* 22(1): 5–6

Spiegel A & Mehlwana A (1997) *Family as social network: Kinship and sporadic migrancy in the Western Cape's Khayelitsha*. Co-operative Research Programme on Marriage and Family Life. Pretoria: Human Sciences Research Council

Stats SA (Statistics South Africa) (2001) *Census 2001*. Pretoria: Stats SA

Steinberg J (2005) *The number: One man's search for identity in the Cape underworld and prison gangs*. Johannesburg: Jonathan Ball Publishers

Steinberg M, Johnson S, Schierhout G, Ndegwa D, Hall K et al. (2003) *Hitting home: How households cope with the impact of the HIV/AIDS epidemic. A survey of households affected by HIV/AIDS in South Africa*. Report commissioned by the Henry Kaiser Family Foundation

Stephens S (1995) *Children and the politics of culture*. New York: Princeton University Press

Steyn M (2001) *Whiteness just isn't what it used to be: White identity in a changing South Africa*. Albany: State University of New York Press

Straker G (1992) *Faces in the revolution: The psychological effects of violence on township youth in South Africa*. Cape Town: David Philip

Streak J, Dawes A, Ewing D, Levine S, Rama S & Alexander L (2007) *The causes, nature and impact of child work and labour in agriculture in South Africa: A study of three purposively selected sites*. Report submitted to the Towards the Elimination of Child Labour Program of the International Labour Organisation. Pretoria: Human Sciences Research Council

Swart-Kruger J (Ed.) (2000) *Growing up in Canaansland: Children's recommendations on improving a squatter camp environment: A site report in the international project: Growing up in cities*. Pretoria: HSRC Publishers

Swart-Kruger J (2001) *Isikhathi Sokulala*: How boys and girls in a South African squatter camp experience bedtime. *International Journal of Anthropology* 16(2–3): 99–111

Swart-Kruger J & Chawla L (2002) 'We know something someone doesn't know': Children speak out on local conditions in Johannesburg. *Environment and Urbanization* 14: 85–96

Tang SC (2002) Childhood experience of sexual abuse among Hong Kong Chinese college students. *Child Abuse and Neglect* 26: 23–37

Taylor N (2007a) Equity, efficiency and the development of South African schools. In T Townsend (Ed.) *International Handbook of School Effectiveness and Improvement*. Dordrecht: Springer

Taylor N (2007b) *How should we think about the 2006 matric results?* Accessed 10 July 2009, http://www.jet.org.za

Thom DP, Louw AE, Van Ede DM & Ferns I (1998) Adolescence. In DA Louw, DM van Ede & AE Louw (Eds) *Human development* (3rd edition). Pretoria: Kagiso

Townsend L & Dawes A (2004) Individual and contextual factors associated with the sexual abuse of children under twelve: A review of recent literature. In L Richter, A Dawes & C Higson-Smith (Eds) *Sexual abuse of children in South Africa*. Cape Town: HSRC Press

Trapido B (2003) *Frankie and Stankie*. London: Bloomsbury Publishing

Van der Berg S (2005) Apartheid's enduring legacy: Inequalities in education. Paper presented at the Oxford University/University of Stellenbosch conference, South African Economic Policy under Democracy (October)

Van der Berg S (2006) *How effective are poor schools? Poverty and educational outcomes in South Africa*. Stellenbosch University Economic Working Paper No. 06/06

Van der Merwe A & Dawes A (2000) Prosocial and antisocial tendencies in children exposed to community violence. *Southern African Journal of Child and Adolescent Mental Health* 12: 29–37

Van der Merwe AC (2006) *Moffie*. Johannesburg: Pen Stock Publishing

Van Kessel I (2000) *Beyond our wildest dreams: The United Democratic Front and the transformation of South Africa*. Charlottesville: University of Virginia Press

Van Zyl Slabbert F, Malan C, Marais H, Olivier J & Riordan R (Eds) (1994) *Youth in the new South Africa: Towards policy formulation*. Pretoria: HSRC Publishers

Varga CA & Makubalo EL (1996) Sexual (non) negotiation. *Agenda* 28: 31–38

Wallerstein JS & Kelly JB (1980) *Surviving the breakup: How children and parents cope with divorce*. London: Grant McIntyre

Ward C (2007a) Neighbourhood indicators: Monitoring child rights and well-being at small area level. In A Dawes, R Bray & A Van der Merwe (Eds) *Monitoring child well-being: A South African rights-based approach*. Cape Town: HSRC Press

Ward C (2007b) *'It feels like it's the end of the world': Cape Town's youth talk about gangs and community violence*. Monograph Series No. 136. Pretoria: Institute for Security Studies

Ward C & Bakhuis K (2009) Intervening in children's involvement in gangs: Views of Cape Town's young people. *Children and Society* online: 1–18, http://www.hsrc.ac.za/CYFSD-publications.phtml

Ward C, Martin E, Theron C & Distiller G (2007) Factors affecting resilience in children exposed to violence. *South African Journal of Psychology* 37(1): 165–187

Weiss E, Whelan D & Gupta GR (1996) *Vulnerability and opportunity: Adolescents and HIV/AIDS in the developing world*. Washington, DC: International Center for Research on Women

Weiss E, Whelan D & Gupta GR (2000) Gender, sexuality and HIV: Making a difference in the lives of young women in developing countries. *Sexual and Relationships Therapy* 15(3): 233–245

Werner E (2000) Protective factors and individual resilience. In JP Shonkoff & SJ Meisels (Eds) *Handbook of early childhood intervention* (2nd edition). Cambridge: Cambridge University Press

Werner E & Smith RS (1989) *Vulnerable but invincible: A longitudinal study of resilient children and youth*. New York: Adams, Bannister, Cox Publishers

Western J (1981) *Outcast Cape Town*. Minneapolis: University of Minnesota Press

Wichstrøm L (1998) Alcohol intoxication and school dropout. *Drug and Alcohol Review* 17: 413–421

Willis P (1977) *Learning to labor*. New York: Columbia University Press

Wilson F (2006) On being a father and poor in South Africa today. In L Richter & R Morrell (Eds) *Baba: Men and fatherhood in South Africa*. Cape Town: HSRC Press

Wilson F & Ramphele M (1989) *Uprooting poverty: The South African challenge*. Cape Town: David Philip

Wood C, Welman M & Netto L (2000) A profile of young sex offenders in South Africa. *Southern African Journal of Child and Adolescent Mental Health* 12(1): 45–58

Wood K & Jewkes R (1997) Violence, rape and sexual coercion: Everyday love in a South African township. *Gender and Development* 5(2): 41–46

Wood K & Jewkes R (2001) Dangerous love: Reflections on violence among Xhosa township youth. In R Morrell (Ed.) *Changing men in southern Africa*. Pietermaritzburg: University of Natal Press/Zed Books

Wood K, Maforah F & Jewkes R (1998) 'He forced me to love him': Putting violence on adolescent sexual health agendas. *Social Science & Medicine* 47(2): 233–242

World Bank (2006) *World development report 2007*. Washington, DC: World Bank

Young L & Ansell N (2003) Fluid households, complex families: The impacts of children's migration as a response to HIV/AIDS in southern Africa. *The Professional Geographer* 55: 464–479

Index

protest action 28, 226, 294–295, 315
public transport *18*, 103, 139, 152

R
race 327
    and class 30, 313
    definitions of 29–31
    and families 49–55
    and friendship 160–164, 313
    and identity 158–159
    and language 159–160, 164–166
    schooling and social integration 157–166
    see also apartheid; segregation, racial
rape 120–121
rebellion 44, 46, 263–267
reciprocity 59–62, 68, 93, 96, 306–310
religion 113
    decision-making about school careers
        238–239
    and personal control 289–290, 301–302
    see also church; morally imbued discourse
research on children 27–29, 31–37
    ethics 35, 39
    ethnographic 32, 33, *35*
    iterative 33
    methodologies 31–40
    participatory 36, 38
    qualitative 32–37
    quantitative 31–32
resilience 94, 201, 226, 237, 294–296, 302
respect
    intergenerational 60–61, 308
    and social danger 128–129
    and subservience 70
    teachers 192–193
    ukuhlonipha 60–61, 308
    see also intergenerational relationships
rights 37, 65, 95, 119
risk 117, 118, 120–121
    behaviour and drop-out from school
        233–234
    perceptions of 102–106, *105*
    social, and HIV/AIDS 118, 284
    see also under dangers
rites of passage 39, 242, 265–267
role models 115, *275*, 289, 291, 325
romantic relationships *see* dating and
        sexual relationships
rumour and gossip *see* gossip and rumour
rural connections 49, 57–59, 95, 107, 147, 307

S
school careers, decision-making
    age of leaving school 231–323
    anti-schooling subculture 247
    attendance 227–230, *227–228*, 234–237
    and domestic conflict 235–236
    'drop-out' rates 230–235, *232*, 236
    and employment 242–244, *243*
    enrolment 229, 230, *231*
    gangs and crime 244–246
    influence of friends and peers 237–240
    initiation rites 242
    knowledge of further education 247, 249
    matric attainment rates 232
    motivations for leaving school 234–249
    perceived value of education 246–252
    premature departure *232*, 232–233
    religious involvement 238–239
    and teenage pregnancy 240–242
schooling 170
    class size 177, 178, 180
    discipline 179–182, 191, 193–197, 199–200,
        307
    facilities 177–178
    fees 177, 178, 179
    funding 171, 177
    grade attainment *173*, 173–174, 180,
        204, 216
    management 180, 181
    mathematics and science *172*, 172, 174–175
    matric *172*, 172–173, 182, 231
    outcomes 171–172
    post-apartheid reforms 170–177
    process of 180–183
    pupil:teacher ratio 178, 181
    resource inequalities 177–180
    skills and qualifications 170, 177, 180, 182,
        185–186
    see also teaching
schooling, social aspects 203–205
    choosing a school 205–209
    class 157–166, 204, 222, 230
    educational expectations 217–223, *217–219*
    fees 206–207
    friendship 223–227
    influence of home and neighbourhood
        209–216
    language of instruction 205–206
    matric ball 224–225
    pre-school *227–228*, 229